Emotion and Religion

Emotion and Religion

A Critical Assessment and Annotated Bibliography

John Corrigan, Eric Crump, and John Kloos

GREENWOOD PRESS
Westport, Connecticut • London

Library of Congress Cataloging-in-Publication Data

Corrigan, John, 1952–
    Emotion and religion : a critical assessment and annotated bibliography / John Corrigan, John Kloos, Eric Crump.
        p. cm.
    Includes bibliographical references and indexes.
    ISBN 0–313–30600–1 (alk. paper)
    1. Emotions—Religious aspects—Bibliography. I. Kloos, John M., 1950– II. Crump, Eric. III. Title.
Z7785.C67 2000
[BL65.E46]
016.2′001′9—dc21   00–035372

British Library Cataloguing in Publication Data is available.

Copyright © 2000 by John Corrigan, Eric Crump, and John Kloos

All rights reserved. No portion of this book may be reproduced, by any process or technique, without the express written consent of the publisher.

Library of Congress Catalog Card Number: 00–035372
ISBN: 0–313–30600–1

First published in 2000

Greenwood Press, 88 Post Road West, Westport, CT 06881
An imprint of Greenwood Publishing Group, Inc.
www.greenwood.com

Printed in the United States of America

The paper used in this book complies with the
Permanent Paper Standard issued by the National
Information Standards Organization (Z39.48–1984).

10 9 8 7 6 5 4 3 2 1

For Jerald C. Brauer

In memoriam

Contents

Preface	ix
Introduction: A Critical Assessment of Scholarly Literature in Religion and Emotion John Corrigan	1
Part 1. Historical Studies	21
Ancient	21
Medieval to 1600	27
1600–1800	39
Nineteenth Century	46
Twentieth Century	52
Surveys	61
Part 2. Social and Behavioral Sciences	69
Psychological Studies	69
Anthropological Studies	86
Sociological Studies	103
Part 3. Theological and Philosophical Studies	121
Theological Studies	121
Philosophical Studies	174
Index of Authors	219
Index of Topics	231

Preface

The study of emotion currently is undergoing a renaissance across the arts and sciences. Some of the most interesting and original contributions have been in the area of religion and emotion. This bibliography documents such work.

Scope. The bibliography is the only one of its kind and is extensive. It is not exhaustive. Works have been selected for inclusion based upon several criteria. Most importantly, a piece of scholarship must have made a significant contribution to the study of religion and emotion through its presentation of data, its innovation in terms of approach or mode of analysis, its interpretation, or its critical engagement of previous work. In some cases, books (and a few articles) have been listed even though only one part of the book directly addresses the topic of religion and emotion, the authors judging that the scholarly discussion in such a book meets one or more of the criteria of significance. Second, in view of the likely readership, the authors have chosen to include scholarship only in English, German, French, and Latin. Third, the bibliography favors recent scholarship over older scholarship. However, works of historical importance, regardless of the date of their authorship, have been included. Fourth, scholarship in certain areas, such as medical science and literary studies, has been admitted to the bibliography only in as much as it intersects with disciplinary categories chosen by the authors in their organization of the field.

Organization. Part One lists historical studies according to several historical periods/categories: (1) ancient (to the eighth century), (2) medieval and early modern, (3) seventeenth and eighteenth centuries, (4) nineteenth century, (5) twentieth century, (6) survey works. Historical studies include research bearing on numerous religious traditions (Jewish, Christian, Muslim, Hindu, etc.) and a broad range of geographical locations.

Part Two enumerates research in the social and behavioral sciences. It organizes scholarship according to three primary areas: psychological studies, anthropological studies, and sociological studies. Works included in this part of the bibliography likewise address a diversity of religious traditions and popular religious expressions globally distributed.

Part Three is divided into two sections, theological works and philosophical studies bearing on religion and emotion. These two sections represent a deep historical tradition of reflection on emotion. The bibliography is here limited to Western intellectual traditions, and, within the section on theology, largely, but not exclusively, to Christianity.

Many works listed in the bibliography blend disciplinary perspectives. Certain historical studies intersect with literary studies or philosophy. Scholarship located under a social sciences heading often draws upon several different fields in exploring religion and emotion, integrating, for example, sociological, psychological, and historical perspectives. Theological and philosophical works have profoundly influenced each other as well as contributed to the development of research in other areas. The authors have organized the bibliography essentially on disciplinary ground, but the borders marking that ground are porous and at times indefinite. Readers accordingly might discover useful annotations for works in sections other than the one or two that are of primary interest to them.

An *Introduction* surveys the scholarship in all three parts of the bibliography, noting predominant themes, the contributions of particular persons, and research clustered around specific emotions. It critically assesses the overall landscape of the study of religion and emotion with a view to locating continuities, junctures, debates, and prospects within the literature.

Names and spelling. Titles in French, German, and Latin have not been translated. Words in these languages and others occasionally have been utilized in annotations, in almost all cases with an English translation.

Indices. The end matter of the book includes a topic index (according to page number) and an author index (by entry number). The former comprehends all major topics, including references to proper names in the annotations. The latter lists all primary authors (including up to the first three authors of co-authored or co-edited works) and editors.

J.C.

Introduction

A Critical Assessment of Scholarly Literature in Religion and Emotion

John Corrigan

The following survey of literature identifies various approaches to the study of religion and emotion with particular regard to prominent areas and themes, the contributions of important historical figures, and specific emotions. Analysis of research patterns in some cases is undertaken with extensive reference to items in the annotated bibliography. The description of investigative trajectories at other times invokes a limited set of examples. Accordingly, this assessment is best utilized as a map of the scholarly terrain, a guide to the dominant features of the landscape. It is an invitation to explore, to search for patterns and prospects beyond those articulated herein, and to envision linkages among the various disciplinary perspectives that currently command the study of religion and emotion.

Historical Studies

Prominent Areas of Research

Scholarly investigation of emotion in the religious past has been distributed across a broad range of topics and themes. However, several areas stand out in relief against this accumulated mass of research, largely because of the number of studies concentrated in those areas, and secondarily because of the depth and sophistication of the analysis redolent in those studies. The four most prominent foci are: Hindu *bhakti*,

Christian revivalism, mysticism (especially Sufist and Christian), and women's experience.

The historical essence of the Hindu devotional movement of *bhakti* is emotion, especially the cultivation of emotion (25). Forms or gradations of the devotees' feelings can be identified (296, 328), while a study of the historical meanings of the Sanskrit term emphasizes love of God (302). Specifically, *bhakti* emerged and developed as the emotional involvement with a deity (334), often as the relationship between lover and beloved (52). The *bhakta* nevertheless has appeared historically in a variety of roles, including the guru, hero, and madman as well as the lover and beloved (257). Some studies have emphasized the range of emotions involved in such devotionalism as it developed over the course of the eighth to sixteenth centuries (53), including, in the case of the sixteenth-century *bhakta* teacher Tukurama, love, guilt, sorrow, and ecstasy, among others (98). The historical diversity of this strand of Hinduism was not without its limits, however, diversity occasionally giving rise to accusations of heterodoxy (112). Historians have stressed the linkage between meditation and emotion in *bhakta* (324, 40), and the best historical studies address the manner in which this devotionalism is framed by sociological and political factors (308). Some historians have argued that *bhakta* in privileging emotion over intellect embodied social revolt against Indian elites (90), while one writer makes a comparison with the Christian gospel of love in its Johannine manifestation (4).

Investigation of the role of emotion in revivalism has focused largely on British and American instances. Christian revivalism involves "ecstatic experiences" that are manifest in the physical exercises of the participants (186). One American history depicted revivalism as a "recharging" of the "emotional power house" that moves the wheels of social life (301), while another stressed emotion as a key element of a cultural revitalization through religious revival (317). Theorizing about the importance of the public and collective display of emotion became a more common aspect of religion in America during the Enlightenment (138). It has been argued that revivalism in England and America valued emotion over intellect (139), but it also has been shown that emotion was conceived as integrated with intellect, social experience, political thought and other aspects of a coherent worldview (137). The theory that revival was merely an emotional response to encounter of the American frontier has been challenged (132). The claim that emotional outpourings that characterized eighteenth-century American revivalism were innovative behavior has been rejected (177). Historians have proposed that revival preaching was deliberately sentimental (182), and revivals were judged by their capability to deliver excitement or heighten psychological tension (188, 197). Conversely it has been argued that nineteenth-century Methodists constructed meeting sites so as to deliberately limit emotion (211), and that revival calmed passion by raising tranquil feelings (214). In America, emotional revivalism is found in locations ranging from Appalachia, where it survives in its eighteenth and nineteenth-century styles (203), to back alleys of the nation's capital, where religion naturally took an emotional form (228). In the nineteenth-century Businessman's Revival, emotion was commodified and offered to God in exchange for favors (187).

Emotion and mysticism were linked in ancient Mediterranean religions, such as the worship of Mithra in Rome (7) and later, most visibly in Christian and Sufi religious life, and in the devotions of the *bhakta*. Mystical ecstasy arises through preparation and the exercise of certain techniques (289). While one observer suggests that mystics "feel a lot and know a little" (290), some historians have concluded that emotion and rationalist philosophy were joined, as in Sufi tradition through the influence of al-Ghazzali (286) and in Christianity as the union of emotionalism with an intellectualist strain of Augustinian devotionalism (312). Mystical religion accordingly can generate theologies

Introduction 3

of feeling (313). Not all mysticism stresses emotion: one historical study claims that St. John of the Cross thought reliance upon feeling a mistake (70).

In the area of women and religion, historians have concentrated their attention on feminized constructions of religious emotion and the role of emotion in women's religious experience. The interpretation of historical instances of such phenomena has moved in several directions. One study concludes that the devotions of women in seventeenth- to nineteenth-century France were characterized more by fear than men's devotions (170), while other studies argue that medieval women experienced status reversal vis à vis males in the course of their emotional religious exercises (50, 113), and that women in eighteenth-century England employed religion as a means to express anger against males who oppressed them (185). Several studies propose that the religious ecstasies of medieval women issued from a profound awareness of the body and of pain, both physical and spiritual (51, 117), with St. Perpetua seeking through martyrdom escape from emotions that tied her to her father (93). Much has been written about women and hysteria, again with varying conclusions. Early Christian female mystics were accused of being hysterics (32), as were European women centuries later (316). Ecstatic (and somnabulant) female preachers in early twentieth-century Finland likewise were called hysterics (283). Although male fear of women led to witchcraft accusations (167), Dr. Edward Jorden was among the first to defend a woman from charges of demonic possession and malfeasance by identifying her as suffering the medical condition of hysteria (129). Women likewise escaped the charge of possession (and mysticism) in late nineteenth-century anti-clerical France through diagnoses of hysteria (193). The emotionality of goddesses has been scrutinized by historians as well. While anger is a hallmark of some Indian and Sri Lankan goddesses (252, 284), the image of an affectionate bond between mother and child was exploited by medieval Franciscan preachers (94). (At the same time, women who used love charms in sixteenth-century Modena were penalized by church authorities [110]). Franciscan and Carthusian preachers remade the figure of Mary as less emotional in the thirteenth to fifteenth centuries. She subsequently became a model for women to rein in their feelings (82), and in Victorian England women rejected as a model a more emotional Mary (190).

Historical Study of Specific Emotions

A substantial portion of historical scholarship has been concentrated on religion and expressions of the emotions of anger, fear, bliss, love, shame/guilt, hatred, mourning, and jealousy. Research also has addressed melancholy (81, 87, 155, 218) and the emotional aspects of laughter (13, 14, 28, 43, 89, 206, 310) in some detail.

The nature of the anger of God in the Hebrew Bible varies from text to text (8) – although one study explains it as the rationalization of the experience of exile (29) – and anger as it is depicted as a whole in the Hebrew Bible suggests its complexity (15). Anger was expressed in a variety of ways, such as in the ritual clapping of hands in ancient Mesopotamia and Israel (23). The early Christian God also was angry (31), like Indian and Sri Lankan goddesses (252, 284), and figures from Greek mythology (where anger was the proper response to the breaking of religious taboos) (38). A female saint's anger is made understandable through consideration of the seventh-century Frankish culture of emotion in which she was situated (115). Cursing by medieval Celtic saints has only the appearance of anger (65), and among Christian monks in the eleventh-century cursing came to be associated with the absence of anger (96). Similarly, swearing in anger was ruled not to be blasphemous in sixteenth-century Spain (145). In Islam, representations of the prophet mark his greatness through reference to his anger (71).

Historical surveys and overviews of fear address its nature and function across a spectrum ranging from "primitive religion" to monotheistic traditions and the Enlightenment (323, 325, 332, 335). Christian fears of divine judgment increased from the thirteenth to eighteenth centuries (299), fears of hell were prevalent in early modern Europe (135), the French feared sorcery in the nineteenth century (189), and the African Igbo in the twentieth century lived a religion characterized by a "dread of the divine," which was a combination of the fear of death and the desire to escape divine wrath (267). The fear of death underlay the popularity of miracle stories in fourteenth century Christianity (74). Christian tragedy historically has featured a blend of horror and guilt (329) and, by raising a "sacred terror" in their readers, various authors have illuminated and driven home the meanings of moral tales in nineteenth- and twentieth-century America (311). In the twentieth century, fear has been linked to religious change in Ghana (277), to the shamanic personality in the Congo (259), and to visions of Mary in Spain (230).

A large number of studies have addressed the experience of joy or bliss, which is depicted in the Upanishads as non-duality and wholeness (305). Joy was associated with the movement from profane to sacred space in ritual in Israelite religion, and it was also connected to spontaneity in ancient Israel (3, 39). One study of bliss in India has likened it to the "oceanic feeling" while another study of Christianity in nineteenth-century Manchester casts joy as the feeling of submission to a higher power (34, 221). In Renaissance Christianity, joy was a key aspect of the cult of St. Cecelia (61).

Love has been a key theological component of Sufism, Christianity, and Hinduism (100). It was actualized in the Hebrew Bible as the faithfulness of vassal to ruler, and in Tamil Shaiva sectarianism as servant-like devotion (36, 280). Courtly love traditions in the Christian West influenced the vision of St. Francis of Assisi as well as medieval women mystics (106, 114), although it has been argued that courtly love was transformed to Christian love by the fourteenth century (56). The history of love in the West is marked by attempts to reconcile religious love with human love, and with love of nature (330, 331), with twelfth–century Cistercians defining *caritas* as both love of God and love of humans (109). Mystical love has been studied utilizing insights from addiction research (70), and eroticism and religious love frequently have been linked, as in Christian devotions to Mary (92).

Guilt appears in historical studies of religion in a number of ways, from expected analyses of the relation of guilt to submission and expiatory sacrifice in Judaism and Christianity (31, 35) to surprising discussions of guilt fantasies which were part of the piety of Afrikaaner women during the eighteenth to twentieth centuries (253). Christian family identity in the ancient Mediterranean was grounded in shame (19), and the nineteenth-century French religious "culture of delirium" arose in response to feelings of guilt (189). Historical research of hatred likewise has taken some anticipated directions, such as in discussion of the importance of hatred of a father in a saint's spiritual development (106), and the hatred of religious groups that are not one's own (262). Jealousy studies range from examinations of the "law of jealousy" in ancient Judaism, which prescribed the ritual handling of suspected adulteresses (17), to analysis of Islamic contexts for friendship as generosity overcoming jealousy (255).

Emotions associated with mourning are important in the history of religion, one study arguing that mourning and weeping have been a key part of Christian mysticism (104), another analyzing the ritual structuring of grief in fourteenth-century Christianity as an "extreme" form of cultural expression (74). The public performance of tears in medieval Spain manifested an inner state of mourning for sin and contrition and was crucial to the ritual of collective repentance (59). In sixteenth-century Judaism weeping also played a crucial role in spiritual development, not as mourning, but as a ritualized means by which a person ascended mystically to the heavens (130).

Themes and Prospects

Historical scholarship has explored the emotional component of religious life in a wide assortment of chronological and geographical settings, and with respect to several religious traditions. The majority of studies focus on the Christian West, but investigations of Hindu, Muslim, and Jewish emotional life have been steadily increasing. Currently there is only minimal historical interest in emotion in Japanese and Chinese religions outside of Buddhism, and although scholars interested in emotion have made a few historical forays into African, Oceanic, and Native American religious life, for the most part those areas remain vastly underexplored as well.

The most important and currently the most promising theme among historians of religion and emotion is gender. Studies of women mystics have been particularly important, and especially those that interweave the themes of gender, body, domination, pain, and escape. Investigations of linkages and resistance to linkages between hysteria and women's religious experience likewise have opened important issues in the historical study of religion and emotion, particularly through reference to psychological and physiological aspects of religious life. Most of the scholarship that attends to gender has focused on fear and anger as specific emotional states, with some attention to the joy of mystical union. There has been comparatively little interest thus far in defining historical manifestations of shame and guilt, hatred, awe, jealousy, and the emotions associated with mourning in historical accounts of women's religious lives. Likewise, research on the ways in which women have practiced religious emotion in a public settings is only a fraction of what it could be given the potential richness of the topic. Some studies have taken the family as a primary context for understanding the historical meanings of emotions connected to worship, faith, and moral action.

Comparative histories of religion and emotion are needed. Only a handful of projects at this time address similarities and differences across religious traditions or historical periods. The ongoing integration of relevant anthropological, sociological, and psychological research into historical investigation should provide some possibilities for remedying that deficiency by fostering the invention of themes that are susceptible to comparative study. More badly needed are historical works that engage the very issue of the definition of emotion in religion. How is emotion as a category conceptualized by religious groups in various historical periods? How is it envalued or disparaged? How is it thought to intersect with intellectual life and action? To what extent is it objectified in religion? Should kinds of emotion (i.e. religious or non-religious) be distinguished?

The historical study of religion and emotion likely will continue to unfold as a project in three parts. First, there is the prospect that it will develop understandings of the historical contexts for the expression and concealment of emotion in various religious settings, with regard especially to specific emotional states of anger, fear, joy, and so forth. Second, indications are that concern with gender and, increasingly, race and ethnicity, will play a major part in historical research of religion and emotion. Analysis of the role of class is desperately needed, but there is little evidence that beyond a handful of studies that historians have engaged it seriously as a category alongside gender, and little reason to suppose that it will appear as prominently in the near future. Third, historians likely will broaden the nature of their cooperative enterprise with scholars whose primary interest is literature, whether that be religious scriptures and mythologies, poetry, fictional narratives, theological/philosophical treatises, or diaries, correspondences and memoirs. The results of that cooperation might appear as a more precise rendering of the emotional lives of religious individuals and groups within a historical setting rendered as a system of feeling rules.

Research in the Social and Behavioral Sciences

Psychological Studies

Psychological research has articulated three primary areas of investigation of religion and emotion. First, psychologists continue to mine a handful of seminal texts by William James, Sigmund Freud, and Carl Jung, and to elaborate and build upon those texts. Second, psychological research has focused on specific emotions in religion, and especially guilt/shame, fear, anger, love, melancholy/depression, and envy. Third, certain themes, including gender, healing, and erotics, and to an increasing extent the physiological aspects of emotional life in religion have organized the work being done in this area.

Interest in the writings of William James has centered on his association of mysticism with emotion (339), the feelings of the solitary heart (388), and on James's assertions that emotion plays a central role in belief (387). Some work proposes that James linked religion with emotion because it seemed to have conflicted with reason (407), while other studies explore feminized emotion in James's thinking as a key to understanding his theory of religion (348). The influence of Freud has been immense, both for his grand claims about the nature of religion as the experience of "oceanic feeling" (369, 372, 414, 415, 521) as for his discussion of discrete components of psychic life, such as penis envy, that have sparked broader discussion of envy and its representation in myth (340). Carl Jung's emphasis on the integration of feeling in religion and his claim that religious beliefs have an emotional foundation have inspired much research. Investigations of collective emotion (376), the manner in which archetypes are constituted by "emotional-dynamic" components (409), and feeling as the core of theological concepts (426), represent several of the ways in which Jung's ideas have shaped psychological research on religion and emotion.

Some studies, following Freud's lead but not always his method of research, conclude that religion raises guilt to excessive levels (369, 423), even though responses to guilt differ among religious groups (336). Guilt is connected with desire in religious attitudes, and it can be connected with remorse in religious contexts as well (441). Shame is associated with Christian views of sexuality and with embrace of Christian systems of reward and punishment (434). Alongside guilt and shame, fear has attracted the interest of researchers, with studies suggesting a range of arguments, including the claims that religion can cause an irrational fear of punishment (423), and both aggravate and reduce fear of death (418), that it is intense among Christian charismatics (354), and that the fear of being abandoned by God can lead to eating disorders (424). The spiritual experience of a near-death incident can be marked by profound fear, rather than joy (364). Some surveys measure relative levels of fear among different religious groups and among different classes of persons within such groups. One such survey found that among Turkish children, religious fears were most frequent (365). It is reported that some religious persons have a fear of psychotherapy (421).

Religion can transform anger (416), and scriptural texts legitimate the expression of anger, which can be therapeutically beneficial (429). Anger as a "demonic" form of power can be used for good (360). Depression, or melancholy, is arguably the most studied emotion among psychological researchers interested in religion. In Christian history, depression was of interest to desert monks, church fathers, and Thomas Aquinas (384), and it might be the source of religious experience (349, 388), that does not mean that its influence is always positive, as in the case of Vincent van Gogh, whose depression and suicide have been linked to his religious vision (405). One psychological study details the interrelationships between religiousness and loneliness (413), while another correlates loneliness with belief in a wrathful God (433), and another concludes that Hindus are lonelier than Christians or Muslims (343).

Studies of religion and emotion increasingly note the importance of gender, whether that be in respect of women's positive feelings during mother-goddess rituals (385), or with regard to religious aspects of depression and guilt in a woman's personality (419). The theme of healing also has been important in recent work. Some research points out the manner in which religious rites provide cathartic release of negative emotions and so foster psychological healing (386). Analysis of specific rituals includes a study of the manner in which Jewish public prayer in the *minyan* alleviates loneliness and restores mental health (430). Emotions associated with sexual desire have been analyzed in connection with spirituality (366), and psychological inquiry that involves physiological research has suggested a variety of ways in which body, emotion, and religion are related, as in the argument that communication between the left cortex and the right cortex of the brain is essential for establishing the feeling component of religion (377).

Anthropological Studies

Anthropological research has focused on healing (including notions of harmony and balance), witchcraft and possession, and gender, with some attention as well to ritual, trance, and the objectification of emotion in religious contexts. In many cases some of these themes are interwoven in field studies. Again, specific emotions that have come under scrutiny are anger, fear, shame/guilt, ecstasy, mourning, and depression/sadness.

Studies of religious healing that substantially address the role of emotion include some which stress the manner in which ritual performances relieve painful emotions (532), as in the healing of despair in Sinhalese Buddhism (527), the ritual healing of depression among Indians of the Pacific Northwest (493), and the shamanic healing of sadness in Malay ritual (501). Others point out various interrelationships of spirit healing and emotion (484), such as the emotional context for healing "soul loss" in Nepal (472), and the linkage between health, holiness and emotion in Afro-Brazilian candomblé and xangô (524). Mourning as a key ingredient of religious healing is explored alongside its equivalent role in psychotherapeutic healing (491). Chinese healing traditions have been studied with an eye to emotion as well (559), and particularly with regard to Chinese emphasis on healing as a process involving the reestablishing of harmony – emotional disorder being correlated with cosmological disturbances and imbalances (469). Harmony likewise is the key to a healthy emotional life among Tamil persons living within a Hindu caste system (468).

The related themes of witchcraft and possession appear often in connection with emotion. "Moth madness" among the Navaho is caused by possession by a witch (506), and the healing of fear and anger in Ecuador requires the overcoming of witchcraft (534). Demon exorcisms in Sri Lanka purge anger and greed (494) while in northern Brazil, spirit possession is linked to ecstasy (485). Recognition of the emotions of witches themselves – especially envy – is important in the culture of the Kenyan Gusii (506). There is also a "gentle madness" among the Mahgreb in North Africa (455) and the holy "madness of the saints" in Bengal (515, 516), both of which are characterized by trance rather than possession. Trance, ritual and ecstasy are elsewhere associated (482, 483), and the emotional components of religious ritual are often explored in anthropological studies, resulting in early theoretical statements, such as Marett's (518), and Goldenweiser's "religious thrill" (481), as well as thickly descriptive work on, for example, how Hindu pilgrims are transformed through the ritual dance of *srngara rasa*, or "erotic emotion" (520).

Anthropological studies that address religion, emotion and gender are numerous, with the majority exploring an aspect of women's lives. Where one study describes the emotional dimensions to male impersonation of the goddess Bhagavati in southern India (462) another explores the joy of female firewalkers who act like men in northern Greece (467). Other women reach emotional peaks in religious exercises elsewhere, as in Finland and Russia, where they ecstatically chant the Karelian lament, a performative rendering of the Karelian religious worldview (549), and among the African Winti, where they exhibit an uninhibited and joyous sexual passion in the *mati* work (556). In some cases women fare less well with regard to emotion, as in the cases of Hindu brides who must deny social relations and be sad for a time (542), and in Polynesia, where the religious valuing of low-level emotional attachments to others is involved in their subordination to men (530). In another case, Sudanese women learn to resist certain aspects of their subordination to men through emotional trance (460). Among Muslims in Malay, where men are viewed as spiritual and women as essentially emotional creatures, women are able to maintain their high status (531).

The objectification and commodification of emotion is an emerging theme in anthropological studies bearing on religion. It can be seen in various instances as part of complex objectifying tendencies in conceptualizations of the self (465, 556). In one case emotion is poetically and ritually rendered as food in local Hindu performances surrounding the worship of Krishna (550).

Studies that address anger focus especially on ritual ways in which anger is reduced among persons in a community. From the ritualized expression of repressed anger in Kenya (487), to Christian talking cures for hidden "bad feelings" in the Solomon Islands (557), to religious antidotes for anger among Hindu worshippers of Kali (523), research underscores the importance of religious ideas and practices in the negotiation of this socially disruptive emotion. The process of curing anger might require a ritual process that rebalances hot and cold, and certain fluids in the body, at the hands of an exorcist (495). At the fringes of such exercises are, on the one hand, such phenomenon as "justifiable anger" (512) and, on the other, the case of ritualized rage expressed in violence against one's enemies (463). The role of religious difference in the outbreak of anger between two groups can take many forms, as between members of rival Buddhist sects (457), or between representatives of two very different religious orientations, such as Christian missionaries and non-Christian Africans (464). A large number of studies that analyze anger also treat fear, but some research is concerned very specifically with fear as a key component of religious life. Frazier's emphasis on the fear of the dead as the fundament of religion (475), and Malinowski's emphasis on the fear of death as the source of emotional tension in religious rites (517) are among the sweeping claims for the role of fear in religion. More recent work examines local dynamics of the religious handling of fears. In Sri Lanka, for example, oracles facilitate the expression of fear among Tamil families suffering the ravages of war (503).

Ecstasy and depression both are frequently connected with spirit possession. Ecstasy, which often is associated with mysticism, can be present among rattlesnake handlers in Appalachian Christian communities (497) as much as in religious dancing in Brazil (485). Ecstastic episodes have been characterized by distinctive neural and hormonal activity (482). The spirit possession that sometimes is associated with ecstatic moments (509) can also characterize conceptualization of states of depression and despair. Despair in Buddhist cultures sometimes is understood in connection with an attack by an evil spirit (527). In India, depression is thought to arise as sadness over the transitoriness of life, of conceptualization of life as a dream state (521). The appearance of sadness in mourning, however, might in fact be emotions of attachment between Andaman Islanders (535). And in Shinto, the lament for a dying person actually might be sorrow for oneself (452). Religious cultures manage mourning in various ways, through ritual practices and rhetorical strategies. Religious singing is a common expression of grief and sadness (471), while specific kinds of singing and weeping at burials leads to the transmogrifying of males into birds (474). In Transylvania, mourning of an unmarried person includes the wedding of that person, so that the deceased may experience what was missed in life (498). Surveys of religious approaches to bereavement frequently address the emotional aspects of the process (470).

Sociological Studies

Sociological research on religion and emotion has grown directly out of Emile Durkheim's studies of social solidarity, which have been enlarged and refined over time by a number of other writers. Aside from this strand of research, a fair amount of effort has been invested in producing what might be called "happiness and satisfaction" measurements among religious persons, and religion and mental health studies. Among the specific emotions that have attracted investigators, anger and fear, together with the emotions involved in mourning, constitute the greater part of religion and emotion studies. There has been some interest in hatred and shame, but comparatively little in ecstasy and guilt.

Durkheim's contribution rests largely in his analysis of collective sentiment in religious ritual, and the role of emotion in the structuring of social order (587). His influence is present in a great many studies, including those that challenge specific parts of his theory. The genesis of solidarity and the sacred in emotion remains a primary theme, even when supplemented by claims for the role of biology (591). Such solidarity establishes the power of the sacred, an "emotional energy" (610), which is maintained through bonds of companionship among members of a community (616), although an emotionally tight-knit community of saints might represent an overly authoritarian solidarity (612). In addition to this aspect of Durkhiem's theorizing, certain ideas of Weber's have proven important to the sociological study of religion and emotion. Chief among these is Weber discussion of charisma in a leader and especially his claim that attraction to such a leader is grounded in feelings of hope, despair or enthusiasm (655). Wach, who evidenced a broad interest in emotion in religion, turns some of the same ground as Weber in treatments of linkages between personal charisma and emotion, but departs from Weber in his attention to the emotional element in the experience of the divine (653). Bellah, and more recently, Wuthnow, have remarked on the element of feeling in belonging to a religious group (566, 608, 656, 657, 658).

Investigators have noticed anger in a variety of religious contexts. Anger appears central to a televangelist's performance (614). Religious persons are angry at their loss in divorce (590). Anger is not avoided by Quakers, but viewed as an indication of the necessity to address problems (566). Gaza Strip teenagers who experience the social disruptions and violence of religious disputes there become angry when they perform religious rites (588). An even higher percentage (two-thirds) become fearful. Fear of death nevertheless is the most common theme of research, whether in the context of studies of near-death experiences (649), or the contemplation of prolongation of life with life-sustaining technology (568). There has also been some interest in fear of emotion, as in the case of French problems in approaching Islam in Algeria (575). In research on mourning, the most common type of study reports the usefulness of religious ritual in ameliorating the emotional trauma of the bereaved (572, 605, 606, 630). Sociologists also have explored the manner in which religion reduces the fear of dying (596).

Sociological literature includes a significant body of research on religious factors related to happiness and to the overcoming of depression and loneliness. The social dimension of religion is linked to low levels of loneliness (609), and so are religious ideas, as in Turkey, where they construct an optimistic view of the world that lessens depression, especially among females (636). Sometimes, however, religion appears to work in precisely the opposite direction, as in the case of adherents to several conservative Protestant denominations, who became more depressed after divorce than members of other groups (590). Religion is linked to satisfaction with life among Portugese-French adolescents (624), it is a source of hope for the sick (611), and it is correlated to physical well-being in gerontological research (603). Reliance upon religion in coping with the murder of a loved one, however, brings mixed results (681), and non-practioners of Santeria in a Cuban-American community show greater personal happiness and satisfaction than practitioners (629).

Gender is an important factor in research about satisfaction with life and especially about one's place in society. While there is a high degree of correlation of mental health and religiosity in women, the same is not true for men (577). California women whose religious lives unfold under the banner of the Religious Right happily and enthusiastically embrace their subordination to men (583), while women in a conservative Southern Baptist group divorce belief from behavior in resisting expectations for their subordination, as a strategy leading to their happiness (628). The repression of sexual passion in Muslim women complicates the possibilities for happiness for both women and men (618).

Theological and Philosophical Studies

The many strands of theological and philosophical inquiry in the West have been interwoven virtually since their beginnings. Certain aspects of this historically shared project have been of particular importance for the study of emotion, and especially in the areas of ethics and virtue, the relationship of affectivity to cognition, and the human body. The following discussion of the theological and philosophical literature registers certain differences in their approaches to emotion, but it suggests as well the manner in which each has informed, criticized, and shaped the other both over time and in specific moments of invention.

Theological Studies

Studies of religion and emotion that focus upon theological ideas in general are less concerned with specific emotions than with understanding the language of emotion, the relation of emotion to cognition and will, the ethical implications of emotional experience, and the ways in which specific writers have approached these issues. The exception is research on ecstasy (see below), and an occasional reference to fear (686, 753, 796, 856), melancholy (729), or despair/anxiety (785, 786, 794, 796, 870). The drift of theological studies of religion and emotion is rather the attempt to define emotion *per se*, and to place it within theological constructions of self.

Theologians and Emotion

Friedrich Schleiermacher is one of the most important theologians concerned with emotions. In several works, Schleiermacher explained the essence of religion as a "feeling of absolute dependence" and sought to describe the relation of feeling to thinking and doing (902, 903). The "feeling of absolute dependence" has come under extensive critical review (883, 892) as the centerpiece of Schleiermacher's thought. One critic has argued that Schleiermacher was essentially correct in positing the feeling, but that he did not have command of philosophical categories necessary for successful articulation of his theory (714). Schleiermacher's "romanticist" theory of religion (663) is variously analyzed as dependent on conceptualization of a relationship between feeling and intuition (742), as grounded in a particular relationship between language and feeling (855), and as understandable essentially as an outworking of Schleiermacher's linking of essence and appearance (908). One study proposes that the meaning of spirit (*Geist*) is the key to understanding the feeling of absolute dependence; another asks whether Schleiermacher's theory is theological or philosophical (804); another criticizes it for de-embedding feeling from culture (877). Some theologians have offered supplementary concepts and descriptions of other kinds of feelings that ought to be clustered with the feeling of absolute dependence (952).

Thomas Aquinas defined the operations of four principle passions (hope, fear, joy, and sadness) in the context of a discussion of body and soul and the concept of grace (925), as well as in other treatises. Interpreters have opened an assortment of pathways to his theory of emotions, generally with reference to another aspect of Thomas's theology. So, one writer notices passions and affections in Thomas's moral theology (752), others concentrate on the affective character of virtue (811, 874), and another on the association of knowledge and love in his theology (765). The place of affectivity in the spiritual life has been an important general consideration of interpreters (874), as has the Thomistic notion of the relation between emotion and cognition (918).

Inquiry into Augustine's thinking about emotion most commonly takes his notion of "the enjoyment of God" (*frui Deo*) as its point of departure (659, 817, 904). Augustine is seen in relation to Greek and Roman philosophy, particularly with regard to ontology in his theory of love (760), which has been called a kind of "Christian Platonism" (685). The "law of love" is seen as the "law of delectation" (926), and the "desire for God" as three complementary and interpenetrating modes of emotional experience (678). Like studies of Aquinas, scholarship on Augustine seeks to place his thinking about emotion in the context of his metaphysics (824), and to address statements about the unity of feeling and knowledge (692).

Bernard of Clairvaux, St. Bonaventure, and Ignatius Loyola all have been important figures in theological studies of religion and emotion. For Bernard, the affections were central to religious experience (792, 896). Scholarship has explored therelation of Bernard's ideas to the courtly love tradition (741), and has addressed in various ways the relationship between love and knowledge, the relation of tradition to localized religious experience, and rhetorical expression in language and the religious affections (741, 793, 897). Exploration of Bonaventure's theology has paid particular attention to the role of emotion in contemplative aspects of religious experience (711, 712). Opinion about Bonaventure's understanding of the relationship of thinking to feeling, however, varies. It has been argued that he envisioned spiritual development as the progressive separation of emotion and intellect on the way to mystical ecstasy (237), while, on the other hand, it has been claimed that cognition and the affections are in harmony in Bonaventure's mysticism (260). Theologians have investigated Ignatius Loyola's *Spiritual Exercises* from a variety of angles, and often with regard to the valuing of religious affectivity inherent in that document (878). The *Spiritual Exercises* are thought to be a "school for the affections," a means to educate and discipline feeling (669), and have been cast as a conceptual model for the linkage of right feelings with right actions (752).

The Protestant Reformation and its aftermath introduced an assortment of fresh perspectives on emotion. Calvin's *Institutes of the Christian Religion*, in its emphasis on renewal of the heart through faith, both addressed emotion directly (686), and, according to one commentator, actually was rhetorically structured in such a way as to cultivate piety – including its emotional elements – in the reader (776). Some interpreters have stressed the affective character of faith in Calvin (840) while others have proposed that faith appears as a mixture of intellect and affections (851). Students of Martin Luther have located the affective element in Luther's concept of faith (707), one writer identifying the affective character of faith as trust (676). While some commentary has pointed to Luther's innovation in addressing the place of emotion in religious life, some also has noticed the indebtedness of Luther to the New Testament, Augustine, and Aquinas (837). Analyses of Luther's writings have underscored the connection between language and affect in the language of his sermons (916, 917).

A key figure for researchers is Jonathan Edwards. His classic *Religious Affections*, which explains the role of the religious affections in spiritual development, lists certain of them, and describes the way in which they connect a person to the Spirit of God, is the cornerstone of his thinking about religion and emotion (719). Together with his aesthetically-oriented definition of virtue as "the affection of the heart to being" (718), and his explication of love as the sum of all virtues (716), Edwards's theory of the affections has drawn enormous critical interest. Edwards's writings have been praised for their complexity and nuance – a kind of thick description (875) – and for their reflexivity, as in the case of Edwards's concern about the possibility of self-deception in the course of emotional religious experience (687). For Edwards, moral action is grounded in the affections (814), reason and emotion are joined in religious experience (766), and beauty is a primary quality of the affective dimension of spirituality (721). Edwards's articulation of the concept of the "sense of the heart" is indebted to Calvin and Augustine, not to early Enlightenment writers (909). Following Edwards, John Wesley stressed affectivity, and one study suggests that Wesley's theology centered on emotional religion as a mediation between orthodoxy and orthopraxy (689, 690, 691).

Kierkegaard's writings are rich in analyses of emotion. The discussion of emotion, and especially love, in *Either/Or* (782) complements and reinforces the analysis of despair, as it increases alongside consciousness and in relation to anxiety and sin (785). The exploration of anxiety as itself a consequence of sin, seen in various ways (786), is also central to Kierkegaard's thinking about religion and emotion. Scholarship has focused on Kierkegaard's correlation of certain moods with the movement of existence from the aesthetic, to the moral, and then to the religious (826), with the specific moods of irony, anxiety, religious melancholy, and despair brought to the foreground (827). Growth in emotions has been seen as growth into an individual before God (887), with faith as a "happy passion" (684), although Kierkegaard's writings have been utilized as well as a basis for understanding the affinity between modernity and melancholy (729).

Leading Themes in Theological Literature on Emotions

One of the most important themes in theological studies of religion and emotion is the language of affectivity. From general theories of language that have applications to religious language (735), to dictionary and journal articles that explicate the meanings of vocabulary about the affections in the Old Testament (726), Pauline literature (773), and the Bible (812), studies of religious language about feeling vary widely in terms of their historical and thematic foci. Most common are analyses of the semantic fields relevant to understanding the language of feeling in specific writers. Studies of Luther that fall within such a category include those that address instances of his biblical exegeses, as in the case of his interpretation of Psalm 6 (916), as well as more broadly cast interpretations, such as the analysis of his creative application of the language of traditions of mystical ecstasy to explanation of the meaning of justification by faith (865). Research likewise focused on individuals includes the exploration of rhetorical strategies and affective language in Bernard of Clairvaux (896, 897), analysis of the linguistics of Wesley's notes on the affections (691), a review of language and "emotional readiness" in Jonathan Edwards's writings (909), and the semantics of divine apathy (*apatheia*) in Western antiquity (736). Broader investigations of theological language about emotion feature an assortment of approaches, in different historical periods, as, for example, a study of the affective character of the language of mystical union in medieval women mystics (828), a historical overview of usage of Augustinian vocabulary about the "enjoyment of God" (790), and a consideration of the anthropology of the Hebrew Bible that examines "feelings" in a detailed fashion (953). Another layer of scholarship is oriented to more general observations, including the claim that the language of faith is the language of the emotions (898), and that the meaning of joy is given in religious language through analogy (732).

The study of ecstasy also has appeared prominently in theological studies. In most cases, such studies provide detailed treatment of the role of emotion in ecstasy, but many also approach ecstasy as a complex and multi-sided phenomenon, in which cognition, contemplation, affectivity, and mystical "knowledge" together constitute the ecstatic experience. Overviews of religious ecstasy demonstrate the interrelatedness of a number of factors (743), and some provide analysis of various broad historical contexts that shape the experience of ecstasy, as in the case of the relationship between ecstasy and rapture in the thirteenth to seventeenth centuries (772), or that of ecstasy and prophecy among Hebrew Bible prophets (757), or in a survey of understandings of ecstasy in the patristic period following the Montanist challenge of "enthusiasm" (788). Several figures loom large in studies of ecstasy. St. John of the Cross is important for his reflection upon ecstatic experience (722), and so is St. Teresa of Avila, who had no explicit theory of ecstasy but profoundly influenced subsequent theorizing about it (931). Carmelites drew substantially upon the reports of both mystics in developing understandings of ecstasy (723). Scholars have explored the place of mystical ecstasy in Bonaventure's theology (879), including in comparison to Thomas Aquinas's thought (918). The theology of Maximus the Confessor likewise has come under scrutiny for itsconceptualization of the role of the emotions in mystical ecstasy (927, 937). And some studies explore the ways in which theorists have conceived linkages between ecstasy and contemplation, as in Dionysius the Areopagite (938), and ecstasy and Christian gnosis, as in Origen (939) and Clement of Alexandria (942).

The relationship of the heart to intellect and cognition, and to the will, has long been of interest to theological writers. Medieval theologians frequently debated the matter. Recent work has tended to reject distinctions between affectivity and intellect, through criticism directed towards questioning the worthwhileness of the two categories, through theorizing of linkages or symbiosis between them, and through historical theology that uncovers more conceptualization of interplay between affect and intellect than was previously recognized. An analysis of the Stoic phrase "apex of the mind" (*apex mentis*), and its reception and transformation by patristic and medieval Christian writers is useful in outlining some of the elements in past debates (768), as is a study of affect and reason in Cistercian theology and spirituality (807). Various writers have rejected the distinction between intellect and affect as fruitless in understanding medieval Christian mysticism (829, 864), while others have redefined these dimensions of spirituality to allow for their reciprocal action, as in Luther and Gerson (869), or other complementary relationships, as in the *Cloud of Unknowing* (841). Studies of the relationship between cognition and the affective faculties in Bernard of Clairvaux, William of St. Thierry, and other twelfth-century writers likewise identify the intertwining of love and intelligence (770), and other symbioses during that period (771).

Some writers have stressed the role of the affections in revelatory experience, in their connection with intellectual and volitional aspects of religion (767) or as constitutive of "emotional knowledge" as a medium of revelation (847), or otherwise as a means to grasp Christian truths (886). Scholarship has proposed the disclosive character of affective states as an aspect of the cognitive character of religion (819), with some writers emphasizing the objectivity of emotional experience in religion (854). Theologians who work with the categories of intellect, affections, and volition largely stress the interrelationship between those three elements (767, 921). Faith accordingly follows as an emotionally constituted phenomenon for some theologians. It is a context of feeling and expression, as trust linked with cognition (833), as an oscillation between fear and gladness (856). Faith and feeling are viewed as two *sui generis*, but interactive, modes of being in the world (866). While fundamental to Christian faith, emotions themselves are understood to be shaped by local narrative (915).

Theological inquiry into virtue, value, and the moral life has intensified its examination of the emotional aspects of those areas. It has been observed that feelings are intrinsically valuational (758), that moral knowledge is born in affectivity (820), and that the "knowing heart" is the basis of moral awareness (821). If emotions are fundamental to any ethics (806, 885), their role has been described in various ways, ranging from an analysis of the moral life as the transformation of the passions in the formation of character (752), to a description of the relation between emotions, interior disposition and action (751), to a constructivist view of emotions in discussion of religious ethics (809). A recent theocentric ethics grounded in affectivity is developed in detailed fashion through a sophisticated analysis of the nature of the religious affections (750). Virtue, for its part, is both affective in its constitution and provokes the affections (872). Historical studies of Aquinas, Erasmus, and other medieval and early modern figures increasingly tend toward revisionist interpretation that underscores the importance of emotion in moral life (762, 763, 946).

Theological reflection on the body sometimes has been entwined with speculation about the place of emotion in religion. The unity of body and soul in writings by Nemesius of Emesa (often misattributed to Gregory of Nyssa) made possible for the central role given the passions in his theological anthropology (853). Recent theological discourse comprehends the issue of the relation of body and soul in a wide variety of ways, including, most commonly, the claim for the mutual influence of body and soul as a foundation for theological recovery of emotions (843), and, less commonly, the location of a phenomenology of the body within an ontology of human being as affectivity (797).

Much debate has centered on the capability/inability of God to feel. A recent study defends the idea of the impassability of God (698), while another, in re-examining the thinking of Origen, declares it to qualifiedly endorse impassability (708). A study of Aquinas's thinking about emotion concludes that God must be impassable because he is incorporeal (1200). Other research moves in the opposite direction, pointing out the emotionality of God in Lactantius (803), arguing that a compassionate God identifies with human suffering (831), and that divine resistance to evil is linked to divine compassion and love (728). An historical examination of divine apathy (*apatheia*) exhaustively tracks its appearances in the first three centuries of Christianity, with frequent reference to Greek and Latin traditions (736).

Religion, Emotion, and Philosophers

Theological and philosophical approaches to emotion are intertwined in a number of ways. Certain historical figures (e.g. Aquinas) and certain themes (e.g. affectivity and cognition) are important to both traditions of investigation, and a more general, centuries-long process of cooperation has created an atmosphere in which scholars may move between theological and philosophical discourses with some ease, should they choose to do so. It nevertheless is useful to view the manner in which philosophical thought has developed in certain ways that are distinct from patterns of theologizing. Such a view discloses not only the place of specific thinkers and themes that are distinct in philosophical writing. It provides perspective on the fluidity and porousness of each tradition, on the ways in which each has reinforced, challenged, or been transformed by the other, and at the same time it underscores the durability and definitiveness of theological and philosophical modes of inquiry. This overview of philosophical writings relevant to the study of religion and emotion accordingly will focus on a somewhat different cast of persons (with a few exceptions) and include a view of some themes that appear more prominently in philosophical literature than in theological.

The importance of Aristotle (966) for theory regarding the relation of emotions to virtue has been articulated in a number of ways (1185), sometimes with reference to specific emotions (1231). Scholarship has observed the importance of his treatment of emotion in the *Rhetoric* for understanding his ethical writings (995), while noting that his definition of *aisthesis* is fundamental to his thinking about emotion itself (1253). A great many studies have commented on the reception and transformation of Aristotelian thought in various historical periods. A study of the place of his theory of the passions in the formation of early modern philosophy is an example (1093). Stoic thought likewise has been of interest to philosophers. The majority of research has concentrated on Seneca, including overviews of the place of emotion in his moral and political philosophy (1000), his understanding of the relation of emotion and action (1089), and his theory of the passions, in one case with particular attention to anger (1033). Scholarship has engaged Stoic theories of the affections of the soul (1040), explored Posidonius's understanding of the passions (1230), and criticized the view of Stoics as intellectualizers of emotion, proposing instead that they made intellect passionate (1119). Kant's debt to Stoicism in the matter of the emotions has been observed as well (1214).

Like Aristotle, Aquinas has been at the center of philosophical study of emotion. Treated most fully in the *Summa* (1242), Aquinas's theory of emotion has been key to subsequent debate about passion, virtue, cognition, ethics, the relevance of emotion to intentionality (1021) and affective language about God (1105). Commentary has explored his understanding of the role of emotion in his arguments about moral judgment and activity (974), his view of the relationship of passion and virtue, in the context of the consubstantiality of body and soul (991), and in his claim for passion as a constitutive element of emotion, alongside a cognitive act of belief or judgment (1035). Scholarship likewise has observed the problems in Aquinas's structuring of the passions (1141), and criticized his theories outrightly for their claiming a cognitive aspect to emotion (1184).

Descartes's *Passions of the Soul* (1012) is fundamental to philosophical discussion of emotion. Scholars have investigated his understanding of interior emotion (980), the passions as "confused" thoughts or perceptions (976), the relation of will to the passions (1043), the various meanings of passions in his writing as perceptions, sensations, and emotions (1011), and as concupiscible/irascible (1160), and the general manner in which he classifies the passions of the soul (981). Much research has attended to physiological versus cognitive theories of emotion in Cartesian thought (1147), to Descartes's theory of the passions against the background of his ideas about the relationship of body and soul (1057), and to embodied passions (1003). A large part of such research refers to his ethics, and especially to the manner in which his ideas intersected with and influenced other ethical theories, such as those generally of sixteenth- and seventeenth-century French moralists (1116), and Cambridge Platonists (1197). Scholars have studied the manner in which Spinoza reworked some of Descartes's ideas about emotion (980), how dualist theories of the soul informed their work (1079), and how Spinoza broke with Cartesian and Aristotelian views of the soul by distinguishing perception and volition (1002). For Spinoza, reason and the passions engaged each other transformatively (1120). Malebranche's reworking of Descartes (976), which likewise linked the passions and ethics, included an emphasis on virtue as the love of immutable order (1048, 1128).

Hume's investigation of the passions and morality (1081), which linked self-love, benevolence, and moral sentiment (1080), was central to his philosophy. Together with his analysis of religion, the origins of which he traced to fear of death, the dread of misery, and anxious concern for happiness (1084), his writings about passion and morality have attracted constant scholarly attention. Scholars have claimed that reason and the passions are psychologically dependent in Hume's philosophy (1192), that the experience of passion is concurrent with the belief (1167), and that he thought calm passions preferable to violent ones in maintaining stability in religious and social life (1088). Commentary on his philosophy has connected passion with causation and aesthetics as well as morality in general (1029, 1087, 1166), and one study has argued that his understanding of the role of sentiment in morality makes him "the women's moral theorist" (972).

Among more recent influential philosophers concerned with religion and emotion is William James, who stressed the priority of religious affectivity over philosophical and theological constructions in his analysis of the nature of religious experience (1096, 1094). He has been criticized for exaggerating the role of emotions in religion (1144). Rudolf Otto likewise stressed emotion, the *mysterium tremendum*, in his analysis of the holy (1155) and as a part of his philosophy of religion (1156). *Angst* is central to Heidegger's philosophy, which proposed that anguish or anxiety apprehends being through nothingness (1069, 1070). It has been criticized for privileging anxiety in his ontology, but has been marshalled against cognitivist understandings of the emotions as well (1252).

Three recent figures who have greatly advanced philosophical discussion of religion and emotion are Max Scheler, Paul Ricoeur and Robert C. Solomon. Scheler's *a priori* linking of religious values with feeling (1205, 1041), articulated especially in studies of sympathy and ressentiment (1203, 1204), stress affective intentionality towards the other in a ethical system where emotions correspond to an objective order of values (1235, 1086). Drawing on Pascal (1061; see also Pascal: 1046, 1116, 1159), and critical

Introduction 17

of Kant's privileging of respect over sympathy (1181), Scheler posits a hierarchy of feelings/values (1207) that has been defended (1226), criticized and reworked (1232), and reinterpreted (1248). Ricoeur sees emotion as an involuntary which sustains voluntary action, preceding and limiting it (1173, 1175, 1182). For Ricoeur, feeling is both intentional and an affection of the self (1174, 1180), and his philosophy of feeling defines the affective fragility of the heart as a locus for human fallibility, and evil (1176). Knowing and feeling are related in metaphorical process (1177). Ricoeur's conversations with Scheler (1181) and Solomon – in the course of which he identifies feeling as a third mode distinct from the passions and emotion (1179) – represent a key part of recent philosophical exploration of emotion in its relation to ethics, judgment, and action. Solomon for his part criticizes Ricoeur's lack of a systematic framework for the analysis of feeling (1222), while defending a cognitivist theory of emotion. Drawing upon Sartre (1222, 1224), Solomon's seminal work proposes that emotions are judgments (1221, 1223), and argues for connections between emotion, intentionality, and rationality (1218).

Debates about the relationship between reason and feeling, such as those imbedded in the writings of Fichte and Jacobi (1021, 1059, 1199), remain important, as does the opposition to feeling as the basis of religion that we find in Hegel (1068) and others. The influence of Francis Hutcheson is still felt in thinking about ethics, the affections, and moral sense (1085). Promising new areas of philosophical study of emotion, value, and ethics include Martha Nussbaum's notion of "narrative emotions" as a middle ground between cognitivist and constructivist theories of the emotions (1151) and Michel Henry's idea of "pathetic" community as the essence of community (1072, 1074, 1075).

Philosophical Topics Bearing on Religion and Emotion

Most prominent among topics in the philosophical literature about emotion are: ethics, reason and cognition, and aesthetics. There has been important recent scholarship as well clustered around the body and physiology.

Research on ethics draws upon the western philosophical tradition in its breadth, beginning with the recovery of a theory of emotion and morality in Galen (1060) and the analysis of passion as therapeutic desire in various Hellenistic schools of ethics (1153), to the significance of the affections for justice in Duns Scotus (1026) and Aquinas's discussion of the ways in which emotions can both support and impair moral judgments (974). There is ongoing debate about Cartesian ethics and the passions (1003), and about linkages of emotion in ethics with religion, as in Schopenhauer (1208). Discussion of feeling as a part of moral psychology/moral philosophy (1258, 1010) has taken a variety of paths. Among the most important are approaches that stress the moral significance of emotions in their own right (1154), emotions as independent bearers of value (1138), and as the primary impetus to moral insight (1062). The irreducibility of affectivity has been suggested as central to understanding how emotions reveal values (1231). The capability of emotions to render moral decisions is described as their role in establishing felt harmonies or felt contradictions (1006), as feelings of comfort or discomfort (1052), and as correct or incorrect emotions in ethical reflection (992). The relationship between emotion and judgment is complex (986). Feminist ethics has focused especially clearly on emotion in ethics, in recoveries of Hume's claim for the role of sentiment (972), and in the appropriation of Descartes by French feminists LeDoeuff and Irigaray (1008). Detailed consideration of the role of affectivity in feminist moral epistemologies (1118) has served as a point of reference for critical engagement with classic theorists (e.g. Kant) and their recent interpreters (1213). More pointed approaches include the claim that suspicion of emotion in the Western epistemological tradition undercuts the epistemic authority of women in the construction of social theory (1091).

Desire (971, 998, 1000, 1049, 1050, 1133) and anxiety (982, 1070, 1073, 1084, 1201) have been central to many philosophical investigations of emotion. Another leading theme in the philosophical literature is cognition, which is inseparable from most research on ethics. The ascendancy of cognitivist views of emotion (1009) includes the general investigation of the cognitive nature of affective states (969), as well as theorizing about the relation of emotions to beliefs through reference to specific emotions such as pride, shame, and guilt (1241). Scholars have focused on emotions as interrelated structures of belief and desires (1050), claiming that feelings are ideational and end in knowledge (1078), on emotion and passivity (1044), and on the integration of affect and cognition with particular attention to moral insight and motivation (1061). It has been argued that emotions presume a dependence on belief (1188), a position sometimes articulated with reference to judgment (1221), or to aesthetics (1216). Dialectical or conflationist theories of emotion and cognition propose the union of intellect and sentiment in consent (1108), and the metaphorical interrelatedness of knowing and feeling (1177). Cognitive theory of affectivity has been formulated *contra* Kantian epistemology (1144), and with reference to Hume and Spinoza (1146). The ambiguities and confounds of such theorizing have been detailed in a study of Peirce's attempt, later set aside, to reduce emotion to cognition (1228), and through the utilization of philosophical concepts drawn from Heidegger to criticize cognitivist theories of emotion (1252).

Philosophical investigation of aesthetics is rich in its approach to emotion, and much of this work directly or indirectly bears on themes relevant to the study of religion. Schopenhauer looms large in this literature, for his notions of pain and pleasure in the experiencing of art (1058) as much as for his linkage of aesthetics, affections and ethics (1211). Hume likewise has been important, for his connection of religion, aesthetics and emotion, particularly with regard to the experience of fear (1087, 1090), as has Spinoza (1216), Hegel – for his ideas about aesthetics and irony (1063) – and Kant, whose discussions of feeling and aesthetics (1158) have influenced much recent phenomenology of affectivity. Philosophers have addressed the way in which art is structured in drama (1013), how it symbolizes feeling (1113, 1115), how belief, intention, and judgment are involved in emotional responses to art (1028), and how, as Dewey argued, emotion is present in "art as experience" (1255). It has been argued that literary truths are presented by aesthetic feeling (1137, 1136). Suzanne Langer has explored the biological aspects of feeling alongside its expression in art (1113).

Discussion of religion and emotion has been closely associated with reflection on the body, especially as understandings of embodiedness and duality have developed out of Cartesianism (1003, 1057), and, most recently, with reference to "living bodiliness" in Michel Henry's philosophy (1106). Henry More's psycho-physiology of the passions (1005) and the investigation generally of body, mind, and emotion in the seventeenth century (1093) are good starting points for recent theories about emotion that value physiological factors. The call for more dialogue with neurobiology (1055) is part of a broadening investigation of the relation of feeling to physiological changes (1114). This broadening has been surveyed with particular attention to physiology and cognitivist analyses of emotion (1126), and includes definitions of the emotional state as a composite of physiological processes caused by a mixture of belief and desire (1215), and as an event essentially at one with physiological change, but described by a different grammar (968). The blending of neurobiology with cognitive science offers one kind of approach *contra* constructivist analyses (1056). Sartre on the other hand criticized construals of emotion as physiological (1202) and it elsewhere has been argued that physiological changes are not necessary components of emotion (1239).

The Study of Religion and Emotion

The study of religion and emotion is a highly visible part of the current renaissance in the study of emotion currently taking place across the arts and sciences. It is important to bear in mind, however, that the study of religion and emotion is to be distinguished to a certain extent from the general surge of scholarly interest in emotion by virtue of its rich and ancient history. Philosophical and theological inquiry into emotion that originated in the ancient Mediterranean has stood as the trunk of a tree that counts many branches of investigation, from medieval scholastic theology, to Cartesian philosophies, to seventeenth- and eighteenth-century emotivist ethics, to recent views of "narrative emotions," historically variant "feeling rules," and the gendering of religion and emotion in various cultural settings. The study of religion and emotion consequently is situated in a remarkably rich context of traditions that inform and direct it, and it is positioned to contribute significantly to the study of emotion generally while it advances understanding of its own interests in myth, ritual, ethics, theology, philosophy, and other aspects of religious life and thought. The trends observed in this assessment of the field accordingly should serve not only as a guide to the exploration of specific topics in religion, but as a point of departure for imagining and inventing new ways in which to define emotion itself, and to explore its place in the web of culture that includes religion as just one of its components.

Part 1

Historical Studies

Ancient

1. **Adler, Elaine June.** "The Background for the Metaphor of Covenant as Marriage in the Hebrew Bible." **Ph.D. diss., University of California, Berkeley, 1990.** Focusing on Hosea, Jeremiah, and Ezekiel, this analysis of metaphor concludes that the relationship of Israel with Yahweh is homologous to that between spouses especially with regard to emotions of love, jealousy and passionate longing.

2. **Alexiou, Margaret.** The Ritual Lament in Greek Tradition. **Cambridge: Cambridge University Press, 1974.** An overview of ritual grief in ancient Greece that proposes that emotion is structured and expressed in the formal laments of funeral rites.

3. **Anderson, Gary A.** A Time to Mourn, A Time to Dance: The Expression of Grief and Joy in Israelite Religion. **University Park: Pennsylvania State University Press, 1991.** Draws upon the Hebrew Bible, rabbinic literature, and historical data in arguing for an assortment of meanings of joy in the ancient Jewish community. The experience of joy is associated with the movement from profane to sacred space in ritual. Ritual serves as both expression and stimulus of emotion, with joy as a representation of cleanness and mourning as acknowledgement of impurity.

4. **Appasamy, A. J.** Christianity as Bhakti Marga: A Study of the Johannine Doctrine of Love. **Madras: Christian Literature Society for India, 1930.** A revised dissertation (Oxford, 1922) that identifies similarities between devotional *bhakti* and the meaning of love in the Gospel of John, with emphases on prayer as communion with the deity and the joy of the mystic.

5. **Aune, David Charles.** "Passions and Desires in the Pauline letters: An Exploration of Paul's Moral Psychology." **Ph.D. diss., Brown University, 1996.** Paul takes a negative view of the passions in some of his writings, depicting them as dangerous appetites, while in other places he asserts that passion and reason are not

opposed and that personal interactions as well as relations with God can be fruitfully conducted when they are grounded in desires. Includes a survey of cognitive and non-cognitive approaches to thinking about passion in Plato, the Stoics, Aristotle, and the Epicureans.

6. Avalos, Hector I. "The Comedic Function of the Enumerations of Officials and Instruments in Daniel 3." Catholic Biblical Quarterly 53 (1991): 580-88. The picturing of pagans as automata, as mechanistic and lifeless in their behavior, is a key feature of Daniel 3. Against the historical background of early Judaism, such mocking constitutes both a socio-religious critique and a depiction that elicits laughter from a Hebrew audience/readership.

7. Bailey, Cyril. Phases in the Religion of Ancient Rome. London: Oxford University Press, 1932. A history of Roman religion from the establishing of worship of local and household deities to the Mithraic liturgy. Emphasis is placed upon the relationship between emotion and mysticism, especially in the republican period and in the worship of Mithras.

8. Baloian, B. E. Anger in the Old Testament. American University Studies, Theology and Religion, no. 99. New York: Peter Lang, 1992. A consideration of various scriptural texts with variously contrasting and overlapping depictions of the anger of God.

9. Bell, Joseph N. Love Theory in Later Hanbalite Islam. Albany: SUNY, 1979. This is an examination of the religious ideas of Ahmad ibn Hanbal (b.780) and their interpretation by four writers during the thirteenth to seventeenth centuries, with particular attention to the manner in which those interpretations apologized for legalistic Islam and discouraged Sufic and erotic conceptualizations of love.

10. Bettini, Maurizio. Anthropology and Roman Culture: Kinship, Time, and Images of the Soul. Translated by John Van Sickle. Baltimore: Johns Hopkins University Press, 1988. Alongside a discussion of emotional components of family relations and the representation of time in ancient Rome, Bettini addresses the manner in which Romans employed natural symbols in picturing the soul. Focus is on the madness of Aristaeus, a powerful God and benefactor of mankind, as an example of the manner in which Roman myth linked the emotional state of a god with the origins of culture.

11. Boer, P. A. H. de. Fatherhood and Motherhood in Israelite and Judean Piety. Leiden: E. J. Brill, 1974. Explores historical aspects of emotional bonding between parents and children, as represented in images of gods and goddesses of ancient Israel.

12. Bremmer, J. N. "Greek Maenadism Reconsidered." Zeitschrift für Papyrologie und Epigraphik 55 (1984): 267-286. Women's participation in the trances of maenadic ritual served as a means for their integration into Greek society by providing an occasion for the expression of emotion for which there was otherwise no outlet.

13. Brenner, Athalya. On Feminism, Anger, and Humour in Biblical Studies. Nijmegen: Katholicke Universiteit, 1994. Essay that suggests certain Biblical texts (interpreted here alongside accounts of Josephus) are meant to stir emotions of joy and to cause laughter. Specific themes of such texts are the ridiculed ruler and sexual ambiguity.

14. ------. "On the Semantic Field of Humour, Laughter and Comic in the Old Testament. On Humour and the Comic in the Hebrew Bible. Edited by Yehuda T. Radday and Athalya Brenner. Bible and Literature series, no. 23. Sheffield: Sheffield Academic Press, 1990. Pp. 39-58. An historical linguistic account of Old Testament words and phrases that proposes that certain Hebrew roots are linked to comic representation in literature – both as mockery of persons and as expression of personages' laughing. Biblical Hebrew, however, has less words relating to laughter than Modern Hebrew or Aramaic.

15. Brice, Eugene W. "A Study of Hatred and Anger in Old Testament Man." Ph.D. diss., Yale University, 1997. Proposes three categories of emotions of hate and anger, including antipathy/indifference, belittlement, and loathing. Violent emotions are expressed in writing, where the interrogative sentence was especially employed, and in the cult. The emotional life of Old Testament man was complex.

16. Davies, Stevan L. "Ascetic Madness." Pagan and Christian Anxiety: A Response to E. R. Dodds. Edited by Robert C. Smith and John Lounibos. Lanham: University Press of America, 1984. Pp. 13-26. Hatred of the body was common in the ancient Mediterranean, and especially pronounced in Christian and Gnostic circles. It was expressed in a wide range of religious myths drawn from Greek and Oriental sources, and points to intense guilt-feelings among a broad section of the population.

17. Destro, Adriana. The Law of Jealousy: Anthropology of Sotah. Brown Judaic Studies, no. 181. Atlanta: Scholars Press, 1989. A blending of historical analysis with literary and anthropological approaches focused on an ancient Jewish rite to which suspected adulteresses had to be submitted. The historical background of the ritual and its setting are considered alongside discussion of jealousy, uncleaness, and the judgment of God.

18. Dodds, E. R. Pagan and Christian in an Age of Anxiety: Some Aspects of Religious Experience from Marcus Aurelius to Constantine. The Wiles Lectures given at the Queen's University Belfast, 1963. Cambridge: Cambridge University Press, 1968. The intellectually feeble world of the third century overflowed with fear and hatred. Disenchantment with the world contributed to an emotional neo-Platonic mysticism.

19. Esler, Philip F. "Family Imagery and Christian Identity in Gal 5:13 to 6:10." Constructing Early Christian Families: Family as Social Reality and Metaphor. Edited by Halvor Moxmes. London: Routledge, 1997. (This collection of essays derives from a conference held in Oslo in 1995.) Esler argues that family identity in the ancient Mediterranean was grounded in notions of shame, particularly shame that arose through the public revelation of interfamily strife. Feelings of shame accordingly shaped the familial aspect of Christian identity.

20. Evans, Arthur. The God of Ecstasy: Sex Roles and the Madness of Dionysos. New York: St. Martin's Press, 1988. A popular history of the participation of persons in the Bacchanalia, with attention to gender and sexuality, Euripides's Bakkhai, and emotions historically connected with sexual desire, warfare, and religious devotion.

21. Farron, S. "The Sentimentality, Romanticism, and Emotionalism of the Ancient Greeks and Romans, with Specific Reference to Aeneid 4." Acta Classica 26 (1983): 83-94. Greeks and Romans in the ancient world were more emotional than persons in the

twentieth century. They brought that emotionality to their interpretation of the myth of Aeneas.

22. Finn, Thomas M. From Death to Rebirth: Ritual and Conversion in Antiquity. Mahwah: Paulist Press, 1997. Explores the meaning of conversion in Graeco-Roman paganism, Judaism, and early Christianity, stressing conversion as largely a matter of cognition. Feeling, and especially awe, was a part of the process, but was not fundamental to conversion.

23. Fox, Nili S. "Clapping Hands as a Gesture of Anguish and Anger in Mesopotamia and Israel." Journal of the Ancient Near Eastern Society 23 (1995): 49-60. A study of the terminology for the expression of rage and grief through the ritual clapping of hands. This behavior calls attention to the actor and frames a particular mood for ritual occasions. Possible magical ritual aspects are associated with clapping.

24. Gager, John G. "The Attainment of Millennial Bliss Through Myth in *The Book of Revelation*. Visionaries and Their Apocalypses. Issues in Religion and Theology, no. 4. Edited by Paul D. Hanson. Philadelphia: Fortress Press, 1983. Explores the historical setting and logic of the *Revelation to John* with reference to expressions of hope and despair in the book. Argues that the religious discourse served as a "time machine" that relocated hearers into a blissful millennial future.

25. Goswami, Bhagabat Kumar. The Bhakti Cult in Ancient India. Chowkhamba Sanskrit Series, vol. 52. Varanasi: Chowkhamba Sanskrit Series Office, 1965. Originally published 1924. History of the religious philosophy of *bhakti* movements in India, with an emphasis on *bhakti* as the cultivation and expression of emotion as a means of embracing life rather than seeking to escape it.

26. Griffin, William Paul. "The Image of God in Joel and Other Selected Prophecies." Ph.D. diss., Emory University, 1996. God, like humanity, is emotional, but certain emotions are more pronounced in God.

27. Guettler, Amy E. "Music as Prayer." Sacred Music 122 (1995): 6-12. Liturgical music functions as prayer because of its capability to express emotion. It becomes sacred in the process.

28. Huidberg, Flemming Friis. Weeping and Laughter in the Old Testament: A Study of Canaanite-Israelite Religion. Leiden: E. J. Brill, 1962. This study connects the emergence of cultic weeping and laughing in the ancient Canaanite cult to forms of weeping in the religion of Israel. Argues for the presence of "laughter" in the poetry and narrative art of Israel, as well as in behavioral aspects of Israelite religion.

29. Latvus, Kari. God, Anger, and Ideology: The Anger of God in Joshua and Judges in Relation to Deuteronomy and the Priestly Writings. Journal for the Study of the Old Testament Supplement Series, no. 279 (Sheffield, UK: Sheffield Academic Press, 1998). Anger as it is represented in these books of the Old Testament can be understood only through the lens of national catastrophe. The Jews did not want to give up on God as their protector, and so they rationalized the meaning of exile, taking it as a consequence of the anger of God at their idolatry.

30. Lonsdale, Steven H. Dance and Ritual Play in Greek Religion. Baltimore: Johns Hopkins Press, 1993. An analysis of the role of dancing that stresses mania as its

essential feature. Ritual dancing, such as that of the Dionysiacs, is an experience of ritual as ecstatic expression. Dancers believed that their god drove them to such an experience.

31. Maccoby, Hyam. The Sacred Executioner: Human Sacrifice and the Legacy of Guilt. Bath: Thames and Hudson, 1982. An overview of human sacrifice in ancient Judaism and early Christianity, with concluding observations about modern anti-Semitism. The Sacred Executioner, who is at the center of myths of human sacrifice, takes upon himself the guilt of mankind, in a ritual of submission to an angry male God.

32. MacDonald, Margaret Y. Early Christian Women and Pagan Opinion: The Power of the Hysterical Woman. Cambridge: Cambridge University Press, 1996. Early Christian understanding of the role of women in the origins of the religion labeled the initiative and invention of women as part of their "hysteria." MacDonald defines sometimes overlapping meanings of hysteria in the early Christian world, including: the gullibility associated with a rustic, sorcery, and the determination to remake the social order. Women's depiction as hysterics is explored with particular attention to their public perception, and especially their perception by non-coreligionists.

33. Mangano, Mark J. "Rhetorical Content in the Amarna Correespondence from the Levant." Ph.D. diss., Hebrew Union College – Jewish Institute of Religion, 1990. Analyzes the manner in which emotions of love, jealousy, joy, fear, hope, compassion, wrath, and distress are conveyed in the Amarna corpus. Appeal to emotion in the correspondence was meant to persuade rulers of a person's loyalty or to provoke political action. The construction of tropes in the corpus is explicitly linked to the expression and manipulation of emotion.

34. Masson, J. Moussaieff. The Oceanic Feeling: The Origins of Religious Sentiment in Ancient India. Dordrecht and Boston: D. Reidel, 1980. This species of psychohistory examines through the lens of psychoanalysis the earliest Sanskrit texts, with particular attention to images of sea and forest, as a means of analyzing the feeling of blissful contemplation referred to in those texts.

35. Milgrom, Jacob. Cult and Conscience: The Asham and the Priestly Doctrine of Repentance. Leiden: E. J. Brill, 1976. Expiatory sacrifice in ancient Judaism was linked to feelings of guilt. Remorse and confession of wrongdoing reduced intentional sin to an inadvertence, thereby rendering it eligible for sacrificial expiation.

36. Moran, W. L. "The Ancient Near Eastern Background of the Love of God in Deuteronomy." Catholic Biblical Quarterly 25 (1963): 77-87. The distinctiveness of the concept of God in Deuteronomy is supported by analysis of the historical context of the discourse about covenant. Love was defined by faithfulness and service of vassal to ruler. Accordingly, love of God is to keep his commandments.

37. Morgan, Michael L. Platonic Piety: Philosophy and Ritual in Fourth-Century Athens. New Haven: Yale University Press, 1990. This study attempts to place Plato's epistemological thinking within the religious framework of ancient Athens, through consideration of Greek religious ideas and especially by examining the language of ecstasy found in the Phaedo. The Symposium is presented as a discourse indebted to a religious vocabulary drawn from the mystery religions and Bacchic worship.

38. Muellner, Leonard. The Anger of Achilles. Ithaca: Cornell University Press, 1996. Proposes that anger (*menis*) is incurred by the breaking of basic religious and social taboos. Whether it be the anger of Zeus, Agamemnon, Achilles, or other figures, *menis* is more than an emotional state. It is a set of actions as well. Appendix 1 is a detailed etymology of *menis*.

39. Muffs, Yochanan. Love & Joy: Law, Language and Religion in Ancient Israel. New York and Jerusalem: The Jewish Theological Seminary of America, distributed by Harvard University Press, 1992. Among these collected articles by Muffs are several treating emotional aspects of religion. There are discussions of God's anger and love in Part I ("God and Man") and a detailed historical analysis of love and joy as metaphors of willingness and spontaneity in Part III ("Law and Metaphor").

40. Narayanan, Vasudha. The Way and the Goal: Expressions of Devotion in the Early Sri Vaisnava Tradition. Washington, D.C.: Institute for Vaisnava Studies, and The Center for the Study of World Religions, Harvard University, 1987. A historical study of *bhakti* from the seventh to twelfth centuries, focused on the expression of devotion in the piety of the Alvars, "those who are immersed in the love of God" (p. 2), and especially love, surrender, and the discipline of *bhakti-yoga* (meditation). The poetry of the Alvars was created in a Tamil language "associated with powerful emotions" (p. 7) that nevertheless was sufficiently precise to allow transition to the commentaries and theological treatises of the Vaisnava tradition, itself a composition of Sanskrit literatures and Alvar poetry.

41. Nilsson, Martin Persson. Greek Piety. Translated by Herbert Jennings Rose. Oxford: Clarendon Press, 1948. A comprehensive overview of the religions of ancient Greece that interprets Dionysiac orgies as escape from the body through a process of purification that was predicated upon extreme emotional practice.

42. Nock, Arthur Darby. Conversion: The Old and the New in Religion from Alexander the Great to Augustine of Hippo. Oxford: Clarendon Press, 1933. This detailed history is grounded in the claim that religious abstractions grow out of and are continuously shaped by emotions. Because worship rested fundamentally upon emotion in pagan religion, it was not refuted by reason. The relation between emotion and worship remained in Christianity but to some extent was altered by a rationalistic discourse.

43. On Humour and the Comic in the Hebrew Bible. Edited by Yehuda T. Radday and Athalya Brenner. Bible and Literature series, no. 23. Sheffield: Sheffield Academic Press, 1990. A collection of fourteen essays -- some less historically oriented than others, and all to a certain extent exegetical -- that explore themes of jokes, laughing, smiling, and humor in the Old Testament. Essays include an analysis of comedy in Job, humor in Old Testament names, Jonah as parody, and Jeremiah 18 as a joke.

44. Pagan and Christian Anxiety: A Response to E. R. Dodds. Edited by Robert C. Smith and John Lounibos. Lanham: University Press of America, 1984. Ten essays from an NEH summer seminar in 1979 that consider Dodds's notion of anxiety and religion in the ancient world. Various essays address emotional aspects of mysticism, prophecy, and the search for religious meaning.

45. Paisley, A. G. The Emotional Life of Jesus. London: James Clark and Company, 1931. This study draws clues from Biblical texts, and some others, about Jesus' experience of seven emotional states, including fellow-feeling, joy, grief, humiliation, indignation, courage, and love. A blend of history, literary criticism, and theology, the book concludes that Jesus' emotional life was fully human.

46. Versnel, H. S. Inconsistencies in Greek and Roman Religion. Studies in Greek and Roman religion, vol. 6. Leiden: E. J. Brill, 1990. A consideration of henotheism, or the tendency to affectionate devotion to one god without denying the authority of other gods. The analysis focuses on Dionysiac ecstatic religion, in the interest of revealing ambiguities and inconsistencies in the religious mentality of the ancients.

47. Yuen, Shing-Chung Royan. "Qing-Hen in the Book of Lamentations: A Rhetorical Analysis of Lamentations from Chinese Perspectives." Ph. D. diss., Graduate Theological Union, 1996. The study of Hebrew laments has been limited by the failure to investigate their emotional elements. The messages of the laments have been misunderstood or only partially understood. The Chinese concept of qing-hen represents the fact of an emotional bonding between persons as well as various emotions associated with lament: regret, resignation, loneliness, grief, sorrow and other emotions. Application of this concept to the analysis of Hebrew laments yields understanding of the level of feeling indicated in the laments, and insight into the literary construction of Lamentations 1-5.

Medieval to 1600

48. Al-Qatam, Abdulla Abdalli. Shi'ite Poetry During the Umayyad Period. Ph.D. diss., University of Utah, 1992. This analysis of Shi'ite belief and emotions as expressed in poetry during the period 661-750 is set within a historical framework that addresses political-religious leadership and the development of concepts of imam, wasi, and mahdi. Primary themes of the analysis are bravery, lamentation, argument and glory.

49. Babés, Leila. "Passion et Ironie dans la Cite. Annaba du Ribat au Reformisme." Maghreb, Machrek 135 (1992): 39-52. Focuses on the devotions to a Muslim saint in Annaba, Algeria from the fifteenth century in discussing the manner in which emotion and reason are interrelated in the Islamic Maghreb. Emotional aspects of devotion are strong but are structured by rationalized worship.

50. Bartlett, Anne Clark. Male Authors, Female Readers: Representation and Subjectivity in Middle English Devotional Literature. Ithaca: Cornell University Press, 1995. The intensely emotional devotions of medieval Christian women, especially nuns, are structured by Christologic passion and nuptial narratives. Though written by males, such narratives became the basis for female assertions of power and self-understanding distinct from the intentions of the male authors.

51. Beonio-Broccheri, Mariateresa Fumagalli. "The Feminine Mind in Medieval Mysticism." Creative Women in Medieval and Early Modern Italy: A Religious and Artistic Renaissance. Edited by E. Ann Matter and John Coakley. Philadelphia: University of Pennsylvania Press, 1994. The religious ecstasies and emotional visions of medieval women mystics was grounded in a keen awareness of the body, and a sense of the painfulness of physicality (which was often relieved in union with God, especially according to the mystical model, "a mixture of emotion and biblical culture" [p. 28]).

52. Bhattacharyya, Manjula. "Medieval Bhakti Movements in Gujarat." *Medieval Bhakti Movements in India: Sri Caitanya Quincentenary Commemoration Volume.* Edited by N. N. Bhattacharyya. New Delhi: Munshiram Manoharlal, 1989. Pp. 97-105. An examination of a form of *bhakti* in a sixteenth-century movement in northern India that cast the relationship of the devotee to the god as that between lover and beloved.

53. Bhattacharyya, N. N., ed. Mediveal Bhakti Movements in India: Sri Caitanya Quincentenary Commemoration Volume. New Delhi: Munshiram Manoharlal, 1989. A collection of thirty essays treating the emergence and transformations of *bhakti* movements in India, from the eighth century to the sixteenth. Some essays focus on saints, others analyze connections/oppositions to Muslim, Jain, and Buddhist groups, while others take etymological approaches. The essays suggest the breadth of conceptions of the emotional aspect of *bhakti*.

54. Binski, Paul. Medieval Death: Ritual and Representation. London: British Museum Press, 1996. An exploration of medieval death culture that analyzes ways of dying and rituals of death largely through reference to images in painting, sculpture, and illustration. Discussion of attitudes towards death and the emotional component of death and dying is interwoven throughout the text.

55. Bisson, Thomas N. "The Organized Peace in Southern France and Catalonia, ca. 1140-ca.1233." American Historical Review 82 (1977): 290-311. Largely an analysis of the terms of political reconciliation, this interpretation proposes that the "sanctified peace" was based fundamentally on the shared religious emotion of the people, as it was vented in waves of popular expressions in the 990's, 1020's, and 1030's.

56. Bowra, Sir Maurice. Medieval Love-Song. The John Coffin Memorial Lecture. London: Athlone Press, 1961. Examines the rigid ideal of love in song within the context of ethical and social aspects of Christianity – especially as represented by the Crusades. Pays particular attention to themes of purity, strength, generosity and devotion. This ideal of courtly love by the fourteenth century was transformed into Christian love as the religious context over time reshaped its primary features. That transformation concluded with the extermination of the love-song.

57. Champakalakshmi, R. "Religion and Social Change in Tamil Nadu (c. AD 600-1300)." Mediveal Bhakti Movements in India: Sri Caitanya Quincentenary Commemoration Volume. Edited by N. N. Bhattacharyya. New Delhi: Munshiram Manoharlal, 1989. Pp. 162-173. Discussion of the ideology of *bhakti* as expressed through emotionally powerful hymns, as a process that joined an urban elite, who were more interested in ideology, with the lives of common folk who embraced the hymns through forms of popular religion. Analysis of key twelfth-century transformations of Saiva and Vaisnava movements with attention to caste identity and the nature of emotional *bhakti* devotion.

58. Christian, William A., Jr. Apparitions in Late Medieval and Renaissance Spain. Princeton: Princeton University Press, 1981. A study of Christian visions in the fifteenth and sixteenth centuries that emphasizes emotion as communication from God, as a moral indicator or signifier, and as a message to be decoded. Emotional response to apparitions was a key form of evidence of the event both to persons receiving the apparitions and those searching the authenticity of them. Analysis focuses on the

emotions of wonder, pleasure, awe, sadness, fear, and distress, (expressions of which are plentiful in the appendices of Spanish language accounts of apparitions).

59. -----. "Provoked Religious Weeping in Early Modern Spain." **Religious Organization and Religious Experience**. Edited by J. Davis. London: Academic Press, 1982. Pp. 97-114. Weeping was part of an economy of sentiment that was thought to influence God in early modern Spain. Tears were evidence of feelings. People were easily moved to tears both because they took weeping to be a way of spiritual advancement and because the outward sign of weeping, on certain public occasions, evidenced the fact of collective repentance. Spiritual directors paid close attention to sudden changes in persons' emotional displays, as increases in expressiveness were considered reliable signs of interior religious life. Ignatius Loyola conceptualized weeping as a religious exercise, invented a discourse for the analysis of emotion, and prescribed exercises for the cultivation of weeping.

60. Cohen, Charles Lloyd. **God's Caress: The Psychology of Puritan Religious Experience**. New York: Oxford University Press, 1986. A study of Puritans' conceptualizations of their relationship with God, and especially the affective dimensions of that relationship. Along the way the analysis treats emotional states such as love, fear of God, repentance, guilt, compunction, conversion and other aspects of heart religion.

61. Connolly, Thomas. **Mourning Into Joy: Music, Raphael and Saint Cecilia**. New Haven: Yale University Press, 1994. Examines the alternating experiences of sadness and joy in Renaissance Christianity with respect to the cult of St. Cecilia, who became a symbol and exemplar of thoroughgoing spiritual reform. Extensive analyses of the ecstasies of historic Christian figures, "music of the heart," Jean Gerson, Dante, and Raphael, this interdisciplinary study illustrates the development of a religious world around a specific emotional process (i.e. mourning into joy). Appendix I is, "Selected Scripture Texts of Mourning and Joy."

62. Coppins, Attracta Anne. "Religious Enthusiasm from Robert Browne to George Fox: A Study of Its Meaning and the Reaction Against it in the Seventeenth Century." D. Phil. thesis, Somerville College, Oxford University, 1983. A historical study of the negative construction of "enthusiasm" in English heresiography, with attention to devotion, biblicism, and prophecy. The discussion of devotion includes analysis of emotional preaching styles, various species of "experimental" religion, and seventeenth-century criticisms of religious enthusiasm as mere emotion. It was not until the twentieth century that enthusiasm lost its specifically religious meaning.

63. Coursen, Herbert R., Jr. **Christian Ritual and the World of Shakespeare's Tragedies**. Lewisburg: Bucknell University Press, 1976. An analysis of six tragedies that argues that an understanding of the ritual of the Christian Eucharist is central to comprehending the historical settings of the plays. Positing the Eucharist as a dramatic archetype structuring an experience of fear, pathos, and purgation, Coursen analyzes the emotional patterns of tragic characters as a performance of religious ritual, in so doing advancing a theory about both the historical meanings of communion and the literary meanings of tragedy.

64. Crane, R. S. "Suggestions Toward a Genealogy of the 'Man of Feeling.'" **Backgrounds to Eighteenth-Century Literature**. Edited by Kathleen Williams. Scranton and London: Chandler Publishing Company, 1971. Pp. 322-349. A survey of writings of Scottish and English moralists that tracks the historical development

of ideas about emotion. In the eighteenth-century various terms were employed to indicate feeling, including "sentiment," "benevolence," and "sensibility."

65. Davies, Wendy. "Anger and Celtic Saints." Anger's Past: The Social Uses of an Emotion in the Middle Ages. Edited by Barbara H. Rosenwein. Ithaca: Cornell University Press, 1998. Pp. 191-202. Argues that Celtic cursing, which included language of a religious nature, was not evidence of anger, but rather a socially sanctioned ritualized expression of a persons' discontent with the denial of honorable status to them.

66. Duby, Georges and Philippe Braunstein. "The Emergence of the Individual." A History of Private Life II. Revelations of the Medieval World. Edited by Georges Duby. Translated by Arthur Goldhammer. Cambridge: Belknap Press of Harvard University Press, 1988. Pp. 507-630. In the course of a lengthy discussion of intimacy, the authors comment on the invention of subjectivity and the expression of sentiments, including through Christian religious devotions. This section of the book allows for a glimpse of religion and emotion linked with other aspects of private life.

67. Erikson, Erik H. Young Man Luther: A Study in Psychoanalysis and History. London, Faber and Faber, 1958. An examination of the historical context, including family situations, schooling, mentoring, and other factors, that surrounded the deeply emotional struggle of Luther on his way to asserting a new theological standpoint. Foremost in this analysis is the psychological view of the father and son relationship.

68. Fairchild, Hoxie Neale. Religious Trends in English Poetry. Vol. I. Protestantism and the Culture of Sentiment. New York: Columbia University Press, 1939. An extensive discussion of the ways in which sentimentalism arose from Puritan and latitudinarian sources, and became the characteristic feature of English poetry in the early eighteenth century. Religious themes occupied a central place in the poetry of the period, which expressed the variable and inconsistent emotional orientation of the sentimentalist. Deism, and eventually Christian evangelicalism, came to be the repository of this emotional quality.

69. Febvre, Lucien Paul Victor. The Problem of Unbelief in the Sixteenth Century, the Religion of Rabelais. Translated by Beatrice Gottlieb. Cambridge, Mass.: Harvard University Press, 1982. A classic work bearing on emotional aspects of religious belief, challenges to the legitimacy of emotion as a component of belief, and the cultural frameworks within which such questions were debated.

70. Garrity, Robert Michael. "Bernard of Clairvaux and John of the Cross: Divergent Views of Human Affectivity in Christian Spirituality." Ph.D. diss., Catholic University of America, 1990. Analyzes human capacity to feel, especially the emotion of love, with regard to two mystics. For Bernard, self-love, interpersonal relations and the integration of affect are key. For John, God and humanity are dissimilar, personal relationships dangerous, self-denial essential to spiritual life, and reliance upon feeling a mistake. This psychohistorical project draws at key points on theories of feeling and self arising from addiction research.

71. Ghazzal, Zouhair. "From Anger on Behalf of God to 'Forbearance' in Islamic Medieval Literature." Anger's Past: The Social Uses of an Emotion in the Middle Ages. Edited by Barbara H. Rosenwein. Ithaca: Cornell University Press, 1998. Pp. 203-230. Anger was a marker for the heroic figure of the prophet in *hadith* literature, and its expression was a fundamental aspect of the governing duties of the caliph.

72. Gildea, Marianna. **Expressions of Religious Thought and Feeling in the *Chansons de Geste*.** Washington, D.C.: Catholic University of America Press, 1943. A historical linguistic study of religious experiences represented in the *Chansons* that draws upon the theories of Rudolf Otto in explaining religious meanings in twelfth- and thirteenth-century France. Organized as a series of analyses of key terms in the medieval text, the book primarily addresses the themes of religious thought and feeling, the object of religious belief, and relations between subject and object.

73. Gilpin, W. Clark. "Sir Henry Vane: Mystical Piety in the Puritan Revolution." **Death, Ecstasy and Other Worldly Journeys. Edited by John J. Collins and Michael Fishbane. Albany: SUNY Press, 1995. Pp. 361-380.** The mid-seventeenth-century religious life of Vane was characterized by an intense, one-sided emotionalism which shaped his social and political vision. It likewise provided a framework and inspiration for his view of history.

74. Goddrich, Michael E. **Violence and Miracle in the Fourteenth Century: Private Grief and Public Salvation. Chicago: University of Chicago Press, 1995.** Focusing on "two primal human emotions," belief in the transcendent and the fear of death, this study argues that miracle stories featuring an escape from violent death characterized the hagiography of fourteenth-century Christianity. Acts of divine intercession, "rescue miracles," are contextualized by a culture for which "extremes of emotional expression had become distinguishing marks" (p. 27).

75. Goldin, Frederick. **The Mirror of Narcissus in the Courtly Love Lyric. Ithaca: Cornell University Press, 1967.** This study of the imagery of the mirror includes an extended meditation on St. Augustine's *De Trinitate*. When the broader history of love poetry is observed, it becomes clear that for Augustine, love and knowledge both exist in the mind as substances, with love drawing the soul to its ideal, which is revealed by knowledge.

76. Greaves, Margaret. **The Blazon of Honour: Studies in Mediaeval and Renaissance and Magnanimity. London: Methuen and Co., 1964.** Surveys the representation of the magnanimous hero from Aristotle to Milton, with particular focus on courtly love, romantic grief, Christian religious symbolism, jealousy, melancholy, and the soul alone before God.

77. Haller, William. **The Rise of Puritanism, or, The Way to the New Jerusalem as Set Forth in Pulpit and in Press from Thomas Cartwright to John Lilburne and John Milton, 1570-1643.** New York: Columbia University Press, 1938. Characterizes Puritan preachers as physicians of the soul who "appealed through the imagination to men's emotions" (25). Puritanism took shape as a religious movement focused on the affections, as an "eagerness for emotional experience and expression" (281), and Puritans manifested deep anxiety about their futures, sometimes becoming melancholic "spiritual weepers."

78. Hamlin, William M. "Attributions of Divinity in Renaissance Ethnography and Romance; or, Making Religion of Wonder." **The Journal of Medieval and Renaissance Studies. 24 (1994): 413-447.** Proposes that the testimony of autoethnographies of New World inhabitants reveals the manner in which native persons chose to represent themselves in accord with descriptions offered by colonists. Natives who were overcome with awe of European explorers observed them as divinities, thereby making religion out of wonder. The emotional element, through a discursive process,

accordingly structured a religious view of the world that included the attribution of divinity to Europeans.

79. Hardison, O. B., Jr. The Enduring Moment: A Study of the Idea of Praise in Renaissance Literary Theory and Practice. Chapel Hill: University of North Carolina Press, 1962. An analysis of the various poetic expressions of praise in the sixteenth century - and their classical precedents - with particular attention to the elegy. Christian types of elegy represented the sadness of mourners as well as the virtue and beauty of the deceased, and employed exclamation and hyperbole in picturing the eternal love and piety of the soul in paradise. Poems on the passion of Christ were rich with lamentation alongside praise.

80. Hardy, Friedhelm. "TirupPan-Alvar: The Untouchable Who Rode Piggyback on the Brahmin." **Devotion Divine: Bhakti Traditions From the Regions of India. Studies in Honor of Charlotte Vaudeville.** Paris: École Française d'Extrême-Orient, 1991 and Groningen: Egbert Forsten, 1991. Pp. 129-154. Analysis of religious ecstasy as the loss of ego-centricity, and, especially of the centrality of the temple to ecstatic devotionalism. The aesthetic element in South Indian Hinduism can be understood in its sensuous material culture which draws devotion by its beauty.

81. Hattur, Matt. "Ravens and Writing-Desks: Riddles and Rituals in England." **Culture Underground: Studies in Ritual and the Subaltern.** Edited by Alice N. Onderlan and Theo Dormuss. Oxford: Port Meadow Press, 1987. Pp. 10-66. A study of humor, religious imagination, and "hearts" in premodern social settings.

82. Hinton, Rebecca Ann. "The Humanization of Mary in the English Religious Lyrics of the Thirteenth, Fourteenth, and Fifteenth Centuries." Ph. D. diss., Miami University, 1990. Images of Christ and Mary began to change in the twelfth century, with both appearing more human. Franciscan and Carthusian preachers nevertheless made an effort to retain some element of the demi-goddess in Mary's appearance, and they did so by rendering her less emotionally expressive, less shaken by her experience of tragedy in the world. In the thirteenth century, sermons and moral essays drew upon the revised image of Mary in urging women to overcome maternal attachments and to rein in their feelings.

83. Ho, Shun-Yee. "Symbolism in the Religious Poems of the *Book of Poetry*." Ph.D. diss., University of Wisconsin-Madison, 1997. Argues that the religious symbolism of the Book of Poetry (c. 1100-600 BCE) is key to understanding the ideas and emotions of the ancient Zhou people. The simplicity and rationality of the religious system's symbolic order is linked to a highly positive view of life and the world.

84. Hollywood, Amy. The Soul as Virgin Wife: Mechthild of Magdeburg, Marguerite Porete, and Meister Eckhart. Notre Dame, IN: University of Notre Dame Press, 1995. The visions and profound emotional experiences of these Christian mystics is linked to their re-valuation of the body, and various conceptualizations of the body in pain.

85. Hughes, Jonathan. The Religious Life of Richard III: Piety and Prayer in the North of England. Thrupp, Gloucestershire: Sutton, 1997. An analysis of the emotional religious life of Richard III set within the context of nostalgic and sentimental devotions to various saints in northern England. An "individualistic, emotive concept of holiness" (p. 22) led to a deemphasis of prayer as a ritualistic means to healing and a reinforcement of religion as an internal matter involving a sense of richness and worth.

86. Jordan, Gregory E. "Traces of Emotion in *The Dream of the Rood.*" Ph.D. diss., University of South Florida, 1996. The emotional is prominent in this Old English poem, which attempted to inculcate a desire for heaven and avoidance of hell. It exploits the emotionality that its audiences have invested in images of God/Jesus, the cross, the church, lordship and other phenomena, and shifts that emotion to a new object, the *Dream of the Rood*.

87. Kaufman, Peter Iver. Prayer, Despair, Drama: Elizabethan Introspection. Urbana: University of Illinois Press, 1996. "Therapeutic despair," an ongoing, introspective emotional process of struggle, was a constitutive feature of Calvinist piety in England. The creative emotional turmoil of religious life is redolent in the literary depictions of self in Shakespeare (and especially Hamlet), John Donne, Christopher Marlow, and Edmund Spenser. In this context the question "to be or not to be" invokes a rich assortment of religious issues involving identity, self-making, and self-valuation.

88. Kim, Man-Poong. "Faithfulness, Guilt, and Shame in the Women of the Yi Dynasty in Korea: With Contemporary Illustrations and Implications for Pastoral Care and Counseling in the Korean Church in the Republic of Korea." Ph. D. diss., Boston University School of Theology, 1989. Analyzes marital fidelity, guilt and shame in Yi women within the context of Christian and neo-Confucian religious ideas, and employs psychohistorical methods to disclose the meanings of emotional life for those women.

89. Klaniczay, Gábor. The Uses of Supernatural Power: The Transformation of Popular Religion in Medieval and Early-Modern Europe. Cambridge: Polity Press, 1990. An approach to a history of popular religion that takes the carnival, and specifically "the culture of popular laughter," as the foundation for medieval religious festivity. Emotions stimulated and shaped by the carnival are fundamental to the vitality of popular religion.

90. Klostermaier, Klaus Konrad. "Will India's Past be America's Future? Reflections on the Caitanya Movement and Its Potentials." Tradition and Modernity in Bhakti Movements. Edited by Jayant Iele. Leiden: E. J. Brill, 1981. Pp. 94-103. Bhakti is both a privileging of emotion over intellect, and the embodiment of revolt of the lower classes against Indian elites. The early sixteenth-century Caitanya movement was a blending of a Buddhist concern for consciousness, traditional Hindu theism, and an elaborate and complex view of emotional life.

91. Konkola, Kari Sueros. "Psychology of Emotions as Theology: The Meaning and Control of Sin in Early Modern English Religion." Ph.D. diss., University of Wisconsin-Madison, 1994. English Protestants believed that religious law was meant to govern emotions as well as thoughts. This analysis of beliefs about the functioning of the emotions focuses on conversion as a means of restructuring emotional life so as to make Protestant devotionalism a pleasant and seemingly "natural" experience. Meditative techniques drawn from medieval praxis provided the basis for emotional change. Pride, envy, anger, and love are chiefly discussed.

92. LeClerc, Jean. Monks and Love in Twelfth-Century France: Psycho-Historical Essays. Oxford: Clarendon Press, 1979. Traces the emergence in the twelfth century

of the notion of human feelings as important and significant, and especially the role of St. Bernard of Clairvaux in refashioning the idea of love of God as a matter of deep personal emotion. Such love was also manifest in mystical relationship with the Virgin Mary, in a devotion that channeled erotic feelings in legitimate Christian expression.

93. Lefkowitz, Mary R. "The Motivations for St. Perpetua's Martyrdom." Journal of the American Academy of Religion 44 (1976): 417-421. The motivations were not entirely doctrinal, and included a strong emotional component. Perpetua sought relief from the close emotional pairing with her father alongside an opportunity to commit a political act that would indict her social environment.

94. Lesnick, Daniel R. Preaching in Medieval Florence: The Social World of Franciscan and Dominican Spirituality. Athens: University of Georgia Press, 1989. Franciscan preaching appealed to the emotions, and the emotionalism that it fanned led to experiential learning. Clerical references to the emotional bond between mother and child were of particular importance in the Franciscan emotional narrative style.

95. Leverenz, David. The Language of Puritan Feeling: An Exploration in Literature, Psychology, and Social History. New Brunswick: Rutgers University Press, 1980. A detailed historical investigation of the ways in which Puritans expressed religious sensibility. Borrowing from Freudian psychoanalytic theory, Leverenz analyzes the utilization of mother-father-child imagery in religious expression, and the emotional aspects of interrelationships between private religious fantasies and public conflicts.

96. Little, Lester K. "Anger in Monastic Curses." Anger's Past: The Social Uses of an Emotion in the Middle Ages. Edited by Barbara H. Rosenwein. Ithaca: Cornell University Press, 1998. Examines liturgical curse formulas, the pairing of opposites (e.g. patience and anger), and various models for emotional life in the monastic context. The highly structured nature of liturgical curses undermined their emotional quality, so that cursing in the eleventh century came to be associated with lack of anger.

97. Lobel, Diana Nicole. "Between Mysticism and Philosophy: Arabic Terms for Religious Experience in R. Yehuda Ha-Levi's Kuzari." Ph.D. dissertation, Harvard University, 1995. Jewish innovator Ha-Levi adapted Arabic terms for religious experience in order to support his theory of direct religious experience grounded in sense-perception, prophecy and love. At the same time he criticized any human striving to overcome the space between the human and the divine. The subjective and emotional aspect of prophecy is key to understanding his creative appropriation of Arabic language about religion.

98. Lokhande, Ajit. Tukarama: His Person and his Religion. A Religio-Historical, Phenomenological and Typological Inquiry. Frankfurt: Peter Lang, 1976. The sixteenth-century poet and *bhakta* preacher cultivated a relationship with the deity as an emotional experience that included love, guilt, sorrow, and ecstasy. Tukurama was a mystic prophet, not a theologian.

99. Lovejoy, David S. Religious Enthusiasm in the New World: Heresy to Revolution. Cambridge: Harvard University Press, 1985. A survey of emotional brands of Christianity from mid-sixteenth century England to late eighteenth-century America that focuses on the connections between religious feeling and various groups' determination to build community, structure politics, and hold power. Religious enthusiasm is rendered as radical emotionalism.

100. Majumdar, Bimanbehari. "Religion of Love: The Early Medieval Phase (c. AD 700-1486)." **Mediveal Bhakti Movements in India: Sri Caitanya Quincentenary Commemoration Volume**. Edited by N. N. Bhattacharyya. New Delhi: Munshiram Manoharlal, 1989. Pp. 1-16. A survey of the emergence of love as a key component in Sufism, Christianity, and Hinduism, from a comparative perspective.

101. Mansfield, Mary C. **The Humiliation of Sinners: Public Penance in Thirteenth-Century France**. Ithaca: Cornell University Press, 1995. The development of Roman Catholic penitential rituals shows overall an attempt to balance the private emotional connection with God with a public display of humiliation, even though at times the private and public aspects of penance were not evenly balanced.

102. Marcus, Ivan C. **Piety and Society: The Jewish Pietists of Medieval Germany. Études sur le Judaisme Médiéval**. Vol. X. Leiden: E. J. Brill, 1981. Jewish pietists practiced a "heart religion" that included, prominently, the fear of God, which leads a person ceaselessly to discover new prohibitions, invent new safeguards, and unselfishly love God.

103. Marten, A. Lynn. "Jesuits and their Families, the Experience in Sixteenth-Century France." **Sixteenth Century Journal** 13 (1982): 3-23. The Jesuit order in France exploited men's experiences of emotional bonds within their families in attracting them to an order that was represented as featuring family-like emotional closeness.

104. McIntire, Sandra. "The Doctrine of Compunction from Bede to Margery Kempe." **The Medieval Mystical Tradition in England**. Edited by Marion Glasscoe. Cambridge: D. S. Brewer, 1987. Pp. 77-90. This study focuses on religious mourning and weeping in the Christian tradition. The emergence of the doctrine of the grace of tears proved central to the development of Christian mysticism.

105. Milhaven, John Giles. **Hadewijch and Her Sisters: Other Ways of Loving and Knowing**. Albany: SUNY, 1993. An exploration of the emotionality of Hadewijch, a thirteenth-century Dutch mystic, that focuses on the manner in which her notion of union with God rested on ideals of embodied love and mutuality. The ideas of other medieval writers, such as Bernard of Clairvaux, are presented as dissimilar cases, as proponents of self-sufficient and disembodied loving.

106. Mockler, Anthony. **Francis of Assisi: The Wandering Years**. Oxford: Phaidon, and New York: E. P. Dutton, 1976. Francis's thinking about the religious calling, as it unfolded over the course of his life, was shaped by his hatred of his father as well as by Francis's embrace of the cultural traditions of courtly love.

107. Monad, Paul Kleber. **Jacobitism and the English People, 1688-1788**. Cambridge: Cambridge University Press, 1989. Into this history of Jacobite rebellions and riots is woven an extensive discussion of religious life, including Jacobite anti-Catholicism, as Monod explores Jacobitism as a movement defined by sympathy, affection and feeling.

108. Netherton, William David. "'Joy Gars Me Jangell': Affective Devotion in the English Writings of Richard Rolle." Ph.D. diss., Texas Tech University, 1997. Fourteenth-century mystic and writer Rolle practiced a faith largely founded on feeling. His audience embraced his depiction of the religious life as fundamentally a matter of affective devotion. Rolle emphasized physical phenomena, as in his sensual descriptions

of the relationship between Jesus and the devotee, as a key aspect of the cultivation of affective piety.

109. Newman, Martha G. The Boundaries of Charity: Cistercian Culture and Ecclesiastical Reform, 1098-1180. Stanford: Stanford University Press, 1996. A key element of the religious culture of the Cistercians was their definition of *caritas* as the ideal love felt by a human for God and for other humans. That notion increasingly was expressed in military and sexual metaphors and inspired an ethos of control, a construction of the boundaries of *caritas*, for Cistercians.

110. O'Neil Mary. "Magical Healing, Love Magic and the Inquisition in Late Sixteenth-Century Modena." Inquisition and Society in Early Modern Europe. Edited by Stephen Haliczer. Sydney: Croom Helm, 1987. The *maleficia ad amorem*, the diabolical use of means in inducing affection, occupied an important role in the religious life of persons in late sixteenth-century Italy. Roman Catholic authorities levied penalties upon those who practiced love magic. Persons of low status were attracted to love charms as a means of sudden transformation of their lives, and most users of love charms were women.

111. Orellana, Sandra L. "Idols and Idolatry in Highland Guatemala." Ethnohistory 28 (1981): 157-177. Pre-colonial Mayan religion explained the universe through recourse to emotion. Because of the emotional core of Mayan religion, it proved strongly resistant to the attempts of Spanish overlords to exterminate it.

112. Pande, Susmita. Medieval Bhakti Movement (Its History and Philosophy). Meerut: Kusumanjali Prakashan, 1989. *Bhakti* is precisely "a full-fledged personal emotion" (p. 1) that is secured from the dangers of unreflective emotionalism by its philosophical basis. This survey considers the teachings of six historical figures, and analyzes the saintly expressions of *bhakti*, including heterdox trends in the movement.

113. Petroff, Elizabeth Alvilda, "The Rhetoric of Transgression in the *Lives* of Italian Women Saints." Body and Soul: Essays on Medieval Women and Mysticism. Edited by Elizabethy Alvilda Petroff. Oxford: Oxford University Press, 1994. Pp. 161-181. This analysis of the emotional dynamics between saintly women and their confessors concludes that the confessional context was a situation that allowed for a reversal of status between the sexes, the women enjoying more authority, and setting the direction and parameters for the encounter, more so than the male clerics.

114. -----. "Gender, Knowledge, and Power in Hadewich's *Strophische Gedichten*. Body and Soul: Essays on Medieval Women and Mysticism. Edited by Elizabethy Alvilda Petroff. Oxford: Oxford University Press, 1994. Pp. 182-203. Religious poems about "lady love" by a female Dutch mystic draw upon a conception of courtly love in expressing the relationship between a person and a female divinity.

115. Peyroux, Catherine. "Gertrude's Furor: Reading Anger in an Early Medieval Saint's Life. Anger's Past: The Social Uses of an Emotion in the Middle Ages. Edited by Barbara H. Rosenwein. Ithaca: Cornell University Press, 1998. Pp. 36-55. This study proposes that the manner of a female saint's anger indicates her celestial marriage to Christ, as well as other key aspects of her social and religious life. According to Peyroux: "When we write histories of the past in which feeling is omitted, we implicitly disregard fundamental aspects of the terms on which people act and interact. . . " (pp. 54-5).

116. Questier, Michael C. <u>Conversion, Politics, and Religion in England, 1580-1625</u>. **Cambridge Studies in Early Modern British History. New York: Cambridge University Press, 1996.** This history of the English Reformation focuses on the emotional experience of conversion, interpreting it as an event that varied from person to person in terms of the details of the crisis. Conversion, however, left a person emotionally excited and on edge, rather than satisfied and stable. The nature of conversion as such informed the factionalism, swings of allegiance, and shifting clergy-laity relations of the time.

117. Riggs, Cheryl. "Julian of Norwich and the Ecstatic Experience." <u>Tradition and Ecstasy: The Agony of the Fourteenth Century</u>. **Claremont Cultural Studies. Ottawa: Institute of Medieval Music, 1997. Pp. 109-122.** The fourteenth century produced religious fervor as powerful as the devotion to Hellenistic mystery cults that distantly preceded it, and the Protestant Reformation that soon followed it. Ecstatic union in Julian was characterized by her pain and left her feeling depressed.

118. Rose, Paul Lawrence. "Two Problems of Bodin's Religious Biography: The Letter to Jean Bautru Des Matras and the Imprisonment of 1569." <u>Bibliothèque d'Humanisme et Renaissance</u> **38 (1976): 459-465.** The emotional residue of Bodin's religious conversion in 1569 led to a religious enthusiasm that caused him to give up his opposition to the Civil War.

119. Rozett, Martha Tuck. <u>The Doctrine of Election and the Emergence of Elizabethan Tragedy</u>. **Princeton: Princeton University Press, 1984.** This historical and literary study analyzes the manner in which Christian feelings of confidence and despair were linked to doctrines of election in Elizabethan drama. Especially important was the intellectual practice of conceiving all of humanity as divided into two distinct groups: the saved and the damned. The Protestant desire for assurance, and the continuous self-examination and comparison with others formed the axis of Elizabethan emotional investment in the doctrine of election.

120. Sanford, A Whitney. "Pilgrimage Within: Paramanand's Lyrics as Play between the Sacred and the Profane." **Ph.D. diss., University of Pennsylvania, 1995.** Cues drawn from the environment arouse emotions, which are culturally and socially constructed, enabling the devotee to join intimately with Krishna. Analysis of the lyrics of sixteenth-century poet-saint Paramanand shows an understanding of the process of sacralization as the investment of *bhava* (emotion) in a person or object.

121. Schoenfeldt, Michael. "The Gender of Religious Devotion: Amelia Langer and John Donne." <u>Religion and Culture in Renaissance England</u>. **Edited by Claire McEachern and Debora Shuger. Cambridge: Cambridge University Press, 1997. Pp. 209-233.** This comparison of the religious aspects in the writing of sixteenth-century authors Langer and Donne focuses on devotional fervor as it both cooperates and competes with erotic desire. Each author presents emotional piety as criticism of a social order (and particularly of Christian orders).

122. Scribner, Bob. "Popular Piety and Modes of Visual Perception in Late-Medieval and Reformation Germany." <u>Journal of Religious History</u> **15 (1988): 448-469.** Reformation criticism of images was directed especially against their potential to excite and overheat the emotions, giving rise to the more "objective" representation that produced an emotionally impoverished "cold gaze."

123. Shobha, Savitri Chandra. **Medieval India and Hindi Bhakti Poetry: A Sociocultural Study.** New Delhi: Har-Anand Publications, 1996. This study addresses the emotional and devotional element in *bhakti* poetry alongside social philosophies (including thinking about the place of women in society), culturally syntheses as reflected in Sufi writings, and the emergence of humanism as the conglomeration of virtues (e.g. affectionate) and the absence of vices (e.g. anger).

124. Smith, A. J. **The Metaphysics of Love: Studies in Renaissance Love Poetry From Dante to Milton.** Cambridge: Cambridge University Press, 1985. The first half of this literary history examines the manner in which notions of sense and innocence were connected to concepts of love by St. Augustine, St. Bernhard, Dante, Petrarch, and other writers, with a particular emphasis on love as attraction and union. The second half of the book is concerned largely with love as immortality in Shakespeare, as a conglomeration of body and soul in Donne, and as a means through nature to eternity in Henry Vaughan.

125. Stevenson, Robert M. **Patterns of Protestant Church Music.** Durham: Duke University Press, 1953. Chapter IV ("Bach's Religious Environment") focuses on the "wellsprings of creative emotion that marked his [Bach's] creative life." The most intimate religious emotions are represented in the cantatas.

126. Taylor, Henry Osborn. **The Mediaeval Mind: A History of the Development of Thought and Emotion in the Middle Ages.** 2 vols. London: Macmillan and Company, 1911. This sweeping history of the coalescence of emotional piety, the "emotionalizing of Latin Christianity" (p. 330), begins with the patristic synthesis of emotion as both the experience of faith and the practice of emotion in everyday life. Pagan, neo-Platonic, Jewish and Christian components all were important to the construction of medieval emotional life. Cultural and "racial" differences determined a certain degree of difference, but overall, by the eleventh century, religious life had become a torrent of emotion in utterances and actions. The detailed historical overview is complemented by chapters on St. Bernard, Francis of Assisi, Aquinas, Bonaventure, Dante, and many other figures.

127. Wanagffelen, Thierry. "Des Meconnus de l'Histoire des Eglises: Penser le Fait Religieux en France au XVIe Siecle hors des Schemas Confessionnels." *Information Historique* 57 (1995): 55-61. Stresses that the history of the Reformation in France must include analysis of the religious feelings of the French.

128. Wiethaus, Ulrike. **Ecstatic Transformation: Transpersonal Psychology in the Work of Mechthild of Magdeburg.** Syracuse: Syracuse University Press, 1996. This exploration of a Beguine's thirteenth-century treatise *The Flowing Light of the Godhead* concentrates on usages of the metaphor of the heart and the experience of ecstasy as distinct from a religious vision.

129. **Witchcraft and Hysteria in Elizabethan London: Edward Jorden and the Mary Glover Case.** Edited and with an Introduction by Michael MacDonald. London: Routledge, 1991. In the extended *Introduction*, MacDonald argues that physician Jorden's insistence that hysteria, and not demonic malfeasance, lay at the bottom of seeming incidences of witchcraft led to the decline of witchcraft accusations in seventeenth-century England. MacDonald examines the case of teenager Mary Glover, who suffered fits and wild displays of extreme anxiety, and whose seeming possession was challenged by Jorden, who identified it as a medical condition or fraud.

130. Wolfson, Eliot R. "Weeping, Death, and Spiritual Ascent in Sixteenth-Century Jewish Mysticism." Death, Ecstasy and Other Worldly Journeys. Edited by John J. Collins and Michael Fishbane. Albany: SUNY Press, 1995. Pp. 209-247. Weeping is a ritual means by which the soul separates from the body, ascends to the higher realm, and experiences a state likened to ecstatic death. The soul is mystically united to the Godhead, and in the process creates an overflow of holy waters which trickle down to the lower realm. Elements of the drama are distinctively gendered.

1600-1800

131. Barker-Benfield, G. J. The Culture of Sensibility: Sex and Society in Eighteenth-Century Britain. Chicago: University of Chicago Press, 1992. This detailed cultural history proposes that "sensibility was a form of religion" (p. 262), and that it was practiced as such especially by women, who conceived their own bodies as its sanctums, made shrines of set tea tables, and constructed the reading of poetry as a devotional ritual. Men were less active than women in the practice of such devotions, but nevertheless were participants in much of the ritual and evidenced investment in its discourse.

132. Boles, John C. The Great Revival, 1787-1805. Lexington: University Press of Kentucky, 1972. A study of the southern camp meeting beginnings of the Second Great Awakening in the United States that explicitly rejects previous interpretations that cast those meetings largely as a cathartic emotional response to the difficulties of life on the frontier. A central belief structure of theological ideas – the 'religious mind" of Southern evangelicals – is the key to understanding the emotionality of the revival.

133. Breitweiser, Robert Mitchell. American Puritanism and the Defense of Mourning: Religion, Grief, and Ethnology in Mary White Rowlandson's Captivity Narrative. Madison: University of Wisconsin Press, 1990. Argues that Rowlandson's narrative represents a challenge to Puritan understanding that life is an allegory, and to the view that the emotional component of life is a mere figure of underlying moral meanings. In the narrative, Rowlandson opposes the religious sublimation of mourning by insisting that her grief is real and that the emotional qualities of the captivity experience are more than conventions.

134. Campbell, Ted A. The Religion of the Heart: A Study of European Religious Life in the Seventeenth and Eighteenth Centuries. Columbia: University of South Carolina Press, 1991. A historical overview of Catholic, Protestant, Orthodox, and some Jewish religious groups that embraced a view of the affections as the means by which the distance between a person and God is overcome. The process in many cases involves repentance and faith as a part of the emotional experience.

135. Camporesi, Piero. The Fear of Hell: Images of Damnation and Salvation in Early Modern Europe. Translated by Lucina Byatt. Cambridge: Polity Press, 1990. Originally published 1987. Focusing on the "syndrome of fear," this study analyzes representations of hell as a sewer, slaughterhouse, place of horrific corruption, and physical pain, among other things. During the late seventeenth and early eighteenth centuries fears of hell lessened as intellectuals subjected the various traditions about its features to scrutiny (e.g. no oxygen within the earth to fuel its fires).

136. Clapper, Gregory S. **John Wesley on Religious Affections: His Views on Experience and Emotion and Their Role in the Christian Life and Theology.** Metuchen: Scarecrow Press, 1989. A survey of emotion in Wesley's theology that addresses specific emotional terms such as "passion," "feelings," and "impulses." The writings of Jonathan Edwards influenced Wesley in his thinking about emotion.

137. Corrigan, John. **The Hidden Balance: Religion and the Social Theories of Charles Chauncy and Jonathan Mayhew.** Cambridge: Cambridge University Press, 1987. Chauncy and Mayhew assembled their theologies in a context of significant social and political change during the middle and latter part of the eighteenth century. Their thinking about the nature of the relationship of reason to emotion was influenced by their perception and interpretation of those changes. They stressed the interconnectedness of emotion with structures of power, authority, private judgment, social status, divine grace and cosmic order.

138. -----. **The Prism of Piety: Catholick Congregational Clergy at the Beginning of the Enlightenment.** New York: Oxford University Press, 1991. Certain Congregationalist theologians in early eighteenth-century Boston ("catholicks") drew upon Enlightenment notions of the coherency and immutability of nature and nature's laws in concluding that the human body was good and useful. Because of perceived linkages between the body and feelings, emotion likewise was valued as it had not been previously. Emotion accordingly played a key part in Catholicks' views of the nature of collective Christian life. Catholick thinking contributed to the emotional revivals of the Great Awakening.

139. Crawford, Michael J. **Seasons of Grace: Colonial New England's Revival Tradition in its British Context.** New York: Oxford University Press, 1991. An investigation of "heart religion" and Protestant revival in the seventeenth and eighteenth centuries that addresses the emotional element in preaching styles, conversion experiences, prayer, and hymnody. Participants embraced a theological standpoint that valued the affective dimension over the intellectual experience.

140. Denby, David J. **Sentimental Narrative and the Social Order in France, 1760-1820.** Cambridge: Cambridge University Press, 1994. Sentimental narratives were at the heart of the French Enlightenment. This interdisciplinary analysis analyzes various kinds of writing, including eighteenth-century religious historiography, reflections on virtue, Protestant morality, and writings that expose the false dichotomy of reason and sentiment. Sentimental texts increasingly substituted for moral treatises and in so doing advanced secularization during and after the Revolution.

141. Didier, Béatrice. "Raison, Sentiment, Réligion dans quelques Articles de l'Encyclopédie." **Europa im Zeitalter Mozarts.** Edited by Moritz Czáky and Walter Pass. Wien: Böhlau Verlag, 1995. Pp. 399-405. An analysis of Diderot's eighteenth-century relating of emotion, religion and reason, with reference to some British writers (Locke, Toland, Tindal), and to notions of the "cruel God" and the "sickness of fanaticism."

142. Dinet, Dominique. "Le ferveur Religieuse dans la France du XVIIIe siecle." **Revue d'Historie de l'Eglise de France** 79 (1993): 275-299. Emotional religion remained a key part of French life during the Enlightenment and in the early nineteenth century.

143. Duncan, Margaret Beaton. "Aspects of the Hero in Eighteenth-Century English Literature." Ph.D. diss., University of California, San Diego, 1990. The sentimental hero arises from a revaluation of feeling that came with related changes in theological, philosophical and scientific thought. Popular understandings of Christian character blended with the traits of sentimental heroes and the resulting profile fit well with perceptions of women in the eighteenth century, leading to an increase in the number of female heroes known for their emotions.

144. Ebersole, Gary L. **Captured by Texts: Puritan to Postmodern Images of Indian Captivity**. Charlottesville: University Press of Virginia, 1996. A historical and literary study analyzing the ways in which emotions framed captivity narratives and were, in turn, framed and given meaning by specific genre expectations. Focus is on the role of emotions in Puritan narratives of the seventeenth and eighteenth centuries, and on the complex system of emotional displays and responses, read as indicators of one's moral character, in the sentimental novels of the eighteenth and nineteenth centuries.

145. Flynn, Maureen. "Blasphemy and the Play of Anger in Sixteenth-Century Spain." *Past and Present* 149 (1995): 29-56. Church authorities recognized that swearing in moments of emotional intensity were not equivalent to blasphemy. Sources include records of testimony of the Spanish Inquistion and religious writings of the time.

146. Funke, Maurice R. **From Saint to Psychotic: The Crisis of Human Identity in the Late Eighteenth Century: A Comparison of Clarissa, La Nouvelle Héloïse, Die Leden des Jungen Werthers**. New York: Peter Lang, 1983. Within literary works by Richardson, Rousseau, and Goethe are complex representations of love and passion, as the characters seek to come to terms with fears of death, pain, suffering, and sex. Religion is a key influence on their development, particularly with regard to feelings associated with sexuality. Arguing that those feelings were spiritualized, Funke links them to the historical context of Christian fervor.

147. Gatyas, Kenton Bernard. "The Struggle for Orthodoxy: Religion, Revivals, and Anglo-American Relations in the British Northern Colonies." Ph.D. diss., University of Illinois-Urbana, 1996. The Great Awakening underscored the importance of emotional conversion to a person's religious status. Churches divided over the issue of emotion in religion. Extreme emotionalism or "enthusiasm" in religion led to debates that resulted in growth of the Church of England in the colonies as persons sought more stable institutional structures for their faith.

148. Gill, Frederick C. **The Romantic Movement and Methodism: A Study of English Romanticism and the Evangelical Revival**. London: Epworth Press, 1937. An analysis of the historical linkages between the rise of an emotional Methodist religion and the emergence of a literature which evidenced authorial interest in emotion and explored styles by which to cultivate and express emotion. Two terms which represented the character of Methodism and Romanticism – and which were variously used both by supporters and opponents of the two movements – are "sentiment" and "enthusiasm."

149. Greene, Donald. "Latitudinarianism and Sensibility: The Genealogy of the 'Man of Feeling' Reconsidered." *Modern Philology* 75 (1977-78): 159-83. The notion of a person as virtuous when acting with universal goodwill towards others emerged from the Christian background of the seventeenth and eighteenth centuries. English latitudinarians did not favor works over faith, and thus are to be counted a key

part of the rise of sentimentalism as the image of the "man of feeling" coalesced around the approval of joy and delight as valuable religious and moral emotions.

150. Greven, Philip. **The Protestant Temperament: Patterns of Child-Rearing, Religious Experience, and the Self in Early America**. New York: Alfred A. Knopf, 1977. There were primarily three kinds of temperament among Protestants in the seventeenth and eighteenth centuries in America: the "self-suppressed," "self-controlled," and "self-asserted." They derived largely from styles of child-rearing and featured a distinctive emotional orientation. Each temperament is linked to a different mode of religious faith as various Protestant religious options developed in America.

151. Gugerli, David. "Protestant Pastors in Late Eighteenth-Century Zurich: Their Families and Society." **Journal of Interdisciplinary History** 22 (1992), 369-385. Clergymen viewed their family life as knitted together by emotion and by marriage as a union of equals, while nevertheless remaining committed to certain traditional views, including the authority of their rank.

152. Hambricke-Stowe, Charles. **The Practice of Piety: Puritan Devotional Disciplines in Seventeenth-Century New England. Published for the Institute of Early American History and Culture. Chapel Hill: University of North Carolina Press, 1982.** Puritans employed a wide assortment of approaches and techniques in constructing a life of piety in the American colonies. Singing, prayer, meditation, formal and informal worship, and the reading of Scripture were the superstructure of everyday religious life. Many of the Puritan devotional disciplines were geared to arousing emotion and to properly channeling it, and to cultivating connections between private and public dimensions of piety.

153. Hamm-Ehsani, Karin. "'Sentimentalism and the Young Ludwig Tieck: A Study of the Effects of the Emotional Culture in the Life and Work of the 'King of Romanticism.'" Ph.D. diss., University of California, Los Angeles, 1996. A psycho-biographical survey of Tieck against the background of eighteenth-century sentimentalism, including its appearances in religion. The transition from sentimentalism to romanticism can be seen in Tieck's work.

154. Havran, Michael J. "The Character and Principles of an English King: The Case of Charles I. **Catholic Historical Review** 69 (1983): 169-208. The religious upbringing of Charles I combined with the emotional character of the man, against a background of specific childhood experiences, to shape his ideas of the Christian ruler.

155. Heyd, Michael "Richard Burton's Sources on Enthusiasm and Melancholy: From a Medical Tradition to Religious Controversy" **History of European Ideas** 5 (1984): 17-44. This essay traces the development of English ideas about religious enthusiasm as a manifestation of melancholy, and places that development in a broader European context.

156. -----, "Medical Discourse in Religious Controversy: The Case of the Critique of 'Enthusiasm' on the Eve of the Enlightenment." **Science in Context** 8 (1995): 133-157. Seventeenth-century enthusiasts increasingly were cast as suffering from melancholy. As chemical and mechanical explanations of health and disease replaced humoral theories, Protestant ministers adapted them to support their claim that enthusiasm was of the body and not the mind, thus enabling church authorities to discontinue the charge of heresy for enthusiasts.

157. Laing, Annette Susan. "'All Things to All Men': Popular Religious Culture and the Anglican Mission in Colonial America, 1701-1750." Ph.D. diss., University of California, Riverside, 1995. Eighteenth-century preacher George Whitefield de-emphasized formal rationalized devotional structures and urged instead a religious culture of emotion on his audiences in British America. Whitefield's successes were the culmination of a half century of religious ferment, as laypersons who embraced a voluntaristic and less formal mode of religious organization challenged and sometimes converted Anglican missionaries. In the process, the laity progressively articulated and reinforced the distinctive perspective that set the scene for the emotional piety of the Great Awakening.

158. Leaver, Robin A. Music as Preaching: Bach, Passions, and Music in Worship. Oxford: Latimer House, 1982. This brief historical consideration of the music of Bach – and especially the Matthew Passion and John Passion – argues that it significantly excited the religious affections and enriched the piety of Christians in the eighteenth and nineteenth centuries.

159. MacDonald, Michael. Mystical Bedlam: Madness, Anxiety, and Healing in Seventeenth-Century England. Cambridge: Cambridge University Press, 1981. A history of popular religious beliefs and practices and their intersection with notions of insanity and healing. Focusing on madness, delirium, the emotional dimensions of membership in a family, and the emotional aspects of mental states, this study interprets religious explanations of such phenomena through analysis of the notes of two thousand cases of mental illness kept by seventeenth-century astrological physician Rev. Richard Napier. Napier's clients organized their understanding of emotional states by associating them with good and evil spirits.

160. -----. "The Fearful Estate of Francis Spira: Narrative, Identity, and Emotion in Early Modern England." Journal of British Studies 31 (1992): 32-61. Francesco Spira, a Venetian lawyer, experienced intense emotions over his conversion during the Inquisition in the sixteenth century. The popularity of the story among contemporaries and afterward is intelligible only by taking emotional life as a culturally constructed phenomenon.

161. Mazzela, David Samuel. "Cynicism and Sentiment in Eighteenth-Century Great Britain: Arguments About Moral Obligation and Social Participation in Religion, Politics, and Poetics, 1660-1832." Ph.D. diss., 1996. The eighteenth-century British took the meaning of "sentimental" to be a generalized love of human beings, and "cynical" to mean the hatred of people. Over time both terms came to be associated with emotional manipulation. This study includes a detailed discussion of the manner in which institutional and intellectual developments in religion contributed to that transformation of meaning.

162. Miller, John. Religion in the Popular Prints 1600-1832. Cambridge: Chadwyck-Healy, 1986. A selection of popular art that illustrates the change from "the emotional intensity and excitement of religion" in the seventeenth century to eighteenth century "reliance on reason" and morality (p.31), and the rediscovery of emotional spontaneity and excitement in Methodism. The book consists of 154 plates with brief commentary on each one, and an extensive introduction.

163. Miller, Perry. The New England Mind: The Seventeenth Century. Cambridge: Harvard University Press, 1953. Originally published 1939. Identifying

an emotional "Augustinian strain of piety" among Puritans who settled in New England, this history explores both the practice of that piety and the ongoing attempts to articulate its intellectual substance. Particularly important to Puritan religious life was the sermon which was preached in a "plain style," or in such a way as to appeal to the emotions.

164. -----. **The New England Mind: From Colony to Province**. Cambridge: Harvard University Press, 1953. A historical study of the manner in which the highly emotional piety of the Puritans in New England decreased in intensity, leading to the splintering of Puritan society, the ascendancy of moral religion, rifts between clergy and laity, and the emergence of a secularized state.

165. Payne, Rodger M. **The Self and the Sacred: Conversion and Autobiography in Early American Protestantism**. Knoxville: University of Tennessee Press, 1998. An analysis of conversion narratives that addresses the subjective aspect of piety and describes the manner in which ideas and emotions were linked through the creative linguistic process of emotion.

166. Porter, Roy. "The Rage of Party: A Glorious Revolution in English Psychiatry?" **Medical History** 27 (1983): 35-50. Political groups in the wake of the Revolution of 1688 characterized religious enthusiasm as madness, as a means of removing enthusiasts who were perceived as an impediment to social consensus.

167. Quaife, G. R. **Godly Zeal and Furious Rage: The Witch in Early Modern Europe**. London: Croom and Helm, 1987. This historical survey of witchcraft proposes that the zeal of church authorities and/or the rage of a woman's neighbors created the early modern witch. Male fear of women, especially older, sexually assertive women, was fundamental to that construction.

168. Rivers, Isabel. **Reason, Grace, and Sentiment: A Study of the Language of Religion and Ethics in England, 1660-1780**. Cambridge: Cambridge University Press, 1991. An analysis of latitudinarian religion, the non-conformist religion of grace associated with Baxter and Bunyan, John Wesley's ideas about Christian love, and the "affectionate religion" of Isaac Watts. The discussion of the rhetoric of affection details defenses of emotional Christianity as intellectually sound and socially useful.

169. Ryder, Mary R. "Avoiding the 'Many-Headed Monster'": Wesley and Johnson on Enthusiasm." **Methodist History** 23 (1985): 214-222. John Wesley's condemnation of religious enthusiasm as a species of pride, unless it was framed by reason and tradition.

170. Sala, Raymond. "La Mort dans le Haut-Vallespir: XVIIe, XVIIIe, et 1ere Moitie du XIXe Siecle: Approche des Sensibilites et des Mentalites Religieuses." **Histoire, Economie et Société** 8 (1989): 613-617. The testimony of archival documents, and especially wills, reveal that the devotions of French Catholic women were characterized by fear more than the devotions of French men in the same period.

171. Seed, Patricia. **To Love, Honor, and Obey in Colonial Mexico: Conflicts Over Marriage Choice, 1574-1821**. Stanford: Stanford University Press, 1988. An explication of the role of the Roman Catholic Church in constructing and fostering specific and interrelated notions of love, will, and honor, with reference to the ways in which courtship and marriage provided a stage for their performance. Church authorities cast love between men and women as an unreliable emotion, promoted arranged

marriages, and urged cognizance of markers of social class as desirable in a prospective partner, over against emotional connectedness between persons.

172. Sharpe, Kevin. "Religion, Revolution, and Rhetoric in Seventeenth-Century England." Huntington Library Quarterly **57 (1994): 255-299.** An historiographical overview that proposes that the emotional element in religion must be investigated in order to shed light on notions of kingship, and the occurrence of regicide.

173. Sommerville, John C. "Religious Typologies and Popular Religion in Restoration England." Church History **45 (1976): 32-41.** Popular religious publications became less emotional in the late seventeenth century, alongside falling interest in social problems.

174. Spurr, John. "'Rational Religion' in Restoration England." Journal of the History of Ideas **49 (1988): 563-585.** The seventeenth-century English reaction against enthusiasm opened the way for rethinking the relation of reason to religion, and set the stage for the rational religion that appeared late in the century.

175. Wainwright, William J. Reason and the Heart: A Prolegomenon to a Critique of Passional Reason. **Ithaca: Cornell University Press.** This intellectual history focuses on emotion and religious belief in Jonathan Edwards, John Henry Newman, and William James. Properly disposed emotions are necessary to capture the force of arguments drawn from non-affective evidence.

176. Ward, W. R. Power and Piety: The Origins of Religious Revival in the Eighteenth Century. **Manchester: John Rylands University Library, 1980.** Tracks mystical and enthusiastic movements, and groups that featured emotional preaching, from the Peace of Westphalia (1648) through the Protestant revivals in the 1740's. Stresses how dispossessed groups -- those denied public standing by the state -- increasingly turned to the cultivation of interiority and affect in their piety.

177. Westerkamp, Marilyn. Triumph of the Laity: Scots-Irish Piety and the Great Awakening, 1625-1860. **New York: Oxford University Press, 1988.** A history of the development and transmission of the emotional rituals that characterized the Great Awakening, beginning with early seventeenth-century Northern Ireland and concluding with the "triumph of the laity" as a consequence of debate and schism within churches. The outpouring of emotion in American revivals during the mid-eighteenth century was not innovative religious behavior.

178. Wolff, Larry. "Religious Devotion and Maternal Sentiment in Early Modern Lent: From the Letters of Madame de Sevigne to the Sermons of Pere Bourdaloue." French Historical Studies **18 1993: 359-395.** Sévigné, known for her mystical devotions, cultivated her "maternal" emotions by drawing upon techniques associated with the seventeenth-century Catholic Reformation in France. The context for some of those techniques was the Lenten culture.

179. Youngs, J. William T., Jr. God's Messengers: Religious Leadership in Colonial New England, 1700-1750. **Baltimore: Johns Hopkins University Press, 1976.** This study of the relations between clergy and laity includes observations on the reception among both groups of enthusiastic religion, and especially ministers' views on the practice of preaching so as to arouse the emotions.

Nineteenth Century

180. Anderson, Marston. "The Scorpion in the Scholar's Cap: Ritual, Memory, and Desire in *Rulin Waishi*." **Culture and State in Chinese History: Conventions, Accommodations, and Critiques**. Edited by Theodore Huters, R. Bin Wong, and Pauline Yu. Stanford: Stanford University Press, 1997. The Confucian classic narrates various characters' metaphorical reconstructions of self. This authorial design is historically linked to earlier Confucian commentary about the role of emotions in human life, and to Confucian rites that originated in emotion.

181. Bland, Lucy. "Rational or Spiritual Love?" The Men's and Women's Clubs of the 1880's." **Women's Studies International Forum** 13 (1990): 33-48. In meetings of men and women in London during the late nineteenth century, considerable time was given over to discussion of relations between the sexes. Differences emerged, including men's questioning the legitimacy of women's notions of spiritual love.

182. Butler, Jonathan M. **Softly and Tenderly Jesus is Calling: Heaven and Hell in American Revivalism, 1870-1920**. Brooklyn: Carlson Publishing, Inc., 1991. Nineteenth-century American revivalist preaching was characterized by a forthright sentimentalism. That approach is especially evident in the work of preachers Dwight L. Moody, Sam Jones, and Billy Sunday.

183. Campbell, John Angus. "Nature, Religion, and Emotional Response: A Reconsideration of Darwin's Affective Decline." **Victorian Studies** 34 (1974): 159-174. Analysis of the life and writings of Charles Darwin reveals the interconnections between his professed decline in emotional range and his similarly professed loss of religious belief and aesthetic appreciation of nature.

184. Christodoulou, Joan. "The Freethinking Christians and the Millennium." **London Journal** 14 (1989): 148-159. An overview of the emotional religion of the Freethinking Christians as they made plans for the dawn of the millennium in the early nineteenth century.

185. Clark, Anna. "The Sexual Crisis and Popular Religion in London, 1770-1820." **International Labor and Working-Class History** 34 (1998): 56-69. Female prophets in London embraced millenarianism as a means by which to express anger at males who oppressed them.

186. Conkin, Paul K. **Cane Ridge: America's Pentecost. The Curti Lectures, University of Wisconsin, Madison, 1989**. Madison: University of Wisconsin, 1990. A survey of the settings, doctrines, institutions, and ritual of the Cane Ridge, Kentucky revivals in the early nineteenth century that argues that ecstatic religion is most often associated with highly formalized or ritualized structures of worship. The ecstatic experiences of persons manifest in the physical exercises of participants in the Cane Ridge meetings demonstrate that "the word *revival* came to mean not just renewed commitment but an intensely affectionate form of religion" (173).

187. Corrigan, John. **Business of the Heart: Emotion and Religion in the Nineteenth Century**. Berkeley: University of California Press, [2001]. During the revival of 1858 in Boston various groups asserted their social identities through their participation in its emotional proceedings. Emotion itself was objectified and exchanged

as a commodity in transactions with God. The Protestant middle class deepened perceptions of difference through their performances of emotion in a fashion distinct from the perceived emotional style of African Americans, Irish and abolitionists. The emotional aspects of religious life are discussed together with the ways in which emotion played a part in reading, the theatre, sports, family life, school, relations between clergy and laity, in the activities of the young men of Boston and in business and commercial enterprises.

188. Cross, Whitney R. **The Burnt-Over District: The Social and Intellectual History of Enthusiastic Religion in Western New York, 1800-1850**. Ithaca: Cornell University Press, 1950. A study of Protestant revivals that connects the intensely emotional piety of upstate New Yorkers with social and economic changes brought by the Erie canal and with new styles of Christian leadership and ritual. Revival participants loved excitement and action and they judged religion by its capability to deliver on both of those fronts.

189. Devlin, Judith. **The Superstitious Mind: French Peasants and the Supernatural in the Nineteenth Century**. New Haven: Yale University Press, 1987. In viewing popular religion, including medicine, witchcraft, demonology, prophecy, and possession, it appears that modes of feeling have changed little over the past four centuries. The nineteenth-century "culture of delirium" promoted hysteria, which occurred specifically as a response to guilt and fears about sorcery and the black arts.

190. Englehardt, Carol Marie. "Victorians and the Virgin Mary: Religion, National Identity, and the Woman Question in England, 1830-1880." Ph.D. diss., Indiana University, 1997. Victorian culture pictured women as emotional rather than rational creatures. They likewise were cast as morally superior to men and naturally maternal. Examination of evangelical Victorians' unwillingness to see Mary as the ideal woman reveals the instability of such thinking about women. Protestants resisted Catholicism because they believed that it would feminize Englishmen.

191. Foster, Lawrence. **Women, Family, and Utopia: Communal Experiments of the Shakers, the Oneida Community, and the Mormons**. Syracuse, NY: Syracuse University Press, 1991. An historical study that addresses emotional aspects of religious life among members of the three groups, including notions of love, trance, and the psychology of family emotion. Much of the analysis is undertaken with an eye to gender roles and differentiations.

192. French, Hal W. **A Study of Religious Fanaticism and Responses to It**. Studies in Religion and Society, vol. 26. Lewiston: Edwin Mellen Press, 1990. Beginning with a Roman definition of *fanaticus*, "to be put into raging enthusiasm by a deity," this study analyzes the ways in which intensity of emotion becomes a marker for persons who believe themselves to be spiritually superior, and, in consequence, adversarial in their relationships with others. The Israeli-Palestinian conflict and nineteenth-century broad church Anglicanism are discussed.

193. Goldstein, Jan. "The Hysteria Diagnosis and the Politics of Anti-Clericalism in Late Nineteenth-Century France." **Journal of Modern History** 54 (1982): 209-239. In the politics of anti-clericalism, the diagnosis of hysteria in women became politicized, leading to medical diagnoses of hysteria where previously demonic possession, mystical ecstasies, or divine vision/intervention had been accepted as defining terms of emotional experience.

194. Gunther, Candy. "The Spiritual Pilgrimage of Rachel Stearns, 1834-1837: Reinterpreting Women's Religious and Social Experiences in the Methodist Revivals of Nineteenth-Century America." Church History 65 (1995): 577-595. Proposes that the emotional dimension of women's religious life and especially the pursuit of love in the nineteenth century is represented in entries in Stearn's journal.

195. Jackson, Hugh. "'White Man Got No Dreaming': Religious Feeling in Australian History." Journal of Religious History 15 (1988): 1-11. The religious feelings -- and other feelings -- of European settlers were reduced in Australia because of the alienation of colonists from the Australian landscape. Before emigrating to Australia, settlers had sensed an intimate linkage with the English countryside that nourished emotional life.

196. Janet, Richard J. "Providence, Prayer, and Cholera: The English General Fast of 1832." Historical Magazine of the Protestant Episcopal Church 51 (1982): 297-317. The fast channeled anxieties and fears about disease and government into more specifically religious forms. Some persons resisted the call to fast, and continued instead with their criticisms of the aristocracy, based upon a notion that God was punishing the people for oppression of the poor.

197. Kent, John. Holding the Fort: Studies in Victorian Revivalism. London: Epworth Press, 1978. The essence of revivalism is "the use of a series of meetings to heighten the psychological tension of a group of people" until it finds "release in an outburst of speech and action" (346). Emotion, and the cultivation of emotion, dominated the methods of revivalists, even when they said it did not. The business of revivals was to excite emotion.

198. Koltun-Fromm, Ken. "Inescapable Frameworks: Moses Hess' *Rome and Jerusalem* and the Recovery of Religion, Tradition, and Identity." Ph.D. diss., Stanford University, 1997. Part three examines Hess's understanding of the emotions in connection with two views of the self that alternated in Hess's thinking, one based on racial theory and the other primarily focused on the construction of Jewish identity through the unfolding of historical events.

199. Kselman, Thomas A. Death and the Afterlife in Modern France. Princeton: Princeton University Press, 1993. Includes various discussions of the "emotional organization" (p. 293) of matters linked to death: burial, grieving, social adjustment, relationships to spirits, and other things. There is extensive discussion of formal religious means for negotiating death as well as folk beliefs and practices.

200. Leiby, James. "Charity Organization Reconsidered." Social Service Review 58 (1984): 523-538. The charity organization movement of the late nineteenth century grounded its agenda not in theories about social service in the modern industrial state, but in a commitment to a notion of community characterized by strong emotional bonds between persons.

201. Lewis, Jan. "'Mother's Love': The Construction of an Emotion in Nineteenth-Century America." Social History and issues in Human Consciousness: Some Interdisciplinary Connections. (New York: New York University Press, 1989). Love is a social construction, and antebellum American motherhood likewise was constructed, as a model of love, understood as self-sacrifice, sinlessness, and benevolence. That love, which they inculcated in their children, comported well with

democratic ideals in shaping American culture, which in the nineteenth century had an evangelical color.

202. Loyer, François. "Le Sacre-Couer de Montmarte: L'Eglise Souffrante et L'architecture Triomphante." Debat 44 (1987): 144-155. The competition for the design of Sacred Heart basilica in 1874, and the selection of Paul Abadie's design, is examined as an instance of the expression of national emotion embodied in a religious site.

203. McCanley, Deborah Vansau. Appalachian Mountain Religion: A History. Urbana: University of Illinois Press, 1995. The region is notable for the emotional quality of its religion. That religion lies largely outside the mainstream, and is grounded in eighteenth-century revival cultures and nineteenth-century camp meeting religion.

204. McKenzie, Alan T. Certain, Lively Episodes: The Articulation of Passion in Eighteenth-Century Prose. Athens: University of Georgia Press, 1990. A survey of theories of the passions in an assortment of contexts, including Edward Gibbon's *The Decline and Fall of the Roman Empire*, the writings of David Hume and Henry Fielding, and in the *Spectator*. The production of eighteenth-century taxonomies of the passions and the development of linkages between feeling and physiology hastened the reconceptualization of morality and character.

205. Mudford, Peter. Memory and Desire: Representations of Passion in the Novella. London: Duckworth, 1996. Proposing that relationships of passion take place as re-enactments of myth, the author reviews ten writings – ranging from Madame de Lafayette to Tolstoy and Gidé – with an eye to defining the distinction between passionate love and Christian love. The primary Christian referents are the myth of the fall, and the distant prospect of harmony after enduring suffering.

206. Polhemus, Robert M. Comic Faith: The Great Tradition from Austen to Joyce. Chicago: University of Chicago Press, 1980. Analyzes how the exercise of comedy in literature – the sense of humor – reveals assumptions about the nature of life, human motivation and desire, and concern about the soul. This self-styled "history of laughter" (p. 5) contextualizes various writings within a Judaeo-Christian worldview in order to understand their complex comic emotionality.

207. Rabinowitz, Richard. The Spiritual Self in Everyday Life: The Transformation of Personal Religious Experience in Nineteenth-Century New England. Boston: Northeastern University Press, 1989. A historical meditation on the nature of religious experience, and especially its emotional components, among New England Protestants, including an analysis of the coalescence of the romantic notions of the self that informed evangelical theology. That theology proposed an understanding of religious life as a union with the divine, accompanied by intense feelings. It led to a religious devotionalism that cared less for moralism than it did for the experiences of the self as they emerged in delimited contexts of engagement with God, specific other selves, and the past of one's own life.

208. Raboteau, Albert J. Slave Religion: The Invisible Institution in the Antebellum South. New York: Oxford University Press, 1978. A historical study that proposes among other things that African traditions were supplemented by and reconciled with Christian traditions, through the common ground of emotion. "The powerful emotionalism, ecstatic behavior" of Christian revivalism were "amenable to the African religious heritage of the slave" (149).

209. Rack, Henry D. "The Decline of the Class Meeting and the Problem of Church Membership in Nineteenth-Century Wesleyanism." Proceedings of the Wesley Historical Society 39 (1973): 12-21. The tradition of the class-meeting, a fundamental component of Wesleyan worship, deteriorated as religious emotion diminished.

210. Rawlyk, G. A. The Canada Fire: Radical Evangelicalism in British North America, 1775-1812. Kingston and Montreal: McGill-Queens University Press, 1994. A history of religious enthusiasm in Canada – with references to the United States as well – that analyzes the manner in which emotion came to be a key component in Protestantism there, especially in conversions, camp-meeting rituals, prayer, and in the orderings of the family and conceptualizations of the individual.

211. Robins, Roger. "Vernacular American Landscape; Methodists, Camp Meetings and Social Responsibility." Religion and American Culture 4 (1994): 165-191. Methodists in the nineteenth century constructed permanent camp meeting sites that were designed to limit the intense emotional quality of spiritual outpourings characteristic of gatherings earlier in the century.

212. Seeley, Paul Alan. "Virile Pursuits: Youth, Religion, and Bourgeois Family Politics in Lyon on the Eve of the French Third Republic." Ph.D. diss, University of Michigan, 1994. A social history and collective biography that described how Catholic mothers were responsible for the character development of their sons, including the formation of patterns of affectivity. The emotional lives of those young men, as they grew into adults, is described, as well as other aspects of Catholic child-rearing, and distinguished from the training of sons in republican bourgeois families.

213. Shaw, Nancy Joy. "Speaking for the Spirit: Cotton, Shepard, Edwards, Emerson." Ph.D. diss., Cornell University, 1988. Affective religiosity is a distinguishing feature of Puritanism. These four writers defended that religiosity in their writings, stressing the importance of emotions and the subjective experience. Emerson adapted Puritan thinking about the self to the transcendental idea of the divinity of the soul.

214. Sizer, Sandra S. Gospel Hymns and Social Religion: The Rhetoric of Nineteenth-century Revivalism. Edited by Allen F. Davis. American Civilization series. Philadelphia: Temple University Press, 1978. The metaphors of gospel hymns – and especially those associated with the Protestant revivalism of Dwight L. Moody – were a "technique of transcendence." By appealing to and cultivating the emotions they conceptually relocated persons from an oppressive urban existence to a place of serene and tranquil feeling. Revivalism accordingly calmed passion by raising it.

215. Spears, Timothy B. "Circles of Grace: Passion and Control in the Thought of John Humphrey Noyes." New York History 70 (1989): 79-103. Noyes's thinking about the organization of society was grounded in his determination to join sexual and spiritual passion.

216. Stubley, Peter. A House Divided: Evangelicals and the Establishment in Hull, 1770-1914. Monograph in Regional and Cultural History. Hull: University of Hull Press, 1995. The emotional piety of evangelicals in Hull – and especially Methodists --

developed in the context of a conflict between the evangelical churches and two "counter-cultures," one antagonistic to religion of any sort, and the other moderately interested in religious education but uninvolved in church or chapel worship exercises. Class differences substantially structured the three cultures, and especially the gulf between the "uninhibited enthusiasm" of the Methodists and the "dignified, orderly ways" of the Wesleyans.

217. Turley, Briane K. **A Wheel within a Wheel: Southern Methodism and the Georgia Holiness Association.** Macon, GA: Mercer University Press, 1999. Explores theological and social aspects of the Holiness movement in nineteenth-century Georgia, with insights into its emotional aspects.

218. Uffenheimer, Rivka Schatz. **Hasidism as Mysticism: Quietistic Elements in Eighteenth-Century Hasidic Thought.** Translated by Jonathan Chipman. Princeton: Princeton University Press, 1993. Quietism tends to force emotional activism to the background of religious practice, both in Hasidic and Christian mysticism. Hasidism explicitly prohibited feelings of regret and despair and downplayed remorse and sadness.

219. Veysey, Lawrence. **The Communal Experience: Anarchist and Mystical Counter-Cultures in America.** New York: Harper and Row, 1973. Historical survey that explores various historical postures associated with the communal experience, and especially the experience of ecstasy. Consideration of the history of radical social movements suggest that fellow-feeling transcends social structures.

220. Viswanathan, Gauri. **Outside the Fold: Conversion, Modernity, and Belief.** Princeton: Princeton University Press, 1998. A study of religious change in colonial India in the nineteenth and twentieth centuries, focusing on conversions to Christianity and intermixed with discussion of conversion in England. In modernity, conversion increasingly is less a matter of belief and more a matter of moods and feelings, so that individual subjectivity is progressively divorced from institutional rationality, and persons' right to belief subsequently diminished. Religious subjectivity is reduced to affect.

221. Wach, Howard M. "A 'Still, Small Voice' from the Pulpit: Religion and the Creation of Social Morality in Manchester, 1820-1850." **Journal of Modern History** 59 (1991): 317-330. Argues that the Unitarian theology of Taylor and others in Manchester fostered a style of religious feeling that functioned to keep the social hierarchy intact, especially by promoting the notion of the "comfort and joy" of submission to higher powers.

222. Watson, Samuel J. "Religion and Motivation in Confederate Armies." **Journal of Military History** 58 (1994): 29-55. Argues for a connection between evangelical southern religion and the effort to maintain morale and unit cohesiveness in the Confederate army, concluding that emotions associated with religion were overlayed onto the soldiers experience in the field, structuring and giving meaning to that experience.

223. Weisberger, Bernard A. **They Gathered at the River: The Story of the Great Revivalists and their Impact upon Religion in America.** Boston: Little, Brown, 1958. A history of the religious enthusiasm among American Protestants in the nineteenth century, with an emphasis on the centrality of emotion in the preaching,

theology, and ritual of participants, and especially on emotion as an antidote to perceived "deadness" in the churches.

Twentieth Century

224. Basu, Helen. "Hierarchy and Emotion: Love, Joy, and Sorrow in a Cult of Black Saints in Gujarat, India." Embodying Charisma: Modernity, Locality and the Performance of Emotion in Sufi Cults. Edited by Pnina Werbner and Helen Basu. London: Routledge, 1998. Pp. 117-139. Argues that emotional constructs are used in the performance of status relationships as part of a counter-hegemonic worldview. Ritualized expression of emotion is opposed to dominant social and moral orders, and in this setting the construction of gender domains as complimentary is fundamental to understandings of saints and heroes as good or evil. The saints are known as "people of the heart," and religious encounter with them is characterized by ecstasy and trance.

225. Beckman, David M. Eden Revival: Spiritual Churches in Ghana. Foreword by William J. Danker. St. Louis: Concordia House, 1975. The Christian pentecostal Eden Revival Church, founded in the mid-twentieth century, was focused on faith healing. Like other spiritual churches in Ghana it featured a noisy, highly emotional worship, especially during the Wednesday night healing service. The blending of Christian and African religious ideas is clothed in a liturgy that fosters ecstatic experiences.

226. Beit-Hallahmi, Benjamin. Despair and Deliverance: Private Salvation in Contemporary Israel. SUNY Series in Israeli Studies. Albany: SUNY Press, 1992. A study of the rise of "new religions" in Israel from est to ISKCON to the Jehovah's Witnesses that takes such religions as offering a more "private" view of salvation than Judaism traditionally understood in Israel. The embrace of private salvationist religions has proceeded in the twentieth century from despair over the relevance and viability of public religion in Israel. New religions are "the cry of the oppressed creature" (187).

227. Bennett, Peter. "In Nanda Baba's House: The Devotional Experience in Pushti Marg Temples." Divine Passions: The Social Construction of Emotion in India. Edited by Owen M. Lynch. Berkeley: University of California Press, 1990. Pp. 182-211. Pushti Marg is a religious path grounded in traditions of worship that excite the emotions as the cowherd companions of Krishna were passionate in their association with him. Pushti Marg conceives the expression of emotion as a matter of taste, as a matter of aesthetics interwoven into enthusiastic devotion. Devotees also believe that actual emotions are embodied in material culture, in the ornaments with which they decorate religious images.

228. Borchert, James. Alley Life in Washington: Family, Community, Religion, and Folk Life in the City, 1850-1970. Urbana: University of Illinois Press, 1980. A history of alley-dwelling African Americans that includes discussion of emotional camp meetings conducted in the alleys. "Like everything else in alley life, religion was a physical and emotional experience" (p. 198) of a high order, as opposed to more formal, conservative, and restrained services in black and white churches alike outside of alley life.

229. Brooks, Charles R. "Hare Krishna, Radhe Shyam: The Cross-Cultural Dynamics of Mystical Emotions in Brindabun." **Divine Passions: The Social Construction of Emotion in India. Edited by Owen M. Lynch. Berkeley: University of California Press, 1990. Pp. 262-285.** Outlines the emotional components of Krishna *bhakti* as practiced in northern India, with a focus on the relationship with Krishna as the most sublime emotional state that a person can experience. ISKON (International Society for Krishna consciousness) is a force working to de-emphasize certain teachings bearing on the cultivation of emotion in the worship of Krishna. The two groups nevertheless have found ways to lessen the doctrinal distance that separates them.

230. Christian, William A., Jr. **Visionaries: The Spanish Republic and the Reign of Christ. Berkeley: University of California Press, 1994.** A history of religion, politics and apparitions of the Virgin Mary in twentieth-century Spain that emphasizes the importance of the testimony of the emotions to claims of visions. Feelings of fear, fright, shame, and awe, together with weeping, were reported as part of a vision, and church officials and members of the communities in which the visions took place carefully searched those feelings in order to distinguish theater and hysteria from sincerity and piety.

231. Damann, Ernst. "Nachchristliche Religiöse Bewegungen in Afrika." **Zeitwende 40 (1969): 99-109.** Religious movements in sub-Saharan Africa in 1872-1935 veered away from traditional Christianity because Christianity could not accommodate the emotionalism of those African churches. The result has been an assortment of emotional, quasi-Christian movements that incorporate indigenous religious beliefs, rituals, and styles.

232. Derné, Steve. **Culture in Action: Family Life, Emotion and Male Dominance in Banaras, India. Albany: SUNY Press, 1995.** A contemporary history that utilizes ethnopsychology and the notion that "strategies of action" only develop over time, in order to analyze relationships within the family. The culture that shapes those relationships is fundamentally religious in content, especially in its reliance on the religious epic *Ramayana*. Hindu men create and recreate joint family living arrangements in which fear of collective authority is valued and one-on-one love is considered dangerous, both perspectives being grounded in religious belief.

233. Domingues, Patricia L. "Women of the New Christian Right: Ideological Hegemony in Process." **Ph.D. diss., University of California, Riverside, 1994.** An analysis of women's willing subordination to men in Christian Right families that draws explicitly on the sociology of emotions in discussing the religious movement's view of social relations, ritualized interaction of persons, and the expression, concealment, and adaptation of emotion. Submissiveness -- including a certain structuring of emotional life -- in a wife is viewed as the performance of a sacred obligation.

234. Doyle, Barry M. "Religion, Politics, and Remembrance: A Free Church Community and Its Great War Dead." **War and Memory in the Twentieth Century. Edited by Martin Evans and Ken Lunn. New York: Oxford University Press, 1997. Pp. 223-238.** Analysis of the collective mourning of Harry Jewson, killed in combat in Palestine in 1917. The Free Church community of Norwich, England, utilizing homoerotic imagery common in the male mourning process, constructed an emotionally-moving image of Jewson as an exemplar of Christian Liberal virtues and Edwardian propriety.

235. Dusenbery, Verne A. "On the Moral Sensitivities of the Sikhs in North America." <u>Divine Passions: The Social Construction of Emotion in India</u>. Edited by Owen M. Lynch. Berkeley: University of California Press, 1990. Pp. 239-261. An analysis of "moral affect"-- and especially shame, honor, and guilt – among Sikhs in North America that reinforces studies by Rosaldo (1983, 1984), Lutz (1983, 1986) and Lynch (1990) that link emotion and morality as culturally constructed aspects of the self. Focuses especially on cross-cultural perceptions and tensions.

236. Erikson, Erik H. <u>Ghandi's Truth: On the Origins of Militant Non-Violence</u>. New York: W. W. Norton, 1969. An historical and psychological exploration of the emotional dynamics underlying the religious perspective of Ghandi, with an emphasis on the emergence of a moral vision from the resolution of developmental and emotional aspects of his life and especially those involving the father-son relationship.

237. Ewing, Katherine P. "A Majzub and his Mother: The Place of Sainthood in a Family's Emotional Memory." <u>Embodying Charisma: Modernity, Locality and the Performance of Emotion in Sufi Cults</u>. Edited by Pnina Werbner and Helen Basu. London: Routledge, 1998. Pp. 160-183. A *majzub* is a person whose action and speech may seem inappropriate or mad, but are frequently thought to be signs that the person has been "burned" by closeness to God. This Sufi idea represents a manner in which expressions of emotion – by the *majzub* – indicate resistance to a hegemonic emotional system in which certain states are considered psychotic while others are enforced as normative. The analysis features a blending of historical and anthropological approaches.

238. Fleischer, Manfred P. "Die Religionsphänomenologie als Hilfswissenschaft der Zeitgeschichte." <u>Zeitschrift für Religions- und Geistesgeschichte</u> 27 (1975): 97-121. Emotions can be abstracted from one set of circumstances and transferred directly into another context when structural similarities are present. Certain sets of feelings have been re-channeled from specifically religious concerns to support a new mythology of the West German state in the twentieth century.

239. Flood, Gervin. "Ritual Dance in *Kerala*: Performance, Possession and the Formation of Culture." <u>Indian Insights: Buddhism, Brahmanism, and Bhakti. Papers from the Annual Spalding Symposium on Indian Religions</u>. Edited by Peter Connolly and Sue Hamilton. London: Luzae Oriental, 1997. Pp. 169-183. An analysis of the *teyattam*, a festival featuring dance-possession rituals that occur at shrines in the area. Arguing that the "religious" can never be separated from the "cultural," Flood draws upon performance theory in identifying "emotional expression" as fundamental to the festival, and especially as enacted violence that renews and purifies the community.

240. Fortes, Meyer. <u>Oedipus and Job in West African Religion</u>. Cambridge: Cambridge University Press, 1959. A study of West African religions, primarily that of the Tallensi, that focuses on ideas of fate in those religions, as a way of addressing the seeming absence of feelings of guilt among the religion's practitioners.

241. Frembgen, Jurgen Wasim. "The *majzub* Mama Ji Sarker: A Friend of God Moves From One House to Another." <u>Embodying Charisma: Modernity, Locality and the Performance of Emotion in Sufi Cults</u>. Edited by Pnina Werbner and Helen Basu. London: Routledge, 1998. Pp. 140-159. An examination of the life of Sufi saint Mama Ji Sarker (b.1910) and his followers that argues that to know the saint is to

experience a blending of emotion alongside the charismatic authority of the saint, so that "charisma and love are intertwined like the warp and weft" of a fabric. This personalized charismatic relationship with the saint is evident in the deep emotional bonds between members of the community.

242. Gerlach, Luther P. "Pentecostalism: Revolution or Counter-Reformation?" Religious Movements in Contemporary America. Edited by Irving I. Zaretsky and Mark P. Leone. Princeton: Princeton University Press, 1974. Pp. 669-699. Discusses aspects of ecstatic religious behavior among Protestants and Roman Catholics, including its relationship to unconventional ideology, its incompatibility with certain structures of expression, and ceremonial dissociation, especially as those features are evident in Haitian pentecostalism.

243. Githieya, Francis Kimani. The Freedom of the Spirit: African Indigenous Churches in Kenya. Atlanta: Scholar's Press, 1997. A socio-historical study that follows the development of African spirit churches from the late nineteenth century to the late twentieth century. Communication with ancestral spirits, a key aspect of the churches' Christian-African blend of theologies, is undertaken through feeling (and is open to anyone).

244. Griffith, R. Marie. "'Joy Unspeakable and Full of Glory': The Vocabulary of Pious Emotion in the Narratives of American Pentecostal Women, 1910-1945." An Emotional History of the United States. Edited by Peter N. Stearns and Jan Lewis. New York: New York University Press, 1998. Pp. 218-240. A study of early Pentecostalism through analysis of the emotional performances that the movement has valued, especially with regard to women praying together. Stressing emotion as social and cultural code, the essay focuses on joy and gratitude among women as important experiences that reinforced belief in the face of public skepticism about the religion.

245. Harrell, David Edwin, Jr. All Things are Possible: The Healing and Charismatic Revivals in North America. Bloomington: Indiana University in the Press, 1975. A history of healing and revivalism in mid-twentieth century America, with a focus on leading figures of the Protestant evangelical movement, and the manner in which they conceived emotion as an essential part of religious life, and invented styles for fostering it.

246. Hilliard, David. "The Religious Culture of Australian Cities in the 1950's." Hispania Sacra 42 (1990): 469-81. Examines the manner in which the expression of religious feeling among a broad spectrum of the Australian population was conditioned by social change, largely in urban contexts in the year during and after the Second World War. Emotion in religion was constructed in accord with a general cultural response to change.

247. Hoffman, Gerhard and Alfred Hornung, editors. Emotion in Postmodernism. American Studies series, vol. 74. Heidelberg: Universitätsverlag C. Winter, 1997. A collection of twenty-essays on American culture that features several useful discussions of religion and emotion, from variously constructed interdisciplinary perspectives, including history. Noel Carroll reviews theories about linkages between emotions and morality, and Rüdiger Kunow discusses the seeming repression of emotion in holocaust writings by Wiesel, Spielgelman, and Kosinski. Other essays addresses emotion in various quasi-religious contexts (e.g. the experience of the Grand Ganyon). Many explicitly criticize Frederic Jameson's celebrated definition of postmodernism as a

cultural movement involving the waning of affect and Jean-Francois Lyotard's absolute distinction between cognition and feeling.

248. Holland, Ronando W. "The Key to Black Politics." Ph.D. diss., Duke University, 1989. Marcus Garvey, Martin Luther King, Jr., and Jesse Jackson exploited traditional African-American involvement in religion in persuading their audiences of the value of certain political goals. Their styles were grounded in the utilization of religious ritual and speech, and featured especially the deployment of emotionally rich religious symbols, as they constructed a "theopolitical symbolism."

249. Holm, Nils G., editor. Religious Ecstasy: Based on Papers read at the Symposium on Religious Ecstasy Held at Abo, Finland, on the 26th-18th of August, 1981. Uppsala, Sweden: Almqvist & Wicksell, 1982. These twenty essays address an assortment of historical, philosophical, and psychological issues having to do with emotion and religion. Nils G. Holm, in "Ecstasy Research in the 20th Century – An Introduction," surveys recent studies of ecstasy and calls for its study as a culture-bound phenomenon. Chapters on the Siberian shaman's technique of ecstasy, emotion in Nepalese séances, linkages between political expression and Muslim performance of ecstasy in Iran, and religious ecstasy in classical Sufism blend historical and anthropological approaches. Elsewhere, studies of Theresa of Avila, Euripedes's *Bacchanals*, and the pre-Christian Gnostic text *Eugnostos the Blessed* illustrate ecstatic techniques from a historical perspective and argue for the "explanatory value of ecstasy" (217).

250. Kerner, Karen. "Japan's New Religion." Japan Interpreter 6 (1970): 135-150. Shinko Shukyu, the "new religions" to which Soka Gakkai belongs, have appeared in twentieth-century Japan as part of a global anti-intellectual, millennialist movement that offers emotional comforts.

251. Kiernan, Jim. "Authority and Enthusiasm: The Organization of Religious Experience in Zulu Zionist Churches." Religious Organization and Religious Experience. Edited by J. Davis. London: Academic Press, 1982. Pp. 169-179. Zulu Zionist gatherings exhibit such intensity of emotion that the display is best characterized as the enthusiastic abandonment of self-control. Prophets and ministers are responsible for overseeing the performance and do so by different means. The minister, especially, is responsible for preventing the performance of religious enthusiasm from reaching a point where it might estrange members or potential members of the group.

252. Kolenda, Pauline. "Pox and the Terror of Childlessness: Images and Ideas of the Smallpox Goddess in a North Indian Village. Mother Worship: Themes and Variations. Edited by James J. Preston. Chapel Hill: University of North Carolina Press, 1982. Pp. 225-250. In India, pox is represented as a hot, capricious, and angry mother. Mothers in Khalalpur are ambivalent about vaccination for their children because they fear that the goddess MotherPox will be angered by attempts to exclude her. Ritual offerings to her help to appease her anger. The model for the emotional makeup of MotherPox are derived from Hindu theory that connects anger and passion in women.

253. Landman, Christina. The Piety of Afrikaans Women: Diaries of Guilt. Praetoria: University of South Africa, 1994. Analysis of religion and emotion in the diaries of seven women, covering the years 1768-1964, that focuses on their cultivation of self-humiliation and self-hate in an effort to please their Christian God. Guilt fantasies and the excessive confession of sins formed a key part of their piety.

Historical Studies

254. Lasch, Christopher. **The Culture of Narcissism: American Life in an Age of Diminishing Expectations.** New York: W. W. Norton, 1978. This study relies on a psychoanalytic approach in arguing that feelings of anxiety and guilt derive from an overweening emphasis on the self in American society, and that the failure of religion in the twentieth century to organize a more humane and moral order is rooted in a psychological problem.

255. Lindholm, Charles. **Generosity and Jealousy: The Swat Pukhtun of Northern Pakistan.** New York: Columbia University Press, 1982. A study of emotion and social relations among the Pukhtun that incorporates discussion of Islam. The religious ideal and worship of the Pukhtun is to establish an immediate and personal relationship with God as a lover or friend. The mutuality and reciprocity of the relationship are key (the master-servant model is rejected) as both parties are expected to dissolve in love for each other. The notions of romance and worship are both derived from the image of the friend as a person who is neither jealous nor excites jealousy.

256. Lynch, Owen M. "The Social Construction of Emotion in India." **Divine Passions: The Social Construction of Emotion in India.** Edited by Owen M. Lynch. Berkeley: University of California Press, 1990. Pp. 3-34. An overview of the constructionist approach to emotion when applied to the Indian notion of rasa (juice, extract, quintessence), especially in the ways *rasa* was reinforced by medieval *bhakti* traditions and theologies of the Vaishnavite sects. Includes suggestions for research.

257. McDaniel, June. **The Madness of the Saints: Ecstatic Religion in Bengal.** Chicago: University of Chicago Press, 1989. A study of "divine madness," *bhakti* ecstasism in various forms, including its ritual and literary expressions, and with consideration of the various roles of the ecstatic as guru, hero, lover, or madman. The devotional self in the form of an ecstatic arises on the heels of the sacrifice of the old self, but the merger of the person and the deity, a symbiotic relationship, sacrifices life in the physical world. The ecstatic accordingly welcomes intense emotions as part of the journey of faith.

258. McDonough, Peter. **Men Astutely Trained: A History of the Jesuits in the American Century.** New York: The Free Press, 1992. A broad history that includes substantial discussion of the manner in which men were trained to control, conceal, express, and negotiate emotion as part of the religious culture of the order.

259. McGaffey, Wyatt. **Modern Kongo Prophets: Religion in a Plural Society.** Bloomington: Indiana University Press, 1983. Historical ethnography of twentieth-century prophetic movements in Kongo leading to a discussion of the religious prophet as a "healed madman," among other things. Focus is on the personality of the prophet, with emphasis on affect and especially on similarities between the shamanic personality and schizophrenia, both of which manifest a certain psychological profile: "the primary condition is a feeling of fear, failure, and guilt" (234).

260. Michel, Patrick. "Les Cultes Populaires en Poligne: Matériaux Pour Une Symbolique Politique." **Archives de Sciences Sociales de Religions.** 51 (1981): 101-119. Emotions can be transferred directly from a religious context to a political one. Argues that Roman Catholic religious devotions in twentieth-century Poland, and especially the devotion to the Blessed Virgin, stimulate and express national feelings, including emotions of pride, hope, and other positive feelings.

261. Minor, John E. "The Mantle of Elijah: Nineteenth-Century Primitive Methodism and Twentieth-Century Pentecostalism." Proceedings of the Wesley Historical Society 43 (1982): 141-149. The broad appeal of the Methodist movement drew in the working class through its proposal of an alternative lay model of church as well as its passionately emotional style, which also appealed to intellectuals.

262. Moore, Leonard J. Citizen Klansmen: The Ku Klux Klan in Indiana, 1921-1928. Chapel Hill: University of North Carolina Press, 1991. Study of a parareligious organization grounded in hatred of Catholics, Jews, African Americans, feminists, immigrants and members of various ethnic and political and occupational groups. The KKK gained control of the state republican party, elected a governor, and won for its candidates a majority in both houses of the legislature, leading Moore to conclude that the Klan was a populist rather than a nativist group.

263. Mulder, J. A. Niels. "A Comparative Note on the Thai and Japanese Worldview as Expressed by Religious Practice and Belief." Journal of the Siam Society 58 (1970): 79-85. Argues that a certain quality of feeling (*rasa*) allows for Javanese experience of the order and unity of the cosmos.

264. Myers, Fred R. Pintupi Country, Pintupi Self: Sentiment, Place, and Politics Among Western Desert Aborigines. Berkeley: University of California Press, 1991. Survey of twentieth-century Pintupi culture includes discussion of morality, ritual, and the sacred in relation to emotional life. Emotion is not merely a physical feeling, but an interpretation of the relationship of a "self" to a set of circumstances. Particular attention is given to happiness, shame, compassion, and emotions involved in identification of a person with specific geographical and political territory.

265. Nasuruddin, Mohammed Ghouse. "Dancing to Ecstasy on the Hobby Horse." Emotions of Culture: A Malay Perspective. Edited by Wazir Jahan Karim. Singapore: Oxford University Press, 1990. Pp. 142-158. An examination of the origins and the recent history and performance of a dance on a bamboo horse, that is undertaken in order to achieve a state of ecstasy, a symbolic, joyous ride into heaven, where the dancer is united with divine spirits. The ritual leads to the similar emotional and spiritual experience for spectators as well.

266. Nelson, Timothy John. "Every Time I Feel the Spirit: Religious Experience and Religious Ritual in an African American Congregation." Ph.D. diss., University of Chicago, 1997. Study of an African Methodist Episcopal church in Charleston, South Carolina that rejects analyses of emotional worship among African American congregations as largely the product of a need for emotional catharsis. Argues instead that the emotional aspects of a worship service are part of a normative cultural construct, and that it constitutes collective action as the performances of virtuosos are interwoven with the performance of the congregation as a whole.

267. Okorocha, Cyril C. The Meaning of Religious Conversion in Africa: The Case of the Igbo of Nigeria. Aldershot: Avebury, 1987. A study of the "religious experience" of the Igbo set within a historical context of conversions to Christianity since 1906. Analysis focuses on "dread of the divine" as the key to Igbo religiosity and addresses the manner in which the Igbo explore various means by which to escape divine wrath, overcome fear of death, and be freed from anxiety.

Historical Studies

268. Parish, Steven M. **Moral Knowing in a Hindu Sacred City: An Exploration of Mind, Emotion, and Self.** New York: Columbia University Press, 1994. Analyzes the manner in which Hindus in the city of Bhaktapur in the valley of the Nepal integrate notions of mind, self, and emotion, and especially the manner in which emotion defines the meaning of a moral person. Specifically addresses emotions of anger, love, fear, and empathy, and discusses the cultural artifacts "heart-god" and "heart-self."

269. Park, George, and Cheryl Brown. "Sacrifical Strategies: Catholic Pilgrims in Time of Devalorizing Service." <u>Newfoundland Studies</u> 7 (1992): 123-142. Argues that the emotional tenor of pilgrimage served as a substitute for deficient quality of family life among Newfoundlanders.

270. Pearson, Roger. "Ancestor Worship in Sub-Saharan Africa." <u>Southern Quarterly</u> 10 (1972): 233-244. Ancestor worship among the Azande, Bantu Zulus, Nuer, and other sub-Saharan groups is undertaken largely out of fear that the spirit of the deceased will visit trouble upon the living unless the living, by their actions, manifest reverence for them. This belief is predicated on the understanding that ancestral spirits cannot know the true feelings and intentions of the living.

271. Pelton, Robert D. **The Trickster in West Africa: A Study of Mythic Irony and Sacred Delight.** Berkeley: University of California Press, 1980. Ashante, Fon, Dogon, and other tribal stories are interpreted with regard to the role of the trickster as a revealer of the facts of change and death, and as a model of the ways in which feeling, and wit, come into play in acknowledging such things.

272. Peters, Larry. **Ecstasy and Healing in Nepal: An Ethnopsychiatric Study of Tamang Shamanism.** Malibu: Undena, 1981. A historical/anthropological analysis of healing rituals that involve a shaman entering a trance, making a diagnosis of a sick person, and supervising a course of therapy that appears "psychotherapeutic." The shaman's experience of ecstasy is fundamental to his authority and effectiveness.

273. Pétursson, Pétur. "Revivalism and Lay Religious Movements on Iceland: A Survey and an Account of the Current State of Research." <u>Scandanavian Journal of History</u> 11 (1986): 335-344. Emotional religion did not take root in Iceland because of the channeling of emotion to other concerns, and especially with the ongoing attempt to obtain independence from Denmark, a project requiring significant emotional resources.

274. Pitts, Walter F. **The Afro-Baptist Ritual in the African Diaspora.** Foreword by Vincent L. Wimbush. New York: Oxford University Press, 1993. Historical approach to Afro-Baptist ritual, which is characterized by preaching geared to produce successive emotional buildups, and, sometimes, multiple "emotional apexes." The roots of that ritual process are African.

275. Sanders, Cheryl J. **Saints in Exile: The Holiness-Pentecostal Experience in African-American Religion and Culture.** New York: Oxford University Press, 1996. The discussion of worship in this study proposes that spirit possession is a key feature of African American religions (including Cuban santéria, Haitian vaudou, and Brazilian candomblé), and that possession always involves some ecstatic forms, especially trance. Such ecstasy is expressed in shouting, holy dance, glossolalia, utterances, and other ways. This "fluid" aspect of worship takes place alongside "fixed forms." Analysis of worship forms is carried out alongside consideration of exile as a key metaphor of African American religious experience.

276. **Shiefflin, Edward L. The Sorrow of the Lonely and the Burning of the Dancers.** New York: St Martin's Press, 1976. A study of the Kabuli of New Guinea that explores in detail the historical background and twentieth-century practice of reciprocity as symbolic action that embodies cultural values. Religion, and especially the religious aspects of the performance of reciprocity, are examined with respect to anger, sorrow, sentimentality, mourning, and nostalgia.

277. **Steemers, J. C. "Cultural Embarrassment and Religious Fear." Religion in a Pluralistic Society. Edited by J. S. Pobee. Leiden: E. J. Brill, 1976. Pp. 97-109.** Commentary on the emotional aspects of religious change in twentieth-century Ghana, as protectors of tribal beliefs and promoters of Roman Catholicism have sought to come to terms with each other.

278. **Steinberg, Mark D. "Workers on the Cross: Religious Imagination in the Writings of Russian Workers, 1910-1924. Russian Review 53 (1994): 213-239.** Religious feelings continued to inform the art of Russian laborers just before and during the revolution.

279. **Tolbert, Elizabeth Dawn. "Women Cry with Words: Symbolization of Affect in the Karelian Lament." Yearbook for Traditional Music 22 (1990): 80-105.** A study in the history of music that focuses on the Karelian lament, a performance found among women in the shamanistic religions of northern Asia and Scandanavia. Performed at funerals and weddings, it represents and excites emotion both through its melody and by the deployment of certain words and grammatical styles.

280. **Trawick, Margaret. "The Ideology of Love in a Tamil Family." Divine Passions: The Social Construction of Emotion in India. Edited by Owen M. Lynch.** Berkeley: University of California Press, 1990. Pp. 37-63. A study of *anpu* (love) that discloses, with reference to a Tamil family, the tradition that love was by nature and by right hidden. Discussion of love as devotion is carried out with reference to notions of master and servant drawn from religious models of relationships, and especially from the discourse of Shaiva sectarianism.

281. **"Trial Balloons." Journal of Modern History 46 (1974): 516-517.** This note suggests that the emotional intensity of religious gatherings is related to how close people sit to one another, with greater expression of emotion, and greater excitement, as proximity to others is increased.

282. **Turner, H. W. History of an African Independent Church. Vol. 1. The Church of the Lord (Aladura), and vol. 2, The Life and Faith of the Church of the Lord (Aladura).** Oxford: Clarendon Press, 1967. An examination of Aladura in four West African countries that highlights baptism by the Holy Spirit, faith healing, dreams, visions and prophecies, ecstatic dancing and trance. Previous scholarly analyses of the religion as unrestrained emotionalism that degraded the individual and the moral and intellectual content of the Christian faith are judged unjust, as is the image of the Negro race as spontaneous, uncontrolled, and emotional by nature.

283. **Voipio, Aarni. Sleeping Preachers: A Study in Ecstatic Religiosity. Suomalaisen Tiedeakatemian Toimituksia Annales Academiae Scientiarum Fennicae, vol. 75.** Helsinki, 1951. A historical survey of ecstatic religion leading up to six cases of Finnish women who sermonized from an apparent state of sleep upon their beds in the early twentieth century. Hysteria is proposed as the proper description of

their condition, although it is likewise described as a trance in which the self "becomes volitionally and emotionally integrated" (72).

284. Weeramunda, A. J. "The Milk Overflowing Ceremony in Sri Lanka." **Mother Worship: Themes and Variations.** Edited by James J. Preston. Chapel Hill: University of North Carolina Press, 1982. Pp. 251-262. The ceremony is performed in Sri Lanka in order to appease the anger of the goddess Pattini, a defeminized goddess who longs to be a male, and whose breasts create fire and destruction.

285. Wijeyewardene, Gehan. **Place and Emotion in Northern Thai Ritual Behavior.** Bangkok: Pandora, 1986. Draws upon Freud, Weber and Levi-Strauss in arguing that religious behavior among Thai Buddhists is fundamentally emotional (at the same time that it promotes control of emotions in meditation). Sexual symbolism is central to the analysis.

Surveys

286. Ali, S. Ameer. "The Mystical and Idealistic Spirit in the Islamic Expression." **The Sufi Mystery.** Edited by Nathaniel P. Archer. London: Octagon Press, 1980. Pp. 192-213. Outlines the manner in which the emotional side of Al-Ghazzali's mystical philosophy developed within the monasteries of the dervishes, with broader commentary on the Sufist linkage between emotional experience – and especially joy/longing – and rationalist philosophy.

287. Arapura, J. G. **Religion as Anxiety and Tranquility: An Essay in Comparative Phenomenology of the Spirit.** The Hague: Mouton, 1972. An historical and philosophical approach to identifying key concepts within the history of religion. The emotional states of anxiety and tranquility define two kinds of religious experiences, with the former manifest especially as conscience and guilt.

288. Aronson, Harvey B. **Love and Sympathy in Theravada Buddhism.** Delhi: Motilal Banarsidass, 1980. Brief survey that focuses on joy, equanimity, loving kindness and compassion, the four sublime attitudes taught by the Buddha, in arguing that Theravada Buddhism promotes social involvement not social withdrawal.

289. Behari, Bankey. "The Way to Ecstasy." **Sufi Studies: East and West: A Symposium in Honor of Idries Shah's Services to Sufi Studies by Twenty-Four Contributors Marking the 700th Anniversary of the Death of Jalahuddin Rumi (A.D. 1207-1273).** Tonbridge, Kent: Octagon Press, 1974. Pp. 183-205. Overview of the "ecstatic condition" as the product of practices carried out in the right manner and with the right preparation, according to the testimony of various historical personages.

290. Bharati, Agehananda. **The Light at the Center: Context and Pretext of Modern Mysticism.** Santa Barbara: Ross-Erikson, 1976. An examination of mysticism in various religious traditions that addresses relationships between feeling and knowing, concluding that mystics "feel a lot but know very little" (59).

291. Bremard, Henri. **Histoire Littéraire du Sentiment Religieux en France depuis la Fin des Guerres de Religion jusqu'a nos Jours.** Vols. 1-11. Paris: Librairie Bloud et Gay, 1916-1933. Sweeping history of religion and emotion in France that is

encyclopedic in approach, and includes numerous and detailed references to saintly figures and writers, some of whom are not French. The focus tends to be on the intellectual aspects of mysticism (especially in volumes 2-7) and other emotional forms of religion. There is also significant discussion of humanism and Christian life in the *ancien regime*, with categorizations of types of sentimentalism in religion. The collection includes a comprehensive Index (see below).

292. ------, **Histoire Littéraire du Sentiment Religieux en France depuis la Fin des Guerres de Religion jusqu'a nos Jours**. **Vols. 1-11. Paris: Librairie Bloud et Gay, 1939.** Index Alphabétique et Analytique par Charles Grolleau. This is an analytical index to the multi-volume history by Bremard.

293. Briffault, Robert. **Reasons for Anger: Selected Essays**. London: Robert Hale, Ltd., 1937. Includes a chapter that argues that "sexual emotion" is closely associated with religious emotion in tribal cultures and in the ancient Mediterranean, and that Christianity as it came to dominate the West has attempted to divorce sex and religion. Schleiermacher's feeling of absolute dependence is in fact similar to the feeling of dependence that emerges in sexual love. Christianity has not been entirely successful because "when the religious emotions surge up, the sexual emotion is never far away" (137).

294. Buehler, Arthur F. **Sufi Heirs of the Prophet: The Indian Naqshbandiyya and the Rise of the Mediating Sufi Shaykh**. **Studies in Comparative Religion. Columbia: University of South Carolina Press, 1998.** An exploration of love of the shaykh, Muhammad, and God in a study of the historical development of Sufism, with attention to the authority of the shaykh, and the manner in which the shaykh guided the spiritual life of his disciples. Spiritual energy is transmitted to the disciple through a bonding of hearts, regardless of the physical distance between the two. Concludes with observations on the redefinition of the Shaykh's role as mediating agent during the last century in Pakistan.

295. Champion, Françoise and Danièle Hervieu-Léger, editors. **De l'émotion en Religion: Renouveaux et Traditions**. **Paris: Centurion, 1990.** This is a collection of six essays of historical sociology generally organized around the themes of routinization, secularization, and spiritual renewal, that explore various roles of emotion within Judaism, Christianity, Islam, Soka Gakkai, and New Age spirituality by focusing on themes of trance, desire, charity, and love, among others.

296. Chatterjee, Chinmayi. **Studies in the Evolution of Bhakti Cult: With Special reference to Vallabha School, Part II**. **Jadavpur University Sanskrit Series, no. 9. Calcutta: Jadavpur University, 1981.** A study of *bhakti* in various schools of Indian thought, with a focus on devotion as feeling. Forms or gradations of devotional feeling are identified, as in the Vaisnava school of Bengal (here listed in order from beginnings to fulfillment): (1) no affection; (2) feeling as slave to master; (3) friendship; (4) parental tenderness towards God; (5) spousal love.

297. Ching, Julia. **Confucianism and Christianity: A Comparative Study**. **Tokyo: Kodansha International, with the cooperation of the Institute of Oriental religions, 1977.** Stresses emotional harmony in Confucianism as the foundation of Confucian spirituality.

Historical Studies 63

298. Coe, David K. Angst and the Abyss: The Hermeneutics of Nothingness. American Academy of Religion Series, no. 49. Chico: Scholars Press, 1985. A work of philosophy and intellectual history that tracks the linkages between angst and religion in ancient near eastern and Greek thought, Gnosticism, medieval mystics, and twentieth-century existentialist writers. Coe concludes that angst is a primal craving to assert transcendence.

299. Delumeau, Jean. Sin and Fear: The Emergence of a Western Guilt Culture 13th - 18th Centuries. Translated by Eric Nicholson. New York: St. Martin's Press, 1990 [1983]. A monumental cultural history of sin, a study in mentalité beginning with late medieval contempt for the world and the decisive emergence of the notion of conscience, through the Christian construction of various orders of sin, to Protestant eschatology. Christian fears of divine judgment, and especially of tortures in the afterlife, intensified over a period of five hundred years, coloring religious life in deeply pessimistic tones, and radically diverting from early Christian worldviews.

300. Denison, J. H. Emotion as the Basis for Civilization. New York: Charles Scribner's Sons, 1928. A sweeping global history that explores the role of emotion in Hinduism, Islam, Japanese religion, Christianity (and especially its connection to the feudal system), and in African and Chinese religions, and among the ancient Greeks and Romans. Denison above all urges the usefulness of emotional bonds in uniting persons in culture, and the analysis of religion and emotion centers on the ways in which religion cultivates emotion for that end.

301. ----- . Emotional Currents in American History. New York: Charles Scribner's Sons, 1932. A far-reaching analysis of American emotional culture, as it has been manifest in industry, commerce, politics, religion, race relations, and class. Religion is an "emotional power house" that charges the culture and supplies "the power that runs the wheels of the social mechanism" (314). Protestant and Roman Catholic emotional styles are distinguished, and revivalism is cast as a "recharging" of the power house. The religions of Mormonism, Theosophy, Spiritualism, the New Mexico *penitentes*, and other religious groups also are briefly examined within the context of religion as an emotional phenomenon.

302. Dhavamony, Mariasusai. Love of God According to Saiva Siddhanta: A Study in the Mysticism and Theology of Saivism. Oxford: Clarendon Press, 1971. A thorough history of the meanings of the Sanskrit term *bhakti*, its various usages in Vedic devotion, Upanishadic theism, in the Mahabharata, in Saivism, and elsewhere, with particular attention to Tamil doctrines, and with a concluding overview of *bhakti* ideas about the God of love, salvation, and the life of the mystic. Related emotional states considered are sorrow for sin, fearlessness, and surrender.

303. Dollimore, Jonathan. Death, Desire and Loss in Western Culture. London: Penguin, 1998. A wide-ranging survey that addresses the manner in which Christianity historically has insisted upon escape from desire (like Gnosticism and Buddhism) and questions the existence of the "person" who possesses "emotion." Dollimore investigates emotions associated with death and eroticism within a context rich in references to religious imagery in literature.

304. Ferguson, Harvie. Religious Transformation in Western Society: The End of Happiness. London: Routledge, 1992. Blending historical sociology and intellectual history, this study of happiness is organized with respect to five topics: faith, belief, morality, passion, and sensuousness. The first three are associated with Christianity. Passion, viewed here as a mode of consumption, is linked to individualism, capitalism, and the modern search for self. Sensuousness is the religious expression of modern life. The experience of happiness has developed over the course of western history in two ways: as an intellectual and ecclesiastical tradition, and as a mystical and emotional variant of Christianity.

305. Gispert-Sauch, G. Bliss in the Upanishads: An Analytical Study of the Origin and Growth of the Vedic Concept of Ananda. New Delhi: Oriental Publishers and Distributors, 1977. An historical/exegetical study of *ananda* (bliss, joy) with references to liturgies, domestic happiness, sexual pleasure, and literary depictions of heaven. Bliss correlates to the experience of non-duality, the "heavenly state" of wholeness.

306. Gorringe, Timothy. God's Just Vengeance: Crime, Violence, and the Rhetoric of Salvation. Cambridge: Cambridge University Press, 1996. A study of the historical intersections of atonement theology with thinking about crime and punishment in the west. Drawing on the work of Norbert Elias, it proposes that theological notions of atonement and expiation are intertwined with the cultural construction of feeling, of "structures of affect" (8). Twentieth-century notions of retributive justice are linked to emotional satisfactions in violence that are represented and practiced through Judaeo-Christian theologies.

307. Hardy, Friedhelm Ernst. "Emotional Krsna Bhakti." 2 vols. D.Phil thesis, Oxford University, 1976. Argues that emotional *bhakti*, which can be traced to the first few centuries C.E. embraces a worldview contrary to other Indian religious views, in that it constitutes emotions, the senses, and sense-objects as positive and meaningful. Accordingly, aesthetics, eros, and ecstasy are fundamental to the relationship between *bhakta* and KRSNA. This religious attitude is the product of creative interpenetration of Tamil and Sanskrit traditions.

308. -----. Viraha-Bhakti: The Early History of KRSNA Devotion in South India. Oxford: Oxford University Press, 1983. A study of "emotional bhakti" which, according to the author, has been long-neglected. Connecting the beginnings of KRSNA *bhakti* with the Bhagavat-Purana, the history includes analyses of various forms of emotional devotion, with an eye to sociological and political factors, and concludes with observations about the participation of the *bhakta* in another person's emotions.

309. -----. The Religious Culture of India: Power, Love and Wisdom. Cambridge: Cambridge University Press, 1994. These twenty-four Wilde Lectures at Oxford University over the period 1985-1987 include seven on "Love – the Rhythms of the Interior World' (191-366). Rich with historical and literary references, the seven lectures focus generally on the "landscape of the heart," and illustrate that terrain with the examples of various god-figures and historical personages.

310. Hyers, M. Conrad. Zen and the Comic Spirit. London: Rider and Company, 1974. Proposes that the expression of emotion in laughter is fundamental to Zen. Such laughter is analyzed as a refusal to absolutize, to attach the self to anything, and as a practice of transcending self. The fullness of the Zen comic vision lies in laughter in the face of misfortune.

311. Ingebretsen, Edward J. Maps of Heaven, Maps of Hell: Religious Terror as Memory from the Puritans to Steven King. London: M. E. Sharpe, 1996. Literary history that tracks the emergence and development of a discourse of terror from writings of early New Englanders (including Jonathan Edwards) through nineteenth and twentieth-century representations of "sacred terror." The use of terror was, for Americans, a "reasonable thing," used to illuminate moral tales and allegories.

312. Knowles, David. The English Mystical Tradition. London: Burns and Oates, 1961. Proposes that in the evolution of Catholic mystical theology, the Dionysiac emphasis on emotion remained strong, and together with the Augustinian strain, which was a "half-intellectual, half devotional, grace-enlightened penetration of Christian truth," informed a range of mystics and contemplatives.

313. Knox, R. A. Enthusiasm: A Chapter in the History of Religion, with Special Reference to the XVII and XVIII Centuries. Oxford: Clarendon Press, 1950. A broad survey of emotional Christianity, with particular emphasis on the period between the rise of the Quakers and the emergence of revivalistic Protestantism, that identifies "mystical" and "evangelical" as the two major types of enthusiasm. Emphasis is on the formation of theologies of feeling, and especially in connection with the issue of divine incarnation.

314. Mansfield, Bruce. "Thinking About Australian Religious History." Journal of Religious History 15 (1989): 330-344. Australian Christianity is characterized by its intellectual and institutional aspects rather than by emotions, or a certain quality of emotion.

315. May, Henry F. Ideas, Faiths, and Feelings: Essays on American Intellectual and Religious History 1952-1982. New York: Oxford University Press, 1983. A collection of ten essays and three extended reviews, many of which, such as "Philip Greven and the History of Temperament," directly address the issue of religion and emotion in American history.

316. Mazzaroni, Christina. Saint Hysteria: Neurosis, Mysticism and Gender in European Culture. Ithaca: Cornell University Press, 1996. This interdisciplinary study explores the construction and deployment of historical linkages between female hysteria and mysticism. Hagiographies are cast as pathographies in light of the emergence of medical theories that cast women as sufferers of the ambiguous and malleable affliction of hysteria. Women's spirituality accordingly was frequently shorn of its religious features, and treated as various species of madness.

317. McLoughlin, William G. Revivals, Awakenings, and Reform: An Essay on Religion and Social Change in America, 1607-1977. Chicago History of American Religion Series. Chicago: University of Chicago Press, 1978. Reflections on the manner in which social change, ideological systems, and emotional expression have been historically linked in enthusiastic, revivalistic religion in America.

318. Nurbakhsh, Javad. Sufism III: Submission, Contentment, Absence, Presence, Intimacy, Awe, Tranquility, Serenity, Fluctuation, Stability. Translated by Terry Graham and Leonard Lewisohn. London: Khaniqahi-Nimatullahi Publications, 1985. Various terms having to do with the emotional life of Sufis (as well as notions of virtue) are explained in detail, sometimes etymologically or with reference to historical factors. Occasionally the author evaluates their usefulness in the discipline and devotions of Sufism.

319. -----. **Sufism: Fear and Hope, Contraction and Expansion, Gathering and Disposition, Intoxication and Sobriety, Annihilation and Subsistence.** Translated by William C. Chittick. London: Khaniqahi-Nimatullahi Publications, 1985. Analysis of emotional states and spiritual conditions relevant to the practice of Sufism, sometimes drawing upon historical background, usually with theological judgments, and with commentary on the dangers of excessive fear.

320. -----. **Sufi Symbolism: The Nurbahksh Encyclopedia of Sufi Terminology. Vol. 2. Love, Lover, Beloved Allusions and Metaphors.** Translated by Terry Graham and Neil and Sima Johnston. London: Khaniqahi-Nimatullahi Publications, 1987. Brief encyclopedic entries of historical meanings of key terms in religion and emotion, including love, delight, crying, ecstasy, serenity, sorrow, shame, etc.

321. -----. **Sufism IV: Repentance, Abstinence, Renunciation, Wariness, Humilty, Humbleness, Sincerity, Constancy, Courtesy.** London: Khaniqahi-Nimatullahi Publications, 1988. Historical/exegetical approach to Muslim sources that analyzes moods and virtues, with some reference to historical disputes over them.

322. Perella, Nicholas James. **The Kiss Sacred and Profane: An Interpretive History of Kiss Symbolism and Related Religio-Erotic Themes.** Berkeley: University of California Press, 1969. A history of the kiss in Christian thought and representation, with commentary on numerous themes, including rapture, delight, love, nuptials, mysticism, and various other emotions and settings for emotion.

323. Pfister, Oscar. **Christianity and Fear: A Study in History and in the Psychology and Hygeine of Religion.** London: George Allen and Unwin Ltd., 1949. A groundbreaking and comprehensive study that defines fear as an emotion observable without the existence of an external threat, and from there outlines its appearance in neurotic and non-neurotic persons, as a problem of collective psychology. With reference to this model it addresses the formation of fear in Jewish history, and follows it through Jesus, St. Paul, the Catholic Church, and various Reformers, to the Enlightenment. In the conclusion, Pfister proposes that the historical "solution" to the "problem of fear" is the therapy of Christian love.

324. Rawlinson, Andrew. "Love and Meditation in the Bhakti Tradition." **The Saints: Studies in a Devotional Tradition of India.** Edited by Karine Schomer and W. H. McLeod. Berkeley: Berkeley Religious Studies Series, and Delhi: Motilal Bunarsidass, 1987. Pp. 53-58. A typology of *bhakti* that takes love and meditation as poles, and argues that the genius of historical *bhakti* saints was to structure a path to salvation that drew upon both.

325. Roche, Aloysius. **Fear and Religion.** London: Sands and Co., 1938. A popular but useful historical survey of religious fear in regards to God, death, hell, purgatory, and old age. Proposes that fear be understood as a religious motive.

326. Rubin, Julius H. **Religious Melancholy and the Protestant Experience in America.** New York: Oxford University Press, 1994. Traces the emergence of the melancholy spirit from the Reformation, through the evangelical piety of early European settlers in America, revivals, and various nineteenth- and twentieth-century Protestant developments. Argues that melancholy was once a commonplace religious condition, but generally came to be recognized as a representation of mental illness.

327. Sharda, S. R. **Sufi Thought: Its Development in Panjab and Its Impact on Panjabi Literature From Baba Farid to 1850 A.D.** Delhi: Munshiram Manoharlal, 1974. Regional history of Sufism that includes extensive discussion of theories of love and the influence of Sufism on Nirguna Bhakti religion. Comments on notions of fear, shame, hope, awe, and the illumination of the heart.

328. Sharma, Krishna. **Bhakti and the Bhakti Movement: A Study in the History of Ideas.** New Delhi: Munshiram Manoharlal, 1987. A revisionist study addressed to historians that challenges interpretations of bhakti that correlate it largely with Vaishnavism, arguing instead that the term refers to abroad spectrum of devotional life. In its essence, *bhakti* is a feeling.

329. Simon, Ulrich. **Piety and Terror: Christianity and Tragedy.** London: Macmillan, 1989. An analysis of the manner in which the relation between feeling and tragedy has changed in the history of the West, and especially in Christianity. The analysis begins with a study of classical tragedy and its appearance in the Old Testament, moving to a commentary on the death of tragedy as a philosophical perspective in the middle ages, its rebirth in the late sixteenth century, and its transformation in the twentieth century as Christian tragedy that blends feelings of horror and guilt with acceptance.

330. Singer, Irving. **The Nature of Love. Volume I: Plato to Luther.** Second edition. Chicago: University of Chicago Press, 1984. A history of the concept of love with emphasis on love as idealization – including erotic idealization and religious idealization – from its appearance in ancient Greek writings, to Luther's notion of *caritas*. Examinations of mysticism, the Christian idea of *agape*, and religious notions of fellowship comprise the majority of the book.

331. -----. **The Nature of Love. Volume II: Courtly and Romantic.** Chicago: University of Chicago Press, 1984. A study of the emergence of courtly love in the West and its transformation to Romantic love, with attention throughout to religious love. Part I addresses medieval attempts to reconcile human with religious love, while Part II traces later successes in harmonizing love of nature with love of God.

332. Smith, Edwin W. **The Religion of the Lower Races. As Illustrated by the African Bantu.** New York: Macmillan, 1923. A classic example of the attempt to explain the functioning of "primitive religion," in this case with reference to the Bantu. It emphasizes the excitement and manipulation of emotion, especially in rituals relating to ancestors and friends. This religion "places the Bantu in continual bondage to fear" (66) of evil spirits, witches, wizards, magic, and taboos.

333. Spae, Joseph J. **Buddhist-Christian Empathy.** Chicago: Chicago Institute of Theology and Culture, 1980. Explores Japanese religious feeling in context of similarities to emotions involved in the Christian religion.

334. Werner, Karel. "Love and Devotion in Buddhism." **Love Divine: Studies in Bhakti and Devotional Mysticism.** Durham Indological Series, no. 3. Edited by Karel Werner. Richmond, Surrey: Curzon Press, 1993. Pp. 37-52. Presents historical evidence for the "deep emotional involvement" (xv) of the Buddha's followers with that deity. That involvement is a significant advantage to them in their efforts to reach Enlightenment. Love and devotion aid salvation, and are part of a path of *bhakti* in Buddhism.

335. Woolley, Geoffrey H. Fear and Religion. London: Ernest Benn, Ltd., 1930.
An inquiry into the nature of fear associated with Christianity, "primitive religion," early Judaism, and modernity, that is somewhat sermonic in tone but is a significant early attempt to interpret and apply Rudolf Otto's Idea of the Holy historically.

Part 2

Social and Behavioral Sciences

Psychological Studies

336. Attivissimo, Donna Ann. "A Constructivist Analysis of the Experience of Guilt: Sex, Religion, and Psychopathology Correlates." Ph.D. diss., Hofstra University, 1995. Averill's social-constructionist model, in which emotions present in the system are there because they serve a function, is used to study the syndrome of guilt. Guilt is very common; most experience it once per week, and it lasts from one hour to half a day. Only <u>responses</u> to guilt differed among religious groups. Atonement was the general response, though many continued to feel guilty after they were forgiven.

337. Averill, James R. <u>Anger and Aggression: An Essay on Emotion</u>. New York: Springer-Verlag, 1982. Within a constructionist perspective, Chapter 4, "Historical Teachings on Anger" (73-101) offers the views of Plato, Aristotle, Seneca, Lactantius, Aquinas, and Descartes. Averill interprets these ideas and their implications in terms of biological, psychological, and socio-cultural theories about anger.

338. Averill, James R. "The Social Construction of Emotion: With Special Reference to Love." <u>The Social Construction of the Person</u>. Edited by Kenneth J. Gergen and Keith E. Davis. New York: Springer-Verlag, 1985. Pp. 89-109. A constructionist study of a romantic ideal, with references to the growth in the west of love as altruistic, to Dante, and to the medieval lady as Virgin Mary. Falling in love is approached as an "emotional syndrome," or an organized set of responses. Behavioral, physical, and cognitive processes are interpreted as emotional within a social context. Love's components are the idealization of the beloved, suddenness of onset, physiological arousal, and commitment.

339. Barnard, G. William. "Exploring Unseen Worlds: William James and the Philosophy of Mysticism." Ph.D. diss., University of Chicago, 1994. Theories of conversion, fascination with "psychical research," interest in the subliminal self, relating radical empiricism and mysticism, and a "field model of the self" are all part of the larger

context of James's work, through which Barnard seeks to analyze mysticism. Chapter 2 explores James's theories on the nature of experience and his understanding of emotion.

340. **Barth, Brigit.** "**Die Darstellung der Weiblichen Sexualität als Ausdrunk Männlichen Uterusneides und Dessen Abwehr.**" Jahrbuch der Psychoanalyse 26 (1990): 64-101. "Womb envy" exists; it is for males what penis envy is in females. But Freud and followers have neglected it. Male envy of the female womb, and all of its power, is a motive for male aggression. Womb envy is woven, unconsciously, in the fabric of society, and it is found in myth, religion, medicine, politics, and linguistics. Finally, it is a mainspring for racism.

341. **Beecher, Marguerite and Willard.** The Mark of Cain: An Anatomy of Jealousy. New York: Harper & Row, 1971. Contemporary reflections on the age-old problem of jealous competition are offered from what is an essentially psychological standpoint, though the book contains many biblical references to Jewish wisdom literature.

342. **Beit-Hallahmi, Benjamin.** Psychoanalytic Studies of Religion: A Critical Assessment and Annotated Bibliography. Westport, Conn.: Greenwood Press, 1996. On emotions, see sections on Religious Experience, Conversion, Rituals, Transition Rites, Ego Psychology, Mother-Worship, and Biographies. This overview of theory and detailed listing of works updates his Psychoanalysis and Religion: A Bibliography. Norwood, Pa.: Norwood Editions, 1978.

343. **Bhogle, Shalini.** "**Perception of Loneliness as an Index of Culture and Age.**" Psychological Studies 36 (1991): 174-79. Comparative study of loneliness in India, related to age, gender, and religion, using the Revised UCLA Loneliness Scale. Hindu families were typically made up of 4 members; Muslim families, 8-20; Christian families averaged 5-6 members. Hindus experienced greatest loneliness, and the emotion was highest among Hindu adolescents. Younger boys were lonelier than first-borns. First-born Christian girls were lonelier than younger ones. Women were less lonely than men.

344. **Blackwell's Encyclopedia of Social Psychology.** S.v. "**Emotional Experience.**" Answers two questions from major theorists of emotion. What is an emotion? Subjective experience. What about emotions makes for their characteristic subjective experiences? Physiology, central and peripheral, action and action tendencies, cognitive tendencies and appraisals. The latter bears directly on the study of religion, since emotional appraisals involve values, goals, and ultimate concerns.

345. **Boden, Margaret A.** "**Wonder and Understanding.**" Zygon: Journal of Religion and Science 20 (1985): 391-400. Wonder is at the heart of religious experience, understanding, for science. The mind has become problematic, and much of it has been seen as superfluous. Science too often denies the mind. Developments in artificial intelligence correct this by leading the psychologist to new appreciation of the human mind – to wonder about the mind.

346. **Campbell, Joseph.** The Hero with a Thousand Faces. Princeton: Princeton University Press, 1968 [1949]. It is the creative hero who guides and saves society, not the reverse. Citing a wide range of sources, the achievement of personal identity, through the adventures of desire and the fear of that discovery, is explored. The psychological integration of feelings is the true object of the hero's quest.

347. Capps, Donald. "Childhood Fears, Adult Anxieties, and the Longing for Inner Peace: Erik H. Erikson's Psychoanalytic Psychology of Religion." **Religion, Society, and Psychoanalysis: Readings in Contemporary Theory**. Edited by Janet Liebman Jacobs and Donald Capps. Boulder, Colo.: Westview Press, 1997. Pp. 127-62. Religion is how the inner space, at first associated with the mother, becomes the center of the true self. Mother-child images of trust, nurture, care, as well as the unrepresented relation of the self to itself, provide the religious sources for a vision of possible wholeness. Anxieties in adults measure how much reconciliation eludes them. Being open to one's self as child, its fears and dangers, measures how much resolve has been achieved.

348. ------. "James's 'Transfigured Nature'": Where Art and Religion Converge." **Journal of Religion and Health** 36 (1997): 109-26. James's appreciation of painting, especially landscapes, played a role in his psychology of religion. Portraits show his distance from religious subjects, but landscapes reveal James's personal use of religion and his self-identification with the religious-minded. The feminine is present in landscape art for James, bringing love, melancholy, and religion's maternal aspect to the fore.

349. ------. **Men, Religion, and Melancholia: James, Otto, Jung, and Erikson**. New Haven: Yale University Press, 1997. "Mourning and Melancholia" and "The 'Uncanny'" by Freud are keys to understanding James's Varieties of Religious Experience, Otto's Idea of the Holy, Jung's Answer to Job and Erikson's Young Man Luther. Melancholia haunted the authors and depended on childhood traumas of a perceived loss of the mother's love. Melancholia may be the psychological source of religious experience.

350. Cherry, Keith, and David H. Smith. "Sometimes I Cry: The Experience of Loneliness for Men with AIDS." **Health Communication** 5 (1993): 181-208. In this small sample of male AIDS outpatients, feelings of existential loneliness were related to religious faith, living in the face of death, and questions about life's meaning. Narratives show that the subjects experienced isolation from society; they felt alienated and stigmatized. The medical establishment was perceived as adding to feelings of loneliness. As their bodies changed, they felt that their relationships were dissolving and in need of restructuring.

351. **Childhood and Selfhood: Essays on Tradition, Religion, and Modernity in the Psychology of Erik H. Erikson**. Edited with Introduction by Peter Homans. Lewisburg, Pa.: Bucknell University Press, 1978. What motivates the self in its development from within? From without? Identity is the key. Psychoanalysis, for Erikson, offers emphatic links among body, ego, and cultural environs, at times, playing a religious role.

352. Coles, Robert. **The Spiritual Life of Children**. Boston: Houghton Mifflin, 1990. Children are by nature soulful, capable of being profane one minute, spiritual the next, thereby revealing much about humanity. Jewish, Christian, Muslim, secular – these children appear, in words and in pictures, to be without fear as they face the idea of God. American, Israeli, Tunisian, and Irish children, among others, express and portray God's wishes, heaven and hell, the devil, skepticism, and faith, with openness and passion.

353. Conn, Walter E. "Self-Transcendence, the True Self, and Self-Love." **Pastoral Psychology** 46 (1998): 323-32. Conn builds on earlier, post-Freudian psychoanalytic

interpretations to theorize that the self is unified in the radical desire for self-transcendence. Relying on Lonergan's model of transcendence, Merton's idea of the true self, and Fromm's notion of the meaning of self-love, Conn posits that the true self is realized in religious experience through the radical desire for transcendence. Further, the meaning of genuine self-love is based in this view of the self.

354. Copestake, David R., and H. Newton Malony. "Adverse Effects of Charismatic Experiences: A Reconsideration." Journal of Psychology & Christianity 12 (1993): 236-44. Cases show the negative effects of charismatic religious experience. Though untypical, anxiety, depression, fear, and mania may be more common than supposed. Such after-effects exacerbate existing conditions, at times requiring hospitalization. Neuropsychological diagnoses given counter the explanations by devotees (lack of faith, unredeemed sin, and demonic possession). Some reactions are like the effects of psychedelic drugs.

355. Coxhead, Nona. The Relevance of Bliss: A Contemporary Exploration of Mystic Experience. New York: St. Martin's, 1985. Reflections on the higher consciousness, a shift in perception "impossible to mistake," feeling over-whelmingly illuminated – from the viewpoints of psychiatry, medicine, and neurophysiology. Bliss is relevant as a civilizing force to address contemporary problems; it will lessen hostility, crime, and lives of lost purpose.

356. Csordas, Thomas J. "The Rhetoric of Transformation in Ritual Healing." Culture, Medicine, and Psychiatry 7 (1983): 333-75. Catholic Pentecostals engage in psychotherapy in their healing rituals. Religious discourse with an affective tone makes for a precondition to healing, shapes an experience of empowerment, and creates the immediate perception of transformation. In so doing, the ritual is both religious and therapeutic. Negative emotions are removed, and a new self-meaning, of the person as whole and holy, is achieved.

357. Darwin, Charles. The Expression of the Emotions in Man and Animals. 3rd ed. With an Introduction, Afterward and Commentaries by Paul Ekman. New York: Oxford University Press, 1998 [1872]. The critical edition complete with plates and appendices (on text changes, photography, and head words) and critical apparatus. For Darwin, emotions are innate, part of biology. Chapter 8, "Joy, High Spirits, Love, Tender Feelings, Devotion" (195-218), contains reflections on affection, devotion, love, and religion, including descriptions of the human face, upturned eyes, and hands pressed palms together.

358. Davis, Charles. Body as Spirit: The Nature of Religious Feeling. New York: Seabury Press, 1976. Zen and Western social psychology inform this study of true religion, which Davis claims is rooted primarily in the affections. Yet he notes that Christianity, especially mysticism, is seen as the enemy of the body. A fundamental trust in the body is wanting. Opposed to an asceticism of punitive discipline, an asceticism of achieved spontaneity is recommended. Sinful egos, wrapped in their cells of selfishness, must learn how to feel, to recover the rhythms of the body, and to release feeling, as an arrow from a bow.

359. De St. Aubin, Ed. "An Examination and Elaboration of the Polarity Theory of Personal Ideology." Ph.D. diss., Northwestern University, 1994. Study of value systems, religiosity, politics, and the emotional foundation of personal ideology. Silvan Tomkins said that conservative, normative ideology is founded on anger, surprise,

disgust/contempt, and excitement, while humanism is structured through joy, distress, shame, and fear. Tomkins's Polarity Theory is confirmed in this sample of 64 adults.

360. Diamond, Stephen. <u>Anger, Madness, and the Daimonic: The Psychological Genesis of Violence, Evil, and Creativity</u>. Albany, N.Y.: State University of New York Press, 1996. This revised dissertation seeks to clarify the depth psychology of Rollo May, especially his contribution to study of "the daimonic." Anger and rage are "daimonic" forms of power, which can be as much about creativity as it is about negative or destructive reactions (the demonic). Humans can choose whether to exercise such power for good or evil.

361. Dick, Lois Chapman. "An Investigation of the Disenfranchised Grief of Two Health Care Professionals Caring for Persons with AIDS." <u>Disenfranchised Grief: Recognizing Hidden Sorrow</u>. Edited by Kenneth J. Doka. Lexington, Mass.: Lexington Books, 1989. Pp. 55-65. Two health-care professionals find difficulty working with AIDS sufferers. They are unable to rise above the ruined lives of their patients, or find comfort in the funerals of those for whom they have cared. Play is impossible, and there is loneliness in a patient's grief. Not even religion offers consolation or solace from the personal devastation.

362. Dunlap, Knight. <u>Religion, Its Functions in Human Life: A Study of Religion from the Point of View of Psychology</u>. New York: McGraw-Hill Book Co., 1946. Chapter 5, "The Role of Desire in Religion" (123-33), considers basic desires for food, protection, rest, activity, excretion, sex, children, fame, and belonging. Among these, the desires for food, drink, and security (from threats of injury, suffering, or death) are deemed most influential in the rise of religion and in its early development.

363. Dunn, Paul. "Natural Enthusiasm: A Western Spiritual Context for the Contemporary Humanistic Orientation in Psychology and Education." Ph.D. diss., University of California, Santa Barbara, 1991. The 1960s humanistic approach to psychology tried to liberate body and emotions from Western bias. Lack of clarity occurred in addressing spiritual ideation within the notion of human experimental capacity. Looking back to Shaftesbury's naturalistic view of religious enthusiasm, and to the Romantics, it seems that recent confusions are nothing new. The critique of dualism and the embrace of an organic approach are part of the trajectory Dunn promotes.

364. Ellwood, Gracia Fay. "Holy Darkness, Holy Light: Toward an Interpretation of Painful Near-Death Experiences." Ph.D. diss., Claremont Graduate University, 1998. Work on Near-Death Experiences (NDEs) is positive, lifting up bodily release and joyous journey in the spirit realm. A few studies reveal painful NDEs, full of feelings of fear, malevolent beings, isolation in a living-hell-of-a-world after the experience. The painful NDEs are reviewed, both the interviews and the interpretations of what such experiences might mean.

365. Erol, Nese, and Nail Sahin. "Fears of Children and the Cultural Context: The Turkish Norms." <u>European Child & Adolescent Psychiatry</u> 4 (1995): 85-93. Three groups of Turkish children were measured by the Fear Survey Schedule for Children. Girls were more fearful than boys, and their fear was more intense and frequent. Fears of death and of separation were the most intense; religious fears were most frequent.

366. <u>The Fires of Desire: Erotic Energies and the Spiritual Quest</u>. Edited by Fredrica R. Halligan and John J. Shea. New York: Crossroad, 1992. Papers from a psychoanalytic conference at Fordham University (1991) on erotic desire, passionate energy, Jungian psychology and spiritual transformation. The question addressed: how does libidinal energy further the spiritual quest?

367. Fragola, Anthony N. **"From the Ecclesiastical to the Profane: Foot Fetishism in Luis Bunuel and Alain Robbe-Grillet."** Journal of the American Academy of Psychoanalysis **22 (1994): 663-80.** Foot fetishism is a central motif for Spanish surrealist Bunuel and French director Robbe-Grillet. Sexual obsession and deviance result from repressive Catholic teachings where sex is guilt. The fetish is a substitute for intimacy, and replacement is due to a fear of castration and anxiety over biological differences. While Bunuel sees it as deviant, religious-based behavior, Robbe-Grillet, the norm that society denies.

368. Freud, Sigmund. The Future of An Illusion. **Garden City, N.Y.: Anchor Books, 1961 [1927].** Religion compensates the masses for those instincts and passions sacrificed for the sake of social life and security. Wish-fulfillment, or illusion, religion rewards and punishes in ways that give people repetitive and deeper feelings of guilt. This is neurotic; science is the modern answer.

369. ------. Civilization and Its Discontents. **New York: Norton, 1961 [1930].** Chapter 1 is the classic response to Romain Rolland's reading of The Future of An Illusion (1927). Rolland agreed with Freud's view of the religion of the masses, but confesses that he has had a sensation of "eternity" – a limitless, boundless, "oceanic feeling," independent of organized religion. This becomes the occasion for Freud to reflect on religion and emotion. Even oceanic feeling is illusory, a narcissistic regression to the mother-infant union.

370. Frey-Wehrlin, C. Toni. **"Widerstand und Anpassung: Die Analytische Psychologie und die Institutionen."** Analytische Psychologie **24 (1993): 288-301.** A bold methodological statement on feeling loyal to a religious based (non-denominational) Jungian psychotherapy, at a time when the currents of depth psychology are disturbed by institutional scrutiny and accountability. Reimbursement to psychologists requires that treatment be proven efficacious through statistically documented cures. Do that without compromising inner loyalty to the principles and ideals behind the therapy.

371. Fromm, Erich. To Have or to Be? **New York: Continuum, 1996 [1976].** Two modes of existence vie for dominion, the having mode and the being mode. The having mode is marked by materialism, aggression, greed, envy, and violence. The being mode is expressed in sharing, pleasure, meaning, and creative activity. It is based in love. Fromm believed that the having mode threatens the psychological and ecological destruction of humanity and nature. The possibilities for a solution rely on altruism and the religious impulse for a "new man" in a "new society."

372. Gallard, Martine. **"De la sensation océanique au sentiment d'être vivant."** Cahiers Jungiens de psychanalyse **84 (1995): 65-75.** Many regard the notion of limitless extension and oneness with the universe to be a source of religiosity. How receptive were Freud and Jung to this sensation (what Freud termed "oceanic feeling")? Jung was more favorable to the thought that one could experience nature directly, achieving an immediate, mystical connection with the infinite. But Freud (interested in sexual desire and self-knowledge) viewed oceanic feeling as illusion. Images of psychic wholeness are sketched.

373. Goldenberg, Naomi R. **Returning Words to Flesh: Feminism, Psychoanalysis, and the Resurrection of the Body.** Boston: Beacon, 1990. Emptiness in contemporary life arises from society's rejection of the body, which contains our physicality and emotions. It also holds our memories – our personal histories – our relationships, and our feelings of the presence of others. The anti-body attitudes and anti-feminism of the religious traditions share blame for this, as does technology. Her Jewish identity is a source of hope, as are the "talking cures" of psychoanalysis and feminism.

374. Greven, Philip. **Spare the Child: The Religious Roots of Punishment and the Psychological Impact of Physical Abuse.** New York: Knopf, 1990. Greven urges non-violent techniques of child-rearing in his review of what physical punishment feels like to children. Discussions of religious, psychological, and secular implications of physical punishment would aid social workers, clergy, therapists, educators, and parents. Greven tries to explain why children have been spanked, and how punishments affect the feelings and behavior of children, both private and public.

375. Hardy, Alister. **The Spiritual Nature of Man: A Study of Contemporary Religious Experience.** Oxford: Clarendon Press, 1979. Collection of first-hand accounts showing an awareness of a benevolent non-physical power greater than that of the self. The accounts are classed in terms of sensory, behavioral, cognitive and affective elements. These deeply felt transcendental experiences point of the spiritual nature of being human.

376. Heisig, James W. **Imago Dei: A Study of C. G. Jung's Psychology of Religion.** Lewisburg, Pa.: Bucknell University Press, 1979. The God-image as a symbol of psychic totality is the central notion in Jung's complex writings on religion. Heisig traces its development, the wide variety of experiences of God, and the content of unconscious projections. Jung classed as an imago Dei any unconscious product that stood for an individual's "highest value." The content of feeling-toned representations is collective emotion.

377. Henry, James P. "Religious Experience, Archetypes, and the Neurophysiology of Emotions." **Zygon: Journal of Religion and Science** 21 (1986): 47-74. The intuitive right-brain makes for warm attachment behavior and for the powerful emotions that fuel cultural expressions of religious ritual. The numinous experiences of the holy include mother-infant and adult bonding. During these sacred moments, neuroendocrines activate ties that last a lifetime.

378. Hill, Peter C. "Affective Theory and Religious Experience." **Handbook of Religious Experience.** Edited by Ralph W. Hood, Jr. Birmingham, Ala.: Religious Education Press, 1995. Pp. 353-77. Hill attempts to explain the conditions under which the full range of emotions is experienced and to identify the religious implications of the emotions. Theories described include bio-social and appraisal theories, conceptualizing affect, cognitive-arousal theory, religious coping, and the influence of affect on cognition.

379. Homans, Peter. **Jung in Context: Modernity and the Making of a Psychology.** Chicago: University of Chicago Press, 1979. Loneliness, low self-esteem, and narcissism shaped Jung's development and approach to religion. The mind became church and society, worlds within a world. His writings have given many the means to order and reflect upon their own inner struggles.

380. ------. __The Ability to Mourn: Disillusionment and the Social Origins of Psychoanalysis__. Chicago: University of Chicago Press, 1989. The process of individuation is the fulcrum for change in ideas, beliefs, and values. After a loss, one tries to return, to mourn, to retrieve. This backward-moving-ness produces a new re-centering of self, or individuation, which leads to a release from the past, and the creation of new meanings and values in the space made empty by the loss. The process is developed into a theory of history to explain how psychoanalysis emerged out of Judeo-Christian culture.

381. Hood, Ralph W., Jr. "Psychoanalysis and Fundamentalism: A Lesson from Feminist Critiques of Freud." __Religion, Society, and Psychoanalysis: Readings in Contemporary Theory__. Edited by Janet Liebman Jacobs and Donald Capps. Boulder, Colo.: Westview Press, 1997. Pp. 42-67. Beginning with the feminist critique of Freud's abandonment of seduction theory, Hood argues that Freud saw the inadequacy of describing fundamentalist religion as illusion; rather he thought the delusional nature of such religion needed to be unmasked. Finally, there is a truth in illusion, the truth of human desire.

382. Huntington, Richard, and Peter Metcalf. "The Emotional Reaction to Death." __Celebrations of Death: The Anthropology of Mortuary Ritual__. Cambridge: Cambridge University Press, 1979. Pp. 23-43. In this opening chapter to their textbook, the authors contrast the theories of Radcliffe-Brown and Durkheim. The Durkheimian approach is illustrated through the Nyakyusa of Tanzania. Examples of emotional reactions to death involve religious ritual, and the chapter concludes with Geertz's study of Javanese funerals.

383. Irvine, Judith T. "Language and Affect: Some Cross-Cultural Issues." __Contemporary Perceptions of Language: Interdisciplinary Dimensions__. Edited by Heidi Byrnes. Washington, D.C.: Georgetown University Press, 1982. Pp. 31-47. Affect is subjective, individual and personal. But it is also socially defined. Person, culture, and communication modes are sorted out for analysis. Among the rural Wolof of Senegal, emotion states signal social identity, thus cultural display of affect is as important as the subjective feeling-state, or more so.

384. Jackson, Stanley W. "Acedia the Sin and Its Relationship to Sorrow and Melancholia." __Culture and Depression: Studies in the Anthropology and Cross-Cultural Psychiatry of Affect and Disorder__. Edited by Arthur Kleinman and Byron Good. Berkeley: University of California Press, 1985. Pp. 43-62. Lead-off essay to a volume of comparative studies covers a wide range of Western approaches to the psychology of depression, from classical Greece to the desert monks and early church fathers to Aquinas and Chaucer's "Parson."

385. Jacobs, Janet L. "Women-Centered Healing Rites: A Study in Alienation." __In Gods We Trust: New Patterns of Religious Pluralism in America__. Edited by Thomas Robbins and Dick Anthony. 2d ed. New Brunswick, N.J.: Transaction Publishers, 1990. Pp. 373-83. Alienation is too common a feeling for women. Even in religious experience, they meet obstacles to self-integration, such as male god-images. A powerful resource for women is the goddess ritual where the mother-daughter bond is strengthened. Symbolic integration by guided meditation affirms the feminine self, and this bond is most significant for healing the effects of self-alienation.

386. ------. "Religious Ritual and Mental Health." **Religion and Mental Health**. **Edited by John F. Schumaker. New York: Oxford University Press, 1992. Pp. 291-99.** Religious rites are described as emotions released in cathartic and collective moments, in this cross-cultural study of the role of ritual in mental health. Anger, grief, and shame are explored in rituals of confrontation, mourning, and confession. Religious rites mitigate anxiety. Mental health results from rituals that have a high relational value, bringing significant others into regular opportunities for expressing various emotions.

387. James, William. **The Will to Believe, and Other Essays in Popular Philosophy. New York: Longmans, Green, and Co., 1897.** Belief involves deliberate volition, also fear, hope, bias, passion, imitation, and partisanship – the pressures of class and society. Thus, we find ourselves not knowing why we believe. The prestige of opinions, the affirmation of desire, Christian feelings, passional work – these go into decisions that cannot be made on intellectual grounds. Emotions play an enormous role in what humans believe.

388. ------. **The Varieties of Religious Experience: A Study in Human Nature. New York: Longmans, Green, and Co., 1902.** Ideas and structures arise out of primary experiences, especially the feelings of the solitary heart. Humans have a religious constitution expressed in a "sense of newness," a cheerfulness, a "readiness for great things," which is coterminous with a higher, expansive order, a MORE. Thus, James's radical empiricism gave rise to mysticism.

389. Janet, Pierre. **De l'angoisse à l'extase: études sur les croyances et les sentiments. 2 vols. Paris: Alcan, 1926-1928.** Janet was one of the best-known doctors at the Salpêtrière. These volumes on anguish and ecstasy, beliefs and feelings crowned a life-long interest in the possible avenues through which the study of religious experience might contribute to psychopathology.

390. Johansson, Rune E. A. "Emotion and Feeling in Nibbana." **The Psychology of Nirvana. London: Allen and Unwin, 1969. Pp. 24-27.** Disinterested calm and undisturbed satisfaction describes nirvana. It is compared to the cool waters of a lake, which would be pleasant in the tropics. In this review of emotion words linked to the goal of Buddhism, nirvana is pictured from an emotional view as happiness, peace, calm, security, kindness, and humility. Because it is also "cool," those feelings should be seen as impersonal and disinterested.

391. Jung, C. G. **Psychology of Religion. New Haven: Yale University Press, 1938.** Feelings projected outward and given religious significance are central to Jung's early attempt to relate the psychological notion of the self to God. He was curious about patients who drew mandalas never having seen one. The circle points toward the integration of feelings and the wholeness of the self. In later works, the process of individuation would unite the human and the divine.

392. ------. Answer to Job. **Psychology and Religion: West and East, Vol. 11 of The Collected Works of C. G. Jung. Translated by R. F. C. Hull. New York: Pantheon, 1958 [1952]. Pp. 355-470.** Job is all about differentiation and individuation. Religious beliefs are psychic facts that need no proof; they are based on numinous archetypes, on an emotional foundation, inaccessible to reason. Christ is the answer to Job, and the purpose of the Incarnation lies in the differentiation in Yahweh's consciousness. That "God can be loved but must be feared" is the psychic truth at the heart of the process of individuation.

393. Kahn, Jack. **Job's Illness: Loss, Grief and Integration, A Psychological Interpretation**. London: Gaskell, 1986 [1975]. Job's story is consistent with that of the obsessed neurotic. Over solicitous for the safety of his children, he is even willing to perform sacrifices for their benefit. From the start, Job claims he is blameless; a perfectionist who has not sinned. But he could not keep all the balls in the air and suffers a breakdown. The calamities are a great loss to Job, but it was his own protest of all deterministic answers about his suffering that made him alter the outcome of his illness. Willingness to admit the human imperfections of a limit to knowledge and power is part of the cure.

394. Kirkpatrick, Lee A. "An Attachment-Theory Approach to the Psychology of Religion." **International Journal for the Psychology of Religion** 2 (1992): 3-28. Attachment theory is the interpretive key for the psychology of religion when applied to adults. The worshipper-God relationship mirrors the infant-mother one, and prayer, God images, and conversion can be better understood using the biological theory of attachment. Psychologists may also benefit from this approach as they help clients with loneliness, stress-management, and relationships.

395. ------. "Attachment Theory and Religious Experience." **Handbook of Religious Experience**. Edited by Ralph W. Hood, Jr. Birmingham, Ala.: Religious Education Press, 1995. Pp. 446-75. Attachment theory updates psychoanalysis, given new developments in evolutionary biology. It posits a behavioral system for humans/primates designed by natural selection to keep infants and caregivers together for reasons of security. These emotions in adulthood have considerable significance for the psychology of religion.

396. Kirschner, Suzanne R. **The Religious and Romantic Origins of Psychoanalysis: Individuation and Integration in Post-Freudian Theory**. Cambridge: Cambridge University Press, 1996. Psychoanalysis rests on a Judeo-Christian base. Modern theories of the self do not pose a radical break from tradition. Through the Bible, theologies of redemption, and Neoplatonism, it is argued that psychoanalytic theories are the latest chapter in a long-running narrative, recently secularized. Not the soul's history, the new pattern is this-worldly – the story of the development of personality, emotional growth, individuation.

397. Kohut, Heinz. "Forms and Transformations of Narcissism." **The Search for the Self: Selected Writings of Heinz Kohut, 1950-1978**. Edited and with an Introduction by Paul H. Ornstein. 2 vols. Madison, Conn.: International University Press, 1978 [1966]. 1: 427-60. "Cosmic narcissism," the religious goal of Kohut's psychology, is a mature state produced by a shift from the self to participation in a supra-individual, timeless existence. The shift, genuine, enduring, creative, results from steady actions by the ego, and it is attainable only by the very few. Resting on the creation of a higher form of narcissism, marked by empathy, humor, and wisdom, it is where one lives without anxiety or elation but bathed in communion with a content-less, supra-ordinate Self.

398. Kristeva, Julia. **Black Sun: Depression and Melancholia**. Translated by Leon S. Roudiez. New York: Columbia University Press, 1989. Melancholia is an abyss of sorrow full of incommunicable grief. Depressives can do nothing about insights glimpsed in brilliant flashes. At their core is love for an attach-ment or a lost love. Women feel loss acutely because they must separate from a mother without losing her love. Art is interpreted via religion and psycho-analysis to describe the "Black Sun."

Depression is compared to the current malaise in the West: its lost values threaten the larger social self with eclipse.

399. **Labouvie-Vief, Gisela. <u>Psyche and Eros: Mind and Gender in the Life Course</u>. New York: Cambridge University Press, 1994.** Growth differs with gender. Rationality is seen as masculine; imagination and emotion are aligned with the feminine. Drawing from mythology, religion, philosophy, and literature, a theory of the maturing mind is framed. The Greek myth of Psyche and Eros illustrates how competition between masculine and feminine parts of the mind might be resolved through a more complementary approach.

400. **Lee, Jae Hoon. <u>The Exploration of the Inner Wounds – Han</u>. Atlanta, Ga.: Scholars Press, 1994.** Departing from Western conceptual approaches to evil, Lee employs depth-psychology in making the inner experience of suffering and pain the key to understanding evil. Such inner pain, called han in Korea, is deemed responsible for emotional and mental imbalances in human relations. Han is a psychological fact not to be abstracted. Lee's model for healing is based on the shaman's role of transforming negative han into positive energy, thereby creating a new wholeness in the person.

401. **Maslow, Abraham H. "Lessons from the Peak-Experiences." <u>Journal of Humanistic Psychology</u> 2 (1962): 9-18.** The word happiness may be too weak to adequately describe mystic religious experience, the moments of profound awe, ecstasy, bliss, even rapture. Moments of purely positive and intense happiness, without doubt or fear or inhibition or self-consciousness are part of the "peak-experience." Ascending to this peak is an excursion into health.

402. **Matsumoto, David. <u>Unmasking Japan: Myths and Realities About the Emotions of the Japanese</u>. Stanford: Stanford University Press, 1996.** Micro study via laboratory research, observation of facial expressions, and inspection of emotion language. A protégé of Paul Ekman and neurocultural theory, Matsumoto holds that, due to biology, emotional expression is universal. Yet, given Japan's modification of overt displays, difference in specific emotions is accounted for by cultural circumstances. These antecedents implicate religion. Japan, the world culture, is as taxing as it is influential. Studies like this are ciphers for understanding cultural factors in emotional display rules.

403. **Mead, George Herbert. <u>Mind, Self, and Society, From the Standpoint of a Social Behaviorist</u>. Edited and With an Introduction by Charles W. Morris. Chicago: University of Chicago Press, 1962 [1934].** The seminal work by a great American pragmatist shows the nexus of mind, self, and society as an interrelated process of social constitution. Attending to language and feelings, with scientific precision, Mead demonstrates that the individual constitutes society as genuinely as the society constitutes the self. Religion is treated only marginally by this social psychologist, however, his work has been a key resource for the psychology of religion and for social ethics.

404. **Meissner, W. W. <u>Psychoanalysis and Religious Experience</u>. New Haven: Yale University Press, 1984.** This exposition of Freud's approach to religion, attending carefully his primary works on the subject, is systematic, apologetic, precise analysis by a leading Jesuit psychoanalytic writer. Freedom is needed for a life of grace; psychoanalysis can focus on negative feelings. With the self's natural vulnerability clarified, a fuller, freer expression of humanity is possible. At this point, the theological

can positively contribute to human existence. Psychoanalysis and religious experience prove complementary.

405. ------. "Vincent's Suicide: A Psychic Autopsy." Contemporary Psychoanalysis 28 (1992): 673-94. Was van Gogh's suicide due to sickness, poverty, and loneliness? Vincent's pact with his brother postponed the suicide, making it possible for van Gogh to continue painting in the service of a high religious ideal. The suicide itself is viewed as a dramatic and final, ritual act for a life motivated by religious vision. Death brought his life of pain and martyrdom, rejection and lost love, to a victorious end because, through it, he achieved the realization of love and greater acceptance from his brother.

406. Mounteer, Carl A. "The Religious Experience of Modern American Film." Journal of Psychohistory 20 (1992): 53-63. "Spiritual science fiction," such as Steven Spielberg's films, offer what organized religion cannot. Human fantasy – the belief in superior beings that like us and want to give us eternal life and bliss – is at the heart of films in this genre. Institutional religion cannot offer such assurance, it is argued, because its authority is rooted in the psychological terror of a wrathful God. Spiritual sci-fi supplants traditional religion, giving filmgoers a more humane experience.

407. Myers, Gerald E. "William James on Emotion and Religion." Transactions of the Charles S. Peirce Society 21 (1985): 463-84. James was intrigued at how the emotional component of mystical and conversion experiences creates the rudiments of a belief; thus, the will to hold that belief is already in place. Myers suspects that James linked religion with emotion because the religious seems to conflict with reason. This raises questions about a psychology of religion approached through a psychology of emotion.

408. The Nature of Emotion: Fundamental Questions. Edited by Paul Ekman and Richard J. Davidson. New York: Oxford University Press, 1994. Though not specifically on religion, this is a valuable volume for religion scholars in that 24 leading emotion theorists address 12 fundamental questions, such as: are their basic emotions? How do they relate to memory? Can they be non-conscious? Can they be controlled? Work on the research edge of both biology and so-called cultural psychology, with helpful summaries after each section.

409. Neumann, Erich. The Great Mother: An Analysis of the Archetype. Translated by Ralph Manheim. Princeton: Princeton University Press, 1963 [1955]. Jungian "archetypes" is made up of "emotional-dynamic components," symbolism, content, and structure. The emotional dynamic is the effect of the archetype, and that is explored by Neumann in positive (love, sympathy, trust) and negative emotions (anxiety, fear, feelings of being over-powered). There is a higher level, as well, one where the feeling tone of the personality is set. These emotion effects are studied as responses to the Great Mother.

410. Nielsen, Stevan Lars, and Albert Ellis. "A Discussion with Albert Ellis: Reason, Emotion and Religion." Journal of Psychology and Christianity 13 (1994): 327-41. Albert Ellis heads the Institute for Rational-Emotive Therapy, at the State University of New York. His therapy holds absolutism to be self-defeating, though this does not necessarily challenge all religious beliefs.

411. Oatley, Keith, and Jennifer M. Jenkins. Understanding Emotions. Cambridge, Mass.: Blackwell Publishers, 1996. This excellent textbook presents

emotion in the Western tradition through cultural understandings, evolution development, and social relations. The discussions of emotion in drama, ritual, and psychotherapy are of special interest.

412. Ostow, Mortimer. "**Apokalyptische Archetypen in Träumen, Phantasien und religiösen Schriften.**" Jahrbuch der Psychoanalyse **23 (1988): 9-25.** The fantasies and nightmares of schizophrenics and borderline patients are related to classic apocalyptic visions: the end of the world, the miraculous regeneration of humankind, and the new heaven-on-earth. Numerous clinical cases show remarkable parallels between the schizophrenic and apocalyptic visions. The dangers of new religious cults that prey upon apocalyptic fears are discussed.

413. Paloutzian, Raymond F., and Aris S. Janigan. "**Interrelationships between Religiousness and Loneliness.**" Psychotherapy Patient **2 (1986): 3-14.** In terms of religion, loneliness seems to be a function of how one's orientation, extrinsic or intrinsic, supports belonging and purpose. Two kinds of loneliness are identified: social and emotional. The social is bound to religiousness through the relation of person to church; emotional loneliness, for a religious person, exists in relation to God. The first is extrinsic, the second intrinsic. Group affiliation and personal belief can be used for therapeutic ends.

414. Parsons, William B. "**The Oceanic Feeling Revisited.**" The Journal of Religion **78 (1998): 501-23.** The oceanic feeling of Rolland is not a fleeting regression to a pre-oedipal narcissism. Rather it is an existential achievement, a continuous mystical state, with ethical and developmental depth. This runs counter to Freud's view but parallel to Heinz Kohut's "cosmic narcissism," or participation in a supraindividual, timeless existence. Finally, the influences on Rolland were decidedly Western.

415. ------. The Enigma of the Oceanic Feeling: Revisioning the Psychoanalytic Theory of Mysticism. **New York: Oxford University Press, in press.** Unexamined.

416. Perry, Bruce F. "**Malcolm X in Brief: A Psychological Perspective.**" Journal of Psychohistory **11 (1984): 491-500.** This portrait of Malcolm X shows that his rebellion against White society and civil authority reflected unresolved tensions with his parents and teachers. Conversion to Islam trans-formed the angry young man into an ascetic. His anger toward his parents was re-focused, more widely, toward Christianity, and his stinging criticism of Black preachers was an extension of his bad feelings about his deceased father.

417. Pomi, Massimo. "**Le merveilleux comme paradigme du religieux implicite dans la culture du 20ème siècle.**" Social Compass **37 (1990): 439-54.** Wonder is seen as unconscious searching and as implicit religion. Carrying the senses over many thresholds, wonder is capable of overpowering words and of leading the spirit into the realm (the abyss) of silence. Pomi relies on Benjamin, Bloch, Heidegger, Jaspers, Kafka, Wittgenstein, and other 20th century Europeans.

418. Pressman, Peter, John S. Lyons, David B. Larson, and John Gartner. "**Religion, Anxiety, and Fear of Death.**" Religion and Mental Health. **Edited by John F. Schumaker. New York: Oxford University Press, 1992. Pp. 98-109.** It appears that religion can increase or decrease anxieties related to the fear of death. Religious participation that is public correlates negatively with anxiety; private religiosity corresponds positively to manifestations of anxiety. Among the aged, high religiosity is associated with lower levels of anxiety.

419. Rajabally, Mohamed H. "Florence Nightingale's Personality: A Psychoanalytical Profile." International Journal of Nursing Studies **31 (1994): 269-78.** In the Nightingale family, the mother dominated a weak father. Sibling rivalry was intense, and loyalties were divided. Florence adopted masculine features due to her parents' wish for a son. She was unhappy, full of self-doubt, guilt, and low self-esteem. She suffered from depression and despair. Her religious visions were often hallucinations. At times, she was suicidal. In this negative portrait, her accomplishments came through manipulating other people.

420. Rank, Otto. Beyond Psychology. **New York: Dover, 1958 [1941].** Rank departed from teacher Freud to explore human ultimates: the fear of death, the desire for immortality, the need for love, and the basis for personality. The failure of rationality to cope with the lack of common belief, hostility, fear and guilt in modern civilization is noted. Psychology beyond the self is examined in the myth of The Double, where the rise of the idea of the Soul and the fear of destruction is found.

421. Rayburn, Carole. "The Religious Patient's Initial Encounter with Psychotherapy." Psychotherapy Patient **1 (1985): 35-45.** Religious patients are fearful of their first encounter with therapy. They tend to perceive their problems as punishment for sin, and may see the process as "brainwashing" by a secular high priest. Amid such irrational beliefs they may fear never being whole. The irreligious therapist and countertransference are problems because therapists are hesitant to deal with value systems. This leads to feelings of anger and aggressiveness in the patient, who may end up lonely and filled with fear.

422. Reimers, Adrian J. "More than the Devil's Due." Cultic Studies Journal **11 (1994): 77-87.** Belief in evil spirits is used to control members of cults. Deliverance prayers are used to pacify new members who begin to take on a victim-like role. The leaders are often the only ones able to recognize Satan, and the followers lose confidence in their own judgments. When one criticizes or leaves the group it is seen as an act of Satan. Fearful members are more dependent on the church group, and their fears are used to keep them obeying the group's demands. Distress continues after a member leaves the cult.

423. Religion and Mental Health. **Edited by John F. Schumaker. New York: Oxford University Press, 1992.** Two views are explored: religion builds security of mind, offering believers hope, purpose, and meaning. The mental health fostered by religion enables people to endure pain and suffering, and religion also provides a measure of control in life. The other view holds that religion harms mental health, raising guilt to excessive levels, repressing anger, and responding to wrongful actions with the fear of punishment and anxiety.

424. Richards, P. Scott, Randy K. Hardman, Harold A. Frost, Michael E. Berrett, Julie B. Clark-Sly, and David K. Anderson. "Spiritual Issues and Interventions in the Treatment of Patients with Eating Disorders." Eating Disorders: The Journal of Treatment & Prevention **5 (1997): 261-79.** Religion and spirituality are vital in diagnosing causes and treating eating disorders. Negative images of God, feelings of shame, unworthiness, and fears of being abandoned by God, factor into eating disorders. Spiritual interventions can be constructively used in treating these diseases, and seven interventions that have been found useful are described, including prayer, spiritual reading, and religious teaching.

425. Rizzuto, Ana-Maria. The Birth of the Living God: A Psychoanalytic Study. Chicago: University of Chicago Press, 1979. Subjects draw images of God and then talk about them. Then, Rizzuto is able to make some remarkable claims. First, she finds no one without a God representation. Second, she finds the concept of God to be "cold" in comparison to the emotional acceptance of God based on interpersonal experiences as these are fleshed out in multiple images. Finally, drawing one's own images of God is highly therapeutic.

426. Ross, Christopher F. J. "Orientation to Religion and the Feeling Function in Jung's Personality Typology." Studies in Religion/Sciences religieuses 21 (1992): 305-20. Variety in religious experience can be accounted for by Jung's feeling function and its impact on belief and practice. Feeling is as important in human psychology as thinking. It illuminates sacred texts, kinds of prayer, suffering, and concepts of heaven and sin. It is not surprising that the Myers Briggs Type Indicator has found a preponderance of feeling types in religious vocations. Jung's feeling function also offers a base for comparative study.

427. Rothko, Christopher Hall. "Religion and Personality: An Examination Across Three Cultures." Ph.D. diss., University of Michigan, 1995. A sample of 104 Jews and 115 Polish Catholics was constituted to learn if a devout religious upbringing benefits the person. A confirmation of earlier work was made, that is, religious Jews and Catholics were significantly happier and less psychotic than non-religious participants. The sample was less obsessive and less psychologically-minded. Extraversion was a trait based in ethnicity more than in religiosity. A Lebanese Shiite study failed due to recruitment problems.

428. Sarbin, Theodore R. "Emotion and Act: Roles and Rhetoric." The Social Construction of Emotions. Edited by Rom Harré. Oxford: Basil Blackwell, 1986. Pp. 83-97. Scant agreement exists over what constitutes emotion – though scholars have classified some 400 action terms related to it. Because emotion is often detached from social context, arbitrarily, a general theory of emotion is probably impossible. Why not drop the word from psychology's lexicon? The study of dramatic roles, rhetorical acts, narrative plots, including religious ones, is more productive.

429. Saussy, Carroll, and Barbara J. Clarke. "The Healing Power of Anger." Through the Eyes of Women: Insights for Pastoral Care. Edited by Jeanne Stevenson Moessner. Minneapolis, Minn.: Fortress Press, 1996. Inability to express anger constructively in American culture is a problem to be addressed. The depressed woman may well be empowered and healed by reclaiming anger, and even rage, over disrespect and abuse. Biblical literature supports righteous indignation, and anger can motivate behavior in the work for justice.

430. Scheidlinger, Saul. "The Minyan as a Psychological System." Psychoanalytic Review 84 (1997): 541-52. Jewish daily, communal prayers, the "minyan," offer psychological nourishment, satisfying the needs of social hunger by providing affiliation, thereby alleviating loneliness. Also, the minyan helps to keep before its members a transgenerational identity, as well as a sense of belonging and self-esteem. A counter to stress, the religious service prevents illness and restores mental health. Finally, the minyan functions as a mother-symbol, reconnecting members with a feeling of that strong bond.

431. Schneider, Carl D. Shame, Exposure, and Privacy. Boston: Beacon, 1977. Shame is not to be rooted out. To bring it to awareness, connecting it with self-restraint, is to make self-government and democracy possible. Shame shows that we are valuing creatures; it shows our social nature. Because shame reveals the self's limits and bears witness to the self's involvement with others, shame can be a guide to authentic self-realization. It is false shame that must be rooted out. Psychology bordering on philosophical anthropology raises spiritual questions of how humanity is related to divinity.

432. Schopen, Ann, and Brenda Freeman. "Meditation: The Forgotten Western Tradition." Counseling & Values 36 (1992): 123-34. Meditation declined in the West, while it has risen in the East. An increase in religious emotionalism led to the demise of Western meditation, coupled with the scientific revolution. Freedom from ideas and thoughts mark Eastern practice, whereas focus on an idea is Western. Psychology, research, and counseling are used to prescribe meditation as a means of treating anxiety, anger, and stress.

433. Schwab, Reinhold, and Kay U. Petersen. "Religiousness: Its Relation to Loneliness, Neuroticism and Subjective Well-Being." Journal for the Scientific Study of Religion 29 (1990): 335-45. West Germans are asked about religious beliefs, behavior, neuroses, loneliness, and well-being. Loneliness is correlated with the idea of a wrathful God; the image of a helpful God correlated negatively with loneliness. Religiosity did not correspond with neuroticism.

434. Shame and Its Sisters: A Silvan Tomkins Reader. Edited by Eve Kosofsky Sedgwick and Adam Frank. Durham, N.C.: Duke University Press, 1995. One of the sisters is anger; here it is considered in light of the Christian system of rewards and punishments. Tomkins explains emotions and behavior through "script theory," and Christianity plays the role of a limitation script.

435. Sheehy, Noel. "Talk About Being Irish: Death Ritual as a Cultural Form." Irish Journal of Psychology 15 (1994): 494-507. Irish death rituals points to a belief in the continued existence after death, they address fear of death and mourning, and they reflect a national Irish identity unchanged by secularization and the waning of organized religion.

436. Sober, Elliot, and David Sloan Wilson. Unto Others: The Evolution and Psychology of Unselfish Behavior. Cambridge, Mass.: Harvard University Press, 1998. Altruism has evolved from natural selection. The authors defend Darwin's group selection theory, giving examples of altruism in the animal and the human world that are self-sacrificing. Concern for others is an ultimate motive that individuals at times have. This analysis of cooperation, based on evolutionary biology, argues that selfishness is not the reason for doing good, group selection is. There are enormous implications for the sociology of religion, and for natural theology, in this claim.

437. Spero, Moshe H., and Roberto Mester. "Counter-transference Envy Toward the Religious Patient." American Journal of Psychoanalysis 48 (1988): 43-55. Dealing with religious patients requires special consideration, especially when envy emerges in the therapist toward the religious patient. This counter-transference needs to

be better understood. Religious patients may doubt the process of psychotherapy, challenging the clinical experience and self-knowledge of the psychiatrist. Four case studies show interpretations and uses of envy in counter-transference reactions to religious patients.

438. Stein, Murray. "Sibling Rivalry and the Problem of Envy." Journal of Analytical Psychology 35 (1990): 161-74. Jungian psychoanalytic theory views envy as the disruption of the ego-self relation. Biblical narratives and religious myths illustrate the transformation into envy of normal jealousy and sibling rivalry. Chronically envious relations and their resolutions are considered.

439. Switzer, David K. "The Remorseful Patient: Perspectives of a Pastoral Counselor." Psychotherapy Patient 5 (1988): 275-90. Remorse is the feeling of pain that accompanies the memory of significant loss. The pain is heightened when patients see themselves as the cause of the loss. A case study of a rigidly religious 56-year old woman shows neurosis, unrealistic guilt, and lasting depression. Switzer concludes that remorse, when it becomes sorrow, cannot be cured, but its dysfunctional role in life can be lowered in a meaningful way.

440. Symington, Neville. Emotion and Spirit: Questioning the Claims of Psychoanalysis and Religion. New York: St. Martin's, 1994. Psychoanalysis shares a goal with religion, transforming the self through constructive emotional acts. As traditional religion is not relevant to modern living, secular science could play a more spiritual role. But psychoanalysis has failed in not having answers to life's meaning and purpose. Hence, a conversation with the wisdom of the great religions is urged.

441. Taylor, Gabrielle. Pride, Shame, and Guilt: Emotions of Self-Assessment. Oxford: Clarendon Press, 1985. In terms of self-assessment, the most significant relationship may be the one between guilt and remorse. Taylor considers the view of Max Scheler that remorse is the emotion of salvation. As such, it is less an other-directed emotion and more for the sake of the self. As the expression of remorse heals the self, it becomes possible to begin life anew.

442. Tomkins, Silvan S. Exploring Affect: The Selected Writings of Silvan S. Tomkins. Edited by E. Virginia Demos. Cambridge: Cambridge University Press, 1995. "Ideology and Affect" (109-67) explores child-rearing practices, informed by Calvinist and biblical traditions. "The Varieties of Shame and Its Magnification" (397-410) examines emotion in relation to Christian views of sexuality.

443. Trevarthen, Colwyn. "Brain Science and the Human Spirit." Zygon: Journal of Religion and Science 21 (1986): 161-200. Moral control in relationships and meaning in human communication are generated by the brain core, which responds to the sounds and sights of emotions. The newborn is mentally prepared to share transcendent states with a feeling partner, and its playful fantasies prefigure adult ritual.

444. Ulanov, Ann Belford. The Female Ancestors of Christ. Boston: Shambhala, 1993. Psychological typology presented as history by this Jungian professor of psychiatry and religion at Union Theological Seminary in NYC. Ulanov sees four biblical women (Tamar, Rahab, Ruth, and Bathsheba) as spiritual mothers to Christ, that is, as part of a deeply felt legacy culminating in Jesus. They also intercede for those contemporary readers seeking models of sacrifice, truths of the heart, and consolations for suffering and injustice.

445. ------. "Envy: Further Thoughts." Journal of Religion and Health 34 (1995): 313-16. Urges toward the good may not always produce goodness. They may also be hidden in acts that are bad. Envy can be described in this way since it is often driven by the desire for the good. Once realized, the dangerous effects of envy can be countered. The work furthers ideas found in Cinderella and Her Sisters: The Envied and the Envying (Louisville: Westminster, 1983).

446. Ullman, Chana. The Transformed Self: The Psychology of Religious Conversion. New York: Plenum Press, 1989. Conversion promises relief from adolescent turmoil, especially from anguish and distress. The experience of emotions is central to bringing about change in the self.

447. Vergote, Antoine. Guilt and Desire: Religious Attitudes and Their Pathological Derivatives. Translated by M. H. Wood. New Haven: Yale University Press, 1988 [1978]. The dialectic of debt and desire explains tensions and conflicts between agent and worldview. Exploring the zone between psychic activity and lived religion accounts for neuroses, an imbalance related to the demonic, and mental health, found in positive religious experience. Lateral meanings in the implications of words provide a key to understanding religious language in a psychoanalytic way.

448. Watts, Fraser N. "Psychological and Religious Perspectives on Emotion." Zygon: Journal of Religion and Science 32 (1997): 243-60. Religion can be seen as an emotional state. Though there has been a tendency to view emotion as disruptive, Watts claims that this need not be true. He agrees with J. Averill that emotions, when they are properly used, can be psychologically creative.

449. Zygon: Journal of Religion and Science 21 (1986): 3-112. The March issue: "Recent Discoveries in Neurobiology – Do They Matter for Religion, the Social Sciences, and the Humanities," includes "Thoughts on the Psycho-biology of Religion" (9-29) by Anthony Stevens, and "The Passionate Mind: Brain, Dreams, Memory, and Social Categories" (31-46) by Robin Fox.

Anthropological Studies

450. Abu-Lughod, Lila. Veiled Sentiments: Honor and Poetry in a Bedouin Society. Berkeley: University of California Press, 1986. Among Muslims of the western desert of Egypt, the women and the young men express their personal feelings through oral lyric poetry. Abu-Lughod had the good fortune of doing fieldwork from within a Bedouin family. As an adoptive daughter, she was able to unveil private sentiments. She found that oral poetry is the vehicle through which women and men express feelings that violate the moral code.

451. ------. "Shifting Politics in Bedouin Love Poetry." Language and the Politics of Emotion. Edited by Catherine A. Lutz and Lila Abu-Lughod. Cambridge: Cambridge University Press, 1990. Pp. 24-45. A young woman suddenly dies when, upon a post-marital visit home, she listens to a cassette of the wounded love poems of a cousin with whom she had grown up. The power of the poems, and their effects, are analyzed in terms of the sexual distance, indeed segregation, created by religious practices of socialization.

452. Akira, Omine. "The Genealogy of Sorrow: Japanese View of Life and Death." **Eastern Buddhist** 25 (1992): 14-29. Truth is made manifest in sorrow. In Shinto, sorrow by the dying person is lament, within the ego shell, for oneself. For Buddhist Shinran, sorrow is the realization that one cannot leave the shell of ego feeling. So, self-pity fades, the bottom falls out of sorrow, and the depth of sorrow is known as an emotion transcended but not negated. No matter the tragedy of life, there is a deeper structure to embrace it and render it meaningful. Sorrow constitutes life at its deepest level.

453. Appadurai, Arjun. "Topographies of the Self: Praise and Emotion in Hindu India." **Language and the Politics of Emotion. Edited by Catherine A. Lutz and Lila Abu-Lughod. Cambridge: Cambridge University Press, 1990. Pp. 92-112.** Praise of the many incarnations of divinity in Hinduism is at the heart of the ritual process in India. Public, formulaic, aesthetic descriptions of the positive attributes of the deity are ritualized in a way that involves both interaction and assessment. Hence, both intimacy and distance play a role.

454. Armstrong, Robert Plant. **The Affecting Presence: An Essay in Humanistic Anthropology. Urbana, Ill.: University of Illinois Press, 1971.** Phenomenological study of feeling, art, and ritual life is cross-cultural in that it begins with reflections on feeling in Japan, but proceeds to explore its primary subject: feeling and ritual art among the Yoruba of Nigeria in West Africa.

455. Babes, Leïla. "Folie douce, vent des ancêtres: la transe au Maghreb." **Social Compass** 42 (1995): 461-76. Contra the claim for two kinds of trance (Islamic and "black African"), mysticism and possession are distinguished. Based on the author's survey, mystic passion is tied to several local cults, while the trance of possession is experienced either as violent suffering or as "a gentle madness." In each case, trance is controlled by ceremonial music and dance. The entire issue (#4) is devoted to non-verbal religious practices.

456. Bailey, F. G. **The Tactical Uses of Passion: An Essay on Power, Reason, and Reality. Ithaca, N.Y.: Cornell University Press, 1983.** Displays of passion and how they can be used to exercise power over others comprise the primary theme. A covert theme is the way reason limits our understanding and managing of the world. Data range from parliamentary debates in India to city council squabbles in California. Emotion and suffering are related to faith, and there are religious implications in sacrifices for the sake of a higher passion.

457. Baroni, Helen J. "Bottled Anger: Episodes in Obaku Conflict in the Tokugawa Period." **Japanese Journal of Religious Studies** 21 (1994): 191-210. Two kinds of conflict are contrasted. General restraint marked the conflicts between Buddhists in the Obaku sect and Rinzai Zen. But conflict escalated so much between an Obaku monk and the member of the Shin sect that the government had to step in to prevent violence. This June-September issue (#2-3) is devoted to "Conflict and Religion in Japan."

458. Bateson, Gregory, and Mary Catherine Bateson. **Angel's Fear: Towards an Epistemology of the Sacred. New York: Bantam, 1987.** Bateson's unfinished book on the unity of mind and nature through the integrating metaphors of religion, completed by his daughter. Experience of the sacred is expressed in terms of the passions of mind, an approach to ecology as holy ground, and the unifying power of love. The book's

breadth challenges disciplines; the study is comparative, philosophical, with sensitivity to local cultures – all within a mystical scope. Instinct and reason join in a desire for the sacred.

459. Bennett, Peter. "In Nanda Baba's House: The Devotional Experience in Pushti Marg Temples." Divine Passions: The Social Construction of Emotion in India. Edited by Owen M. Lynch. Berkeley: University of California Press, 1990. Pp. 182-211. Pushti Marg is a religious path grounded in traditions of worship that excite the emotions as the cowherd companions of Krishna were passionate in their association with him. Pushti Marg conceives the expression of emotion as a matter of taste, as a matter of aesthetics interwoven into enthusiastic devotion. Devotees also believe that actual emotions are embodied in material culture, in the ornaments with which they decorate religious images.

460. Boddy, Janice. Wombs and Alien Spirits: Women, Men, and the Zar Cult in Northern Sudan. Madison, Wis.: University of Wisconsin Press, 1989. Muslim women meet alien spirits who enlighten them on Western economic encroachment, the rise of formal Islam, and other issues confronting their Sudanese village. Through the cult of spirit possession, women are able to speak a common metaphorical language about life, including their own subordination to men. Thus, the cult serves a feminist discourse about self-esteem, emotional and body integrity, and trance performance.

461. ------. "Spirit Possession Revisited: Beyond Instrumentality." Annual Review of Anthropology 23 (1994): 407-34. Bibliographic review of recent works on spirit possession covers therapy, religion, communication, psycho-analysis, gender, power, and embodiment. A new turn is afoot in anthropology toward situated knowledge, imagination and creativity, and the relation between self and world. Emotions abound in these new areas of study.

462. Caldwell, Sarah Lee. "Oh Terrifying Mother: The Mudiyettu Ritual Drama of Kerala, South India." Ph.D. diss., University of California, Berkeley, 1995. In this ritual theatre, males impersonate the fierce goddess Bhagavati (Kali). The drama lasts all night, including song, drums, costume, and rice-flour paintings. The experience of possession by the actors is Caldwell's focus, and mudiyettu is interpreted as transformation of feminine/agricultural power, male trauma over feminine sexual passion and emotion, an oppressive means of marginalizing women, and as a potent rite with transforming healing powers.

463. Chagnon, Napoleon A. Yanomamö: The Fierce People. New York: Holt, Rinehart and Winston, 1968. The fierce people of Venezuela and Brazil seem full of a rage spilling into violence in order to get what they want. They frighten, disgust, and excite Chagnon. At its center, Yanomamö social order is based on ritual violence, in particular, the raiding of enemy villages to steal women. The escalation of disputes and the brinkmanship of settlement is not unfamiliar, but the Yanomamö display values opposed to the Judeo-Christian-Islamic meanings of what is good and desirable.

464. Comaroff, Jean. Body of Power, Spirit of Resistance: The Culture and History of a South African People. Chicago: University of Chicago Press, 1985. Though mainly about power and resistance, many emotions arise from conflicts between the Tshidi (South Africa-Botswana) and Christian mission-aries, in particular, evangelical Methodists. Exchanges among parties in these modern religious movements include economics and beliefs, as well as emotions of frustration and anger.

465. Crapanzano, Vincent. "Kevin: On the Transfer of Emotions." American Anthropologist 96 (1994): 866-85. Kevin is a white Rhodesian who lives in South Africa. He tells of being a charismatic Christian and a veteran of terrorist warfare. His story is crafted to have an effect on the ethnographer, like a testimony. It is dialogical, an exchange in the game, "who has the emotion?"

466. Culture and Depression: Studies in the Anthropology and Cross-Cultural Psychiatry of Affect and Disorder. Edited by Arthur Kleinman and Byron Good. Berkeley: University of California Press, 1985. Cultural perspectives, cognitive science, communications and behavior theory, epidemiological measurement in cross-cultural studies, and attempts to integrate anthropology and psychiatry for the sake of better understanding depression. Buddhism is studied, as are traditional African societies and American Indian communities.

467. Danforth, Loring M. Firewalking and Religious Healing: The Anastenaria of Greece and the American Firewalking Movement. Princeton: Princeton University Press, 1989. A northern Greek ritual of firewalking and possession expresses psychological and social problems in ways that produce health and joy. Ritual therapy transforms those who identify with the possessing spirit and empowers them with what is needed for healing. Most firewalkers are women who act like men through metaphor and ritual in order to gain increased power. Anastenaria is compared to the New Age firewalking movement in America.

468. David, E. Valentine. Fluid Signs: Being a Person the Tamil Way. Berkeley: University of California Press, 1984. A person's relationship to the cosmos is either balanced or seeking equilibrium. "Fluid signs" are cultural symbols marking the relations of ranked substances that underlie the Hindu caste system and move between them. When disjunction occurs, fluid signs help to reestablish a healthy emotional life among the Tamil.

469. Davis, Scott. "The Cosmobiological Balance of the Emotional and Spiritual Worlds: Phenomenological Structuralism in Traditional Chinese Medical Thought." Culture, Medicine, and Psychiatry 20 (1996): 83-123. Structural analysis of emotional disorder focuses on the classical Chinese medical text Ling Shu, especially the chapter, "Grounding Spirit," in order to explore the convergence of the inner life of human emotions with cosmology. Ritual performance, including rhythmical, quasi-musical modeling, functions therapeutically to stabilize disorder and restore harmony.

470. Death and Bereavement Across Cultures. Edited by Colin Murray Parkes, Pittu Laungani and Bill Young. London: Routledge, 1997. The essays in this volume are arranged by cultural/historical conceptual frame, major world systems of belief and ritual, and practical implications. Religions include Hinduism, Buddhism, Judaism, Christianity, and Islam. The book is intended to inform health-care professionals and to help them with their patients.

471. Desjarlais, Robert R. "Poetic Transformations of Yolmo 'Sadness.'" Culture, Medicine, and Psychiatry 15 (1991): 387-420. Devout members of a Mahayana Buddhist sect in Nepal come to terms with loss by singing. A song of sadness is examined to show how it soothes the Sherpa's grief over a death. In exploring the transforming poetics in relation to other texts, the argument is made that emotional discourse reflects personal/communal experience, and thus it is felt emotion, not merely a rhetorical strategy.

472. ------. **Body and Emotion: The Aesthetics of Illness and Healing in the Nepal Himalayas**. Philadelphia: University of Pennsylvania Press, 1992. To heal "soul loss," when a frightened spirit takes flight, leaving the body heavy, without energy, shaman divine how the spirit was lost, where it has wandered, and how to retrieve it. Then, the life-force is ritually called back to the body.

473. Ebersole, Gary L. "The Function of Ritual Weeping Revisited: Affective Expression and Moral Discourse." History of Religions 39 (2000): 211-246. A strong critical analysis of some previous lines of interpretation of ritual weeping, with particular attention to a Japanese tale from the ninth-century *Nihon ryoiki*. Stresses the function of ritualized tears as the expression of cultural and moral values and calls for a rethinking of the role of weeping in communal life.

474. Feld, Steven. **Sound and Sentiment: Birds, Weeping, Poetics, and Song in Kaluli Expression**. Philadelphia: University of Pennsylvania Press, 1982. An ethnographic study of a Papua New Guinea culture as sound system of symbols in and through which a people's ethos is arrayed. Suggestive for religion is imitation of mourning birds (dove & warbler): weeping at burial moves women to song; their song moves men to tears; men compose songs and sing them in the forest as boys-become-birds; becoming a bird is the core metaphor of Kaluli aesthetics. Analysis involves performance, songs of loss and abandonment, and the symbols of an avian world that has become the world of myth and feelings.

475. Frazer, James George. **The Fear of the Dead in Primitive Religion**. 3 vols. New York: Arno Press, 1977 [1933]. For Frazer, belief in an after-life is almost universal, and it is both a comfort to sorrow and a sign of human vanity. These Trinity College lectures expand on the fears in archaic societies that the dead will return. Prohibitions, barriers of fire, taboos, destroying the property of the dead, even mutilating and maiming their bodies, show that the "primitive" attitude about the spirits of the dead was one of fear, not affection.

476. Geertz, Clifford. The Religion of Java. Chicago: University of Chicago Press, 1960. Comprehensive study of Javanese religion centered in a analysis of Java's core ritual, the Slametan, or communal feast. Given in response to most any occasion, the feast offers an opportunity for participants to pledge their cooperation and mutual support. No matter the circumstance, the embarrassed, polite, even muted manner of conduct shows the value of the ceremony, which, in the process, reduces conflict, tension, and uncertainty.

477. ------. "Deep Play: Notes on the Balinese Cockfight." The Interpretation of Cultures. New York: Basic, 1973. Pp. 413-53. Stakes in deep play are high when men behave irrationally. Deep play is unlocked in a ritual fight, and the values of Bali society emerge. The more the contest is between status equals, the deeper it gets; and the deeper the play, the more intimate the relation between man and cock, the finer the cock, and the greater emotion displayed. Bets are high, and one bets with one's kinship group. Having been ignored, Geertz's flight from a vice squad reversed village perception of him, and that change points to Balinese values regarding outsiders. Again, the cockfight was the cultural key to feelings.

478. ------. "Religion As a Cultural System." The Interpretation of Cultures. New York: Basic, 1973. Classic definition of religion as a symbol system acting "to establish powerful, pervasive, and long-lasting moods and motivations." Symbols induce

dispositions, inclinations to perform certain acts or to experience certain feelings. The moods induced by sacred symbols range from melancholia to exultation, from self-pity to self-confidence. The motive has meaning in terms of an end; moods mean something with reference to the circumstances from which they spring.

479. George, Kenneth M. "Violence, Solace, and Ritual: A Case Study from Island Southeast Asia." Culture, Medicine, and Psychiatry 19 (1995): 225-60. Headhunting links ritual violence with grief and mourning. But, it is more complex, and thereby suggestive for religious studies. Cases from highland Sulawesi suggest that communities find resolution in ritual. Expressing communal mourning plays a greater role in motivating violence than does personal catharsis. In fact, individual emotion is re-figured collectively as "political affect." The songs, vows, gestures, and ritual noise help people move beyond grief. Generative sites for violence and solace are found in ritual form.

480. ------. Showing Signs of Violence: The Cultural Politics of a Twentieth-Century Headhunting Ritual. Berkeley: University of California Press, 1996. Discursive analysis, contra Rosaldos, of headhunting in upland communities of Bambang. Collective overcoming of loss happens in ritual uttering of vows and oaths. A disfigured head (actually a coconut but standing for both Bakhtin's "grotesque other" and the wealthy coastal peoples) is left to rot, demonizing the victim, further heightening the revenge laid to the coastal enemy. Thus, the humbled uplanders are restored to the status, authority, and virtue that they feel they have lost. George's analysis bears on religion, generally, and he discusses, specifically, the interpretive spins on headhunting by Christians and Muslims.

481. Goldenweiser, Alexander. "Spirit, Mana, and the Religious Thrill." History, Psychology, and Culture. New York: Knopf, 1933. Pp. 377-84. Setting aside origins, the association of spirit with the religious thrill, or heightened emotional tone, is emphasized. What leads to the conceptualization of the world of spirit is also involved in the early association of that spirit world with the religious thrill, and it is the role of mana, or impersonal magical power, to cause the religious thrill. This psychological relationship is seen as the basis for the study of archaic religions.

482. Goodman, Felicitas D. Ecstasy, Ritual, and Alternate Reality: Religion in a Pluralistic World. Bloomington, Ind.: Indiana University Press, 1988. Theoretical, ethnographic, and neurophysiological study of religious trance that altered state of consciousness that leads to ecstasy. Trance is signaled, and the human response is easily observed: deep breathing, sweat, trembling, twitching, and extraordinary vocal patterns. A barrier is felt, and some pass over into a tremendous peak experience. When trancers awake, they report overwhelming joy and intense euphoria. Ecstatic hormonal and neural activity is described.

483. ------. Where the Spirits Ride the Wind: Trance Journeys and Other Ecstatic Experiences. Bloomington, Ind.: Indiana University Press, 1990. This autobiographical book extends Goodman's project of exploring religious trance; here she provides a less objective but more interesting set of notes written from the viewpoint of a participant observer. A Protestant from Mexico, Goodman was trained at Heidelberg and at Ohio State. Her first-hand narratives of spirit journeys in New Mexico and elsewhere go to the heart of ecstatic religiosity in a most illuminating and exciting way: from the inside.

484. Goodman, Felicitas D., Jeannette H. Henney, and Esther Pressel. **Trance, Healing, and Hallucination: Three Field Studies in Religious Experience**. New York: John Wiley & Sons, 1974. Possession trance, spirit healing, and altered states of consciousness, are explored in three groups: the American Shakers, the Brazilian Umbanda, and a Pentecostal movement in the Yucatán.

485. Halperin, Daniel Tzvi. "Dancing at the Edge of Chaos: An Ethnography of Wildness and Ceremony in an Afro-Brazilian Possession Religion." Ph.D. diss., University of California, Berkeley, 1995. Violent trances and wildness in Tambor de Mina Northern Brazilian dance and spirit possession are analyzed through Victor Turner's ideas of ritual process. Ecstatic anti-structure and psychophysiological liminality are viewed against the larger backdrop of socio-economic turbulence.

486. Harner, Sandra, and Warren W. Tryon. "Psychological and Immunological Responses to Shamanic Journeying with Drumming." **Shaman** 4 (1996): 89-97. Several mood inventories were employed to determine if shamanic journeying and drumming produce certain psychological and immunological responses. Anxiety, confusion, depression, fatigue, mood disturbance, stress, and tension-anxiety were measured and found to be significantly lower after drumming. With some qualification, salivary immunoglobulin responded to certain psychological states associated with shamanic journeying.

487. Harris, Grace Gredys. **Casting Out Anger: Religion Among the Taita of Kenya**. Cambridge: Cambridge University Press, 1978. In rituals of casting out anger, the Taita are reconciled to one another. Metaphor combines landscape and emotion: hot and cool graphically point to the human condition before and after the ritual. Anger is not bad, but when resentment is unspoken there is danger, and it must be ritually expelled.

488. Hayward, Douglas James. "Christianity and the Traditional Beliefs of the Mulia Dani: An Ethnography of Religious Belief among the Western Dani of Irian Jaya, Indonesia." Ph.D. diss., University of California, Santa Barbara, 1992. A missionary for 20 years, Haywood knows about the exchanges between the Dani tribe and evangelical Christianity. Each chapter documents further introduction of Christianity, and how it was transformed. The Dani, upon conversion, destroy the sacred objects of their cult, but they continue to fear that those objects are still being used. Part of the Melanesia cargo movement, these people have shaped Christianity to meet their own needs.

489. Heelas, Paul. "Emotion Talk across Cultures." **The Social Construction of Emotions**. Edited by Rom Harré. Oxford: Basil Blackwell, 1986. Pp. 234-66. Emotion talk is part of a public code, and each society writes its own rules for speech. Private emotions vary even more dramatically across cultures, but, because they are private, they form obstacles to study. Religious emotion clearly has a social dimension; its codes of expression prove the best starting point.

490. Henderson, David. "Emotion and Devotion, Lingering and Longing in Some Nepali Songs." **Ethnomusicology** 40 (1996): 440-68. Embodiment theory sheds light on Nepali songs of divine praise. Musical design and pronouns without clear antecedents establish the dialectic between satisfying individual participants and a sense of disembodiment from the presence of self. So, love and longing enter the music. From

the theoretical view, a very thin line divides individual experience and the social expression of devotion.

491. Homans, Peter. "Once Again, Psychoanalysis, East and West: A Psychoanalytic Essay on Religion, Mourning, and Healing." History of Religions **24 (1984): 133-54.** Mourning is at the heart of the psychoanalytic approach to religion and of religious healing. Homans expands on this idea by reviewing Sudhir Kakar's psychoanalytic theory of religious healing in India, and its complex sociological context. Healing here involves reintegrating the patient into community and the collective myth. By comparison, history, psychology, and religion are contextualized, deepened, and changed.

492. Jang, Nam Hyuck. "Shamanism in Korean Christianity: Evaluating the Influence of Shamanism on Perceptions of Spiritual Power in Korean Christianity." Ph.D. diss., Fuller Theological Seminary, 1996. Shamanism shapes views of spiritual power in Korean Christianity, where folk religion has taken the gospel and mixed it with fears of dark powers, a capricious system of rewards and punishments, weak ethics, magic, and self-proclaimed messiahs. For Jang, this is a detriment to the saving power of the gospel, and he suggests ways to introduce the Christian message into Korean shamanistic contexts.

493. Jilek, Wolfgang G. Indian Healing: Shamanic Ceremonialism in the Pacific Northwest Today. **Surrey, B.C., Canada: Hancock House, 1982.** Ceremonial healing of native Americans in the Pacific Northwest employs spirit dancing, possession, and trance. Using the terms of the physiology and psychology of altered states, this study argues that anomic depression and relative deprivation are countered in the therapeutic process of shamanic ritual.

494. Kapferer, Bruce. A Celebration of Demons: Exorcism and the Aesthetics of Healing in Sri Lanka. **Bloomington, Ind.: Indiana University Press, 1983.** Sinhalese Buddhists and their demon exorcisms are examined to understand how people in southern Sri Lanka, especially peasants and the urban working class, comprehend the world. Emphasis on ritual healing, its music, dance, drama, and trance states disclose key transformations in self-identity and social behavior. In the celebrations of demons the basic emotions of anger, desire, greed, hunger, passion, and violent rage are exposed and reconciled.

495. ------. "Sorcery's Passions: Fear, Loathing, and Anger in the World." The Feasts of the Sorcerer: Practices of Consciousness and Power. **Chicago: University of Chicago Press, 1997. Pp. 221-60.** Chapter 7 considers how the body and the world become unbalanced, leading to emotional disturbance. The demons at play are very violent, attacking the body, ruling the graveyard, consuming the human in intense sexual longing. The exorcist must cool the heat of emotional excess within the body of the victim. Balancing bodily fluids is one way to reestablish harmonic unity with the world.

496. Khair, Gajanan S. "The Importance of Being First: Reflections on the First Chapter of the Bhagavadgita." Journal of Studies in the Bhagavadgita **2 (1982): 106-14.** Views on the Bhagavadgita differ since the premier chapter is often overlooked. Arjuna, the common man, has problems of suffering, sorrow, and deciding the right action. His problems are rooted in human nature, self-righteousness, tending toward evil. Yoga is the answer: it remakes a person and, thus, leads to right behavior, proper thinking and feeling, and happiness.

497. Kimbrough, David L. **Taking Up Serpents: Snake Handlers of Eastern Kentucky.** Chapel Hill, N.C.: University of North Carolina Press, 1995. Exciting participant observation of Holiness worship, combined with oral history of the emergence of snake handling in Appalachia. Ecstatic possession overcomes the worshippers who speak in tongues and dance wildly. Some get bit. Photos suggest emotion at the brim of ecstasy.

498. Kligman, Gail. **The Wedding of the Dead: Ritual, Poetics, and Popular Culture in Transylvania.** Berkeley: University of California Press, 1988. A community's grief is made bearable and meaningful through a wedding of the dead in northern Transylvania. Life-cycle rituals in Maramures incorporate illness, untimely death, upheaval in the family, bringing these events into a comprehensible perspective. The death wedding is a symbolic marriage that takes place during the funeral of a young, unmarried person, giving that person in death what he or she was denied in life.

499. Kracke, Waud H. "A Psychoanalyst in the Field: Erikson's Contributions to Anthropology." **Childhood and Selfhood: Essays on Tradition, Religion, and Modernity in the Psychology of Erik H. Erikson.** Edited by Peter Homans. Lewisburg, Pa.: Bucknell University Press, 1978. Pp. 147-88. Erikson's work on the emotional development of the self from childhood to adulthood has value for religious studies and anthropology, especially the study of the Sioux of North America.

500. Kratz, Corinne A. "Amusement and Absolution: Transforming Narratives During Confession of Social Debts." **American Anthropologist** 93 (1991): 826-51. Confessions of Oriek youth in Kenya contrasted with Catholic confession. In initiation, just prior to circumcision, the Oriek publicly confess their social debts. An intermediary questions initiates and announces wrong doings to the crowd. In translating the confession, the announcer recasts the narrative in ways that amuse the audience and absolve the initiates, moving them into adult company and status.

501. Laderman, Carol. **Taming the Wind of Desire: Psychology, Medicine, and Aesthetics in Malay Shamanistic Performance.** Berkeley: University of California Press, 1991. Ritual healing depends on magical diagnoses. When the cause is angin (air, wind, stomach winds), the source of illness is said to be internal, part of the patient's person. Such sickness can lead to a sadness of heart. The "inner winds" come close to Western ideas of temperment. When angin is expressed, people can lead productive, untroubled lives, hence the goal of ritual healing among the Malay.

502. **Language and the Politics of Emotion.** Edited by Catherine A. Lutz and Lila Abu-Lughod. Cambridge: Cambridge University Press, 1990. Using "embodiment theory," which has religious import, performances, poems, songs, conversations, and narratives are seen not as symbolic texts to be analyzed but as everyday social practices with real consequences. The interplay between the politics of daily life and the emotion talk uncovered in fieldwork is explored in terms of power and social relations in which emotion language plays a key role.

503. Lawrence, Patricia B. "Work of Oracles, Silence of Terror: Notes on the Injury of War in Eastern Sri Lanka." Ph.D. diss., University of Colorado at Boulder, 1997. Study of the religious life and suffering of the minority Tamil families caught within the military boundaries of Sri Lanka. Between security forces and separatist Tigers, they must confront the horror of disappearances, mass execution, and torture. Socializing outside the household is confined to religious ceremonies and

resurgence in the cult of local Hindu goddesses. These trance oracles help shattered families express what is difficult to say.

504. Lazarus, Richard S., and Bernice N. Lazarus. "How Biology and Culture Affect our Emotional Lives." Passion and Reason: Making Sense of Our Emotions. New York: Oxford University Press, 1994. Pp. 174-97. Factory workers, merchants, millionaires, sharecroppers, and academics have different value systems, patterns of beliefs, and commitments. Assessing meaning in life determines the emotion(s) to be aroused. How culture controls the emotion expressed is shown in contrasting U.S. and Japan; Yanomamö and Tahitians. Egyptian Muslim, Coptic Christian, and Indian Hindu cultures are cited.

505. Leavitt, John. "Meaning and Feeling in the Anthropology of Emotions." American Ethnologist 23 (1996): 514-39. Are emotions biological or cultural? This review, including a critique of Western concepts by Russian psychologist L. S. Vygotsky, routes the meaning/feeling divide. For Vygotsky, one school of thought on emotions starts from the body, another from the mind. So, there are two distinct approaches. Translation of emotion in religious ritual is required of the ethnologist, not just the meaning but the "feeling-tones." Because both are embedded or inscribed in ritual occasions, ethnographic descriptions are fuller, more resonant than any theory of emotions could be.

506. LeVine, Robert A. "Properties of Culture: An Ethnographic View." Culture Theory: Essays on Mind, Self, and Emotion. Edited by Richard A. Shweder and Robert A. LeVine. Cambridge: Cambridge University Press, 1984. Pp. 67-87. Human emotions, as well as those attributed to witches, those systems of goods and values that produce envy, as well as witchcraft claims, and the religious figures who can intervene on behalf of the Kenyan Gusii – these contexts are needed to interpret meanings in this African culture. The organization of various aspects of culture is what the ethnographer sorts through in order to understand. Just as Gusii meanings are woven into social order, religion, and medicine, so each culture has its own network of meanings.

507. Levy, Jerrold E., Raymond Neutra, and Dennis Parker. Hand Trembling, Frenzy Witchcraft, and Moth Madness. Tucson, Ariz.: University of Arizona Press, 1987. Navajo hand trembling, or "moth madness," can be both epilepsy and pseudo-seizure. The latter is a kind of hysteria of psychic origin caused by anxiety and distress, but the Navajo do not readily distinguish between the two diseases. Young women are special victims of hand trembling, which is often explained as spirit possession by witches who must be exorcised by magic.

508. Levy, Robert I. "Emotion, Knowing, and Culture." Culture Theory: Essays on Mind, Self, and Emotion. Edited by Richard A. Shweder and Robert A. LeVine. Cambridge: Cambridge University Press, 1984. Pp. 214-37. Emotion mobilizes culture, and its study sheds light on the slippery forms of "culture" transmitted through time. The more emotion is linked to historical and psychological phenomena in specific communities, the more visible will be the culture described, and this has implications for the study of religion. For Levy, local forms must be the focus, since both emotion and culture are problematic and resist the simplification of general theory. Sadness in Tahiti shows how local "knowing" is, and how complex "culture" can be.

509. Lewis, I. M. Ecstatic Religion: An Anthropological Study of Spirit Possession and Shamanism. Harmondsworth, Eng.: Penguin, 1971. Classic study of ecstatic

emotional states, distinguishing between central and marginal possession cults; the former support the status quo, while the latter dissent on behalf of the oppressed, especially women.

510. Link, Hilde K. "Where Valli Meets Murukan: 'Landscape' Symbolism in Kataragama." Anthropos 92 (1997): 91-100. Study of a "grammar of love" in Old Tamil myth, and its relation to a sacred place, Kataragama, the Sri Lankan pilgrimage site that harbors Hindu, Buddhist, and Muslim places of worship. Valli is a girl from the jungle who meets Lord Murukan on a sacred hill.

511. Lock, Margaret. "Cultivating the Body: Anthropology and Epistemologies of Bodily Practice and Knowledge." Annual Review of Anthropology 22 (1993): 133-55. Bibliographic review from Durkheim's Elementary Forms to "Embodiment Theory" to the "Cultural Construction of Self and Other," but focusing mainly on recent work, such as the debate between M. Rosaldo and R. Desjarlais on whether emotion is cultural rhetoric or internal experience.

512. Lutz, Catherine A. "The Domain of Emotion Words on Ifaluk." American Ethnologist 9 (1982): 113-28. Classes and analyzes emotion words among members of a Southwest Pacific atoll. Meanings examined include love, fear, happiness, guilt, shame, compassion, sadness, and justified anger. Emotions of good fortune are at the apex of word groups, and the words in this group cannot be uttered in mixed company. Of interest to religious studies are fago, Ifaluk for compassion/love/sadness, and the emotion of "justifiable anger." Lutz's work on vocabularies of emotion has put her at the forefront of comparative studies in emotion.

513. ------. Unnatural Emotions: Everyday Sentiments on a Micronesian Atoll & Their Challenge to Western Theory. Chicago: University of Chicago Press, 1988. Emotions are "embodied thoughts" leading to intensely meaningful cultural, social, and personal constructions. The Western view that emotions are irrational, feminine, and natural is not a universal view, and such precepts will obscure beliefs about persons and feelings of fear, grief, envy, and love, until emotion is appreciated as ideological practice. The comparison between Ifaluk emotions and Western ideas, especially fago and "justifiable anger," is developed further, with implications for religion.

514. Lutz, Catherine and Geoffrey M. White. "The Anthropology of Emotions." Annual Review of Anthropology 15 (1986): 405-36. More than 10 years old, but this review of the literature still merits careful study. Tensions between divergent poles of inquiry show why the field is so dynamic. The question of universals is addressed in depth, as is the cultural and social construction of emotions – both with import for the study of religion. In this essay a cross-cultural psychology emerges, reanimating the too often mechanical images social science has of being human.

515. McDaniel, June. "Emotion in Bengali Religious Thought: Substance and Metaphor." Emotions in Asian Thought: A Dialogue in Comparative Philosophy. Edited by Joel Marks and Roger T. Ames. Albany, N.Y.: State University of New York Press, 1995. Pp. 39-63. This ethno-psychology compares early Indian traditions valuing mental control over distracting emotions to later devotional traditions where the love of a deity is highlighted. In the latter, emotions are valued, though they must be directed and, ultimately, transformed.

516. "Magic." <u>Encyclopedia of Religion</u>. Vol. 9. New York: Macmillan Publishing Company, 1987. Pp. 81-115. A discussion of magic in eight periods and geographical regions rich in references to emotion, from spells to restrain anger to magical inducements of envy and fear.

517. Malinowski, Bronislaw. <u>Magic, Science and Religion</u>. Garden City, N.Y.: Doubleday, 1954 [1948]. This most famous emotion theorist among the classic functionalists, did fieldwork in Melanesia with the Trobriand Islanders. Magic and religion, in the field, are related to the anxieties and the fears of daily life. Both magic and religion are cathartic. They release ritual participants from the emotional stresses and strains of life. The ultimate and most powerful source of emotional tension underlying all religious rites was the fear of death.

518. Marett, R. R. <u>The Threshold of Religion</u>. London: Methuen, 1914. An early emotional theorist, Marett criticized Tylor and Frazer for their views that early humans were dispassionate and overly rational. Religion and magic were much more about affective states in which rationality was suspended. Further, ritual stemmed directly from emotions, not from an ideal super-structure.

519. ------. <u>Psychology and Folk-Lore</u>. London: Methuen, 1920. Religion is vital to humanity as persons strive and progress. What characterizes religious consciousness, everywhere and at all times, is that the human can draw upon a power that makes for (and wills) righteousness. All a person need do is supply some fear, shyness, and humility. This universal belief exists, but more: it is universally helpful to the highest degree.

520. Marglin, Frédérique Apffel. "Refining the Body: Transformative Emotion in Ritual Dance." <u>Divine Passions: The Social Construction of Emotion in India</u>. Edited by Owen M. Lynch. Berkeley: University of California Press, 1990. Pp. 212-36. Hindu Temple (Jagannatha in Puri, Orissa, in eastern India) pilgrims are emotionally, cognitively, and spiritually transformed by the ritual dance called "tasting of srngara rasa," meaning "erotic emotion."

521. Masson, J. Moussaieff. <u>The Oceanic Feeling: The Origins of Religious Sentiment in Ancient India</u>. Dordrecht, Holland: Reidel, 1980. Masson applies psychoanalysis to the Indian tradition. The term "oceanic feeling" (used by Freud in <u>Civilization and Its Discontents</u> [1930]) was derived from Sanskrit and coined by Romain Rolland. Key features of the term are feelings of sadness, a sense of loss over life's transitoriness, feelings of world-weariness, and the perception of human existence as a dream state. These emotions are tied to the image of the sea, and to India.

522. Masson, Jeffrey Moussaieff, and Susan McCarthy. <u>When Elephants Weep: The Emotional Lives of Animals</u>. New York: Delacorte, 1995. Animals lead complex emotional lives, laughing, suffering, falling in love, and being lonely. They experience disappointment; they feel despair, anger, joy, shame, and compassion. Do they have a religious impulse? The authors leave the question open-ended after illustrating their systems of justice, modes of communication, and acts of worship. A person kneels humbly in prayer; a dog rolls over and bares its belly – each submits to a higher being.

523. Menon, Usha, and Richard A. Shweder. "Kali's Tongue: Cultural Psychology and the Power of Shame in Orissa, India." <u>Emotion and Culture: Empirical Studies of Mutual Influence</u>. Edited by Shinobu Kitayama and Hazel Rose Markus.

Washington, D.C.: American Psychological Association, 1994. Oriya Hindus interviewed said the local icon of Kali, Great Mother Goddess, represents the female power that both gives energy to the world and, when unchecked, leads to disaster. This power can only be regulated within, through lajya (displayed by biting the tongue, and inadequately translated as modesty or shame). This complex emotion is the chief antidote for destructive anger. To be full of lajya is to be moral; to develop this emotion is to become civilized.

524. Motta, Roberto. "Le geste et le corps dans la religion afro-brésilienne." Social Compass 42 (1995): 477-86. Afro-Brazilian hedonism may fit well in post-modern society, which values emotion, passion, body, and gesture. In its traditional forms (candomblé and xangô) this popular religion is centered in the body and in gesture, through dance and trance and animal sacrifice. Unlike the West, an intense linkage exists between body and soul, health and holiness.

525. New Directions in Psychological Anthropology. Edited by Theodore Schwartz, Geoffrey M. White, and Catherine A. Lutz. Cambridge: Cambridge University Press, 1992. The state of psychological anthropology, its methods and relations to other disciplines. The claim about cognition, that knowledge is acquired through interaction, is affirmed throughout, and there is significant evidence mustered that cultural knowledge is emotional and social, tied to personality, politics, and religious ritual.

526. Obeyesekere, Gananath. Medusa's Hair: An Essay on Personal Symbols and Religious Experience. Chicago: University of Chicago Press, 1981. Fire walkers, female ecstatics, are studied at Kataragama, a pilgrimage site in Sri Lanka. Of special interest is the meaning of their matted hair. Each snakelike lock is intended to represent a penis, thus matted hair is a symbol of the god's power. The Medusa, through her hair, asserts a denial of castration, and, by extension, a rejection of the demands of local authorities, including husbands. These expressions, it is argued, help to eliminate unconscious feelings of guilt.

527. ------. "Despair and Recovery in Sinhala Medicine and Religion: An Anthropologist's Meditations." Healing and Restoring: Health and Medicine in the World's Religious Traditions. Edited by Lawrence E. Sullivan. New York: Macmillan, 1989. Pp. 127-48. Meditation and spirit possession are reactions to and expressions of despair in Buddhist cultures. In the former, despair holds meaning through the practice of self-mastery techniques; in the latter, hopelessness is seen as an attack by an evil spirit.

528. ------. "Language and Symbolic Form in Psychoanalysis and Anthropology." The Work of Culture: Symbolic Transformation in Psychoanalysis and Anthropology. Chicago: University of Chicago Press, 1990. In the fourth part of his fourth Morgan Lecture (1982), Obeyesekere engages theologians Charles Taylor and Paul Ricoeur in order to think through the possibility of a "vocabulary of emotions" that might apply across cultures. The lecturer is hopeful, though he urges that work be done translating words and studying nonverbal symbolic actions in the absence of emotion words.

529. Ortner, Sherry B. High Religion: A Cultural and Political History of Sherpa Buddhism. Princeton: Princeton University Press, 1989. A dialectic between feeling "big" and feeling "small" – being powerful and being altruistic – is at work both in the founders of monasteries in Nepal and in the non-elite who work to support the monks and

nuns. The elite (objectively "big" people) depend on a subjective response from the small people for material support and for legitimacy. In the process, the Darjeeling workers are empowered.

530. ------. "Rank and Gender." **Making Gender: The Politics and Erotics of Culture**. Boston: Beacon, 1996. Pp. 59-115. Polynesia is hierarchical. Persons are ranked by religious values in a "prestige system" which is promoted by a low-level of emotion attachment. Lessening emotion leaves sibling bonds stronger than marriage ones. Harmony appears to flourish, and sexual activity is high. But, women are subordinated as wives and much controlled. Sexual jealousy often leads to violence, more to preserve status than any emotional tie.

531. Peletz, Michael G. **Reason and Passion: Representations of Gender in a Malay Society**. Berkeley: University of California Press, 1996. "Reason" and "spirituality" are aligned with Malay men and "passion" and "animality" with women. This surprises because of the relatively high status of Malay women. This culture is matrilineal and it is based on an exchange of men, not women. Thus, the construction of gender rests not on kinship structures but on symbolic systems of prestige and virtue among these Muslims of Negeri Sembilan.

532. **The Performance of Healing**. Edited by Carol Laderman and Marina Roseman. New York: Routledge, 1996. Essays from the perspective of medical anthropology on ritual healing, shamanistic performance, magical diagnostic techniques, and poetic dramas enacted to relieve painful emotions.

533. Priest, Robert Joseph. "Defilement, Moral Purity, and Transgressive Power: The Symbolism of Filth in Aguaruna Jivaro Culture." Ph.D. diss., University of California, Berkeley, 1993. Ethnography in northern Peru finds symbols of dirt and defilement which, in the context of sickness and death, appear to be very much about death-anxiety. Filth affect and disgust are related to oral ingestion, food symbolism, homicide, and sex. Priest's theory relies on Paul Ricoeur, Victor Turner, and James Brain; it stands in contrast to that of Mary Douglas.

534. Quiroga, Diego. "Saints, Virgins, and the Devil: Witchcraft, Magic, and Healing in the Northern Coast of Ecuador." Ph.D. diss., University of Illinois at Urbana-Champaign, 1994. Communal rituals, arrullos, order the cosmos into the divine domain and the human domain, which is the realm of the devil. The rituals empower marginal sectors helping people overcome feelings of alienation and fragmentation. Ecuadoran healers, curanderas, draw on cosmic energy to treat illnesses based in fear, frustration, anger, and incongruities.

535. Radcliffe-Brown, A. R. **The Andaman Islanders**. New York: Free Press, 1964. Society is a system of shared sentiments. Weeping expresses feelings of attachment between persons. Society among these islanders is highly domestic, thus social bonds are of the utmost importance. Reciprocal weeping shows mutual emotions, and mourners weeping over the dead are reunited with the living after the burial. When only one party weeps, the sentiment still affirms attachment, despite the change in social bonds. In either case, sentiment is to be distinguished from sadness and other spontaneous outbursts of emotion.

536. Rosaldo, Michelle Z. **Knowledge and Passion: Ilongot Notions of Self and Social Life**. Cambridge: Cambridge University Press, 1980. Emotions relate self to

local culture; they are physiological and cognitive in that they are linked to moral/ideological attitudes – hence their relevance for religion. Culturally constituted attitudes shape cognition and everyday life. Language is more than a system of classifications. Common discourse, habits of conversation, and daily expression are worthy of study because meaning is "bound up with use." Person, act, and cultural environs are all linked through emotions.

537. ------. "Toward and Anthropology of Self and Feeling." Culture Theory: Essays on Mind, Self, and Emotion. Edited by Richard A. Shweder and Robert A. LeVine. Cambridge: Cambridge University Press, 1984. Pp. 137-57. This emotion studies pioneer assumes persons to be social first, individuals second; there is no human psychic unity, no genetic mind. Each culture – each religious culture – must be viewed on its own terms. Scholars are reminded that their own mental ties to culture will limit their ability to understand others. With no way to class emotions universally, the only recourse is to study the terms and frames of the cultures that shape personalities. See entry number 546.

538. Rozin, Paul, Linda Millman, and Carol Nemeroff. "Operation of the Laws of Sympathetic Magic in Disgust and Other Domains." Journal of Personality and Social Psychology 50 (1986): 703-12. Contagion produces disgust via a sterilized cockroach in a glass, or on a laundered shirt once worn by a disliked person (once in contact, always in contact). Similarity links object to image, so that darts are inaccurately thrown at photos of friends, and fudge in the shape of dog feces disgusts. These laws of sympathetic magic were first described by Frazer and Mauss.

539. Shweder, Richard A. "Menstrual Pollution, Soul Loss, and the Comparative Study of Emotions." Thinking Through Cultures: Expeditions in Cultural Psychology. Cambridge, Mass.: Harvard University Press, 1991. Pp. 241-65. Cultural prohibitions raise the question of whether emotional functioning is common or peculiar. This essay posits the problem of "soul loss," claiming there is a soul to lose that we all know by intuition. Also, the act of touching, though it varies greatly across cultures, shares similar emotions and meanings.

540. ------. Thinking Through Cultures: Expeditions in Cultural Psychology. Cambridge, Mass.: Harvard University Press, 1991. Individuals and traditions combine in creative interaction; psyches and cultures "make each other up." This is a clue to the uniqueness of people, but a question raised throughout this work is one of psychological unity across cultures: is there a human nature, an emotional currency, to search for? The answer remains as mysterious as the complexity of Hindu culture, used to illustrate the problem.

541. ------. "The Cultural Psychology of the Emotions." Handbook of Emotions. Edited by Michael Lewis and Jeannette M. Haviland. New York: Guilford Press, 1993. Pp. 417-31. A review of the basic disciplinary questions, with special reference to Hindu culture and the display of lajya, the way a woman avoids contact with certain people. Often translated as "shame" or "modesty," lajya is seen as an emotional performance and a moral state.

542. ------. "True Ethnography: The Lore, the Law, and the Lure." Ethnography and Human Development: Context and Meaning in Social Inquiry. Edited by Richard Jessor, Anne Colby, and Richard A. Shweder. Chicago: University of Chicago Press, 1996. Pp. 15-52. Moral order is not merely power order, yet any social

ordering of people that is moral must needs be a power ordering. Hindu society expects a vulnerable and sad time in the life of a new bride. She is isolated from nearly everyone in her life. Her integration into a new moral community requires a religious denial of social relations, and the life stage, "jouvana," is a well-marked social status.

543. Shweder, Richard A., and Edmund J. Bourne. "Does the Concept of the Person Vary Cross-Culturally?" Culture Theory: Essays on Mind, Self, and Emotion. Edited by Richard A. Shweder and Robert A. LeVine. Cambridge: Cambridge University Press, 1984. Pp. 158-99. People have different world views, and their world views influence, in a decisive way, how people function cognitively and emotionally. Differences in thought are not "deficits" in skills or data or processing. What one thinks about is wrapped up in how one thinks, and culture, including religion, mediates thinking processes and their objects.

544. Siegel, Lee. Laughing Matters: Comic Tradition in India. Chicago: University of Chicago Press, 1987. Siegel shows how Indian culture and religion are expressed in and through emotion. Laughter is present in erotics, in mirth, in misery, in love, in joy, and in seriousness.

545. Spiro, Melford E. "Religious Systems as Culturally Constituted Defense Mechanisms." Culture and Human Nature: Theoretical Papers of Melford E. Spiro. Edited by Benjamin Kilborne and L. L. Langness. Chicago: University of Chicago Press, 1987 [1965]. Pp. 145-60. Clinically, Burmese buddhist monks appear filled with emotional conflicts. But, their tradition offers institutional means of conflict resolution, and it functions to prevent the creation of private defenses, which would magnify individual psychological problems.

546. ------. "Some Reflections on Cultural Determinism and Relativism with Special Reference to Emotion and Reason." Culture Theory: Essays on Mind, Self, and Emotion. Edited by Richard A. Shweder and Robert A. LeVine. Cambridge: Cambridge University Press, 1984. Pp. 323-46. An elder statesman decries determinism. Culture is now so unique that cross-cultural study is impaired. What if Ilongot philosophers deem headhunting more valuable than feeding the starving Ifugao? Spiro, for one, would stand with Buddha, Christ, Isaiah, Laotzu, Socrates, and Gandhi. Contemporary currents (the enculturated only can understand a system) undermine the possibility of history. How might we ever hope to understand the French Revolution, for instance? We must be continually critical in our scrutiny of relativism. Cf. entry number 537.

547. Squarcini, Federico. "Gesture Language as a Vehicle in the Expression of Emotion: A Phenomenological Investigation of the Use of Non-Verbal Expression in Monotheistic Gaudiya Vaisnava Tradition." Social Compass 42 (1995): 451-60. Non-verbal communication stirs up emotions. Gesture language is central to the Gaudiya Vaisnava tradition of 15th century Bengal, long linked with bhakti. Hands and fingers communicate the service offered to the deity.

548. Tan, Leshan. "Theravada Buddhism and Village Economy: A Comparative Study in Spisong Panna of Southwest China." Ph.D. diss., Cornell University, 1995. Buddhism in Yunnan Province was undermined by atheist propaganda and by a market economy. In most of South East Asia, nirvana is release from the cycle of rebirth through annihilation of self and its passions, but for the Tai Lue, nirvana is the top level of heaven, the best place to live. Religious merit is sought for prestige and glory, not for

happiness in another world. Merit-making religion offers chances for networking and enhancing one's economic status. Lavish spending for religious rites is all about this-worldly desires.

549. **Tolbert, Elizabeth Dawn.** "The Musical Means of Sorrow: The Karelian Lament Tradition." **Ph.D. diss., University of California, Los Angeles, 1988.** The Karelian lament, or itkuvirsi, is a woman's folk ritual in eastern Finland and Russian Karelia, with roots in ancestor worship and Eurasian shamanism. The lament is a processual metaphor for Karelia's worldview; its sounds and forms make up a symbolic system that expresses the cosmology of Karelian folk religion. Ecstatic performance, unusual text, and improvisation, and a technique of "musical masking" signal the presence of the sacred.

550. **Toomey, Paul M.** "Krishna's Consuming Passions: Food as Metaphor and Metonym for Emotion at Mount Govardhan." **Divine Passions: The Social Construction of Emotion in India.** Edited by Owen M. Lynch. Berkeley: University of California Press, 1990. Pp. 157-81. In bhakti, emotion is woven through interactions, human and divine, and among members of the sect, which show a deep cultural concern for reciprocity; this dynamic is best found in the symbolic practices surrounding food.

551. **Torgovnick, Marianna. Primitive Passions: Men, Women, and the Quest for Ecstasy.** New York: Knopf, 1997. Wide-ranging challenge to western assumptions about rationality that have kept passionate desires repressed. Through descriptions in 20th century literature of violent and non-rational acts, including cannibalism and human sacrifice, the author argues for the merging of "primitive passion" and ecstasy into contemporary life. Dinesen, Fossey, Gide, Jung, Lawrence, O'Keefe, and native-American voices are employed.

552. **Turner, Victor. The Forest of Symbols: Aspects of Ndembu Ritual.** Ithaca, N.Y.: Cornell University Press, 1967. Religious symbols have two poles of meaning, one is physiological and "orectic," that is, what one longs for, grasps after, relating to desire or appetite, the other pole is related to moral norms, the basic principles that govern society. The drama of ritual causes an exchange between the orectic and normative poles. Biology becomes ennobled; morality takes on emotional significance. In the process, what is necessary is rendered desirable. Duty becomes what one wants to do.

553. ------. **The Drums of Affliction: A Study of Religious Processes Among the Ndembu of Zambia.** Oxford: Clarendon Press, 1968. Virilocal marriage harmonizes with patrilineal descent to create stability and deep lineages. In the Ndembu, virilocal marriage is linked to matrilineal descent (the women bring the men home), creating an incompatibility, shifting patterns of cultivation, and acute tension. Rituals of affliction redress these strains and restore an orderly functioning in group life, by requiring the stranger to be the focus of the time, money, and energy required of public rites, thereby bringing him into society.

554. **Tuzin, Donald. The Cassowary's Revenge: The Life and Death of Masculinity in a New Guinea Society.** Chicago: University of Chicago Press, 1997. Ritual killing of an old tyrant in Melanesia, who had ruled through fear and terror and also trained the young for survival, brings a secret men's cult to an end. The anthropologist who observed the outpouring of emotions at this parricide returns 13 years later to discover

that his role in that supreme act of repudiation is now part of a religious and apocalyptic legend.

555. Ueno, Yuji. "Eastern Philosophy and the Rise of the Aikido Movement." Ph.D. diss., University of Toronto, 1995. Aikido, a martial art based on the religious idea of ki (or ch'i), raises questions about the origin and nature of religious phenomenon. Ueno examines the motives for joining and remaining in the group. He finds that Aikido's rise and persistence are conditioned culturally and socially. Suffering, both physical and emotional, leads members to deeper experiences, as do the religious methods used in the discipline.

556. Wekker, Gloria. "'I Am Gold Money' (I Pass Through All Hands, But I Do Not Lose My Value): The Construction of Selves, Gender and Sexualities in a Female, Working Class, Afro-Surinamese Setting." Ph.D. diss., University of California, Los Angeles, 1992. Winti folk religion and cosmology inform Creole selves, sexuality, and gender. The mati work, a peculiar institution in which women have multiple sexual partners, both male and female, appears to have no stigma attached to it. Open and joyous sexual passion, especially for other women, raises psychological and feminist questions. The author claims participant observation for her methodology.

557. White, Geoffrey M. "Emotion Talk and Social Inference: Disentangling in Santa Isabel, Solomon Islands." Disentangling: Conflict Discourse in Pacific Societies. Edited by Karen Ann Watson-Gegeo and Geoffrey M. White. Stanford: Stanford University Press, 1990. Pp. 53-121. These evangelized Island people express solidarity in Christian terms and resolve conflict by talking out their hidden "bad feelings." This is called "disentangling," and it is practiced publicly. Recasting ceremonial life into a Christian frame leads participants to compare "disentangling" to Holy Communion; both represent moral cleansing, in that personal conflicts are expiated.

558. Whitehouse, Harvey. Inside the Cult: Religious Innovation and Transmission in Papua New Guinea. New York: Oxford University Press, 1995. Whitehouse was made into a cargo god by the people of Baining; he and his wife were "white-skinned ancestors." Two factions, with their own modes of religiosity, were in tension: the "doctrinal mode" of the ruling, centralized Pomio Kivung, and the "imagistic mode" of the enthusiastic village cult. The latter, sparked by upstart prophets, evoked intense emotions but failed to organize. In the short term, the climactic outburst enlivened life in the bush.

559. Wu, David Y. H. "Psychotherapy and Emotion in Chinese Medicine." Cultural Conceptions of Mental Health and Therapy. Edited by Anthony J. Marsella and Geoffrey M. White. Dordrecht, Holland: Reidel, 1982. Pp. 285-301. Chinese traditions regarding cosmic symbolism and energy inform this view of psychotherapy. Ying-Yang, ch'i, and feng-chüe are related to emotions, psychic balance, and health. Disease symptoms are culturally patterned, so is emotion. Recognition of this truth should help in both research and diagnosis.

Sociological Studies

**560. Allen, Robert Raymond. "Singing in the Spirit: An Ethnography of Gospel Performance in New York City's African-American Church Community." Ph.D.

diss., University of Pennsylvania, 1987. Gospel performance by the southern black church community in NYC is treated as a ritual extension of Sunday worship. In this public experience, emotion and sacred symbols come together. Basic tenets of "old-time religion" become emotionally convincing in song as members are reminded of rural identity, lives of hard work, and respect for family and the elderly. "Hard" gospel with a shouting-style is a post-war response to dislocation, expressing a new attempt at urban community.

561. Ashforth, Adam. "Of Secrecy and the Commonplace: Witchcraft and Power in Soweto." Social Research 63 (1996): 1183-1234. Rises in commerce in occult divinations, magical remedies, and spiritual solace point to questions of state power, violence, and daily life in Soweto, Johannesburg, South Africa. The political liabilities of how people protect themselves from evil are central to how politics, from household to state, is constituted. Jealousy is the source of hate that lies behind the desire to harm others through witchcraft. Given the secrecy at the heart of power, can the new regime be open?

562. Bellah, Robert N. "Civil Religion in America." Daedalus 96 (1967): 1-21. There is a religious dimension to "the American Way of Life." Though it is used to mask "petty interests and ugly passions," it is also used to instill feelings of loyalty and patriotism, and it is the vehicle for the Presidency to express religious sentiments. The civil religion is inculcated through public education, voluntary associations, historic places, hymns, and holidays.

563. Bellah, Robert N., Richard Madsen, William M. Sullivan, Ann Swidler, and Steven M. Tipton. Habits of the Heart: Individualism and Commitment in American Life. Berkeley: University of California Press, 1985. The culture of "utilitarian individualism" is pervasive in white middle-class America. Its counterpart, "expressive individualism," has become a vital mode of feeling, enabling many to view commitment (in marriage, work, politics, and religion) as benefits to individual happiness rather than as moral imperatives.

564. Berger, Peter L., and Thomas Luckman. The Social Construction of Reality: A Treatise in the Sociology of Knowledge. Garden City, N.Y.: Doubleday, 1966. When emotions are part of the internalization of reality, society becomes a subjective phenomenon. In this seminal work, the sociology of religion plays a key role in the construction of knowledge, as well as in the development of sociological theory. The treatise is the cornerstone for the constructionist approach to emotions.

565. Brown, Michael F. The Channeling Zone: American Spirituality in An Anxious Age. Cambridge, Mass.: Harvard University Press, 1997. Participant-observation of New Age practitioners, who are called "channels," often women, finds them dealing in financial affairs, emotional problems, and career choices. Baby Boomers who join new religious movements are the largest cohort in this fringe phenomenon, which speaks to self-fragmentation and social anxiety.

566. Brutz, Judith L. "Development of Pacifism in Quakers." Ph.D. diss., Iowa State University, 1988. A pattern is found in pacifist families. It begins with an embrace of pacifism, and it continues until the ideals and values of pacifism are fully understood and lived. The peace orientation shifts from opposition to war and violence to building relationships. Conflict management changes from a closed to an open system

in several ways, including an approach where anger is no longer avoided but is seen as an indicator of problems to be solved.

567. Call, Vaughn R. A., and Tim B. Heaton. "Religious Influence on Marital Stability." Journal for the Scientific Study of Religion 36 (1997): 382-92. Of all factors related to religiosity, frequency of church attendance has the greatest positive influence on marital satisfaction and stability. The religious beliefs of the wife regarding commitment to the marriage and non-marital sex impact stability more than the husband's beliefs.

568. Carmel, Sara, and Elizabeth Mutran. "Wishes Regarding the Use of Life-Sustaining Treatments among Elderly Persons in Israel: An Explanatory Model." Social Science & Medicine 45 (1997): 1715-27. For this study, 1000 Israelis, 70 years of age and older, were asked about life-sustaining treatments (LST). Most wanted to prolong life, if health was good; few wished for LST if they had severe illness. Negative experiences with death lowered the desire to prolong life. Wishes for LST were predicted by feelings about life and death, fear of dying, religiosity, and the will to live. The more religious, the more the subjects wanted to prolong life. Those who feared death did not want LST.

569. Carroll, Michael P. "Stark Realities and Eurocentric/Androcentric Bias in the Sociology of Religion." Sociology of Religion 57 (1996): 225-39. The theory of religion of Rodney Stark and William Bainbridge is assessed. Carroll claims that Western culture separates rationality and emotion because emotion threatens progress. Feminist critiques of Eurocentrism and Androcentrist bias are used to find Stark/Bainbridge dependent on 19th century assumptions.

570. Champion, Françoise, and Danièle Hervieu-Léger. De l'émotion en religion: renouveaux et traditions. Paris: Le Centurion, 1990. Does breakup of the great doctrinal synthesis mean an end to sentiment in modern society? The authors argue that although the religious imagination does not find the old synthesis plausible, its very multiplicity is evidence for the privatization of beliefs, a movement away from the control of religious institutions. Intriguing question: is an emotional revival of religion a sign of the end of secularization, or the end of religion?

571. Clark, Candace. Misery and Company: Sympathy in Everyday Life. Chicago: University of Chicago Press, 1997. Patterns of and rules for receiving and giving sympathy. American social order and the role sympathy plays in promoting solidarity are viewed within the frame of the sociology of emotions. Biblical figures as "sympathy entrepreneurs" and "socioemotional economies of modern Judeo-Christian societies" are cited, but secular models of benevolence have replaced older forms. Sympathy display in ritual functions to celebrate the social order and, at the same time, uplift society's members as per Durkheim.

572. Clulow, Christopher F. "Divorce as Bereavement: Similarities and Differences." Family & Conciliation Courts Review 28 (1990): 19-22. Effects of divorce last. Much depends on how the breakup is handled by partners, children, and associates. The economic, emotional, and legal bonds are easier to deal with when one partner dies, and feelings of grief, sorrow, and anger differ for death than for divorce. Ritual helps to heal the bereaved. Sadly, little social or psychological support is available when a spouse is lost due to divorce.

573. Collins, Randall. "On the Micro-Foundations of Macro-Sociology." **American Journal of Sociology** 86 (1981): 984-1014. The theory of "interaction ritual chains" (based on Durkheim, Goffman, and Weber) seeks to explain emotions at the local level, even as they are linked to society at large.

574. ------. "Stratification, Emotional Energy, and the Transient Emotions." **Research Agendas in the Sociology of Emotions**. Edited by T. D. Kemper. Albany, N.Y.: State University of New York Press, 1990. "Emotional energy" is the natural substrate made up of enthusiasm and confidence. It is this exultant energy that is present in ritual. It is this substrate and its emotions that emerge in ritual interaction.

575. Colonna, Fanny. "Un Regard aveuglé: anticléricalisme par excès d'humanisme universaliste en Algérie." **Anthropologie et sociétés** 20 (1996): 59-83. On the French views of Islam in Algeria, there has been much misunderstanding. The author finds an anticlericalism present in the French, one that is based in three fears: the fear of the Ancient Regime, the threat of religion to the republic, and the positivist fear of emotion and irrationality.

576. **Community in America: The Challenge of *Habits of the Heart*. Edited and Introduced by Charles H. Reynolds and Ralph V. Norman. Berkeley: University of California Press, 1988.** Response to Bellah's 1985 book on the feelings and values of white, middle-class Americans, by social scientists, ethicists, feminists, historians, and literary critics. The longing for community in America has a religious dimension to it, and the participants reflect on narrative, culture, practical reason, religious practice, and public moral discourse. Bellah answers his critics.

577. Crawford, Mark E., Paul J. Handal, and Richard L. Wiener. "The Relationship between Religion and Mental Health/Distress." **Review of Religious Research** 31 (1989): 16-22. Of the 226 subjects interviewed, high religious subjects were less distressed and better adjusted, psychologically, than medium and low religious subjects. Women (136) showed significant statistical correlation between a high degree of religiosity and mental health, and the results were clinically meaningful, too. This was not the case with males.

578. Davidman, Lynn. "The Personal, the Sociological, and the Intersection of the Two." **Qualitative Sociology** 20 (1997): 507-15. The value of qualitative sociology on individual and group experiences can be greater than a religious studies or a psychological approach. Women convert to Orthodox Judaism for the sense of identity and tradition, community solidarity, gender clarity, and family maintenance. Secondly, mother loss impacts children, and, food becomes a symbolic manifestation of the mother's caring. Her loss shapes the individual. In each case, self-understanding is accelerated and profound interpretations of society are developed.

579. **Death and Dying: A Bibliographical Survey**. Edited by Samuel Southard. New York: Greenwood Press, 1991. A reliable resource for social-scientific, as well as other disciplinary, studies related to the theme of religion and emotion, on grieving, bereavement, and mourning, up to 1991.

580. DiBlasio, Frederick A. "The Role of Social Workers' Religious Beliefs in Helping Family Members Forgive." **Families in Society** 74 (1993): 163-70. Social workers with strong religious beliefs have higher regard for forgiveness attitudes than non-religious ones. However, regarding forgiveness techniques, forgiveness and

depression, anger and forgiveness, and openness over religious issues, there seems to be little difference. Non-religious social workers appear fully capable of responding to clients' religious issues – and willing to do so.

581. Dillon, Michele. "The Persistence of Religious Identity among College Catholics." Journal for the Scientific Study of Religion 35 (1996): 165-70. Patterns of collective loyalty among Catholics are replicated at a non-Catholic, private university among Catholic undergraduates. These young American Catholics qualify church authority, not fully accepting it. Regular attendance corresponds more with affirming Catholic teachings on sexuality. Church going offers a constant for differentiating moral values and political opinions.

582. Docking, Jeffrey R. "A Comparative Analysis of the Interpretation of Racism in George Kelsey, Reinhold Niebuhr, and Martin Luther King, Jr." Ph.D. diss., Boston University, 1996. Kelsey (who influenced King) viewed racism as idolatry righted in religious conversion. Niebuhr disagreed; he saw racism as a will-to-power related to the human need for control and security. Racism cannot be solved because no cure exists for human nature. Only by balancing power can racism be checked. King thought many factors converge to give rise to racism – sin, hatred, capitalism, ignorance, and fear.

583. Domingues, Patricia L. "Women in the New Christian Right: Ideological Hegemony in Process." Ph.D. diss., University of California, Riverside, 1994. Covert participant-observation is used at a women's bible group in Southern California to learn why women of the New Religious Right "willingly adopt and enthusiastically support" an ideology of subordination. The sociology of emotions, especially emotion management and interaction ritual, is used.

584. Domino, George, and Yoshitomo Takahashi. "Attitudes toward Suicide in Japanese and American Medical Students." Suicide & Life-Threatening Behavior 21 (1991): 345-59. The Suicide Opinion Questionnaire is used to compare attitudes among 80 male and 20 female Japanese medical students and an equal number of their American counterparts. Japanese students were more likely to think suicide a right, within normal bounds. Americans believed it to show anger and aggression. Males felt suicide inversely related to religious values and commitments; females believed it to be an impulsive act.

585. Duff, Robert W., and Lawrence K. Hong. "Age Density, Religiosity and Death Anxiety in Retirement Communities." Review of Religious Research 37 (1995): 19-32. Two views of death anxiety hold that, 1) being surrounded by many vulnerable retirees increases fear, and 2) high religiosity lowers anxiety. The first claim is found false, at least for six west-coast communities surveyed. But, attendance at religious worship is linked to low death anxiety, though private practices, personal religiosity, and social activities are not. These findings support Durkheim's view of the efficaciousness of shared religion.

586. Durkheim, Emile. Suicide. London: Routledge, 1952 [1897]. Protestants have consistently higher rates of suicide than do Catholics or Jews. Among Protestant groups, the pietistic sects have had consistently higher rates of suicide than others. Cultural differences account for this contrast. It is argued that individualism was greatest in pietistic sects, and, as the person feels less solidarity with the group, the likelihood of suicide increases.

587. ------. **The Elementary Forms of the Religious Life.** New York: Free Press, 1965 [1912]. It is the effervescence of interaction that individuals recollect in symbols; this feeling is at the heart of shared classifications of the world. The unanimous sentiments of believers cannot be illusion: one in league with the sacred is stronger, feeling more force within. Life's trials are endured, even conquered, because ritual lifts the individual above the miseries of being human. Intense emotion and social order go hand in hand; ritual integrates the individual, and emotion flows from social structure. Collective consciousness is the highest form of psychic life. This is most true of death rituals where others are pressed to bring their feelings into line with the bereaved.

588. El-Helou, Mohamed W., and Peter R. Johnson. "The Effects of the Palestinian Intifada on the Behaviour of Teenagers in the Gaza Strip." **Journal of Child & Youth Care** 9 (1994): 63-70. The mass-scale uprising against the military occupation of the Gaza Strip (intifada) has affected teens in troubling ways. Interviews of 61 teens on personal experience, emotions, and coping mechanisms found subjects fearful, anxious, angry, and hateful. Yet, only one exhibited signs of post-traumatic stress disorder. Two thirds felt that religious rites made them fearful; 40% became angry when they performed such rites.

589. Ellison, Christopher G. "Religious Involvement and Subjective Well-Being." **The Journal of Health and Social Behavior** 32 (1991): 80-99. National survey data shows correlation between religiosity and long-term, life satisfaction, as well as to short-term, affective, happiness. Both satisfaction and happiness were improved by strong faith, which also cushioned negative events. Strength of belief is particularly valuable to the elderly and the uneducated where it adds to life satisfaction, but not to happiness. Church attendance does not directly correlate with well-being, though it does enhance religious belief.

590. Erben, Andreas. "Predictors of Divorce Adjustment among Members of Three Conservative Protestant Denominations." Ph.D. diss., Andrews University, 1997. Most of the 360 divorced men and women, from Lutheran, Seventh Day Adventist, and Church of the Nazarene, showed high self-esteem and low attachment. However, they perceived themselves to be more depressed than what has been reported for the general population. Most of the subjects experienced anger at their loss.

591. Fisher, Gene A., and Kyum Koo Chon. "Durkheim and the Social Construction of Emotions." **Social Psychology Quarterly** 52 (1989): 1-9. Cited as authority for the social constructionist approach to the emotions, Durkheim, in his writings, saw the central role biology plays in constituting emotions. Social solidarity is shaped by the intense arousal present in human gatherings. Mechanical solidarity is preserved by instinctive emotional reaction (choler) to violations of shared sentiments.

592. Frank, Robert H. **Passions Within Reason: The Strategic Role of the Emotions.** New York: Norton, 1988. Intriguing argument that employs economic theory to show that pursuit of self-interest ends in failure and that moral behavior accrues unintended benefits. Chapters on altruism, fairness, love, and human decency will be of interest to scholars of religion.

593. Galanter, Marc. **Cults, Faith, Healing, and Coercion.** New York: Oxford University Press, 1989. Charisma is at the heart of the cult, and it raises the level of social cohesiveness through powerful emotional experiences. Cultic behavior and its norms make for ongoing, regular activities; vulnerability in the emotional state of a member occurs when that routine is disrupted. Likewise, on joining a group, the level of symptoms associated with neurotic distress decline. Galanter takes a "systems approach" to analyze the structure and functioning of modern cults, especially the Unification Church.

594. García-Ruiz, Jesús. "Modernité et sociétés paysannes: le rôle du religieux dans la recomposition des identités au Guatemala." **Archives de sciences sociales des religions** 42 (1997): 73-95. Evangelism is a reaction to repressive Christian-Mayan beliefs fostered since the colonial period. In the 1930s, a Catholic action movement ruptured rural Guatemalan society by challenging those rigid beliefs. Opposed to 1950s communism and the authoritarianism of the 1960s, the action movement polarized politics and families. In response, peasants turned to evangelism, expressing mass emotion.

595. Goffman, Erving. "Fun in Games." **Encounters: Two Studies in the Sociology of Interaction**. Indianapolis, Ind.: Bobbs-Merrill, 1961. Pp. 17-81. Games are fun when we are fully engaged in them. They give us opportunities to experiment with roles, and mistakes made in a game do not have the same consequences as mistakes in life. The measure of wholehearted engagement reveals a social dimension in gaming, and happiness is all about being fully engaged. When one would rather be elsewhere, happiness diminishes and inner conflict sets in; this opens the door to some painful experiences. A re-working of Freud's Psychopathology of Everyday Life (1901) this is an important essay on the nature of happiness with profound implications for religious ritual.

596. Goodman, Elizabeth Kushi. "Dying in Japan: Japanese Folk and Religious Beliefs about Death." Ph.D. diss., City University of New York, 1994. The case is made that the Japanese do not share the same fears about death that Western people have. The consolations, in the face of death, are offered by Japanese religion and by traditional lore. These consolations appear to ameliorate the fear of dying. Interviews with the people of Shikoku bear this out – and these people are seen as representative of common Japanese attitudes.

597. Graham-Pole, John, Hannelore Wass, Sheila M. Eyberg, Luis Chu, and S. Olejnik. "Communicating with Dying Children and Their Siblings: A Retrospective Analysis." **Death Studies** 13 (1989): 465-83. Mothers' open talk with dying children helped those children. Mothers who communicate openly with dying children also talk more openly with siblings. After those conversations, siblings were markedly sadder, angrier, more in denial, and more fearful than were the dying children. Mothers' moving beyond grief and bereavement correlates highly with religiosity, and surviving children are more emotionally adjusted, due to greater openness about death.

598. Grasmick, Harold G., Robert J. Bursik, and John K. Cochran. "'Render unto Caesar what is Caesar's': Religiosity and Taxpayers' Inclinations to Cheat." **Sociological Quarterly** 32 (1991): 251-66. Religious identity and the frequency of church attendance affect the inclination to cheat on taxes. These two factors inhibited more than did conservative ideology, gender, race, or socioeconomic standing. It appears that the sanction of shame is the operative emotional force and self-imposed punishment that inhibits cheating on taxes, as well as other illegal behavior.

599. Greeley, Andrew. **Ecstasy: A Way of Knowing**. Englewood Cliffs, N.J.: Prentice-Hall, 1974. Half of all Americans have had at least one ecstatic or mystical

experience. Ecstasy is non-verbal, direct knowledge, fused with intense emotion, and it is not always positive. Some cannot experience it, some can learn to experience it; others cannot avoid it. Positive ecstasy involves feelings of joy, detachment, total loss of fear or anxiety, soaring, and a sense of goodness and love. Triggers are art, nature, childbirth, sex, and religion.

600. Greer, Bruce A., and Wade C. Roof. "'Desperately Seeking Sheila': Locating Religious Privatism in American Society." **Journal for the Scientific Study of Religion** 31 (1992): 346-52. The General Social Survey first asked questions about personal religiosity in 1988. Using Bellah's term "Sheilaism" for privatized religion, the survey found that private religion varied in inverse proportions to feelings of loyalty to religious institutions. Most privatized in their religiosity were people in the Pacific states and New England, and they were white, male, young, and liberal Protestants.

601. Hagerty, Bonnie M., Reg A. Williams, James C. Coyne, and Margaret R. Early. "Sense of Belonging and Indicators of Social and Psychological Functioning." **Archives of Psychiatric Nursing** 10 (1996): 235-44. Belonging is gauged in 379 college students in terms of community involvement, church attendance, depression, loneliness, anxiety, conflict, social support, and suicidal tendencies. Social and psychological functioning is closely related to a sense of belonging, experienced more strongly by young women than by young men.

602. Hamilton, Malcolm B. **The Sociology of Religion: Theoretical and Comparative Perspectives.** London: Routledge, 1995. "Religion and Emotion" (45-70), Chapter 4 of this textbook, reviews classic social scientific theories, including those of Marett, Malinowski, Freud, Jung, and Spiro.

603. **Handbook of Emotion, Adult Development, and Aging.** Edited by Carol Magai and Susan H. McFadden. San Diego, Calif.: Academic Press, 1996. Chapter 19, "Religion, Emotions, and Health," reviews current gerontological research on religion, its influence on physical well-being, and the relationship between attachment theory and religion.

604. Hochschild, Arlie Russell. **The Managed Heart: Commercialization of Human Feeling.** Berkeley: University of California Press, 1983. Based on C. Wright Mills' idea of "The Great Salesroom," this creative study examines the emotional exchanges between the private life of modern individuals and the commercial goods of the economic order. When people agree to treat their emotions as merchandise, they pay a high price. The model of gift exchange comes closest to the classic religious view of persons exalted. Of interest is Appendix A, "Models of Emotion: From Darwin to Goffman" (201-22).

605. Imber-Black, Evan. "Rituals and the Healing Process." **Living Beyond Loss: Death in the Family.** Edited by Froma Walsh and Monica McGoldrick. New York: Norton, 1991. Pp. 207-23. Mourning rites differ from culture to culture, due to beliefs. Bounded by space and time, death rituals offer a sense of safety and order. This psychological phenomenon is widely shared across cultures, and so, where contemporary life lacks authentic rites, the therapeutic process, helping the grief-stricken with loss, is aided by attention to ritual in holiday celebrations or in newly created ones like the AIDS quilt.

606. Janowiak, Sharon Marie. "Bereavement Experiences of African Americans: The Use of Focus Groups." Psy.D. diss., Indiana University of Pennsylvania, 1995.

Focus groups made up of church-going African Americans discussed six themes: church community, bereavement rites, expressions of emotion, belief in an afterlife, natural or accidental death, and social support. Emotions (sadness, anger) and grieving rituals are universal. The role of church community seems to be distinctive of African Americans (value of extended family, extravagant funerals, the practice of putting a wreath on the door of the deceased).

607. Javalgi, Rajshekhar G., Bob D. Cutler, and Naresh K. Malhotra. " Print Advertising at the Component Level: A Cross-Cultural Comparison of the United States and Japan." Journal of Business Research **34 (1995): 117-24.** Visual advertisements are analyzed comparatively according to content (visual appeal, attractiveness of content, people portrayed). The Japanese seek to build brand loyalty first, and they do so by building feelings of friendship. Religious affiliation is most influential when the culture is isolated from outside forces.

608. Jensen, Lene Arnett. "Habits of the Heart Revisited: Autonomy, Community, and Divinity in Adults' Moral Language." Qualitative Sociology **18 (1995): 71-86.** Bellah's conclusion that Americans use individualism to express cherished values is qualified. Self-interest, individual rights, and personal feelings are found among young middle-class Americans. But midlife and older adults speak of community, commitment, and even divinity at a rate, and to a level, that would surprise, and, probably please, Bellah.

609. Johnson, Doyle Paul, and Larry C. Mullins. "Subjective and Social Dimensions of Religiosity and Loneliness among the Well Elderly." Review of Religious Research **31 (1989): 3-15.** Different dimensions of religiosity and loneliness among older persons are examined. Interviews with 131 residents of a high-rise for low-income elderly included controls for social contacts, satisfaction with social contacts, and depression. The social dimension of religiosity was significantly connected to low levels of loneliness; the subjective (personal spirituality) dimension was not.

610. Kemper, Theodore D. "Sociological Models in the Explanation of Emotions." Handbook of Emotions. **Edited by Michael Lewis and Jeannette M. Haviland. New York: Guilford Press, 1993.** Following Durkheim, religious rituals provide the occasions for people to express a variety of shared emotions, and this is the source for what Randall Collins has called "emotional energy," which consists of enthusiasm and confidence, putting the exultation into ritual.

611. Klenow, Daniel J. "Emotion and Life Threatening Illness: A Typology of Hope Sources." Omega **24 (1991-1992): 49-60.** Hope sources for persons with life-threatening illnesses are put into a typology. Religion, medicine, self-discipline, fallibilism, renewal and deception by others (false hope) are major sources, and they are divided into cognitive and behavioral dimensions.

612. MacDonald, Jerry P. "'Reject the Wicked Man,' Coercive Persuasion and Deviance Production: A Study of Conflict Management." Cultic Studies Journal **5 (1988): 59-121.** Study of a utopian, tightly knit, new religious movement and its conflict management techniques. A model of deviance production and coercive persuasion shows how the group creates crises of loyalty that serve to pigeon hole nonconformists, expelling some, while shoring up group feeling. For Durkheim a cloister of saints could be overly authoritarian.

613. **Mallimaci, Fortunato.** "Les Courants au sein du Catholicisme argentin: continuités et ruptures." Translated from the Spanish by Jean Bunel. <u>Archives de sciences sociales des religions</u> 40 (1995): 113-36. Given rapid change as Argentina modernizes, the basic tenets of life are shifting. Three kinds of Catholicism are in play: total Catholicism, marked by a lack of tolerance, emotion Catholicism, charismatic and volatile, and pluralistic Catholicism, which is located somewhere between the two extremes. It is suggested that this latter form may bring the most benefits to Argentines.

614. **Martycz, Virginia Kennedy.** "Identification as Process: A Rhetorical Study of Three Televangelists as Social Intervenors." Ph.D. diss., Ohio State University, 1991. A social intervention model sheds light on televangelism. Jim Bakker employed an "anomaly masking" strategy where the needs of each are met and exchanged through the group as advocate. Hope is high. Jimmy Swaggart used a ploy of "anomaly featuring," stressing group needs, and threat. Anger is central. Pat Robertson used "anomaly masking," where individual needs advocate group needs, and integrity. A theology of action is present.

615. **McGoldrick, Monica, Rhea Almeida, Paulette Moore Hines, Nydia Garcia-Preto, Elliott Rosen, and Evelyn Lee.** "Mourning in Different Cultures." <u>Living Beyond Loss: Death in the Family</u>. Edited by Froma Walsh and Monica McGoldrick. New York: Norton, 1991. Pp. 176-206. Irish, Hindu, Puerto Rican, African-American, Jewish, and Chinese families are at the center of this study, which seeks to inform practitioners working with the dying and the dead. What happens after death, appropriate lengths of time for mourning and integrating the loss, roles and behavior for men and women, stigmatized and traumatic deaths, and how to minimize negative impact are considered.

616. **Mellor, Philip A., and Chris Shilling.** "Lorsque l'on jette de l'huile sur le feu ardent: sécularisation, <u>homo duplex</u> et retour du sacré." <u>Social Compass</u> 45 (1998): 297-320. Sociology separated the religious from any foundational relationship with human sociality. Recent returns to the sacred help us to appreciate more fully Durkheim's ideas of embodiment and the sacred. The "fiery furnace" of society, made of effervescent and sacred bonds, is rooted in the dual nature of the human. New interest in the vigor of the religious ("refueling" the "fiery furnace") will coax sociologists to a new look at the bonds of companionship which constitute society and express our embodied nature.

617. **Miller, William Ian.** <u>The Anatomy of Disgust</u>. Cambridge, Mass.: Harvard University Press, 1997. Disgust, the flip side of shame and humiliation, along with contempt, are used to identify others as lower, and oneself as higher, in social status. Along the way, Christian ascetic traditions and saintliness are approached from the angle of the social and political theories developed by Erving Goffman.

618. **Minces, Juliette.** "La Sexualité de la femme musulmane." <u>Psychanalystes</u> 40 (1991): 63-70. Islamic women are forced to repress sexual passion. The men fear and despise their women as promiscuous, inferior, and deceitful. Women are a necessary evil, but are rejected as persons and used as objects. The sexual needs of Muslim women are ignored since their expression would disgust the men. Husbands in this cultural system are not free but frustrated; at times they are forced into masturbation, homosexuality, and celibacy because women (except for prostitutes) are often unavailable to them.

619. Morris, Linda Louise. "The Nature and Meaning of Near-Death Experiences to Patients and Critical Care Nurses." Ph.D. diss., University of Illinois at Chicago, 1998. Emotions of near-death experience (NDE) are studied in both patient and critical care nurse. Sights, sounds, sensations are reported, and after NDE, a search to find meaning takes place. This is a time of frustration, relieved only once a new way of looking at the world is achieved. This awakening often involves a spiritual quest for the purpose of life. A new life course with shifting priorities is traced in the patients and in their nurses, who feel more compassionate, more comfortable in crises.

620. Mosher, Robert E. "Pentecostalism and Inculturation in Chile." Missiol. D. diss., Pontificia Universitas Gregoriana, 1995. Pentecostalism is the Christian faith of many of Chile's poor; it is filled with emotion, enthusiasm, trances, healing, and spirit possession. The experience of anomie is behind the process of inculturation in Chile, that and a sense of being wronged. Three areas are explored: spirituality, women's roles, and community. Emotional religion is experienced as vindication of oppression.

621. Myers, Scott M. "An Interactive Model of Religiosity Inheritance: The Importance of Family Context." American Sociological Review 61 (1996): 858-66. Parents in 1980 and their adult offspring in 1992 were used to look at religiosity inheritance: effects of childhood, family, and parental influence, how parents transmit religiosity, and how adult offspring modify that inheritance. Marital happiness was a factor in transmission, as were moderate strictness in child rearing and a working husband/nonworking wife unit. Recent experience affects religiosity of offspring, but it does not reduce parental influence or that of family context.

622. Nadeau, Janice Winchester. Families Making Sense of Death. Thousand Oaks, Calif.: Sage Publications, 1998. Pp. 159-90. Religious meanings of death experiences are within the class of ultimate meanings. They are divided into the following types: revelation, reunion and reward; death as a test; God causing the death; and general statements about faith in God. These are all ways that people make sense of the death of a family member, with each way corresponding to a different set of feelings affecting the course of bereavement.

623. Nelson, Timothy, J. "Sacrifice of Praise: Emotion and Collective Participation in an African-American Worship Service." Sociology of Religion 57 (1996): 379-96. Participant observation of African Methodist Episcopal (AME) Church finds emotional worship. "Feeling rules" guide behavior (shouting and mutual encouragement). The collectively desired goal of experiencing God sustains vitality, and group identity, including racial identity, is shored up.

624. Neto, Felix. "Predictors of Satisfaction with Life among Second Generation Migrants." Social Indicators Research 35 (1995): 93-116. Second generation Portuguese adolescents born in France were studied for psychological acculturation and life satisfaction. Religion, friendship, and ethnic identity significantly enhanced satisfaction. Negatives include feeling marginal, social anxiety, and loneliness. Strongest predictors were loneliness and health.

625. Park, Kristin. "The Sacrifice Theory of Value: Explaining Activism in Two Sanctuary Congregations." Sociological Viewpoints 12 (1996): 35-50. A Quaker Meeting and a United Methodist Church participated in the sanctuary movement for Central American refugees. They are studied using the sacrifice theory of value – only through self sacrifice can persons affirm themselves and show the public those beliefs

and values that are not empirically verifiable. Cost and risk are incentives to action. This finding runs counter to rational-choice theory. Once sanctuary participation is routinized, an economy of gratitude replaces the sacrifice of value.

626. Parrott, W. Gerrod, and Rom Harré. "Embarrassment and the Threat to Character." The Emotions: Social, Cultural and Biological Dimensions. Edited by Rom Harré and W. Gerrod Parrott. London: Sage Pub., 1996. Pp. 39-56. Feeling shame does not cause people to cover their bodies; rather, according to this constructionist view, customs for covering the body result in feeling shame. Styles range from bare feet in China to the backs of Turkish hands to Alaskan lips to breasts in Bali and of freely nursing Muslim women.

627. Pevey, Carolyn, Christine L. Williams, and Christopher G. Ellison. "Male God Imagery and Female Submission: Lessons from a Southern Baptist Ladies' Bible Class." Qualitative Sociology 19 (1996): 173-93. Is Christianity misogynistic? The image of God is male, wifely submission is preached, and women are often kept out of leadership roles. This case study tries to discern how Christian women sustain self-esteem and experience happiness. It finds a considerable disconnect between their beliefs and reported practices. These women employ various strategies to subvert the expectation of submissiveness.

628. Piette, Albert. "Implication paradoxale, mode mineur et religiosités séculières." Archives de sciences sociales des religions 38 (1993): 63-78. The relation between context-specific religious practices and the individual's minimal adherence to ritual, symbol, and belief is shaped into a typology in order to explain distracted attention, ordinary emotion, and secular values.

629. Puig, Maria Elena. "Perceived Social Support, Subjective Well-Being, and the Practice of Santeria among Four Immigrant Waves: A Comparative Study of Cuban-Americans in Dade County, Florida." Ph.D. diss., Barry University School of Social Work, 1997. 30% of the sample practiced Santeria. Perceptions of well-being did not vary significantly, one wave to another. But, non-practitioners showed a greater happiness and personal satisfaction than did those who practiced Santeria. In terms of social support for family, those who practiced Santeria had less support than those who did not. Santeria asserts that it provides a system of help; that claim was not born out empirically.

630. Ramsey, Janet Lauchnor. "Gracious Encounters: Listening to Women Who Listen for God." Ph.D. diss., Virginia Polytechnic Institute and State University, 1995. Religious faith has empowered older Lutheran women to survive life crises and losses. They integrated affective religiousness into their everyday lives, enabling them to better express their emotions.

631. Rieff, Philip. The Triumph of the Therapeutic: Uses of Faith After Freud. New York: Harper & Row, 1966. Modern dissolution of a system of common belief is answered, for better or worse, by therapeutic conceptions of the self. Jung's psychology is a new language of faith; Wilhelm Reich's religion of energy positions the therapist as contemporary martyr; D. H. Lawrence's therapeutic intellectual is the new mythmaker.

632. ------. The Feeling Intellect: Selected Writings. Edited with Introduction by Jonathan B. Imber. Chicago: University of Chicago Press, 1990. Essays on Freudian psychoanalysis, religion and politics, political faith, and character extend Rieff's thesis

that social science is filling a religious role in modern life, especially as social scientists attend to human feelings.

633. Riesèbrodt, Martin. **Pious Passion: The Emergence of Modern Fundamentalism in the United States and Iran.** Translated by Don Reneau. Berkeley: University of California Press, 1993. Fundamentalism is an urban movement aimed against the loss of patriarchy and its replacement by depersonalized norms. Of concern is a vast shift in all social relations and institutions. Fundamentalisms are radical-traditionalist movements that seek, passionately, to restore the older, personal and paternal, forms of order.

634. Riesman, David. **The Lonely Crowd: A Study of the Changing American Character.** New Haven: Yale University Press, 1950. Americans once assumed and internalized adult authority. This "inner-directed" character is reminiscent of the Puritans and their ethic of old. Middle-class Americans are "other-directed," their character is more a product of their peers. Persons continue to respond to peers throughout adult life, not merely in overt acts of conformity but in the deeper way of the quality of feelings. Ironically, the American is a lonely member in a crowd, not really close to others, or to one's self. At least the older Americans had company within – the internalized parents.

635. Sabini, J., and M. Silver. "Envy." **The Social Construction of Emotions.** Edited by Rom Harré. Oxford: Basil Blackwell, 1986. Pp. 167-83. Many ways in which we experience envy is discussed. One is as transgression from moral order. One of the seven deadly sins, envy is somehow more demeaning, less pleasurable, nastier than the rest. The others implicate behavior that is evil only when excessive, and each of the other sins has its own natural goal that is inappropriately achieved. With envy, one demeans another, but that is only a secondary, more overt goal. The true goal of envy is self-restoration, but it is done at the expense of the other, and that is why it is perverse.

636. Sahin, Nesrin H., Ayseguel Durak Batiguen, and Nail Sahin. "Reasons for Living and Their Protective Value: A Turkish Sample." **Archives of Suicide Research** 4 (1998): 157-68. Study of reasons for living that guard against loneliness and depression, feelings often related to suicide. Cultural factors, among the Turkish sample, such as moral and religious values, are contrasted to the West. Those more optimistic about life were less likely to be depressed and lonely. Females in this Turkish sample were significantly more optimistic, a fact that runs counter to most international findings.

637. Scharlach, Andrew E., and Esme Fuller-Thomson. "Coping Strategies Following the Death of an Elderly Parent." **Journal of Gerontological Social Work** 21 (1994): 85-100. Friends, peers, and family members who have experienced the loss of a parent were seen as especially important resources to the 83 adults interviewed. Daughters reported receiving more help from friends, religion, and family, than did sons, who found work to be most helpful in coping with their grief.

638. Schervish, Paul G., Raymond J. Halnon, and Karen Bettez Halnon. "Culture and Emotion in Christmas: The Elementary Forms of the Spiritual Life." **The International Journal of Sociology and Social Policy** 16 (1996): 144-70. Explores anxieties that families experience at Christmas. At the center of the study are questions about human actions that "advance blessing" or "deter curse"; suggestions are made on how to heighten the former.

639. Shuman, Carolyn R., Glenn P. Fournet, Paul F. Zelhart, and Billy C. Roland. "Attitudes of Registered Nurses Toward Euthanasia." Death Studies 16 (1992): 1-15. Fear of death and attitudes toward euthanasia (EUT) were examined in registered nurses. Religious commitment, belief, more experience, and seeing death as an end led to opposition to EUT. Nurses endorsing euthanasia were politically liberal, worked with dying patients, and believed their patients should take responsibility for health-care decisions.

640. Simmel, Georg. "Faithfulness and Gratitude." The Sociology of Georg Simmel. Edited by Kurt Wolff. New York: Free Press, 1950. Pp. 379-95. Faithfulness is like momentum, in that, a committed, persistent relationship is maintained after its original emotions are gone. It can also produce appropriate emotions even if they were not originally present. Gratitude arises through interactions. In gift giving, gratitude is felt for the giving more than for the gift itself. Gratitude rises as the division of labor in society increases.

641. Simpson, Michael A. Dying, Death and Grief: A Critical Bibliography. Pittsburgh, Pa.: University of Pittsburgh Press, 1987. Thanatological bibliography spanning 1979-1989. Topics include practical care for the dying, funerary customs (American, Athenian, Chinese, Bornean, Eskimo, Japanese, Maori), ethics and moral philosophy, suffering, pain, hospices, death rituals, elegies, mourning, loneliness, dirges, and the end of the world.

642. Slater, Philip E. The Pursuit of Loneliness: American Culture at the Breaking Point. Boston: Beacon, 1970. Relevance for religion in this classic critique lies in the spheres of popular religious impulses and secularization. Americans must triumph over each other, and worship technology. These go hand in hand in consumer society. Slater points to the hole in modern culture made by a loss of meaning and by subservience to technology. The happiness of TV reflects off sullen faces. We are self-deceived by consumer emotions, and we are alone together.

643. The Sociology of Emotions: An Annotated Bibliography. Edited by Beverley Cuthbertson-Johnson, David D. Franks, and Michael Dornan. New York: Garland, 1994. Chapters, "Emotions in General Sociocultural Context," (3-18) and "Emotions in Specific Sociocultural Groups, Settings and Rituals" (19-42) are good resources for students of religion. "The Classification of Emotions," (141-216) contains a list of three dozen or so specific emotions.

644. Sorokin, Pitirim. Altruistic Love. Boston: Beacon, 1950. A comparative study of Catholic saints and American "good neighbors." The latter were mainly middle-class, middle-aged women from large families who provided sympathy and who alleviated boredom, grief, and loneliness in others.

645. ------. The Ways and Power of Love: Types, Factors and Techniques of Moral Transformation. Boston: Beacon, 1954. A Russian sociologist, banished by the Bolsheviks, spent 31 years in the US and founded Harvard's Research Center in Creative Altruism. With an extraordinary historical range, primarily in the service of a comprehensive description of what he called "the royal road of all-giving creative love," Sorokin aimed to describe the consistent practice of this emotion way. Of interest: the creative types who became great altruists, the techniques and conditions fostering love (confession, conversion, prayer, and self-mastery arts, like yoga). His work was grounded in the deep conviction that only altruistic love can save the world from destruction.

646. **Starzomski, Rosalie C. "Resource Allocation for Solid Transplantation: Toward Public and Health Care Provider Dialogue." Ph.D. diss., University of British Columbia, 1997.** Qualitative study on health resource allocation shows beliefs, values, and reasoning of members in 34 consumer and health-care provider groups. Processes included "deliberative," "examined emotion," and "emotional" reasoning. Moral reasoning was not a function of education or gender. Decision patterns depended on religion, family upbringing, ethnicity, and culture.

647. **Stein, Michael. "Gratitude and Attitude: A Note on Emotional Welfare." Social Psychology Quarterly 52 (1989): 242-48.** Status, reciprocity, and emotions are examined in the context of a Catholic food pantry and soup kitchen. The author and staff members expect gratitude from patrons. When ingratitude is expressed, eliciting anger from volunteers, the author points to status differences and feelings of powerlessness to explain the "attitude."

648. **Strongman, K.T., and Strongman, L. "Maori Emotion." The Emotions: Social, Cultural and Biological Dimensions. Edited by Rom Harré and W. Gerrod Parrott. London: Sage Publications, 1996. Pp. 200-203.** Closed Maori society has carefully guarded cultural borders. Maori emotion in ritual and lore shows the difficulties of cross-cultural study, and it presents a challenge to Anglo-Western scientific methods. Collisions and collusion of two very different cultures must be acknowledged at the outset. Building a vocabulary of emotion words is recommended.

649. **Sutherland, Cherie Olga. "A Very Different Way: A Sociological Investigation of Life After a Near-Death Experience." Ph.D. diss., University of New South Wales, 1992.** Results of interviews with near-death experiencers show changes occurring after the event. Subjects no longer fear death, and they hold firm beliefs in the afterlife. Psychic sensitivities increase, and a strong interest in spiritual growth is reported, though subjects move away from loyalty to organized religion. A more positive view of self emerges, one that is more accepting of others, more compassionate, more loving.

650. **Thoits, Peggy A. "The Sociology of Emotions." Annual Review of Sociology 15 (1989): 317-42.** Recent work goes beyond the level of concepts and broad perspectives. At both macro and micro levels, emotion is still treated as a dependent variable, although its role as an intervening and independent variable in social and cultural contexts is gaining ground; this is especially so with gender roles, small groups, social movements, and stress. Areas where little is known are cited, and a call for more empirical research is made. Implied is a fine-tuning for emotion studies in the sociology of religion.

651. **Thompson, Martie P., and Paula J. Vardman. "The Role of Religion in Coping with the Loss of a Family Member to Homicide." Journal for the Scientific Study of Religion 36 (1997): 44-51.** Emory Medical School study of religious coping in 150 Atlanta families who lost members to murder. Spiritual coping, religious support, avoidance, pleading, good deeds, and discontent were examined. Higher religious coping was expected to correlate with less distress. The sample showed high level religious coping, and it was positively related to well-being. But, religious coping related

negatively to pleading, deeds, and discontent. For homicide, religious coping related to poorer mental health.

652. Victor, Jeffrey S. "Fundamentalist Religion and the Moral Crusade against Satanism: The Social Construction of Deviant Behavior." Deviant Behavior 15 (1994): 305-34. Fundamentalism plays a vital role in the construction of satanic cult crime because it needs scapegoats to support its ideology. Symbolic interactionist study of the dynamics of moral crusades shows how collective processes work to create deviance. Deep sources of social stress activate hunts for satanists, especially when a perceived threat is linked to a legend. Claims of crusaders reach an audience willing to see evil in society.

653. Wach, Joachim. Sociology of Religion. Chicago: University of Chicago Press, 1944. The range of religious expressions involve impulses and emotions shared, by degree, in religious experiences. An emotional relation to the deity is present in bhakti. Extreme expressions are found in American revivalism, and in the emotional starvation that gives rise to sectarianism. Personal charisma appeals directly to the emotions, and it is present in the history of great founders, such as Mohammed, and in reformers, prophets and seers.

654. Weber, Max. "The Social Psychology of the World Religions." From Max Weber: Essays in Sociology. Translated, Edited, and with Introduction by H. H. Gerth and C. Wright Mills. New York: Oxford University Press, 1946. Pp. 267-301. Practical impulses for action, implied in the "economic ethic," are explored in world religions (Confucian, Hindu, Buddhist, Christian, Islamic). After considering the theory of "resentment" in class-determination, and the attempts of religious ethics to evaluate and explain suffering, Weber argues that the justification of good fortune plays the greatest role in actions related to religion. This leads to ideas about authority where "status honor" is shored up and action is based on official duty. This principle and the mutual esteem of status equals, drive economic ethics in the world religions.

655. ------. On Charisma and Institution Building: Selected Papers. Edited and with an Introduction by S. N. Eisenstadt. Chicago: University of Chicago Press, 1968. Charismatic authority is based as much (or more) on the emotional needs of the group as it is on the magnetism of the leader. Hope, despair, and enthusiasm are bases for attraction within a possible following, into which the outspoken, visionary might tap. Despair for the precarious, hope for the comfortable but uninspired, enthusiasm for those swept up in emotionally charged religious assemblies.

656. Wuthnow, Robert. Acts of Compassion: Caring for Others and Helping Ourselves. Princeton: Princeton University Press, 1991. For this sociologist of religion, Americans' altruistic feelings are best understood in stories of human kindness. Good stories hold up a vision of what society can be, and they help people to locate themselves in a web of feeling. Although personal fulfillment is one reason to volunteer, it is not the proper goal for that action, rather it is a worthy bi-product of works that affirm the religious truth of love for neighbor.

657. ------. Sharing the Journey: Support Groups and America's New Quest for Community. New York: Free Press, 1994. Wuthnow's search for the sacred in America involves a movement of small emotional support groups for nurturing individual needs, managing conflict, deepening faith through prayer, and sharing stories about spiritual life and common values.

658. ------. **After Heaven: Spirituality in America since the 1950s. Berkeley: University of California Press, 1998.** Do Americans feel at home in the universe? Institutional religion in the 1950s made for such feelings, but, new spiritual quests, partial and elusive, have come to the fore. Americans see themselves as spiritual without being religious. A profound change has taken place in how the sacred is understood. Lost faith in comprehensive forms that could make them feel more at home in the cosmos arises in competing glimpses of the sacred, in practical wisdom, in journeys — all subject to negotiation.

Part 3

Theological and Philosophical Studies

Theological Studies

659. Agaësse, Paul. "La *"fruitio"* augustinienne." **Dictionnaire de Spiritualité Ascétique et Mystique, Doctrine et Histoire,** Vol. 5: Faber - Fyot. Paris: Beuachesne, 1964. Pp. 1547-1552. The article discusses the nature of the Augustinian distinction between conceptions of *frui* (enjoyment) and *uti* (use) and its theological employment in connection with the investigation of *frui Deo* (the enjoyment of God). It an important rubric for understanding Augustine's treatment of the emotions and affectivity.

660. Anderson, Douglas R. "An American Argument for Belief in the Reality of God." **International Journal of Philosophy of Religion** 26 (1989): 109-118. Drawing upon the writings of the American philosophers Emerson, James, and Peirce, Anderson argues that the consummation of religious belief in God requires the integration of the aspects of feeling, willing, and reason in such a way as to be applicable to all aspects of life.

661. Archimandrite Chrysostomis. **The Ancient Fathers of the Desert: Translated Narratives from the Evergetinos on Passions and Perfection in Christ. Translated by Mikros Euergetenos. Brookline, Mass.: Hellenic College Press, 1980.** This collection of narratives concerning the passions and perfection in Christ from the desert fathers of the early Church is an excellent resource for understanding the theological issues concerning the passions and the spiritual life in Christ that arose and proved to be influential in the rise of monasticism.

662. Archimandrite Sophrony of the Tolleshumnt Knights. "De la nécessité des trois renoncements chez St. Cassian le romain et St. Jean Climaque." In **Studia Patristica, Vol. V: Papers presented to the Third International Conference on**

Patristic Studies held at Christ Church, Oxford, 1959 - Part III: Liturgica, Monastica et Ascetica, Philosophica. Edited by F. L. Cross. Texte und Untersuchungen zur Geschichte der altchristilichen Literatur, Bd. 80. Berlin: Akademie-Verlag, 1962. Pp. 393-400. This lecture examines the various formulations concerning the necessity of the three ascetic renunciations in order to attain Christian perfection in John Cassian and Johann Climacus. The lecture discusses the locus of the renunciation of the passions of the flesh in each of the figures.

663. Baillie, John. The Interpretation of Religion: An Introductory Study of Theological Principles. New York/Nashville: Abingdon Press, 1956. Baillie presents an interpretation of the nature of religion and religious faith in light of an understanding of theology as a comprehensive theory of religion. He addresses the topic of religion and the emotions in critical discussion of other theories of religion, the "romanticist" theory of religion (Schleiermacher) and that of theological intuitionism (Troeltsch and R. Otto). In light of those critiques, he articulates an understanding of religion as a moral trust in reality that is grounded in the consciousness of value, such that the religious inadequacy of feeling alone, its being too subjective and indefinite for a basis for faith in God, is overcome.

664. Baker, Robert O. "Pentecostal Bible Reading: Toward A Model of Reading for the Formation of Christian Affections." Journal of Pentecostal Theology 7 (1995): 34-48. The article presents a Pentecostalist hermeneutics of Scripture for the formation of Christian affections.

665. Barth, Karl. Church Dogmatics, Vol. I/1: The Doctrine of the Word of God. Translated by G. W. Bromiley and Edited by G. W. Bromiley and T. F. Torrance. Edinburgh: T. & T. Clark, 1975. In his discussion of "the Word of God and Experience," Barth argues that it is not necessary to emphasize any one anthropological locus of experience, whether it be affective, voluntative, or cognitive, as that which makes the experience of the Word of God possible. Nor is it necessary, for Barth, to regard certain anthropological loci with fundamental suspicion or distrust as the locus of possible religious experience of the Word of God. Rather Barth contends that the various anthropological loci of experience are to be understood as a totality determined by the Word of God that affects the whole person.

666. Baumgärtel, F., and J. Behm. "*kardia.*" Theological Dictionary of the New Testament. Vol. 3: 606-609. Basic reference work explicating the various understandings of "kardia" (heart) in the Old and New Testaments.

667. Bayer, Oswald. "Staunen, Seufzen, Schauen: Affekte der Wahrnehmung des Schöpfers." Jahrbuch für biblische Theologie 5 (1990): 191-204. "Amazement" (*Staunen*) and "groaning" (*Seufzen*) are presented as integral aspects of "gazing/observing" (*Schauen*) or the perception of God the Creator in Scripture according to Bayer. Bayer's argument is presented as a critique of the suspicion in Protestant theology concerning the perception of God the Creator as implying a natural theology to the detriment of a theology of the cross. For Bayer, the perception of the Creator in creation is an affective perception and not a passionless knowledge.

668. Becker, Aimé. "Poesie et mystique: le theme Claudelien des sens spirituels." Revue des sciences religieuses 43 (1969): 118-148. The essay examines the relation between poetry and mysticism in terms of an examination of the poetry and essays by Paul Claudel. It is especially concerned with explicating Claudel's appropriation of the

category of the "spiritual senses" from the Catholic theological tradition. The essay provides rich material for a discussion of the relation between aesthetics and mysticism in light of the role of affectivity with regards to the "spiritual senses."

669.   Bedard, André. **"Naître à la liberté: Les «Exercices» de saint Ignace comme «*schola affectus*»."** Science et Esprit 25 (1973): 379-408. The essay is an analytical and rich exposition of the *Spiritual Exercises* of Ignatius of Loyola as a "school of the affections" for the education/instruction and discipline of the affections.

670.   Beintker, Horst. **"Christologosche Gedanken Luthers zum Sterben Jesu bei Auslegung von Psalm 8 und Psalm 22 im Kommentar von 1519 bis 1521 und verwandten Texterklärungen."** Archiv für Reformationsgeschichte 77 (1986): 5-30. An expanded and slightly changed version of "Gottverlassenheit und Transitus durch den Glauben. Eine Erschließung der Anfechtungen des Menschen Jesus nach Luthers Auslegung der Psalmen 8 und 22." Evangelische Theologie 45 (1985): 108-123]. The essay explicates the theological significance of the humanity of Christ in Luther's treatment of the tribulation and temptations of Jesus in the divine abandonment of the cross. It demonstrates the significance of Luther's exegesis of the Psalter and its affective language is utilized christologically and soteriologically in terms of the "blessed exchange" [selige Tausch] or "joyful exchange" [fröhlichen Wechsel].

671.   ------. **Die Überwindung der Anfechtung bei Luther. Eine Studie seiner Theologie nach den *Operationes in Psalmos* 1519-1521.** Theologischen Arbeiten, Bd. 1. Berlin: Evangelische Verlagsanstalt, 1954. A classic work in modern studies of the theology of Luther devoted to the topic of the "overcoming of *Anfechtung* (*tentatio/tribulatio*)" in his theological anthropology. Distinguishing between satanic *Anfechtung* and *Anfechtung* by God, Beintker sees the divine *Anfechtung* as a divine action, part of the work of justification as mortification that leads to the overcoming of *Anfechtung* through faith in vivification. The understanding of the state of the Christian before God as *simul iustus et peccator* is understood as the tensive union of faith and *Anfechtung*, as the simultaneous union of hope and fear.

672.   Bell, David N. **The Image and Likeness: The Augustinian Spirituality of William of Saint Thierry.** Cistercian Studies Series, No. 78. Kalamazoo, MI: Cistercian Publications, 1984. An excellent study of the Augustinian character of the spirituality of William of St. Thierry's theological anthropology. It amply attends to the understanding of ecstasy in both Augustine and William and the related issue of the relation between love, affectivity (*affectus/affectio*), and intellect in William's affirmation of *amor ipse intellectus est*. Particularly helpful is his discussion of the three forms of "affection" as active, passive, and cooperative.

673.   Bernard, Charles-A. **"Fruits du Saint-Esprit."** Dictionnaire de Spiritualité Ascétique et Mystique, Doctrine et Histoire, Vol. 5: Faber - Fyot. Paris: Beuachesne, 1964. Pp. 1569-1575. The article presents (1) the understanding of "fruit" in the New Testament, (2) the sense of "fruits of the Spirit" in Paul (especially Galatians 5:22-23 - "The fruit of the Spirit is charity, joy, peace, patience, kindness, generosity, faithfulness, gentleness, and self-control."), and (3) a theological reflection influenced by Thomas Aquinas. The Pauline sense of "fruits of the Spirit" indicates a classical Scriptural context for later theological treatment of affectivity and the importance of pneumatology for Christian theological discussions of the emotions.

674. **Bernard, Charles André, S.J.** "Symbolisme et conscience affective." Gregorianum 61 (1980): 421-448. Following the research of Gilbert Durand, Bernard contends that affective consciousness is involved in the creation and the contemplation of symbols because symbols are founded in terms of an interaction between the basic drives of the human subject and its relation to the world. Symbols have both a representative function and an affective content. The movement of affective consciousness is an integral component of faith, hope, and charity in the ontological affirmation of the objective content of revelation.

675. ------. Théologie affective. Cogitatio fidei, 127. Paris: Editions du Cerf, 1984. A major Catholic systematic presentation of spiritual theology in terms of the centrality of affectivity! It intertwines both historical and systematic concerns in its presentation, which also draws upon the contributions of other disciplines. It is the systematic sequel to Bernard's *Théologie symbolique* (Paris: Téqui, 1978).

676. **Bieritz, Karl-Heinrich.** "*Verbum facit fidem*: Homiletische Anmerkungen zu einer Lutherpredigt." Theologische Literaturzeitung 109 (1984): 481-494. The essay discusses the rhetorical character of Luther's theory of homiletics through the representative consideration of a sermon by Luther. In the course of his analysis of the relation between rhetoric and homiletics, Bieritz discusses the affective character of faith as trust in relation to Luther's utilization of classical rhetoric, especially the rhetoric of Quintillian.

677. **Blowers, Paul M.** "Gentiles of the Soul: Maximus the Confessor on the Substructure and Transformation of the Human Passions." Journal of Early Christian Studies 4 (1996): 57-85. Blower's essay is a superb analysis of Maximus the Confessor's presentation of a teleology of the passions in which the passions are not negated, but rather considered as the crucial contingent vehicle in and through which incarnational grace transforms or transfigures human nature. Showing how Maximus advances the theological discussion beyond that of the Cappadocians, especially Gregory of Nyssa, Blowers provides an explication of Maximus' scriptural image of the passions as the "gentiles" on a microcosmic scale within the macrocosmic plot of the divine economy of human salvation.

678. **Bochet, Isabelle.** Saint Augustin et le Désir de Dieu. Paris: Études Augustiniennes, 1982. A magisterial study of the internal coherence of Augustine's doctrine of the "desire of God." The work is divided into three parts: the errance of desire, the elan of desire, and the accomplishment of desire. The study provides three interrelated contexts within the unity of the topic of the desire of God for Augustine's systematic treatment of the passions and the affections of the human heart. It privileges Augustine's *Enarrationes in Psalmos* in relation to the Confessions, his sermons on the Gospel of John, and De Trinitate in its presentation of the desire of God.

679. **Bondi, Richard.** "The Elements of Character." The Journal of Religious Ethics 12 (1984): 201-218. Noting the emphasis upon both character and the power of narrative, Bondi seeks to present a more comprehensive language of character in order to present a necessary and reasonable role for the language of character in the articulation of the affective and contingent aspects of human experience. In presenting a phenomenology of the self in relation, Bondi seeks to redress a lacuna in Hauerwas' advocacy of a fit between the language of character and narrative. He notes four elements of character to be attended to: the capacity for intentional action, involvement with the passions and character, subjection to the accidents of history, and the capacity of

the heart. He contends that affections and passions are the emotional counterparts to virtues and vices, not simply their analogues.

680. Browning, Don S. Atonement and Psychotherapy. Philadelphia: The Westminster Press, 1966. Browning explores the possibility of utilizing psychological analogies for the purposes of the theological construction of a doctrine of God. Three models of the atonement (Irenaeus, Horace Bushnell, and Anselm of Canterbury) are examined in relation to the essence of the psychotherapeutic relation. Browning proposes an understanding of the doctrine of the atonement in terms of unconditional empathic acceptance in spite of guilt and explores its implications for a doctrine of God, Christology, and of God's relation to the world.

681. ------. "William James's Philosophy of the Person: The Concept of the Strenuous Life." Zygon 10 (1975): 162-174. Browning examines William James' philosophy of the person in terms of two dimensions, romanticism and asceticism, and their joint influence in his portrayal of the significance of strenuous moods for the strenuous life. He links James' understanding of the strenuous life with his understanding of a finite God the chief, but not sole causal influence in a pluralistic and evolving world.

682. Brunner, Emil. Man in Revolt: A Christian Anthropology. Translated by Oliver Wyon. New York: Charles Scribner's Sons, 1939. Brunner discuses feeling or the affective within his theological anthropology in terms of the nature of being human (the psycho-physical unity of personality) and in relation to faith. Though feeling, for Brunner, has its legitimate place in the human's experience of his/her relation to God, he contends that feeling "merely" accompanies the spiritual act of faith, but is not determinative of faith itself. It cannot be ascribed any special theological significance in relation to faith as the human's relation to God. Brunner's position is illustrative of Neo-Orthodox theological wariness concerning feeling and the emotions.

683. Bultmann, Rudolf. Theology of the New Testament. Translated by Kendrick Grobel. New York: Charles Scribner's Sons, 1951, 1955. Classic discussion of Pauline anthropology and the interconnections between the fundamental anthropological concepts of body, psyche, pneuma, life, mind, and heart. Significant attention is given to the voluntary and affective character of the heart which Bultmann sees as the dominant difference between Paul's use of heart and mind, even though Paul can also use mind as synonymous with heart. He also sees a nuance of this difference in Paul's distinction between interior and exterior character of the human self, implying the possibility of the hiddenness of the interior self and a disjunction between the words of the mouth and the heart.

684. Burgess, Andrew J. Passion, "Knowing How," and Understanding: An Essay on the Concept of Faith. American Academy of Religion Dissertation Series, No. 9. Missoula, MO: Scholars Press, 1975. Burgess examines the interrelations between the concepts of knowing, believing, and feeling, centering around Kierkegaard's notion of "faith is a happy passion" expoused by his pseudonymous author, Johannes Climacus. The first chapter examines the conflict between reason and the passions in Descartes, Spinoza, and Hume, contrasting this with dispositional analyses in contemporary analytical philosophy. The third chapter presents the dispositional analyses in terms of the distinction between "knowing that" and "knowing how" and compares these discussions with Climacus' position in Kierkegaard. Finally, he examines the question of the possibility of communication between believers and sceptics in light of the implications of Kierkegaard's presentation of faith as a "happy passion" in relation to the "unhappy passion" of offense.

685. Burnaby, J. *Amor dei*: **A Study of the Religion of St. Augustine**. **The Hulsean Lectures for 1938. London: Hodder & Stoughton, 1938.** Burnaby's study is the classic work on love in Augustine's "Christian Platonism," diametrically opposed to Anders Nygren's interpretation of Augustine and the caritas tradition in Christian theology. Particularly noteworthy is his explication of the relations between will, affection, and desire in relation to love. The work also includes a valuable treatment of "pure love" in Bernard of Clairvaux, Thomas Aquinas, Duns Scotus, Luther, Francis de Sales, Fénélon, and Bishop Butler.

686. Calvin, Jean. **Calvin: Institutes of the Christian Religion**. **Two vols. Edited by John T. McNeil and trans. and indexed by Ford Lewis Battles. The Library of Christian Classics, Vols. XX-XXI. Philadelphia: The Westminster Press, 1960.** Calvin's classic work addresses the topic of the emotions in terms of his discussion of piety, both natural and Christian. In terms of Christian piety, Calvin frames his discussion in light of justification and sanctification. Calvin emphasizes the renewal of the heart through justification through faith by grace alone. Particularly significant is his treatment of faith in relation to true fear and reverence of God and its significance for the Chistian life as "the denial of ourselves" through the mortification of the passions of the flesh.

687. Chamberlain, Ava. "Self-Deception as a Theological Problem in Jonathan Edward's "Treatise concerning Religious Affections." **Church History 63 (1994): 541-556.** Chamberlain presents the evolution of Edwards' recognition of the close connection between emotional religious experience and the possibility of self-deception or hypocrisy that was inadvertently encouraged by experimental religion's emphasis upon the religious affections. The article explicates the theological steps Edwards took in order to address this problem and his increasing emphasis upon persevering Christian practice or action as a safeguard against self-deception with regards to the religious affections.

688. Chatillon, Jean. *"Cordis affectus* au moyen âge." **Dictionnaire de Spiritualité Ascétique et Mystique, Doctrine et Histoire, Vol. 2, pt. 2: Communion fréquente (fin.) - Cyrille de Scythopolis. Paris: Beauchesne, 1949, 1950, 1952, 1953. Pp. 2288-2300.** Article examines the strange and ambiguous conjunction of the terms *affectus-affectio* and *cor* in the spiritual literature from the sixth century to the sixteenth centuries of the common era. Overall, while usually used as synonymous with the expression *affectus mentis*, *animi* or *animae*, Chatillon identifies three factors contributing to an emphasis upon the affective sense of the phrase: (I) the rise of affective spirituality locating the interior or contemplative experience within the heart, distinct from intellectual knowledge; (2) the effort by certain scholastics to reduce the ambiguity of the phrase by deliberately eliminating the intellectual sense in favor of the affective sense; and (3) devotion to the heart of Christ as the symbol of the love of God.

689. Clapper, Gregory S. *"Orthokardia*: The Practical Theology of John Wesley's Heart Religion." **Quarterly Review: A Scholarly Journal for Reflection on Ministry 10 (1990): 49-66.** Clapper discusses the significance of Wesley's practical theology of Christianity as a heart-religion for the postmodern world. He stresses Wesley's theology as centered on 'orthokardia' (the right heart) and its affections as a essential mediation between orthodoxy and orthopraxis. The essay also discusses the

understanding of rationality of the affections in Wesley and the greater emphasis upon the contingency of the Christian religious affections than occurs in Schleiermacher's notion of feeling of absolute dependence.

690. ------. "True Religion" and the Affections: A Study of John Wesley's Abridgement of Jonathan Edwards' *Treatise on Religious Affections.*" Wesleyan Theological Journal 19 (1984): 77-89. Article discusses Wesley's claim that "True religion, in great part, consists in holy affections" in relation to Wesley's editorial abridgement of Edwards' treatise. Brief exposition of Wesley's abridgement of Edward's' treatise on the religious affections is given, noting both what Wesley deleted and what he retained from Edwards. He notes that Wesley deleted the second and the third of Edwards' signs of truly gracious saving religious affections, namely, their objective ground in the nature of divine things and the loveliness of the moral excellency of divine things.

691. ------. John Wesley on Religious Affections: His Views on Experience and Emotion and Their Role in the Christian Life and Theology. With an Introduction by Don E. Saliers. Pietist and Wesleyan Studies, No. 1. Metuchen: Sacarecrow Press, Inc., 1989. The book is a detailed study of Wesley's theology as affection-related in understanding Christianity as a religion of the heart containing certain distinctive patterns of affectivity. Clapper analyzes Wesley's notes on both the Old and New Testaments on the Scriptural significance of the affections, noting the linguistic dimensions of its vocabulary concerning the affections. In his analysis of Wesley's sermons, he discerns the entire pattern of salvation in terms of a process of gaining and intensifying the pattern of affections manifesting the saving grace of God. The book ends with a discussion of the import of Wesley's affective theology for contemporary theology.

692. Cleary, M. "Augustine, Affectivity and Transforming Grace." Theology 93 (1990): 205-212. The article presents a clear and lucid analysis of the importance attributed to affectivity in Augustine's dispute with Pelagius, especially in his treatise *The Spirit and the Letter*. The author emphasizes Augustine's critique of the claim for the all-sufficiency of knowledge in Pelagius' emphasis upon the role of law, teaching, and example and his affirmation of the necessity of the unity of knowledge and feeling in the dynamics of grace and freedom.

693. Cognet, Louis. "Le coeur chez les spirituels du 17e siècle." Dictionnaire de Spiritualité Ascétique et Mystique, Doctrine et Histoire, Vol. 2, pt. 2: Communion fréquente (fin.) - Cyrille de Scythopolis. Paris: Beauchesne, 1949, 1950, 1952, 1953. Pp. 2300-2307. The article discusses the senses given to the "heart" by the "spiritualists" in the seventeenth-century, for example, Francis de Sales, Louis Lallemont, Saint-Cyran, Arnauld, Nicole, and Madame Guyon. It is especially good in its analysis of the relation between the affective and the intellectual elements emphasized in the use of the metaphor of the heart, especially the developing tendency of the sentimentalization of the heart.

694. Colish, Marcia L. The Stoic Tradition from Antiquity to the Early Middle Ages, Vol. II: Stoicism in Christian Latin Thought through the Sixth Century. Studies in the History of Christian Thought. Leiden: E. J. Brill, 1985. A superb study examining the reception of Stoicism in Christian Latin authors that methodologically overcomes the weaknesses of topical approaches, source research, and biases in favor of classical antiquity. The author examines the Christian Latin authors in their own right rather than as passive mediums of transmission of classical Stoicism.

Prominent in her examination is the reception and transformation of Stoic understandings of the passions and the affections in the Latin Apologists, Ambrose and Jerome, Latin Christian poets, John Cassian, Hilary of Poitiers, Augustine, and Gregory the Great.

695. Conn, Walter E. "**Affectivity in Kohlberg and Fowler.**" **Religious Education** 76 (1981): 33-48. The essay compares and contrasts the understanding of the role and significance of affectivity in Kohlberg's theory of moral development and James Fowler's theory of faith-development. He argues, despite first impressions of their respective claims, that Kohlberg's theory of moral development is more deeply rooted in affectivity than is Fowler's theory which, while asserting that affectivity is a central dimension of religious faith, actually eliminates it from his analysis of faith in a cognitive-structural approach.

696. ------. "**Bernard Lonergan's Analysis of Conversion.**" **Angelicum** 53 (1976): 362-404. The article presents an exposition of Lonergan's notion of conversion as intellectual, moral, and religious. He examines the affective character of Lonergan's depiction of the transition from moral to religious conversion.

697. ------. **Christian Conversion: A Developmental Interpretation of Autonomy and Surrender.** New York/Mahwah: Paulist Press, 1986. Conn presents a developmental model of conversion, combining a philosophy of self-transcendence with a critical appropriation of developmental psychology, in order to evaluate Christian conversion. Drawing upon the work of Piaget, Kohlberg, Fowler, Erikson, and Kegan, Conn understands developmental transitions as conversions in the drive for self-transcendence. Conversion is presented as moral, cognitive, and affective. Utilizing insights from Lonergan, affective conversion is seen as critical for the movement from the moral stage to the religious stage in Christian conversion.

698. Creel, Richard E. **Divine Impassability: An Essay in Philosophical Theology.** Cambridge: Cambridge University Press, 1986. Creel's work provides a helpful delineation of the basic aspects involved in a discussion of divine impassability (nature, will, knowledge, and feeling) and presents a defense of the notion of divine impassability in light of modern critiques. He presents a critique of emotional passibilism in relation to God, especially as found in the wok of Charles Hartshorne.

699. Crouzel, Henri. **Origen.** Translated by A. S. Worrall. San Francisco: Harper & Row, Publishers, 1989. Crouzel's excellent systematic overview of Origen's life and thought locates the primary locus for a discussion of the emotions within the rubric of spirituality, encompassing Origen's anthropology, doctrine of knowledge, mysticism, and treatment of asceticism and ethics. Crouzel provides a clear differentiation of Origen's trichotomous understanding of the human as spirit, soul, and body from Plato's, noting that for Origen the soul has a higher element (the intellect or heart as the governing faculty bearing the spiritual senses) and the lower element (which is the source of the instincts and the passions). Origen's trichotomy is further explicated within the dynamic movement from pre-existence of the soul to the fall, to existence after the fall, to death, to resurrection, and to the apocatastasis.

700. Culligan, Kevin. "**Saint John of the Cross and Modern Psychology.**" **Studies in Formative Spirituality** 13 (1992): 29-48. Culligan examines parallels and affinities between St. John of the Cross' psychology of the passions and the affections and that of modern psychology.

701. **D'Arcy, Martin C. The Mind and the Heart of Love: Lion and Unicorn. A Study in Eros and Agape.** New York?: Henry Holt, 1947. Written in reaction to De Rougemont and Anders Nygren's portrayal of the irreconcilability between love as *agape* and *eros*, D'Arcy presents a Catholic defense of the mutuality between *agape* and *eros* through an examination of the sense of love in the Western tradition. Some of the topics covered are courtly and passionate love, love in relation to reason and the will, love and sympathy, and the scholastic philosophical and theological traditions on the relation of love and intellect (especially Thomas Aquinas on the connaturality between love and intellect).

702. **Dechanet, J.-M., O.S.B.** "*Amor ipse intellectus est.* La doctrine de l'amour-intellection chez Guillaume de Saint-Thierry." **Revue du moyen âge latin 1 (1945):** 349-374. The article examines the evolution of William of St. Thierry's understanding of the relation between love (as affection) and intellection in terms of his famous formulation of love-intellection. The author contends that this notion involves the fusion of love and intellection, but one without confusion.

703. **Delitzsch, Franz. A System of Biblical Psychology. Translated by Robert Ernest Wallis. Clark's foreign Theological Library, Fourth Series, Vol. XIII. Edinburgh: T. and T. Clark, 1890.** A classic and once standard reference for biblical anthropology which would be judged as being too influenced by systematic theological concerns, but still a useful reference for the treatment of the emotions in relation to a trichotomous understanding of biblical psychology (especially in relation to the meanings of soul and heart in the Bible).

704. **De Wette, Wilhelm Martin Leberecht. Ueber Religion und Theologie: Erläuterungen zu seinem Lehrbuche der Dogmatik. Second ed. Berlin: In der Realschulbuchhandlung, 1821.** Influenced by J. F. Fries, De Wette, a colleague of Schleiermacher at the University of Berlin, argues that religion is virtuous action inspired by feeling informed by the self-knowledge of that which is aesthetically noble and beautiful. Of the three forms of human certainty, knowledge, faith, and intimation (*Ahnung*), De Wette contends that faith in conjunction with *Ahnung* and its aesthetically-associated feeling (*Gefühl*) in order to give rise to religion. Religious feeling is presented in terms of the aesthetic ideas of inspiration, submission, and worship.

705. **De Wette, Wilhelm Martin Leberecht. Ueber die Religion, ihr Wesen, ihre Erscheinungsformen und ihren Einfluss auf das Leben; Vorlesungen. Berlin, G. Reimer, 1827.** This text is De Wette's systematic analysis of feeling (in relation to intuitive reason) as the basis of religion and the tracing of its development from fetishism to polytheism and nature religion, culminating in its most complete manifestation in Christianity. The work includes discussions of Jacobi, Fries, Schleiermacher, and Hamann as discoverers of the distinctive category of religious feeling.

706. **Diederich, Martin. Schleiermachers Geistesverständnis: Eine systematisch-theologische Untersuchung seiner philosophischen und theologischen Rede von Geist. Forschungen zur systematischen und ökumenischen Theologie, Bd. 88. Göttingen: Vandenhoeck & Ruprecht, 1999.** Diederich examines the philosophical and theological understandings of "spirit" (*Geist*) in both the early as well as the mature Schleiermacher. The examination of the development of Schleiermacher's understanding of both divine and human spirit provides an invaluable presentation of the larger thematic contexts in which Schleiermacher presents his understanding of the essence of religion as the feeling of absolute dependence, especially that of pneumatology.

707. Dockhorn, Klaus. "Luthers Glaubensbegriff und die Rhetorik." **Linguistica Biblica** 3 (1973): 19-39. Dockhorn's essay presents a critique of Gerhard Ebeling's hermeneutical interpretation of Luther's theology and its portrayal of faith in terms of its neglect of the influence of the rhetorical tradition upon Luther. Dockhorn argues that there are significant affinities between rhetoric and its attention to the emotions and affectivity and Luther's understanding of faith.

708. Doi, Kenji. "Ist Gott leidenschaftlos? *Pathos* und *apatheia* bei Origenes." **Theologische Zeitschrift** 54 (1998): 228-240. The article examines the understanding of the impassability of God in Origen. The author seeks to demonstrate that God, for Origen, suffers on account of God's love for human beings precisely because God is incapable of sufering. His argument is developed in terms of Origen's affirmation of the personality of God. His conclusion is that God in relation to Godself is both unable and incapable of suffering, but that God in relation to others is able to suffer in love.

709. Dorner, Isaak August. **Divine Immutability: A Critical Reconsideration. Translated by Robert R. Williams and Claude Welch with an Introduction by Robert R. Williams. Fortress Texts in Modern Theology. Minneapolis: Fortress Press, 1994.** Dorner's essay is a magisterial interpretation and critique of the classical understanding of divine immutability, arguing that God is not immutable in all respects and that God as love requires reciprocity between God and the world such that God can be affected by the world. Dorner contends that the affirmation of the immutability of divine love does not entail divine apathy.

710. ------. **System of Christian Ethics. Edited by A. Dorner and translated by C. M. Mead and R. T. Cunningham. Edinburgh: T. & T. Clark, 1906.** Dorner gives prominent attention to affectivity or the faculty of feeling in his discussion of the psychical elements in the moral constitution of being human (feeling, will, and cognition) and to the passions in his discussion of the virtuous purity and beauty of the Christian character in its realization of the good. Feeling involves feeling of self and intellectual and practical, feelings. He notes that thought cannot determine the will apart from the feelings. One of the few German Protestant systematicians to attend to the issue of the emotions or affectivity.

711. Doud, Robert E. "The Biblical Heart and Process Anthropology." **Horizons: The Journal of the College Theological Society** 23 (1996): 281-295. The article presents an integration of a biblical theology of the heart (as represented in the theoogy of Karl Rahner) and the categories of Whitehead's metaphysical understanding of human selfhood as process.

712. Dreyer, Elizabeth. "*Affectus* in St. Bonaventure's Theology." In **Franciscan Studies, Vol. 20. Edited by Conrad L. Harkins and Roumald Green. St. Bonaventure, NY: St. Bonaventure University, 1986. Pp. 5-20.** The essay presents the significance of *affectus* in Bonaventure's theology in terms of its relations to contemplation, the Trinity, the virtues, and the spiritual gifts of the Holy Spirit.

713. ------. "Bonaventure the Franciscan: An Affective Spirituality." In **Spiritualities of the Heart: Approaches to Personal Wholeness in Christian Tradition. Edited by Annice Callahan, R.S.C.J. New York/Mahwah, N.J.: Paulist Press, 1990. Pp. 33-44.** The essay focuses on two topics that are central to Bonaventure's presentation of the Christian spiritual life: the role of *affectus* in relation

to Bonaventure's pneumatology and the centrality of *affectus* and its roles in mystical experience, especially its contemplative aspects.

714. Dupre, Louis. "Toward a Revaluation of Schleiermacher's Philosophy of Religion." Journal of Religion 44 (1964): 97-112. The essay affirms Schleiermacher's fundamental insight into the essence of religion as the feeling of absolute dependence as essentially correct, but that Schleiermacher lacked the philosophical categories to successfully articulate it. Dupre illustrates this in terms of Schleiermacher's vagueness in distinguishing between religious experience and aesthetic feeling.

715. Dupuy, Michel. "Perfection chrétienne." In Dictionnaire de Spiritualité, Vol. 12, pt. 1: Pacaud - Photius. Paris: Beauchesne, 1984. Pp. 1074-1146. The article presents an exposition of the theological understanding of Christian perfection, an important theological locus for the consideration of emotions, in particular significant historical periods: the biblical period, the early church fathers, the Middle Ages, and the 16th-17th centuries. It provides ample bibliographic resources, both in terms of primary sources as well as secondary sources.

716. Edwards, Jonathan. "Charity and Its Fruits." In Ethical Writings. Edited by Paul Ramsey. The Works of Jonathan Edwards, Vol. 8. New Haven/London: Yale University Press, 1989. Pp. 123-397. Edwards' examination of charity or love is presented in fifteen sermons explicating Paul's "hymn to love" in I Corinthians 13. Edwards presents Christian love as that dispostion or affection that is the chief sum of the virtues, comprising love of self, love to God, and love to other persons. He discusses the virtuous affection of love in relation to the affections of sincerity, envy, humility, and anger.

717. ------. "Distinguishing Marks of a Work of the Spirit of God." In The Works of Jonathan Edwards. Vol. II. With a Memoir by Sereno E. Dwight and revised and corrected by Edward Hickman. Edinburgh: the Banner of Truth Trust, 1986. Pp. 257-277. This work presents a criteriology for distinguishing between the marks of the work of the Spirit of God, including both the common and the saving operations of the Holy Spirit. Whereas Edwards' treatise on the religious affections is concerned with the nature and the signs of the gracious saving operations of the Holy Spirit and, thus, truly gracious saving affections, this essay presents Edward's' treatment of those religious affections in conjunction with both the common and saving operations of the Spirit.

718. -------. "Dissertation II. The Nature of True Virtue." In Ethical Writings. Edited by Paul Ramsey. The Works of Jonathan Edwards, Vol. 8. New Haven/London: Yale University Press, 1989. Pp. 537-627. Edwards' essay contends that the nature of true virtue lies in the "affection of heart to Being," such that virtue is the beauty or excellence of the qualities and exercises of the heart. The dissertation is important in light of Edwards' critique of the positions of Francis Hutcheson on sympathy and David Hume's notion of instinctual kind affections as natural affections.

719. -------. Religious Affections. Edited by John E. Smith. The Works of Jonathan Edwards, Vol. 2. New Haven: Yale University Press, 1959. Edwards' classic work on the religious affections is concerned with presenting the nature of saving gracious affections and the signs of gracious operations of the Spirit of God as a criteriology for distinguishing between uncertain signs and distinguishing signs of truly gracious religious affections. For Edwards, "true religion, in great part, consists in holy

affections" (e.g., fear, hope, love, hatred, desire, joy, sorrow, gratitude, compassion, and zeal). An indispensable and influential work for a pneumatological consideration of the affections.

720. **Elder, E. Rozanne. "William of St. Thierry: Rational and Affective Spirituality." In The Spirituality of Western Christendom. Edited by E. Rozanne Elder with an Introduction by Jean Leclercq. Kalamazoo: Cistercian Publications, Inc., 1976.** The essay examines William of St. Thierry's thought on the differences between rational and affective approaches to God, situating his position in between the contrasting positions of Abelard and Bernard of Claivaux. The author argues that, though William exalts love over reason in the ascent to God, he is of the conviction that the two faculties cannot be separated, "each must be treated and considered with the other and within the other" (William of St. Thierry).

721. **Erdt, Terrence. Jonathan Edwards, Art and the Sense of the Heart. Amherst: University of Massachusetts Press, 1980.** Erdt examines the notion of the "sense of the heart" in Jonathan Edwards' theology in light of the tradition of the Calvinist psychology of the heart and its *sensus suavitatis* as the foundation for the development of Edwards' theological aesthetics. A valuable study of Edwards' theology and the relation between his discussion of religious affections and the treatment of beauty in his theological aesthetics.

722. **Eulogio De La Virgen Del Carmen. "L'Extase chez S. Jean de la Croix." Dictionnaire de Spiritualité Ascétique et Mystique, Doctrine et Histoire IV/2: Espagne - Ezquerra. Paris: Beauchesne, 1961. Pp. 2160-2164.** The article presents a succinct, synoptic account of the systematic understanding of ecstasy in the thought of St. John of the Cross.

723. **Eulogio De La Virgen Del Carmen. "L'Extase dans L'École Carmélitaine." Dictionnaire de Spiritualité Ascétique et Mystique, Doctrine et Histoire IV/2: Espagne - Ezquerra. Paris: Beauchesne, 1961. Pp. 2164-2171.** The article surveys the later Carmelite reception and understanding of the analysis of ecstasy in Teresa of Avila and John of the Cross. It provides a helpful bibliography and notes the various tendencies in later Carmelite thought as to which receives greater or lesser emphasis, ecstasy in relation to the cognitive and intellectual faculties or the appetitive faculties.

724. **Evans, Donald. The Logic of Self-Involvement: A Philosophical Study of Everyday Language with Special Reference to the Christian Use of Language about God as Creator. The Library of Philosophy and Theology. London: SCM Press, Ltd., 1963.** Evans examines the logic of self-involvement in performative speech and expressive speech. Expressive speech is verbal expression of feeling, opinion, and intention. He compares them in terms of similarities and differences: whereas expressions of opinion and intention are performative utterances, the expression of feeling is self-involving, but not performative.

725. ------. **Struggle and Fulfillment: The Inner Dynamics of Religion and Morality. Philadelphia: Fortress Press, 1979.** The book examines the nature of the struggle in religion and morality as the conflict between the "attitude-virtue" of basic trust and the "attitude-vice" of basic untrust. The constitutive elements of trust are assurance, receptivity, fidelity, hope, and passion ("allowing oneself to feel and to express one's most profound and intense feelings, rather than deceiving oneself that these do not exist and falling into apathy" [p. 20]), and those of distrust are anxiety, wariness,

idolatry, despair, and apathy. Trust as passionate participation is further distinguished from "angelic," "megalomaniac," and "daimonic" enthusiasms.

726. Fabry, Heinz-Josef. "*leb; lebab* [heart]." In **Theological Dictionary of the Old Testament, Vol. VII: *k͑ - *lys*. Edited by G. Johannes Botterweck, Helmer Ringgren, and Heinz-Josef Fabry. Grand Rapids: Eerdmans Publishing Company, 1978. Pp. 399-437.** An exhaustive philological study of the senses of the words for "heart" in the Hebrew Scriptures, especially in relation to the anthropological senses and the senses when applied to God. The anthropological senses are categorized in terms of personal identity, the vital center, the affective center, noetic center, and the voluntative center. It provides a detailed presentation of the use of the heart in relation to various affections.

727. Farley, Edward. **Good and Evil: Interpreting a Human Condition. Minneapolis: Fortress Press, 1990.** Farley's work is probably the most significant work by a contemporary Protestant systematic theologian that, in an interpretation of the human condition, attends to the "passions/emotions" in a systematic manner and not just in passing. He presents a discussion of the elemental passions of personal being as the embodied passions of subjectivity, of the interhuman, and for reality. Each of the passions is discussed in terms of their essential character, their corruption and redemption.

728. Farley, Wendy. **Tragic Vision and Divine Compassion: A Contemporary Theodicy. Louisville: Westminster/John Knox Press, 1990.** Farley interprets the problem of evil and suffering as located within the context of the tragic. In disagreement with classical theodicies articulated on the basis of divine impassability, she presents a constructive theodicy affirming the divine resistance to evil and suffering in terms of a phenomenology of compassion and love.

729. Ferguson, Harvie. **Melancholy and the Critique of Modernity: Søren Kierkegaard's Religious Psychology. London: Routledge, 1995.** The book examines the affinity and connections between modernity and melancholy on the basis of a comprehensive examination of the writings of Kierkegaard. Kierkegaard's work is presented within the context of a social and historical theory of melancholy which attends to critical perspectives on the physiognomy of the rise of modernity.

730. Fields, Stephen, S. J. "Balthasar and Rahner on the Spiritual Senses." **Theological Studies** 57 (1996): 224-241. The essay is an examination of the differences between Karl Rahner and Hans Urs von Balthasar's theologies in light of their different evaluations and interpretations of Bonaventure's doctrine of the spiritual senses.

731. Fiering, Norman. **Moral Philosophy at Seventeenth-Century Harvard: A Discipline in Transition. Chapel Hill: The University of North Carolina Press, 1981. [Chapter Four: The Passions and the Science of the Inward Man" (pp. 147-206)].** In his history of moral philosophy at Harvard University in the 17th century, Fiering examines the topic of "The Passions and the Science of the Inward Man" (pp. 147-206). His discussion includes an excellent treatment of piety and emotion in Puritanism, the understanding of the passions/emotions in New England theology, and the interrelations between theological and philosophical theories concerning the passions. The study is an important resource for the contextual consideration of Jonathan Edwards, especially in terms of his discussion of the work of Thomas Shepard.

732. Fiorenza, Francis. "Joy and Pain as Paradigmatic for Language about God." In Metz, Johann Baptist/Jossua, Jean-Pierre, Eds. Theology of Joy. Concilium: Religion in the Seventies. New York: Herder and Herder, 1974. Fiorenza argues that religious language constitutes the discernment of the meaning of joy and pain within an understanding or conviction of the general order of life and existence. For Christian theology, he contends that religious language concerning the joy and pain of God is paradigmatic in terms of how this language functions in its social and performative nature. Contra Kitamori and Moltmann, Fiorenza argues that the language of joy and pain cannot be understood directly of God, but only indirectly through the language of analogy.

733. Fowler, James W. Becoming Adult, Becoming Christian: Adult Development and Christian Faith. San Francisco: Harper & Row, 1984. Fowler examines the intersection between adult developmental theories of vocation and his developmental theory of the stages of faith. Fowler understands emotions not as transient feelings, but rather as a "deep-going, pervasive, and long-lasting set of fundamental dispositions of the heart." He identifies four clusters of Christian affections: (1) gratitude and giving thanks; (2) holy fear and repentance; (3) joy and suffering; and (4) love of God and neighbor.

734. Frankenberry, Nancy. "The Empirical Dimension of Religious Experience." Process Studies 8 (1978): 258-276. Frankenberry draws upon the philosophical and theological perspective of the thought of Whitehead in order to explicate the empirical dimension of religious experience that emerges from the fusion of physical and conceptual feelings and in relation to the valuational and generic contrast between the one and the many. The article is an essay in the tradition of empirical theology.

735. Franklin, Stephen T. Speaking From the Depths: Alfred North Whitehead's Hermeneutical Metaphysics of Propositions, Experience, Symbolism, Language, and Religion. Grand Rapids: Wm. B. Eerdmans Publishing Co., 1990. Franklin's monograph is probably the most meticulous and systematic presentation of Whitehead's theory of language in relation to propositions, symbolism, perception, and religion available. It offers an excellent discussion of the relation between language and pre-linguistic, foundational experience in terms of Whitehead's metaphysics that is significant for wider discussions of the relation between language, feeling, and affectivity. He suggestively develops the implications of his analysis of language for a consideration of the nature of religion and religious language.

736. Frohnhofen, Herbert. *Apatheia tou Theou*. Über die Affektlosigkeit Gottes in der griechischen Antike und bei den griechischsprachigen Kirchenvätern bis zu Gregarios Thaumaturgos. Europäische Hochschuleschriften, 23/318. Frankfurt am Main: Peter Lang Verlag, 1987. The monograph is a superb and comprehensive historical-theological examination of the conception of divine apathy and the theological problems which it raised in the first three centuries of the early church. The first part examines the semantic fields of the word *apatheia* and the understanding of divine apathy from the Presocratics to Plotinus in the Greek philosophical tradition, as well as in the Latin traditions. The second part discusses divine apathy in relation to ebionism, docetism, and Christian gnosticism and the response of the early apologists. The third part examines the understanding of divine apathy in Clement and Origen, Gregory Thaumaturgos, and Tertullian as the divine sublimity beyond passion.

737. Gemünden, Petra von. "La culture des passions à l'époque du Nouveau Testament: Une contribution théologique et psychologique [paper presented at Univ. of Geneva, Jan. 27, 1994]." Études Théologiques et Religieuses 70 (1995): 335-348. Von Gemünden presents a theological and psychological overview of the cultural context within which the New Testament arose as a culture of the passions.

738. Gillepsie, V. "Mystic's Foot: Rolle and Affectivity." In The Medieval Mystical Tradition in England: Papers read at Dartington Hall, July 1982. Edited by Marion Glasscoe. Exeter Medieval English Texts and Studies. Exeter: University of Exeter, 1982. Pp. 199-230. The article examines the fourteenth-century English mystical theologian, Richard Rolle, in terms of the intersection between Rolle's understanding of the theological significance of affectivity and the literary techniques used to present the drama of the process of conversion and affection in the Christian life.

739. Gilman, James E. "Reenfranchising the Heart: Narrative Emotions and Contemporary Theology." Journal of Religion 74 (1994): 218-239. Gilman outlines a theory of the emotions in order to argue that narrative and emotions mutually condition one another - emotions mediating a practical kind of universal truth and narratives mediating meanings peculiar to a faith community. "Narrative emotions," Gilman contends, provide the basis for overcoming the bias of modernity against the emotions and the dilemma of theology in the face of modernity, the tension between particularity of meaning for a particular faith community and truth in terms of universal intelligibility.

740. Gilmour, John. "Art and the Expression of Meaning." Process Studies 13 (1983): 71-87. Article exposes deficiencies in the philosophy of mind guiding expression theories of art. Ideas from Whitehead and Merleau-Ponty provide the basis for cultural analysis of artistic expression. This cultural basis for both feeling and expression is contrasted with accounts of creativity beginning from private, subjective states of consciousness. Author concludes that Whitehead himself is guilty of a version of foundationalism, even though his theory of symbolic reference counts against such an approach.

741. Gilson, Étienne. The Mystical Theology of St. Bernard. Translated by A. H. C. Downes. Cistercian Studies Series: No. 120. Kalamazoo: Cistercian Publications, 1990. The classic and masterful analysis and examination of Bernard of Clairvaux's mystical theology by one of the giants of medieval studies. Particularly significant for the topic of the affections are his discussion of the relation between love and knowledge, mystical union, and the process of the rectification of the will in Bernard's theology. The volume also includes two appendices containing rich treatments of Bernard's theology in relation to the courtly love tradition and notes on the mystical theology of William St. Thierry.

742. Graf, Friedrich W. "Ursprüngliche Gefühl Unmittelbarer Koinzidenz des Differenten: Zur Modifikation des Religionsbegriffes von Schleiermacher." Zeitschrift für Theologie und Kirche 75 ((1978): 147-186. The article provides an excellent examination of the modifications in Schleiermacher's understanding of the concept of religion in the various editions of On Religion: Speeches to its Cultured Despisers and the historical context for those changes. The article traces the different explications of the relation between feeling (*Gefühl*) and intuition (*Anschauung*) and the progressive emergence of the preponderance of the concept of feeling in the definition of religion in later editions.

743. Gratton, Henri. "Psychologie et Extase." Dictionnaire de Spiritualité Ascétique et Mystique, Doctrine et Histoire IV/2: Espagne - Ezquerra. Paris: Beauchesne, 1961. Pp. 2171-2182. The article provides an overview of ecstasy as a psychological phenomenon. Various aspects of a psychological consideration of ecstasy are discussed in relation to the criteriological categories of abnormal, normal, and supranormal, and the anthropological variables of instinctive-affective evolution, existential, cultural-social conditioning factors, and intellectual or mental factors. The article draws upon primarily Catholic reflection on the mystical aspects of ecstasy and the French psychological and psychiatric traditions. Prominent attention is given to the role of the affections and their importance in such considerations.

744. Gregg, Robert C. Consolation Philosophy: Greek and Christian *Paideia* in Basil and the Two Gregories. Patristic Monograph Series, No. 3. Philadelphia: The Philadelphia Patristic Foundation, Ltd., 1975. In light of an examination of the rhetorical genre of *consolatio* in Greek and Latin writings of the Hellenistic period, Gregg establishes the indebtedness of Basil of Caesarea, Gregory of Nyssa, and Gregory of Nazianzus to those traditions in their consolatory epistles, orations, and sermons. A chapter on the problem of "appropriate grief" in relation to consolation is addressed through a discussion of 'apathy' and 'metriopathy.' The final two chapters concentrate on the distinctive Cappadocian theological perspectives on consolation and the affections and the distinctive differences between such a Christian perspective and the Hellenistic tradition on consolation.

745. Gregory of Nyssa. "On the Making of Man." In Select Writings and Letters of Gregory, Bishop of Nyssa. Trans., with Prologomena, Notes, and Indices, by William Moore and Henry Austin Wilson. A Select Library of Nicene and Post-Nicene Fathers of the Christian Church, Second Series, Vol. V: Gregory of Nyssa: Dogmatic Treatises, Etc. Grand Rapids: Eerdmans Publishing Company, 1954. Pp. 387-427. Drawing upon Paul's arguments in I Corinthians, Gregory of Nyssa recognizes three divisions of dispositions in his theological anthropology: the carnal, the "natural," and the spiritual. The attributes of human nature, acquired through the composition of the human as soul and body by reason of the animal mode of generation, become passions when transferred to human life. Human reason, when it becomes the servant of the passions through the love of pleasure, cultivates and lends its cooperation to the passions, producing the vices. If reason assumes sway over the passions, each of the vices is transmuted to a form of virtue.

746. ------. The Soul and the Resurrection. Trans. and Introduced by Catharine P. Roth. Crestwood: St. Vladimir's Seminary Press, 1993. The passions of anger and desire, for Gregory, belong neither to the essence of the soul nor are they of the body. They are rather only among the varying states of the soul. The resurrection of the dead, as the restoration of the human to its original state, is the culmination of the process of purification such that the attributes of the soul will spiritually manifest all that belongs to human nature as the image of God. Gregory argues that there will be spiritual emotions in the next world drawn to fruition in the blessed passionlessness of divine love, otherwise there would be no true virtue or love of God.

747. Groves, Nicholas. "*Mundicia cordis*: A Study of the Theme of Purity of Heart in Hugh of Pontigny and the Fathers of the Undivided Church." In One Yet Two: Monastic Tradition East and West. Orthodox-Cistercian Symposium, Oxford University, 26 August - 1 September 1973. Edited by M. Basil Pennington, O.C.S.O. Cistercian Studies Series, No. 29. Kalamazoo: Cistercian Publications, 1976. The

essay examines the affinities between the Eastern Orthodox and Cistercian understandings of the purity and the cleanness of the heart as being both moral and spiritual. The figures in the Eastern Orthodox tradition that are examined are Evagrius Ponticus, John Cassian, and Hugh of Pontigny serves as the representative of Cistercian spirituality. The article highlights the transition in meaning that occurs between these two poles in the shift from the use of *apatheia* to that of *puritas* in Cassian and the shift from *puritas* to that of *mundicia* in Hugh of Pontigny's sermons.

748. Guillaumont, Antoine. "Notion de 'coeur' chez les auteurs spirituels grecs à l'époque ancienne." **Dictionnaire de Spiritualité Ascétique et Mystique, Doctrine et Histoire**, Vol. 2, pt. 2: Communion fréquente (fin.) - Cyrille de Scythopolis. Paris: Beauchesne, 1949, 1950, 1952, 1953. Pp. 2281-2288. The article examines the signification of *kardia* (heart) amongst Greek ascetic writers from the fourth to the seventh centuries in the common era, chiefly as representing both the interiority of the human and the entire human. The author sees two influences operating in the elaboration of the senses of the heart: the influence of biblical language in both a general sense (of the interior of the human as the locus for the affective, moral, religious, and intellectual life) and a more specialized sense (designating the locus of intelligence and wisdom); and the influence of especially Stoic philosophy. It provides a careful discussion of the relation between *kardia* and soul (*psyche*) and spirit (*nous*).

749. Gustafson, James M. **A Sense of the Divine: The Natural Environment from a Theocentric Perspective.** Cleveland, Ohio: Pilgrim Press, 1994. Gustafson highlights the significance and importance of "natural piety" for treatments of nature within a theocentric perspective. Affective responses to the natural environment can evoke a sense of the divine. A theocentric perspective, Gustafson maintains, informs and empowers a sense of radical dependence upon powers of the natural environment that bear down and sustain us and upon the power of God.

750. ------. **Ethics from a Theocentric Perspective**, Vol. 1: **Theology and Ethics.** Chicago: University of Chicago Press, 1981. In his theological ethics, Gustafson contends that theology is a way of construing the world and life in the world in relation to the divine, as a theocentric construal of god in relation to the world and the human. Such a construal is persuasive only in relation to the context of religious affections "evoked by a power or powers that limit and sustain life in the world." Gustafson understands affectivity to be identified in terms of (1) sense or awareness, (2) attitude, (3) disposition, (4) emotion, (5) object-relatedness, and (6) directional. He identifies six 'senses' or affections: the senses of dependence, gratitude, obligation, remorse and repentance, possibilities, and direction. His theocentric ethics, thus, is an ethics within the limits of the affectivity of piety.

751. Häring, Bernard, C.S.S.R. **The Law of Christ - Moral Theology for Priests and Laity**, Vol. 1: **General Moral Theology.** Translated by Edwin G. Kaiser, C.PP.S. Westminster: the Newman Press, 1961. A classic study in modern Catholic moral theology that gives systematic attention to the emotions or affectivity. Häring presents a phenomenology of the emotions (*Gesinnung*) in relation to the interior disposition and spirit that is prior to, accompanies, and sustains action in order to impart value and depth to it. It is further treated within his moral theology in his discussions of the sins of the heart and sins of action, the capitol sins (pride, envy, anger, avarice, lust, intemperance, and spiritual sloth), contritions of love and fear, and the cardinal virtues (especially fortitude, temperance, and humility).

752. **Harak, G. Simon. Virtuous Passions: The Formation of Christian Character.** New York: Paulist Press, 1993. Harak's thesis is that the virtues involve not only right action, but also right feelings. He argues that the fundamental task of the moral life is the transformation of the passions in the formation of character. He examines the biological foundation of the passions in order to claim that any account of the virtues must begin with the acknowledgment of the embodied and interrelational character of human nature. An exposition of the role of the passions and the affections in the moral theology of Thomas Aquinas and in the *Spiritual Exercises* of Ignatius Loyola complement and build upon his earlier analysis and critique of Descartes.

753. Hartshorne, Charles. **"Science, Insecurity, and the Abiding Treasure." Journal of Religion** 38 (1958): 168-174. Hartshorne contends that science and technology cannot provide security if such a security means the absence of religion. In contrast to claims that the origin of religion lies in human weakness and fear and that religion provides an illusory security, Hartshorne argues that religion can counter fears arising from insecurity and provide ideas and ideals for facing the danger and ambiguities of the future with courage and with joy in light of the divine cherishment of the passing moment in the memory of divine love.

754. Hausherr, Irénée. **Philautie: De la tendresse pour soi à la charité selon Saint Maxime le Confesseur. Oreitalia Christiana Analecta; 137. Rome: Pont. Institutum Orientalium Studiorum, 1952.** A classic study of Maximus the Confessor's treatment of the problem of "self-love" in relation to divine grace. An examination of the topic in Maximus' predecessors in classical philosophy (e.g., Plato, Aristotle, Plutarch, and Philo of Alexandria) and in the Christian theological tradition (e.g., Clement of Alexandria, Origen, Hippolytus, Eusebius, Basil, Gregory of Nazianzus, and Pseudo-Denys the Areopagite, and others) prefaces the presentation of Maximus' position. The monograph examines the psychogenesis of self-love, the corruption of self-love in terms of the passions through the vices of sin, and the converting transformation of the passions through divine grace.

755. **Hegel, Hinrichs, and Schleiermacher on Feeling and Reason in Religion: The Texts of Their 1821-22 Debate.** Edited, translated, and with Introductions by Eric von der Luft, also including a new critical edition of the German text of Hegel's "Hinrichs Foreword." Studies in German Thought and History, Vol. 3. Lewiston: The Edwin Mellen Press, 1987. Von der Luft provides critical introductions and translations of Hegel's "Foreword" to Hinrich's book on the relation of religion to "systematic knowledge, both of which were critiques of the first edition of Schleiermacher's dogmatics and its claims concerning the relation between feeling and philosophical reason as being antithetical to the objective of the truth claims of the Christian religion.

756. Hermann, Wilhelm. **The Communion of the Christian with God: Described on the Basis of Luther's Statements.** Ed. with an Introduction by Robert T. Voelkel. Lives of Jesus Series. Philadelphia: Fortress Press, 1971. Hermann's classic monograph is significant as an illustration of the theological suspicion of the affections in terms of a Protestant critique of Catholic mysticism, which Hermann sees as focusing on the interiority of emotional feelings severed from the objective power (namely, the man Jesus) and the contents of faith that do not end in mere feeling.

757. Heschel, Abraham J. **The Prophets.** Vol. II. Harper Torchbooks. New York: Harper & Row, Publishers, 1971. Heschel presents an understanding of the

Hebrew prophets through an analysis and description of what it means to think, feel, respond, and act as a prophet. The volume begins with a presentation of the prophetic theology of pathos and discussions of the philosophy of pathos (in terms of pathos and apathy, reason and emotion, and the anthropological significance of emotion in the Bible). Heschel's reflections also touch upon the problems of anthropathy as a moral problem, the meaning and mystery of wrath as an aspect of divine pathos, prophetic sympathy, and the relation of prophecy and ecstasy. A classic amongst studies of the prophets.

758. **Hildebrand, Dietrich von.** Ethics. **Chicago: Franciscan Herald, 1953.** The book is a systematic axiological ethics of value and motivation. Influenced by Scheler's phenomenological analyses of the feeling of sympathy, von Hildebrand sees feelings as intrinsically valuational in being correlated with values. Feelings are the receptive response to values. He accords them a central place in his discussion of cooperative freedom and in the relation of the sphere of response to the other spheres of actions and virtues.

759. ------. **The Heart: An Analysis of Human and Divine Affectivity. Chicago: Franciscan Herald, 1977.** Von Hildebrand's treatise is a systematic attempt to recover the significance of the "heart" and its affectivity over against its relative neglect in favor of analyses of the intellect and the will. Part One is devoted to an analysis of the human heart in relation to the difference between non-spiritual and spiritual affectivity, the "tender" and vulnerable character of affectivity, affective hypertrophy and atrophy, and heartlessness. Part Two is devoted to a christological discussion of the affectivity of the person of Jesus as the God-man, the union of human and divine affectivity. Part Three discusses the transformation of the human heart in the Christian in light of divine love.

760. **Hoffman, W. Michael.** "Structure and Origin of the Religious Passions." **International Journal for Philosophy of Religion** 8 (1977): 36-50. The essay discusses the structure and the origin of the religious passions and the question of their interrelation or intermingling in terms of a distinction between direct and indirect religious emotions. The essay presents a critique of Hume's account of the relation between rationality and the emotions and draws upon Rudolf Otto's phenomenological analysis of the numinous as *tremendum et fascinans*, correlating them respectively with the direct religious emotions of "suffering" and joy.

761. **Hoffmann, Manfred.** Erkenntnis und Verwirklung der wahren Theologie nach Erasmus von Rotterdam. **Beiträge zur historischen Theologie, Bd. 44. Tübingen: J. C. B. Mohr, 1972.** An outstanding study of the early theology of Erasmus as *philosophia Christi*. Hoffmann explicates the implications of the rhetorical and hemeneutical background for Erasmus' Christian humanist portrayal of the human. He gives great importance to the central place of the affections and their variety in Erasmus' thought, the character of the education of the affections for the ethical way of virtue, and the affections as the place of intersection for his hermeneutics and ethics.

762. ------. **Rhetoric and Theology: The Hermeneutic of Erasmus. Toronto: University of Toronto Press, 1994.** A richly detailed analysis of Erasmus as a rhetorical theologian, complementing his previous work on Erasmus. Particularly significant is his discussion of the correlation between Erasmus' scriptural hermeneutics and his understanding of the role of the affections in speech and interpretation, recalling the classical functions of rhetoric to teach, delight, and to move the will. Hoffmann presents an important study of the relation between not only language and the affections, but also

of the goal of speech and interpretation as being the interrelating of *ethos* and *pathos* for the advantage of moral virtue.

763. Holmer, Paul L. Making Christian Sense. Spirituality and the Christian Life. Philadelphia: Westminster Press, 1984. For Holmer, making Christian sense of our lives involves the fashioning and nurturing of distinctive Christian emotions in light of Christian teachings (in sermons, the Bible, and liturgy) in order to cultivate the virtues and give shape to and motivate the actions of the will. Holmer draws upon both Kierkegaard and Wittgenstein in this primer of Christian psychology.

764. Hölte, Ragnar. Béatitude et Sagesse: Saint Augustin et le problème de la fin de l'homme dans le philosophie ancienne. Paris: Études Augustiniennes, 1962. A classic monograph on beatitude and wisdom in Augustine's thought in relation to ancient Greek and Roman philosophy. It provides a rich context for the evaluation of Augustine's understanding of the affections in relation to his analyses of *fruitio* and love (as *amor, caritas,* and *dilectio*) in the presentation of his philosophical and moral anthropology. Hölte's treatment of the ontological presuppositions of Augustine's psychology of love clearly delineates the hierarchy of movements of the soul in animal life, the active life, and the contemplative life.

765. Horváth, Tibor, S.J. *Caritas est in ratione*: Die Lehre des hl. Thomas über die Einheit der intellektiven und affektiven Begnadung des Menschen. Beiträge zur Geschichte der Philosophie und Theologie des Mittelalters. Texte und Untersuhungen, XLI/3, 1966. The monography explicates the phrase *caritas est in ratione per quandam affinitatem voluntatis ad rationem* in the theology of Thomas Aquinas. In light of an exposition of the natural determination of the relation between intellect and the will, it is concerned with explicating the unity of the intellective and the affective pardoning of human beings by supernatural grace. The treatise is a detailed examination of the unity between knowledge and love in Thomas Aquinas' psychology in light of the effects of grace as *caritas*, the end of which is blessedness whose essence is in God and has been perfectly revealed in the hypostatic union. Particular attention is given to the notion of habit in light of the Thomistic understanding of nature and grace and the role of the theological virtues in the transformation of the affections of the will.

766. Hutch, Richard A. "Jonathan Edwards' Analysis of Religious Experience." Journal of Psychology and Theology 6 (1978): 123-131. The article examines Edwards' appraisal of religious experience in the context of his cultural and historical setting, psychological understanding of humnan nature, and theological analysis of religious experience. The author concludes that Edwards presents an integrated and holistic analysis of the role of reason and emotion in religious experience, which overcomes antithetical construals of the relation between reason and emotion in religious experience.

767. Inge, William Ralph. Faith and Its Psychology. New York: Charles Scribner's Sons, 1910. A classic exposition of faith that gives central attention to faith as feeling, the aesthetic ground of faith, and faith as the harmonious spiritual development of the interrelation between intellectual, volitional, and affective dimensions of faith.

768. Ivánka, Endre von. "*Apex mentis*. Wanderung und Wandlung eines stoischen Terminus." Zeitschrift für katholische Theologie 72 (1950): 129-176. The article presents the roots of the Stoic philosophical phrase ("apex of the mind") and the

769. Javelet, Robert. "L'Extase chez Les Spirituels du XIIe Siècle." Dictionnaire de Spiritualité Ascétique et Mystique, Doctrine et Histoire IV/2: Espagne - Ezquerra. Paris: Beauchesne, 1961. Pp. 2113-2120. The article surveys the understanding of ecstasy in the spiritual writers of the twelfth-century of the common era. The article looks at Bernard of Clairvaux, Richard of St. Victor, William of St. Thierry, and Hugh of St. Victor.

770. ------. "Intelligence et amour chez les auteurs spirituels du XIIme siècle." Revue d'ascétique et mystique 37 (1961): 273-290 and 429-450. An excellent essay examining the relation between love and intelligence in the major spiritual writers of the twelfth-century. Many of the issues examined are analogous to many current discussions of the cognitive character of the emotions.

771. ------. "Psychologie des auteurs spirituels du XIIe siècle." Revue des sciences religieuses 33 (1959): 18-64, 97-164, 209-268. The essay is a detailed and systematic treatment of the psychology of the human soul in Bernard of Clairvaux, the Victorines, and William of St. Thierry. It presents an excellent analysis of the relation between the cognitive and affective faculties of the human soul.

772. Jetté, Fernand. "Tradition Spirituelle du 13e au 17e Siècle." Dictionnaire de Spiritualité Ascétique et Mystique, Doctrine et Histoire IV/2: Espagne - Ezquerra. Paris: Beauchesne, 1961. Pp. 2131-2151. The article examines the understandings of the expressions "rapture" (*raptus*) and ecstasy (*excessus mentis*) in the spiritual traditions concerning the interior and the spiritual life from the 13th-15th centuries and from the 16th-17th centuries. The article contends that the difference between the two periods lies in the development of an increasing attention to the subjective and psychological aspects of rapture and ecstasy within theological considerations. It provides an excellent overview of the locus of the consideration of affectivity and the emotions and the degrees of their relative importance within the figures covered in these two periods.

773. Jewett, Robert. Paul's Anthropological Terms: A Study of Their Use in Conflict Settings. Arbeiten zur Geschichte des Antiken Judentums und des Christentums, Bd. X. Leiden: Brill, 1971. A standard reference work for understanding the Pauline anthropological terms of flesh, body, conscience, spirit, mind, soul, inner and outer man. Jewett examines each term in relation to the history of research on each term and an exegetical analysis of the senses and use of each term in Paul's writings. He emphasizes the centrality of 'heart' (kardia) for Paul's anthropology as the center of one's thoughts, desires, passions, and affections. It is particularly helpful in relation to the question of the interrelation between terms stemming from the Hebraic tradition and those from the Hellenistic tradition, such as in the tension between a dichotomous anthropology of body and spirit/soul (I Cor. 7:34, 5:4; II Cor. 7:1) and a trichotomous division of body, soul, and spirit (I Thess. 5:23).

774. Joest, Wilfried. Ontologie der Person bei Luther. Göttingen: Vandenhoeck & Rueprecht, 1967. The monograph is probably the major exposition of Luther's theological anthropology in modern Luther studies. It presents Luther's understanding of the ontology of the human person in terms of a relational ontology of the human rather than as a substantial ontology as in medieval philosophy and theology (as in Thomas

Aquinas, Gabriel Biel, and John Gerson). Joest discusses Luther's critique of trichotomous understandings of the constitution of the human being in favor of the Pauline antithesis of flesh and spirit. The antithesis is presented as the fundamental movement of the self in relation to God. This movement is explicated affectively in terms of the relations between *nisus* and *affectus*, *passio* and *raptus*. These are dimensions of the ex-centric and responsatory character of being a person in relation to God.

775. Johnson, Elizabeth. She Who Is: The Mystery of God in Feminist Theological Discourse. New York: Crossroad Publishing Company, 1992. Johnson, in her presentation of a feminist liberation theology that draws upon the resources of classical theology, argues for the legitimacy of using women's experience and language arising from women's interpreted experience for describing the Christian experience of God. The experience of conversion is fundamental for emancipatory speech about God. On this basis, Johnson argues for the reclamation of the pathos of the suffering God of compassion over against the classical apathic and omnipotent God.

776. Jones, Serene. Calvin and the Rhetoric of Piety. Columbia Series in Reformed Theology. Louisville: Westminster/John Knox Press, 1995. Jones presents a rheorical analysis of John Calvin's *Institutes of the Christian Religion*. She contends that Calvin's text and theology are rhetorically structured so as to shape, cultivate, and affect Christian piety, including its dispositional emotions.

777. Jung, Patricia Beattie. "Emotion." In Dictionary of Feminist Theologies. Edited by Letty M. Russell and J. Shannon Clarkson. Louisville: Westminster/John Knox Press, 1996. P. 83. This dictionary article highlights feminist theologies' affirmation of the full spectrum of feelings and emotions as integral to human wholeness over against the denigration and suppression of the emotions in much of traditional theology. Emotions are integral elements of embodied existence. Redemption, for feminist theology, consists not in the negation of emotions but rather in their transfiguration and fulfillment that occurs through their integration with other emotions and reason.

778. ———. "Sanctification: An Interpretation in Light of Embodiment [Bibliography]." Journal of Religious Ethics 11 (1983): 75-95. An account of character is developed on the basis of Ricoeur's philosophy of the will. Particular attention is paid to the role of the bodily involuntary in the process of character-formation in order to augment the interpretation of the moral meaning of sanctification developed by Hauerwas. And its neglect of the affections or feelings. When interpreted in light of corporeality, Jung argues that sanctification entails not only a perceptual transformation but also an affective change in the agent's value orientation, the competent retraining of the agent's emotions, and the gracious triggering of an adoptive disposition toward the agent's incarnate situation.

779. Kaufmann, Gordon D. In Face of Mytstery: A Constructive Theology. Cambridge: Harvard University Press, 1993. Kaufman addresses feelings within a consideration of subjectivity, experience, and freedom in his construction of the concept of the human. Feelings are subjective conditions of human agency that emerge in interaction with objective preconditions for agency. He highlights the relation of feelings to self-reflexivity and how feelings as modes of self-awareness are influenced by the historicity and evolution of socio-cultural patterns of belief as imaginative construction.

780. Keaty, Anthony W. "Newman's Account of the Real Apprehension of God: The Need for a Subjective Context." Downside Review 114 (1996): 1-18. Keaty critiques interpretations of Newman's account of the real apprehension of God as one within an objective context of internal perceptions and external objects. In light of Newman's assertion in his "Essay in Aid of a Grammar of Assent" that a person instinctively identifies the presence of God in the feelings which arise from conscience, he argues that Newman's understanding of real apprehension of God is more appropriately understood within the subjective context of personal aspiration for right relationship with God. Such an account would also do greater justice to the dialectical relation between feelings of conscience and language in terms of Newman's notion of the relation between those feelings and Scripture.

781. Kierkegaard, Søren. Concluding Unscientific Postscript to *Philosophical Fragments*. Ed. and trans. with Introduction and Notes by Howard V. Hong and Edna H. Hong. Kierkegaard's Writings, XII.1-2. Princeton: Princeton University Press, 1992.

782. ------. Either/Or. Parts I and II. Ed. and trans. with Introduction and Notes by Howard V. Hong and Edna H. Hong. Kierkegaard's Writings, III and IV. Princeton: Princeton University Press, 1987. Kierkegaard's classic pseudonymous work presents the aesthetic and the ethical stages of existence and the interrelation between them. An important aspect of this work is his literary portrayals of the character of love in each of the stages in its multifaceted character. A wealth of insights on various emotions, passions, and feelings are presented.

783. ------. Stages on Life's Way: Studies by Various Persons. Ed. and trans. with Introduction and Notes by Howard V. Hong and Edna H. Hong. Kierkegaard's Writings, XI. Princeton: Princeton University Press, 1988. This work by Kierkegaard is the sequel to *Either/Or*, presenting his vision of the three stages or spheres of human existence: the aesthetic, the ethical, and the religious. Kierkegaard's attentiveness to the "affective" in each of the stages of existence is correlated with his literary sensitivity to the genres appropriate to the indirect communication requisite for the presentation of each of the stages with its distinctive moods and affections. Especially to be noted is the "Letter to the Reader" from Frater Taciturnus that discusses the dialectical movement from one stage to another.

784. ------. Works of Love. Ed. and translated by Howard V. Hong and Edna H. Hong. Kierkegaard's Writings, XVI. Princeton: Princeton University Press, 1995.

785. ------. The Sickness unto Death: A Christian Psychological Exposition for Upbuilding and Awakening. Ed. and trans. with Introduction and Notes by Howard V. Hong and Edna H. Hong. Kierkegaard's Writings, XIX. Princeton: Princeton University Press, 1980. Classic discussion of despair in relation to anxiety and sin, presented in terms of an understanding of the human being as spirit. Despair as a complex sickness of the self as spirit is articulated in terms of the human being as a synthesis of the infinite and the finite, the temporal and the eternal, and freedom and necessity – whether it be conscious or unconscious. Despair increases in intensification in the progression from being unconscious to consciousness, and it is further intensified in terms of various gradations of consciousness of self before God (e.g., offense, resignation, defiance).

786. ------. The Concept of Anxiety: A Simple Psychologically Orienting Deliberation on the Dogmatic Issue of Hereditary Sin. Ed. and translated by Reidar

Thomte in collaboration with Albert Anderson. **Kierkegaard's Writings, VIII.** Princeton: Princeton University Press, 1980. Kierkegaard describes the nature and forms of anxiety in an ontological understanding of the self as a synthesis of body, soul, and spirit, but always in relation to the issue of hereditary sin. Anxiety is explicated as (1) the condition of the possibility of hereditary sin (and qualitatively distinct from fear by being related to nothing); (2) the anxiety of spiritlessness, fate, and guilt as the consequences of that sin "which is absence of the consciousness of sin"; (3) the anxiety of sin, whether about evil or the good (as in the demonic); and, finally, (4) as saving through faith.

787. Kinneavy, James L. **Greek Rhetorical Origins of Christian Faith: An Inquiry** New York: Oxford University Press, 1987. The author argues that a substantial part of the concept of faith found in the New Testament can be found in the Hellenistic Greek rhetorical tradition of the concept of persuasion. Kinneavy presents (1) a semantic argument for the compatibility between faith and persuasion, (2) a historical argument for the rhetorical framework's influence upon the Christian conception of faith, and (3) an analytical argument presenting the embodiment of the rhetorical context in various books of the New Testament.

788. Kirchmeyer, Jean. "Extase chez les Pères de L'Église." **Dictionnaire de Spiritualité Ascétique et Mystique, Doctrine et Histoire IV/2:** Espagne - Ezquerra. Paris: Beauchesne, 1961. Pp. 2087-2113. The article surveys the understanding of ecstasy in the patristic period subsequent to the period of the early church's response to the phenomenon of Montanism and the problem of "enthusiasm." In relation to the Eastern church, it examines in particular the Alexandrian school (Clement and Origen), early exegetical work in relation to the topic of ecstasy, treatments of spiritual life in relation to ecstasy (Gregory of Nyssa, Evarius Ponticus, Pseudo-Dionysius the Areopagite, Macarius, and Maximus the Confessor), and the relation between asceticism and ecstasy in emergent monasticism. From the Latin West, the article looks at Cassian and Gregory the Great.

789. Koehler, Théodore. "Thème et vocabulaire de la 'fruition divine' chez Guillaume de Saint-Thierry." **Revue d'ascétique et mystique** 40 (1964): 139-160. Koehler's essay is a superb consideration of the notion of divine fruition and the vocabulary invoked in William of St. Thierry's understanding of the notion of the love of fruition in the antithesis of desire and fruition. The essay explicates the systematic relation of *affectus* to that of fruition.

790. ------. "La *'fruitio'* dans le moyen âge latin." **Dictionnaire de Spiritualité Ascétique et Mystique, Doctrine et Histoire,** Vol. 5: Faber - Fyot. Paris: Beuachesne, 1964. Pp. 1547-1569. This article presents a superb historical overview of the mystical and speculative evolutionary paths of the reception of the Augustinian vocabulary of *frui-uti* to describe eternal beatitude (*fruitio patriae*) and the mystical experience of God in life on earth (*fruitio viae*) in representative figures in the Latin Middle Ages. Koehler notes where these two independent paths also intersected one another, especially in Bonaventure and Gerson. The representative figures treated are the following: Bernard of Clairvaux, William of St. Thierry, Hugh of St. Victor, Bonaventure, Thomas Aquinas, Ruysbroeck, Tauler, Henry Suso, Jean Gerson.

791. ------. "La théologie mystique de la 'fruitio Dei' chez Ruusbroec L'Admirable." **Revue d'ascétique et de mystique** 40 (1964): 289-310. The article explicates the theological structure of the divine fruition in the thought of the mystical

theologian, John Russbroec. The author discusses the role of the affections in his consideration of fruition and love and of the relation between fruition and consolations of divine affection.

792. Köpf, Ulrich. **Religiöse Erfahrung in der Theologie Bernhards von Clairvaux**. **Beiträge zur historischen Theologie 61. Tübingen: J. C. B. Mohr Verlag, 1980**. This book is an excellent historical-theological study of the understanding of "religious experience" and its systematic significance in the theology and spirituality of Bernard of Clairvaux. It examines the understanding of the conditions of the possibility and the various stages and presuppositions of religious experience, the material side or that which is experienced, and the experiencing subject. Köpf provides an excellent account of Bernard's theological anthropology, locating the affections as a central organ of religious experience.

793. ------. "Wesen und Funktion religiöser Erfahrung - Überlegungen im Anschluß an Bernhard von Clairvaux." **Neue Zeitschrift für systematische Theologie und Religionsphilosophie 22 (1980): 150-165**. The essay examines the problems in the concept of religious experience in contemporary theology. The author examines the work of Bernard of Clairvaux and its understanding of the characteristics of religious experience, highlighting the centrality of the affections in religious experience. The essay concludes with the question as to whether or not such a traditional and classical understanding of affectivity is sufficient for the localization of religious experience.

794. Körtner, Ulrich H. J. **The End of the World: A Theological Interpretation**. **Translated by Douglas W. Stott. Louisville: Westminster/John Knox Press, 1995.** The book presents a sustained interdisciplinary analysis of the phenomenon of apocalyptic anxiety and hope, utilizing literary studies, the history of religions, philosophy (e.g., Bloch, Heidegger, Sartre, Jaspers, and Kierkegaard), and psychology, in order to develop a theology of anxiety, more specifically, the anxiety of faith as the sublation of apocalyptic anxiety. Apocalyptic anxiety involves both world-anxiety and self-anxiety. A masterful study of anxiety and theological interpretation of anxiety (heavily influenced by Tillich and Kierkegaard)!

795. Koteskey, Ronald L. "Toward The Development of A Christian Psychology: Emotion." **Journal of Psychology and Theology (1980): 303-313**. The article presents a Christian perspective reinterpreting various psychological theories concerning the emotions (e.g., James-Lange, Cannon-Bard, and Schachter-Singer), which emphasize either the physiological or cognitive aspects of emotions. It argues that the controversy between physiological and cognitive theories is fruitless in light of a theological anthropology emphasizing the unified character of being human in relation to God and world. The article concludes with brief theological analyses of the emotions of love, joy, peace, awe, hate, sorrow, jealousy, and anger.

796. Kreuzer, Johann. "Vom Abgrund des Wissens. Denken und Mystik bei Tauler." In *Scientia* **und** *ars* **im Hoch- und Spätmittelalter. 2. Halbband. Edited by Ingrid Craemer-Ruegenberg and Adreas Speer. Miscellanea Mediaevalia: Veröffentlichungen des Thomas-Instituts der Universität zu Köln, Bd. 22/2. Berlin: Walter de Gruyter, 1994. Pp. 633-649.** The essay explicates the relation between thinking and mysticism in Tauler in terms of the experience of fear and anxiety (*Angst*) in relation to the abyss of knowing and the resurrection to life through mystical "releasement" (*Gelassenheit*) through the illumination of eternity.

797. Kühn, Rolf. "Le corps retrouvé: une phénoménologie subjective radicale appliquée à une investigation sur la corporéité." <u>Revue des Sciences Philosophique et Théologique</u> 72 (1988): 557-568. The essay is a systematic presentation of Michel Henry's phenomenology of the body within an ontology of human being as affectivity. The author also indicates the theological significance of Henry's discussion.

798. ------. "Leben aus dem Sein: Zur philosophischen Grundintuition Edith Steins." <u>Freibürger Zeitschrift für Philosophie und Theologie</u> 35 (1988): 159-173. The article examines Edith Stein's seminal work on the problem of empathy and its significance for her philosophical work and her appropriation of the Thomist philosophical and theological traditions.

799. ------. "La vie affective en psychologie et en philosophie: l'apport de V. Frankl et de S. Weil à une théorie thérapeutique du sentiment." <u>Revue des Sciences philosophiques et théologiques</u> 69 (1985): 548-562. The article examines the affinities between Frankl and Simone Weil's understandings of the affective life and the implications for philosophy and theology of a therapeutic theory of sentiment.

800. Kunz, Erhard. <u>Glaube - Gnade - Geschichte: Die Glaubenstheologie des Pierre Rousselot, S.J.</u> Frankfurter Theologische Studien, Bd. 1. Frankfurt am Main: Verlag Josef Knecht, 1969. Particularly noteworthy in this excellent study of Rousselot on love, faith, and the relation between nature and grace is the presentation of Rousselot's understanding of the relation between love and knowledge, especially in its discussion of the affective connaturality of knowledge as "sympathetic knowledge" (*Sympathieerkenntnis*). Sympathetic knowledge is the telos of all discursive knowledge in the spiritual life and is characterized as intimate and essential, direct and not discursive, affective, and infallible.

801. Lacroix, Jean. <u>Le Désir et les désirs</u>. Collection SUP. Paris: Presses Universitaires de France, 1975. Lacroix examines the political utopias of Rousseau, Saint-Simon, the young Marx, and Fourier in terms of their depiction of human desires for happiness, and the relation between passions and desires (in e.g., Lyotard and Marcuse). He situates these within the dialectic between the desire of God and desires (as found in the thought of Maurice Blondel) as the fundamental context for the evaluation of human desires and passions.

802. Lactantius. "The Divine Institutes." In <u>The Ante-Nicene Fathers: Translations of the Writings of the Fathers down to A.D. 325, Vol. VII: Lactantius, Venanius, Asterius, Victorinus, Dionysius, Apostolic Teaching and Constitutions, Homily, and Liturgies.</u> Edited by the Rev. Alexander Roberts and James Donaldson. Revised and chronologically arranged, with Brief Prefaces and Occasional Notes, by A. Cleveland Coxe. American Reprint of the Edinburgh Edition. Grand Rapids: Eerdmans Publishing Company, 1985. Pp. 9-223. Lactantius critiques the Stoics for their view of affections as diseases of the soul, offering an Aristotelian defense of the passions and affections within a Christian theological exposition of worship of God as involving the right use of the affections [see Bk. IX, especially chapters 14-19].

803. ------. "A Treatise on the Anger of God." In <u>The Ante-Nicene Fathers: Translations of the Writings of the Fathers down to A.D. 325, Vol. VII: Lactantius, Venanius, Asterius, Victorinus, Dionysius, Apostolic Teaching and Consitituitions, Homily, and Liturgies.</u> Edited by the Rev. Alexander Roberts and James

Donaldson. Revised and chronologically arranged, with Brief Prefaces and Occasional Notes, by A. Cleveland Coxe. **American Reprint of the Edinburgh Edition. Grand Rapids: Eerdmans Publishing Company, 1985. Pp. 259-280.** This treatise is directed mainly against Epicureans and Stoics who contended that human deeds could not produce emotions of pleasure or anger in God. Lactantius argues that God's love of the good entails God's hatred of evil.

804. Lamm, Julia A. "The Early Philosophical Roots of Schleiermacher's Notion of *Gefühl*, 1788-1794." Harvard Theological Review **87 (1994):67-105.** Lamm presents an excellent historical study of the early genesis of Schleiermacher's understanding of feeling antecedent to the publication of his *Speeches on Religion* in 1799. Particularly interesting is her presentation of the influence of Spinoza upon Schleiermacher in correcting aspects of the Kantian critical philosophy in terms of ontology. The essay closes with questions concerning the significance of Schleiermacher's early philosophical thought on feeling as philosophical rather than theological.

805. Land, Steven J. Pentecostal Spirituality: A Passion for the Kingdom. **Journal of Pentecostal Theology Supplement Series 1. Sheffield: Sheffield Academic Press, 1993.** In his constructive theological interpretation of the Pentecostal tradition, Land understands the character or fruit of the Spirit to be Pentecostal affections. Those affections are objective, relational, and dispositional gifts of the apocalyptic outpouring of the Spirit. Land analyzes in particular three affections and their attendant affections: gratitude (praise, thanksgiving); compassion (love, longing); and courage (confidence, hope). He also examines the importance of discernment for the identification, cultivation, and preservation of true affections, the power of prayer to shape and express the affections, and the claim that the chief affection is the passion for the kingdom of God.

806. Laney, James T. "Characterization and Moral Judgments." Journal of Religion **55 (1975): 405-414.** The article argues for the inadequacy of any ethics that does not attend to the importance of feeling and the emotions within and emergent from ordinary experience. Moral reflection must not only attend to the moral analysis of the categorization of reason, but also to the reflection occurring in the process of characterization of the moral life in an ethics of virtue or character and in novels.

807. Langer, Otto. "Affekt und *ratio*." In Zisterziensische Spiritualität: Theologische Grundlagen, funktionale Voraussetzungen und bildhafte Ausprägungen im Mittelalter. **Compiled by Clemens Kasper and Klaus Schreiner. Studien und Mitteilungen zur Geschichte des Benediktinerordens und seiner Zweige. Ergänzungsband; 34. St. Ottilien: EOS Verlag, 1994.** Langer's essay is a superb articulation of the understanding of the relation between affect and reason in the Cistercian theological and spiritual traditions.

808. Lash, Nicholas. Easter in Ordinary: Reflections on Human Experience and the Knowledge of God. **Charlottesville: University Press of Virginia, 1988.** Lash provides valuable theological reflections on the significance of affectivity in religious experience and the knowledge of God in the course of his discussions of the essence of religious experience in relation to William James, contemplation and piety in mysticism and theology, Hegel, Kant, Fries, and Schleiermacher, and Von Hügel's notion of the "fringe of feeling" in experience and religion.

809. Lauritzen, Paul. "Emotions and Religious Ethics." __Journal of Religious Ethics__ 16 (1988): 307-324. The essay challenges the traditional dichotomy between reason and emotion, arguing that the recovery of the cognitive structure of emotion provides a basis for the reassessment of the role which emotions play in the moral life. The article sketches the significance of constructivist theories of the emotions for religious ethics in terms of its explanatory aid in accounting for how religious understandings of human life and history bring about significant transformations in the life of the believer. This is illustrated in terms of the effect of religious conceptions of the moral life have upon the emotion of anger.

810. ------. "Reflections on the Nether World: Some Problems for A Feminist Ethic of Care and Compassion." __Soundings: An Interdisciplinary Journal__ 75 (1992): 383-402. Saluting the effort of feminist ethics to recover the importance of the emotions for the moral life, the author seeks to show that the promise of feminist ethics of compassion and care can only come to fruition if it avoids reinforcing traditional stereotypes of women, reason, and emotion. He argues that feminist ethics must attend to a fundamental consideration of the constructivist character of the emotions and the question of the social practices in which particular emotions are embedded.

811. ------. __Religious Belief and Emotional Transformation: A Light in the Heart__. Lewisburg: Bucknell University Press, 1992. The book is a systematic exposition of the relation between religious belief and emotional transformation. The argument draws upon constructivist theories of the emotions which conceive of the emotions primarily as culturally constructed rather than as biologically basic.

812. Lefèvre, André. "Usage Biblique [of *cor* et *cordis affectus*]." __Dictionnaire de Spiritualité Ascétique et Mystique, Doctrine et Histoire__, Vol. 2, pt. 2: Communion fréquente (fin.) - Cyrille de Scythopolis. Paris: Beauchesne, 1949, 1950, 1952, 1953. Pp. 2278-2281. The article surveys the usage of "heart" and its various semantic fields and their relations to other vocabulary in the Bible. It gives great attention to the locus of sentiments and affections vis-à-vis the intersecting semantic fields associated with the words "heart" and "soul."

813. Levy, Eric P. "The Two Natures of Christ: Suffering Victim and Pitying Witness." __Toronto Journal of Theology__ 5 (1989): 57-62. The essay presents an interpretation of the two natures of Christ in the affective categories of suffering and pity.

814. Lewis, Paul. "The Springs of Action": Jonathan Edwards on Emotions, Character, and Agency." __Journal of Religious Ethics__ 22 (1994): 275-297. The essay discusses the Edwardsean claim that religious affections are the "springs of action" in terms of their intrinsic significance in the formation of moral character and the agency of such a character. The author relates Edwards' thought to contemporary discussions of moral agency and character.

815. Lilla, Salvatore R. C. __Clement of Alexandria: A Study in Christian Platonism and Gnosticism__. Oxford Theological Monographs. Oxford: Oxford University Press, 1971. The author presents a historical critique of those positions which either stress Clement's dependence upon Stoicism or the Christian character of his thought (as in Völker's interpretation), even if his language is borrowed from Greek philosophy. Lilla attempts to demonstrate the cultural and philosophical background for Clement's understanding of the passions and the moral life as being that of Philo, Middle Platonism, and Neoplatonism. He argues that Clement diverges from these influences in

his affirmation of Christ the Logos as the one who has the task of healing the passions through educating the soul unto gradual perfection.

816. Lonergan, Bernard. **Method in Theology**. New York: Herder, 1972. Lonergan presents an affective understanding of religious conversion as the sublation of moral and intellectual conversion. Religious conversion is understood as operative grace, namely, "being grasped by ultimate concern" and "other-worldly falling in love." Operative grace as religious conversion is the replacement of the heart of stone by the heart of flesh that initiates the gradual movement towards the transformation of the whole of one's living and feeling.

817. Lorenz, Rudolf. "Die Herkunft des augustinischen *frui Deo*." **Zeitschrift für Kirchengeschichte** 64 (1952-1953): 34-60. The essay is a classic historical-theological study of the origins and structure of Augustine's notion of the enjoyment of God and its systematic importance for Augustine's thought.

818. Macquarrie, John. **Principles of Christian Theology**. Second Edition. New York: Charles Scribner's Sons, 1977. Macquarrie's systematics is divided into three sections: philosophical, symbolic, and applied theology. Within his philosophical theology, he discusses the dialectic of constitutive and fundamental affections of anxiety and hope in relation to the polarities of human existence: possibility and facticity, rationality and irrationality, responsibility and impotence. This forms the background for his analysis of revelation and the necessary role of affective moods in revelatory experience. He argues for the trustworthiness of insights or awareness that are mediated through affective states, which are intertwined with cognition and volition.

819. ------. **Studies in Christian Existentialism: Lectures and Essays**. Philadelphia: Westminster Press, 1965. In "Feeling and Understanding" (pp. 31-42), Macquarrie argues for the theological relevance of religious feeling and the disclosive character of affective states. Utilizing phenomenological insights from Heidegger's analyses of feeling, he maintains that the belongingness of existential understanding to feeling is a presupposition for the affirmation of the cognitive character of religion and that disclosive feeling-states are a presupposition of religion. He underscores the apologetic importance of attending theologically to feelings as significant in arising from and disclosing the structures of human existence which can only rest in God. In "The Seven Gifts of the Holy Ghost" (pp. 247-273), he explores the significance of affections in application to a particular theological topic, namely, the spiritual gifts of the Holy Spirit.

820. Macquire, Daniel C. "The Feel of Truth." In **The Moral Choice**. Garden City: Doubleday & Company, 1978; Minneapolis: Winston Press, 1979. Pp. 281-308. Macquire analyzes affective knowledge and its practicality by understanding feeling and character as conduits of truth. For Macquire, moral knowledge is born in awe and affectivity.

821. ------. "The Knowing Heart and the Intellectualistic Fallacy." In **The Moral Revolution: A Christian Humanist Vision**. San Francisco: Harper & Row, 1986. Pp. 254-270, 287-289. The essay argues for the affective basis of moral awareness and knowledge through a critique of what Macquire terms the "intellectualistic fallacy" in ethics. The essay examines the role of practical reason in Thomas Aquinas and his treatment of the affective component of moral knowledge in terms of connaturality. It also examines the development of the topic of affective knowledge of the good and the

sacred in the seventeenth-century commentator upon Thomas, John of St. Thomas, as preparatory for Macquire's own proposals.

822. Mantzaridis, Georgios I. **The Deification of Man: St. Gregory Palamas and the Orthodox Tradition.** Translated by Liadain Sherrard with a Foreword by Bishop Kallistos of Diokleia. Contemporary Greek Theologians, no. 2. Crestwood: St. Vladimir's Seminary Press, 1984. This book is devoted to an explication of deification of the human as found primarily in the theology of St. Gregory Palamas. It provides a very helpful analysis of the topic of "dispassion" (*apatheia*) in relation to the moral aspects of deification in the Christian life's practice of asceticism and its "sorrowful joy" (the transformation of sorrow into joy). Dispassion is the conversion of the human soul from evil passions that arise from the misuse of the powers of the soul, the submission of the incensive and appetitive faculties to intelligence of the heart.

823. Maurer, Wilhelm. **Der junge Melanchthon zwischen Humanismus und Reformation.** Vol. 2: **Der Theologe.** Göttingen: Vandenhoeck & Ruprecht, 1969. Maurer's study of the early Melanchthon's theology (as influenced by both the humanist tradition and the Reformation theology of Luther) provides superb analyses of (1) the role and significance of the emotions or affections in his theological anthropology in relation to sin and grace and (2) the relation between faith and rapture (*raptus*) in light of the work of the Spirit. Maurer amply documents both the influence of Jean Gerson upon Melanchthon's understanding of the affections as well as his departures from various aspects of Gerson's position.

824. Maxsein, A. *Philosophia cordis.* **Das Wesen der Personalität bei Augustinus.** Neues Forum. Salzburg: Otto Müller Verlag, 1966. The author presents a systematic (possibly too systematic) interpretation of Augustine's theological anthropology as a philosophy of the heart. Despite its possible over-systematization as a dialogical personalism, the book presents extensive discussion of Augustine's understanding of the affections and passions and their interrelation to other aspects of Augustine's thought, namely, his metaphysics of knowledge and doctrine of illumination.

825. McCandless, J. Bardarah. "Christian Commitment and a 'Docetic' View of Human Emotions." **Journal of Religion and Health** 23 (1984): 125-137. Paper focuses on biblical passages which are susceptible to three forms of "docetic" interpretation: denial of unpleasant feelings often in the name of Christian joy; with possible damaging emotional or physical consequences; denial of human development and the possible influence of the past on the present emotional and religious experience; and denial of human value through passive acceptance of what seems to be inevitable by saying "Thy will be done."

826. McCarthy, Vincent A. **The Phenomenology of Moods in Kierkegaard.** The Hague/Boston: Nijhoff, 1978. A systematic discussion of Kierkegaard's phenomenology of moods and their significance in the dialectical unfolding of the stages of human existence, from the aesthetic to the moral to the religious. McCarthy's book is a finely nuanced treatment of Kierkegaard's multifaceted analysis of moods and their ambiguities.

827. ------. "Psychological Fragments: Kierkegaard's Religious Psychology." In **Kierkegaard's Truth: The Disclosure of the Self.** Edited by Joseph H. Smith. Psychiatry and the Humanities, Vol. 5. New Haven: Yale University Press, 1981. Pp. 235-266. An excellent survey of Kierkegaard's religious psychology which pays

particular attention to moods related to reflection and self-consciousness. McCarthy identifies four moods of religious subjectivity that have no external object and are essentially about the self: irony as the mood of rebellion against finitude; anxiety as the mood of possibility; "religious melancholy" (the mood of longing for the infinite); and despair as the mood of sin-consciousness.

828. McGinn, Bernard. "The Abyss of Love: The Language of Mystical Union among Medieval Women." In The Joy of Learning and the Love of God: Studies in Honor of Jean Leclercq. Edited by E. Rozanne Elder. Cistercian Studies Series: No. 160. Kalamazoo: Cistercian Publications, 1995. Pp. 95-120. McGinn's essay presents the increased emphasis upon the affective character of the language for mystical union amongst medieval women mystics in distinction from more intellectual emphases in mystical theology of the medieval period.

829. ------. "Love, Knowledge, and Mystical Union in Western Christianity: Twelfth to Sixteenth Centuries." Church History 56 (1987): 7-24. The essay is a superb presentation of the Christian conceptions of mystical union with God in relation to the various accounts of the union and interaction between love and knowledge. McGinn concludes, at the end of his survey, that the contrast between "intellectual" and "affective" mysticism is not a helpful category.

830. ------, ed. Three Treatises on Man: A Cistercian Anthropology. Cistercian Fathers Series: No. 24. Kalamazoo: Cistercian Publications, 1977. The volume presents three Cistercian treatises in theological anthropology: William of St. Thierry's "the Nature of Body and Soul," Isaac of Stella's "Letter on the Soul," and the anonymous "Treatise on the Spirit and the Soul." McGinn's introduction helpfully sketches the background of these texts, citing the influence of Gregory of Nyssa and Nemesius, and their place in anthropological discussions in the twelfth century. The treatises present the diversity in Cistercian formulations and the different loci for the consideration of the emotions.

831. McWilliams, Warren. The Passion of God: Divine Suffering in Contemporary Protestant Theology. Macon: Mercer University Press, 1985. McWilliams examines the topic of the "passion of God" in relation to the representative work of Jürgen Moltmann, James Cone, Geddes MacGregor, Kazoh Kitamori, Daniel Day Williams, and Jung Young Lee. He argues that the compassionate love of God identifies with human anguish and misery in the passion of God, in marked opposition to traditional notions of divine impassability. He proposes the consideration of God as "wounded healer."

832. Meland, Bernard. "The Appreciative Consciousness." In Essays in Constructive Theology: A Process Perspective. Edited by Perry LeFevre. Chicago: Exploration Press, 1988. Pp. 105-124. Drawing upon the thought of William James, Whitehead, Henry Nelson Wieman, and Dewey, Meland seeks to amplify the meaning and condition of appreciative awareness beyond a restriction to the confines of a strictly cognitive event. Central to this expansion of the meaning and condition of appreciative awareness is the role of affectivity in relating the cognition of events and their relation to the self within a feeling-context. Affective discrimination of events within its context allows for the disciplined, mutual working of mind and sensibilities, such that legitimate awareness can be extended to aesthetics and religion.

833. ------. **Faith and Culture**. New York: Oxford University Press, 1953. Within the premise of immanence Meland seeks to present a reconstruction of the theological orientation of liberal theology such that it can avail itself of the dynamic of the Christian faith as its organizing principle. The volume presents an analysis of the nature and role of faith as a context of feeling and expression, the structure of experience. For Meland, faith is understood to be appreciative awareness, "the attitude of trust assuming an explicit cognitive concern" (p. 120).

834. ------. "Religious Awareness and Knowledge." In **Essays in Constructive Theology: A Process Perspective**. Edited by Perry LeFevre. Chicago: Exploration Press, 1988. Pp. 225-256. Within the tradition of empirical theology, Meland examines the relation between awareness and knowledge, the specific nature of religious awareness, and the character of religious knowledge arising from religious awareness. Feeling and emotion are crucial to the difference between awareness and knowledge in terms of an awareness of intensified meaning. Religious awareness is a particular form of attention disclosing a distinctive pattern of relations, namely, those marked by the felt insight of the good, "the growth of connections making for mutual value and meaning" as the over-plus of the empirically given.

835. ------. "The Significance of Religious Sensibility and Wonder in Any Culture." In **The Secularization of Modern Cultures**. New York: Oxford University Press, 1966. Pp. 116-140. In light of the process of secularization as a dissipating force, rendering all historic religions and their specific sensibilities problematic and apparently irrelevant in a technological age, Meland argues for the relevancy of such sensibilities in light of the elemental sense of wonder and joy as religious sensibility, intrinsic to the dimensions of human existence. Such a sensibility has to do with "the response of wonder and sensitivity to what inheres in the human structure as an intimation of A-More-Than-Human-Reality, to which the human structure is elated as creature to ground, and toward it has instinctive outreaches" (p. 136).

836. Meslin, Michel. **L'Expérience humaine du Divin: Fondements d'une anthropologie religieuse**. Théologie et sciences religieuses: Cogitatio fidei 153. Paris: Les Éditions du Cerf, 1988. Presenting a religious anthropology in interdisciplinary dialogue (as the sequel to his earlier study *Pour une science des religions* [Paris: Seuil, 1973]), Meslin affirms the affective character of religious experience and its human subject, in relation to the sacred. The analysis is presented in relation to the thought of Schleiermacher, Rudolf Otto, and William James.

837. Metzger, Günther. **Gelebter Glaube. Die Formierung reformatorischen Denkens in Luthers erster Psalmenvorlesung, dargestellt am Begriff des Affekts**. Forschungen zur Kirchen- und Dogmengeschichte, Bd. 14. Göttingen: Vandenhoeck & Ruprecht, 1964. Metzger's book is concerned with the topic of the affections as an integral element in the early Luther's theology as found in his early lectures on the Psalms. After examining the historical background of the topic of the affections in antiquity, the New Testament, Augustine, and Thomas Aquinas, Metzger analyses the centrality of the notion of "affectus" in Luther's exegesis in relation to faith (i.e., the interrelation between fides, intellectus, affectus, and credere), to christology and soteriology, and in connection with the hermeneutical question of the understanding of Scripture.

838. Milhaven, J. Giles. "Asceticism and the Moral Good: A Tale of Two Pleasures." In **Asceticism**. Edited by Vincent L. Wimbush and Richard Valantasis

with the assistance of Gary L. Byron and William S. Love. New York: Oxford University Press, 1995. Pp. 375-394. Giles presents a fascinating discussion of the question of what pleasures are worth having for themselves through a comparison of Plato's discussion in *Philebus* and the mystical theology of the Beguine of the Low Countries in Europe in the early thirteenth century, Hadewijch. The essay, especially in its presentation of Hadewijch, discusses the relation between feeling, pleasure, and the good.

839. Miller, Randolph Crump. "Meland: Worship and his Recent Thought" ["Reply B. E. Meland"]. American Journal of Theology and Philosophy 5 (1984): 96-106. Sketching the development of Meland's theological thought in light of his reception of the work of William James, G. B. Smith, Henry Nelson Wieman, and Whitehead, the essay explicates Meland's understanding of worship as grounded in "appreciative consciousness" of God as creative passage, the depth-dimension encompassing suffering and tragedy. The affective character of appreciative awareness, especially in worship, means that one is responsive to that "which is more than we can think."

840. Millet, Olivier. "*Docere/Movere*: Les catégories rhétoriques et leurs sources humanistes dans la doctrine calvinienne de la foi." In *Calvinus Sincerioris Religionis Vindex*: Calvin as Protector of the Purer Religion. Edited by Wilhelm H. Neuser and Brian G. Armstrong. Sixteenth Century Essays & Studies, Vol. XXXVI. Kirksville: Sixteenth Century Journal Publishers, Inc., 1997. Pp. 35-52. The essay presents a rhetorical approach to the theology of Jean Calvin in terms of the humanist tradition which informed Calvin's theology, namely, Lorenzo Valla, Erasmus, Dolet, Budé, and Bucer. It provides an excellent account of the intersection of theological anthropology and rhetorical anthropology in relation to the affective character of faith in Calvin.

841. Minnis, Alastair J. "The Sources of *The Cloud of Unknowing*: A Reconsideration." In The Medieval Mystical Tradition in England: Papers read at Dartington Hall, July 1982. Edited by Marion Glasscoe. Exeter Medieval English Texts and Studies. Exeter: University of Exeter, 1982. Pp. 63-75. Minnis presents the *The Cloud of Unknowing*'s affirmation of the superiority of the power of affection over that of the understanding in relation to the long-standing medieval debate on the nature of theology as being either affective or rational and intellectual. He specifically discusses the influence of Thomas Gallus and his version of Victorine spirituality (especially that of Richard of St. Victor). The essay provides a superb analysis of the relation between intellectus and affectus in Gallus, Richard of St. Victor, and *The Cloud of Unknowing*.

842. Miquel, P. "Περα: Contribution à l'étude du vocabulaire de l'expérience religieuse dans l'oeuvre de Maxime le Confesseur." Studia Patristica, Vol. V: Papers presented to the Fourth International Conference on Patristic Studies held at Christ Church, Oxford, 1963 - Part I: Editiones, Critica, Philologica, Biblica. Edited by F. L. Cross. Texte und Untersuchungen zur Geschichte der altchristilichen Literatur, Bd. 92. Berlin: Akademie-Verlag, 1966. Pp. 355-361. The essay is a nuanced study of the manifold meanings associated with the word which Maximus the Confessor uses for "experience." The author examines in particular the relation and differences between knowledge and experience, items central to comprehending Maximus' understanding of the role of affectivity in religious experience.

843. **Moltmann, Jürgen. God in Creation: A New Theology of Creation and the Spirit of God. The Gifford Lectures 1984-1985. Translated by Margaret Kohl. San Francisco: Harper & Row, 1985.** Recalling Friedrich Oetinger's thesis that "embodiment is the end of all God's works, " Moltmann presents a theological anthropology that emphasizes the perichoretic pattern of body and soul in contrast to those anthropologies that emphasize the primacy and sovereignity of the soul over the body such as in Plato, Descartes, and Karl Barth (who argues for "the ministering body of a ruling soul"). In light of understanding creation as being "in the Spirit of God," Moltmann contends that a correlative holistic anthropology can construe the perichoretic relation between body and soul in terms of a relationship of community, partnership, and mutual influence such that there can be a theological recovery of the emotions and feelings.

844. ------. **The Spirit of Life: A Universal Affirmation. Translated by Margaret Kohl. Minneapolis: Augsburg Fortress Publishers, 1992.** Moltmann's pneumatology is founded upon a recovery of the dimensions of experience and their implications through the overcoming a false alternative between divine revelation and the human experience of the Holy Spirit. Even though Moltmann does not systematically address the topic of the emotions or present extensive examination of particular emotions, his work theologically enables the recovery of crucial theological loci that were traditionally of the utmost importance for a consideration of the emotions by theologians.

845. **Montmasson, E. "La Doctrine de L'ΑΠΑΘΕΙΑ d'après Saint Maxime." Échos d'Orient 14 (1911): 36-41.** The article examines the various senses of "apathy" in the thought of Maximus the Confessor. Apathy is neither the radical annihilation of the passions nor the constant habitual struggle against the violent assaults of concupiscence. The author explicates four basic senses to apathy in Maximus: abstention from all vicious corporeal acts, purity of spirit, purity of heart, and deliverance from useless or indifferent thoughts.

846. **Morel, Georges. Le Sens de l'existence selon Saint Jean de la Croix, Vol. II: Logique. Théologie, t. 36. Paris: Aubier Éditions Montaigne, 1960.** Morel's is a magisterial study of the logical structure of the movement of mystical experience in the theology of St. John of the Cross. He provides a superb analysis of St. John's treatment of the nature of spiritual sentiments, their relation to the will and the understanding, and the distinction between those pertaining to the will and those pertaining to the substance of the soul.

847. **Morissey, Michael P. "Reason and Emotions: Modern and Classical Views on Religious Knowing." Horizons: The Journal of the College Theology Society 16 (1989): 275-291.** The essay considers the work of John Macmurray in order to recover the authentic character of human emotional life for the sake of the possibility of authentic religious knowledge. Relating Macmurray's personalist thought to Plato's myth of the erotic soul and Pascal's "reasons of the heart," Morissey presents a retrieval of the notion of "emotional knowledge" (beyond the infamous dualism between reason and emotion) that will be the condition for authentic human love and the medium for divine revelation.

848. **Mouroux, Jean. The Christian Experience: An Introduction to a Theology. Translated by George Lamb. New York: Sheed and Ward, Inc., 1954.** The book presents a philosophical inquiry into the nature of experience and a theological inquiry into the possibility and the nature of religious and specifically Christian religious experience. Moureaux contends that Christian spiritual experience is not an affective experience, but rather an integration of an affective experience. Integration of affective

experience means not the negation, but rather, in Christian terms, the purification and "assumption" of feeling. He draws upon Thomas Aquinas in treating affectivity in relation to the three supernatural virtues of faith, hope, and charity and St. John of the Cross in relation to "spiritual feeling."

849. **Mueller, John J., S.J. "Appreciative Awareness: The Feeling-Dimension in Religious Experience."** Theological Studies **45 (1984): 57-79.** Mueller utilizes the thought of Bernard Meland on "appreciative knowledge" in order to examine the particular manner in which a person in the feeling dimension of religious experience is in communication with God. The essay also provides a helpful analysis of the understanding of "feeling" in Meland's theology, informed by the Anglo-American tradition of empirical theology.

850. ------. Faith and Appreciative Awareness. **Washington, D.C.: University of Press of America, 1981.** Mueller's monography is a systematic presentation of the theology of Bernard Meland that focuses on Meland's interpretation of faith in terms of "appreciative awareness."

851. **Muller, Richard A. "*Fides* and *Cognitio* in Relation to the Problem of Intellect and Will in the Theology of John Calvin."** Calvin Theological Journal **25 (1990): 207-224.** The article examines the question of the relation between faith and knowledge in relation to Calvin's understanding of intellect and will. It presents a critique of intellectualist interpretations of Calvin's understanding of faith and argues for the importance of the interpretation of the fiducial character of faith in light of the affections of the will as heart. He argues that Calvin's conception of faith as *cognitio* combines *cognitio intellectiva* with *cognitio affectiva*.

852. **Nellas, Panayiotis.** Deification in Christ: Orthodox Perspectives on the Nature of the Human Person. **Translated by Norman Russell with a foreword by Bishop Kallistos of Diokleia. Contemporary Greek Theologians, no. 5. Crestwood: St. Vladimir's Seminary Press, 1987.** Nellas presents a systematic examination of the Orthodox understanding of deification and the nature of the human person. It provides an excellent overview of the topic, especially in terms of its discussion of the passions and dispassion (*apatheia*) in the nature, the living, and the fruits of the spiritual life of the Christian. He understands deification as the "Chrisification" of the human and the emotions in the transformation of creation through grace into ecclessial communion.

853. **Nemesius of Emesa. "On the Nature of Man." In** Cyril of Jerusalem and Nemesius of Emesa. **Edited by William Telfer. The Library of Christian Classics, Vol. IV. Philadelphia: The Westminster Press, 1955. Pp. 203-453.** Often ascribed to Gregory of Nyssa in church history, Nemesius's treatise is a theological anthropology undertaken as an apologetic for providence in relation to classical thought, both philosophical and medical. His discussion of the passions is founded upon an account of the unity between the soul and the body. Passions pertain to the irrational part of the soul susceptible to reason and are divisible into the passions of concupiscence and anger. Further division elicits four forms: desire, pleasure, fear, and grief.

854. **Niebuhr, H. Richard. "Toward the Recovery of Feeling." In** Theology, History, and Culture: Major Unpublished Writings. **Edited by William Stacy Johnson with a Foreword by Richard R. Niebuhr. New Haven: Yale University Press, 1996. Pp. 34-49.** This previously unpublished lecture is the third and final lecture of the Cole lectures delivered at Vanderbilt University by Niebuhr under the general title

of "Next Steps in Theology." At the end of his career, Niebuhr addresses the theological issues that need to be addressed for the sake of a new reformation "as the old man's bequest to the young theologians. . .." This lecture follows the lecture on the issue of the renewal of symbols or toward new symbols. Referring to Jonathan Edwards, Niebuhr urges the future recovery of the validity of the emotions, suggesting the conviction of the objectivity of emotional experience in that "emotional relations to otherness," to objective being, are prior in meaningfulness to intellectual relations.

855.   Niebuhr, Richard R. "Schleiermacher on Language and Feeling." Theology Today 17 (1960): 150-167. The essay discusses the interrelationship between language and feeling in Schleiermacher's thought as integral to appreciating the theological significance given to preaching in his work. Failure to take into account the intimate relation between language and feeling, Niebuhr argues, leads to one-sided distortions of Schleiermacher's theology.

856.   ------. "The Widened Heart." Harvard Theological Review 62 (1969): 127-154. In terms of the affectional character of faith, Niebuhr presents an affective understanding of justification by grace through faith in terms of a twofold tonality of being in the world, as an oscillation between two simultaneous encompassing affections. The human of faith is a *homo duplex* of fear and gladness. Niebuhr utilizes insights from Edwards, Coleridge, Schleiermacher, and Calvin.

857.   ------. Experiential Religion. New York: Harper and Row, Publishers, 1972. This book is a collection of essays concerning the experiential forms and contents of faith, rather than doctrinal and dogmatic definitions of faith, and the manifestations of God. Niebuhr explicates religion in experience as "the feeling of being totally affected, of being set upon behind and before, within and without. . .." Niebuhr attempts to recover faith in affective terms as (1) awakening, (2) suffering, and (3) unifying and suffusing in terms of the scope of faith as suffering.

858.   ------. "Dread and Joyfulness: The View of Man as Affectional Being." Religion in Life 31 (1962) 443-464. Niebuhr seeks to redress the failure of much Protestant theology after Edwards to attend to the affective character of the subjective conditions of faith, focusing rather on the volitional and cognitive elements. He examines the following exceptions to this tendency in modern Protestantism: Kierkegaard and Bultmann, amongst the existentialists; and Coleridge and Schleiermacher amongst the Romantic tradition. Niebuhr argues that both traditions are important for recovering the religious significance of dread and joyfulness.

859.   Noble, H.-D. "Passions." Dictionnaire de théologie catholique contenant l'exposé des doctrines de la théologie catholique, leur preuves et leur histoire. Edited by É. Amann et al. Vol. 11/2: Ordéric vital - Paul (Saint). Paris: Librairie Letouzey et Ané, 1932. Col. 2211-2241. A systematic article that presents a Thomistic understanding of the passions.

860.   Noffke, Suzanne, O.P. "Catherine of Sienna: The Responsive Heart." In Spiritualities of the Heart: Approaches to Personal Wholeness in Christian Tradition. Edited by Annice Callahan, R.S.C.J. Mahwah: Paulist Press, 1990. Pp. 64-78. The essay explicates Catherine of Sienna's understanding of the responsive character of the heart in terms of affectivity.

861. Nuttall, Geoffrey F. "The Holy Spirit in Puritan Piety." In **The Puritan Spirit: Essays and Addresses**. London: Epworth Press, 1967. Pp. 95-103. Nuttall's essay is a concise and succinct presentation of the essential lineaments of Puritan piety in light of its emphasis upon pneumatology. He highlights the Puritan underscoring of the stress upon the Spirit's transformation of the flesh and its passions.

862. ------. **The Holy Spirit in Puritan Faith and Experience.** With a New Introduction by Peter Lake. Chicago: University of Chicago Press, 1992. This book is an acknowledged classic in the field of Puritan studies, presenting the spectrum of the different facets of Puritan theology and piety. It is an essential aid for construing the topic of the religious emotions, passions, and affections in light of the relation between Word and Spirit, the role of experience (and the interrelations between reason and will), and the question of external media for the working of the Spirit.

863. Nygren, Anders. **Agape and Eros.** Translated by Philip S. Watson. Philadelphia: The Westminster Press, 1953. Nygren's classic work is devoted to (1) a study of the Christian idea of love in the New Testament in utter contrast to the Hellenistic idea and (2) a history of the confusion of *agape* and *eros* in the history of the Christian idea of love up to the Reformation and its critique of that confusion, namely, in Luther. Nygren presents the relation between these two motifs in terms of opposition, radically critical of the confusion in the *caritas* tradition that has been influential in considerations of religion and emotions. Though much criticized, his position is still indicative of the theological reasons that inform suspicions concerning the topic of religion and the emotions.

864. Oberman, Heiko A. "Die Bedeutung der Mystik von Meister Eckhart bis Martin Luther." **Die Reformation: Von Wittenberg nach Genf.** Göttingen: Vandenhoeck und Ruprecht, 1986. Pp. 32-44. Oberman presents a survey of the understanding of Christian mysticism from Meister Eckhart to Luther, focusing on the methodological pitfalls and problems attending the question of mysticism, especially that of the collapse of the difference between mystical faith and mystical theology. Oberman critiques the tendency of phenomenology of religion approaches to mysticism to overlook the specificity of Christian mysticism. He argues that categorizations of mysticism as affective or rational-intellectual are not helpful.

865. ------. "*Simul gemitus et raptus*: Luther und die Mystik." **Die Reformation: Von Wittenberg nach Genf.** Göttingen: Vandenhoeck und Ruprecht, 1986. Pp. 45-89. Oberman's essay is a classic examination of the problem (notorious in Luther studies) of the relation of Luther's theology to the mystical theological tradition. He demonstrates how Luther could explicate his doctrine of the Christian as being *simul iustus et peccator* in the affective vocabulary of the mystical tradition as *simul gemitus et raptus*. Oberman argues that Luther transposes the affective language of the mystical tradition of ecstasy from being predicated of love to being predicated of the justification of the sinner through faith.

866. Olthius, James H. "Straddling the Boundaries between Theology and Psychology: The Faith-Feeling Interface." **Journal of Psychology and Christianity** 4 (1985): 6-15. Imminent anger is no longer the separation of theology and psychology, but their fusion into an amalgam which, depending on the mix, is a theologized psychology or a psychologized theology. Paper suggests a way to look at psychology and theology which avoids either a psychologistic reduction of faith to feelings or a theologistic reduction of feelings to faith. Faith and feelings are seen to be two sui

generis modes of being in the world; psychology is defined as the study of sensitive or emotional way of being in the world. Since every human act partakes in all ways of being in the world, including faith and sensitivity, theology and psychology are able in interdisciplinary cooperation to address the interaction of faith and feelings in every human act even as they approach the study from their own unique points.

867. Owen, John. "Of Communion with God the Father, Son, and Holy Ghost, Each Person distinctly, in Love, Grace, and Consolation; of The Saint's Fellowship with the Father, Son, and Holy Ghost Unfolded." In The Works of John Owen, Vol. II. Edited by William H. Goold. Edinburgh: Banner of Truth Trust, 1965 [1657]. Owen's treatise presents the affective as a critical dimension of the spiritual communion between God and God's saints effected through the work of the Spirit and as founded within the nature of the imminent Trinity and the relations between the persons of the Trinity.

868. ------. "ΠΝΕΥΜΑΤΟΛΟΓΙΑ or, A Discourse concerning the Holy Ghost: Wherein An Account is Given of His Name, Nature, Personality, Dispensation, Operations, and Effects; His Whole Work in the Old and New Creation is Explained; The Doctrine concerning It Vindicated from Oppositions and Reproaches." In The Works of John Owen, Vol. III-IV. Edited by William Goold. Edinburgh: Banner of Truth Trust, 1965 [1674]. The passions and the religious affections were of crucial importance for Puritan theology. Owen's classic pneumatology provides an exemplary case of the systematic importance that the affections held for Puritan theology in terms of the Spirit's working the transformation of human affections in justification and sanctification. Particularly interesting is Owen's discussion of the "consequential affections" of the believer's communion with Christ in a "conjugal" relation.

869. Ozment, Steven E. Homo Spiritualis: A Comparative Study of the Anthropology of Johannes Tauler, Jean Gerson and Martin Luther (1509-1516) in the Context of Their Theological Thought. Studies in Medieval and Reformation Thought 6. Leiden: E. J. Brill, 1969. Ozment provides a helpful treatment of *affectus* in relation to the theological anthropologies of Gerson and Luther, especially in relation to the reciprocal operation of *intellectus* and *affectus*.

870. Pannenberg, Wolfhart. Anthropology in Theological Perspective. Translated by Matthew J. O'Connell. Philadelphia: Westminster Press, 1985. Pannenberg examines feelings, moods, and passions in terms of identity and nonidentity as a theme of affective life within a presentation of the social character of being human. His analysis is preparatory for a discussion of alienation and sin and guilt and consciousness of guilt. Feeling is understood to be foundational for every self-consciousness and for self-transcendence as openness to the world. Pannenberg also discusses and criticizes the Kierkegaardian understanding of the relation between anxiety and sin, arguing for anxiety as a consequence of sin. Pannenberg is one of a few systematic theologians who systematically attends to the topic of feeling/emotion in relation to religion.

871. Porter, Jean. The Recovery of Virtue: The Relevance of Aquinas for Christian Ethics. Louisville: Westminster/John Knox Press, 1990. Seeking to recover the importance of virtue for theological ethics, Porter utilizes the theological thought of Thomas Aquinas for a treatment of the affective character of the virtues.

872. Pourrat, P. "Affections." **Dictionnaire de Spiritualité Ascétique et Mystique, Doctrine et Histoire**, Vol. 1. Paris: Beauchesne, 1932-1937. Pp. 235-240. The article encapsulates a succinct examination of the notion of the affections, the various types of affection, and role of the affections in the spiritual life. The article underscores the reliance of the spiritual affections upon ideas and their connection with the virtues. Virtues are presented as themselves affective and as provoking affections.

873. Preul, Reiner. **Reflexion und Gefühl: Die Theologie Fichtes in seiner vorkantischen Zeit**. Theologische Bibliothek Töpelmann, Bd. 18. Berlin: Walter de Gruyter, 1969. Preul examines the theology of Fichte and its development in his pre-Kantian period between 1780 and 1790. He traces the emerging tension and separation between reflection and feeling in Fichte's thought such that religion – especially as a religion of the heart, founded in the convincing power of feeling – becomes only a subsidiary element with an only subjective validity in relation to ethics. The book is an important contribution in historical theology not only for Fichte studies, but also for a determination of the context for the theological emphasis upon feeling in Schleiermacher and others in the period of the *Atheismus- und Pantheismusstreiten*.

874. Principe, Walter, C.S.B. "Affectivity and the Heart in Thomas Aquinas' Spirituality." In **Spiritualities of the Heart: Approaches to Personal Wholeness in Christian Tradition**. Edited by Annice Callahan, R.S.C.J. Mahwah: Paulist Press, 1990. Pp. 45-63. The essay provides an exposition of Thomas' understanding of the heart and affectivity in the spiritual life. The essay significantly relates Thomas' exegesis of the heart in Scripture with his systematic reflections on the passions and the virtues.

875. Proudfoot, Wayne. "From Theology to a Science of Religions: Jonathan Edwards and William James on Religious Affections." **Harvard Theological Review** 82 (1989): 149-168. The article examines the differences in Edwards' theological and William James' phenomenological approach to the problem of religious affections. It suggests the more illuminating character of Edwards' treatment and analysis of the complexity of the evaluation of religious affections in terms of a thick description than that of James' attempt to discern a common element within the varieties of religious experience.

876. ------. "Religious Experience, Emotion, and Belief." **Harvard Theological Review** 70 (1977): 343-367. In light of a consideration of Aristotle, Hume, and Wittgenstein on affective or emotional experience, Proudfoot presents a critique of phenomenological approaches to religion and emotion. He argues that such experiences assume particular beliefs and judgments concerning the world and that it is plausible that such cognitive attitudes are more fundamental than are affective attitudes or emotions. For Proudfoot, the recourse to emotional experience cannot circumvent the Kantian insight that all experience is informed and mediated by cognitive concepts and judgments that structure the world.

877. ------. **Religious Experience**. Berkeley: University of California Press, 1985. Proudfoot's examination of the history of the development of the concept of religious experience beginning with Schleiermacher and a critical analysis of the viability of such a notion for apologetic purposes. Proudfoot criticizes Schleiermacher's claim that sense or feeling is independent of culture and includes an awareness of reality originally given in experience. He contends that affective experience is not independent of concepts and beliefs and provides a helpful consideration of the similarities and differences between

the rules for the identification of emotions and those for the identification of religious experience.

878. Rahner, Karl. <u>The Dynamic Element in the Church</u>. Quaestiones Disputatae. New York: Herder and Herder, 1964. Rahner presents a detailed analysis of "the logic of concrete individual knowledge" in the spiritual exercises of Ignatius Loyola [Chapter 3] in relation to the question of the problem of relating universal essential principles to the individual in a concrete situation. Rahner discuses the affective character of the discernment of spirits in relation to the "non-conceptual" experience of God and the nature and certainty of such experience.

879. ------. "The Doctrine of the 'Spiritual Senses' in the Middle Ages." In <u>Theological Investigations</u>, Vol. XVI. Translated by David Morland. New York: Crossroad/Seabury, 1979. Pp. 104-134. Rahner examines the further development of the notion of the "spiritual senses" in the mystical theology of Bonaventure. He discuses the notion in relation to Bonaventure's discussion of the operations of the soul as acts of both the intellect and the will in a state of grace through the virtues, the gifts of the Holy Spirit, and the blessings of beatitude. Prominent in his discussion is his explication of mystical ecstasy and its transformation of the *apex affectus* in the experience of God and divine grace.

880. ------. "The Doctrine of the 'Spiritual Senses' according to Origen." In <u>Theological Investigations</u>, Vol. XVI. Translated by David Morland. New York: Crossroad/Seabury, 1979. Pp. 81-103. Rahner historically examines the locus of Origen's treatment of the "spiritual senses" in relation to the overall system of Origen's theological thought, especially as regards the ascetic and mystical ascent of the soul.

881. ------. "Faith between Rationality and Emotion." In <u>Theological Investigations</u>, Vol. XVI. Translated by David Morland. New York: Crossroad/Seabury, 1979. Pp. 60-78. Rahner transposes the topic of faith between rationality and emotions into the topic of faith between rationality and freedom. He contends that freedom and its irreducible originality with respect to rationality constitutes the very essence of emotion as caused (motivated) freedom. Though at root faith, emotion and rationality are a unity, derivative tensions exist between them. Rahner explicates this in relation to the irreducible distinction between *fides qua* and *fides quae*. It is an important essay for Rahner's understanding of the affections and the non-conceptual experience of unfathomable mystery that is experienced at the root of rationality and freedom.

882. Reynolds, Terence Paul. <u>The Coherence of Life without God before God: The Problem of Earthly Desires in the Later Theology of Dietrich Bonhoeffer</u>. Lanham: University Press of America, 1989. The book is a study of the re-evaluation of earthly desires, passions, and affections that the author argues takes place in the later theology of Bonhoeffer, especially after 1939 in his posthumously published *Ethics* and *Letters and Papers from Prison*. Though acknowledging the sinfulness of all dimensions of human life, Bonhoeffer is understood as affirming theologically the relative value of the natural life in its intrinsic goodness as penultimate, encouraging secular desires for the good things of earthly life for their own sake.

883. Roberts, Robert C. "The Feeling of Absolute Dependence." <u>Journal of Religion</u> 57 (1977): 252-266. Roberts presents a critical analysis of Schleiermacher's notion of the feeling of absolute dependence in terms of questions concerning its

character as feeling, whether everyone has that feeling, the conditions under which one may be said to have that feeling, whether it implies God, and what God is precisely implied if it implies God.

884. ------. "**The Logic and Lyric of Contrition.**" <u>Theology Today</u> 50 (1993): 193-207. Roberts presents a construal of contrition as the pivotal centerpiece and moving force in the process of repentance and the formation of a new self. Contrition is a gracious affection configured by the gospel, related to but distinguishable from neighboring emotions of fear, regret, embarrassment, and guilt. It is distinguishable from them in that it is constituted in terms of the logic of distinctive Christian propositions or beliefs.

885. ------. "**Emotions among the Virtues of the Christian Life.**" <u>Journal of Religious Ethics</u> 20 (1992):37-68. Roberts argues that the emotions are an integral element in the structure of the Christian virtues. The paper distinguishes four kinds of virtue: emotion virtues, behavioral virtues, virtues of will power, and attitudinal virtues. Roberts attempts to demonstrate that analysis of a Christian virtue from each of the last three kinds of virtue reveals its structural dependency upon what he terms the Christian emotions.

886. ------. "**Emotions as Access to Religious Truths.**" <u>Faith and Philosophy</u> 9 (1992): 83-94. The essay contends that emotions (namely, joy, hope, contrition, and gratitude) are fitting for grasping central Christian truths. Emotions are simultaneously concern-based construals and propositional attitudes. As such, Christian emotions are fundamental and central in Christian knowledge because they (1) use central Christian propositions, (2) are perceptions, (3) embody concerns befitting Christian truths.

887. ------. "**Kierkegaard on Becoming an "Individual.**" <u>Scottish Journal of Theology</u> 31 (1978): 133-152. Roberts presents Kierkegaard's emphasis on the problem of becoming an individual in relation to the emotions. More specifically, the essay explicates Kierkegaard's depiction of the problem of becoming a Christian as involving the growth in the Christian emotions, a feature of which is growth in becoming an individual, namely, as one before God.

888. ------. "**Psychotherapeutic Virtues and the Grammar of Faith.**" <u>Journal of Psychology and Theology</u> 15 (1987): 191-204. The article presents a method for the integration of secular psychotherapies into Christian practice through the recognition of the importance of the virtues and the affections in the Christian grammar of faith, recognizing both the continuities as well as the discontinuities between Christian and secular psychotherapies. It is presented in a case study of Albert Ellis's rational-emotive therapy, which serves as the secular counterpart for a presentation of a distinctively Christian rational-emotive therapy informed by the grammar of faith. Roberts relies upon the work of Kierkegaard for his analysis.

889. ------. <u>Spirituality and Human Emotion</u>. Grand Rapids: Eerdmans Publishing Company, 1982. Influenced by Kierkegaard, Roberts engages in what he terms "an exercise in therapeutic Christian reflection" upon the human condition with regards to the emotions. He understands emotions to be concern-based construals or ways of seeing oneself and the world. Christian emotions are concern-based construals determined by Christian concepts and the scheme or pattern of beliefs giving rise to those concepts. Christian emotions are fruits of the Spirit as concern-based emotions, whose

concern is the passion or desire to live free of the evils of sin and death. The specific Christian emotions or fruits of the spirit examined are gratitude, hope, and compassion.

890. ------. **Taking the Word to Heart: Self and Other in an Age of Therapies.** **Grand Rapids: Eerdmans Publishing Company, 1993.** The book presents a Christian theological and critical analysis of various psychologies and psychotherapies (especially of Heinz Kohut) and a constructive Christian theological construal of the psychology inherent in the Bible and the Christian tradition (especially Thomas Aquinas and Kierkegaard) in dialogue with secular psychologies and therapies. Roberts understands therapy as a "heart-forming word."

891. **Robb, Paul V., S.J.** "Conversion as a Human Experience." **Studies in the Spirituality of Jesuits** 14 (1982). The article gives a presentation of the dynamics of the conversion of the heart. The interior world of the heart is understood as a locus of affections with their opposites and contradictions. Conversion involves the transformation of self in light of an antecedent affective self-knowledge of ones' sinfulness manifest in the affective experience of opposites and the affective knowledge of Christ. The essay draws upon the work of Bernard Lonergan, St. Theresa of Avila, and the spiritual exercises of Ignatius of Loyola.

892. **Rohls, Jan.** "Frömmigkeit als Gefühl schlechthinniger Abhängiglkeit: Zu Schleiermachers Religionstheorie in der "Glaubenslehre."** In **Internationaler Schleiermacher-Kongress Berlin 1984.** Vol. 1. **Edited by Kurt-Victor Selge. Schleiermacher-Archiv, Bd. I/1. Berlin: Walter de Gruyter, 1985. Pp. 211-252.** An excellent presentation of Schleiermacher's construal of piety as the feeling of absolute dependence within his theory of religion and its theological significance for Schleiermacher's dogmatics.

893. ------. "Sinn und Geschmack fürs Unendliche" – Aspekte romantischer Kunstreligion." **Neue Zeitschrift für systematische Theologie und Religionsphilosophie** 27 (1985): 1-24. The essay contains a valuable discussion of feeling and the advent of both the religion of art in German Romanticism and the autonomy of art in which aesthetic experience is understood as the "sense and taste for the infinite." Rohls presents the emergence of the centrality of the concept of feeling in terms of the intersection between religion and art, theology and Romantic aesthetics. Schleiermacher and De Wette are presented as interpreting religion and religious experience in terms of aesthetic categories.

894. **Rousselot, Pierre.** **Pour l'histoire du problème de l'amour au Moyen-Age.** **Beiträge zur Geschichte der Philosophie des Mittelalters VI/6. Münster: Aschendorffsche Buchhandlung, 1908.** Rousselot's monograph is devoted to a history of the theological discussions of the problem of love in medieval theology and philosophy, especially concerning the relation between love, knowledge, and will. While some elements of his analysis have been disputed and challenged and Rousselot in his later thought advanced beyond certain positions in this earlier work, it still presents a rich and rewarding discussion of the conceptions of the relation between cognitive and affective in medieval discussions of love.

895. **Ruello, Francis.** "Le Dépassement mystique du Discours théologique selon Saint Bonaventure." **Recherches des Sciences Religieuses** 64 (1976): 217-270. This is the introductory essay to a bibliographical review of publications devoted to Bonaventure on the occasion of the seventh centenary of Bonaventure. It addresses the

question of the relation between theological speculation and mystical theology in Bonaventure's thought and argues, in light of an analysis of the structure of Bonaventure's *Iteinerarium* and in comparison with the mystical theology of Thomas Gallus, that the progression of theological speculation is an "ascension" in stages towards mystical ecstasy through the separation of *affectus* and *intellectus*.

896. Sabersky, Dorothy. "*Affectus Confessus Sum, et non Negavi*: Reflections on the Expression of Affects in the 26th Sermon on the Song of Songs of Bernard of Clairvaux." In the Joy of Learning and the Love of God: Studies in Honor of Jean Leclercq. Edited by E. Rozanne Elder. Cistercian Studies Series: No. 160. Kalamazoo: Cistercian Publications, 1995. Pp. 187-216. The essay presents a detailed analysis of the significance of the affections for Bernard and the stylistic use of figures of speech employed in a particular sermon on the Song of Songs.

897. ------. "*Nam iteratio affectionis expressio est*. Zum Stil Bernhards von Clairvaux." Cîteaux 36 (1985): 5-20. A comprehensive and detailed presentation of the interrelationship between rhetorical expression in language and the religious affections in the theology of Bernard of Clairvaux.

898. Saliers, Don E. "On the Distinctiveness of Christian Emotions." Weavings 6 (1991): 6-16. Understanding the language of faith as the language of emotions, Saliers explicates the distinctiveness of Christian emotions in terms of a pattern of being in the world gratefully, joyfully, peacefully, and compassionately. He argues that Christian emotions have a paradoxical character distinguishing them from emotions related to a therapeutic search for self-fulfillment.

899. ------. "Prayer and Emotion: Shaping and Expressing Christian Life." In Christians at Prayer. Edited by John Gallen, S.J. Liturgical Studies. Notre Dame/London: University of Notre Dame Press, 1977. Pp. 46-60. The essay contends that prayer, especially in its communal forms, both shapes and expresses persons in terms of depth emotions. Prayer gives articulation to the Christian affections, providing emotion capacities to perceive the world as God's. The language of prayer as the expression of religious faith is the language of emotions in relation to the range of elemental patterns in life, namely, birth and death, sin and terror, gratitude and heartbreak, despair and hope, wretchedness and happiness.

900. ------. "Religious Affections and the Grammar of the Prayer." In The Grammar of the Heart: New Essays in Moral Philosophy and Theology. Edited by Richard E. Bell. San Francisco: Harper and Row, 1988. Pp. 188-205. The essay examines the linguistic character of religious affections in terms of the correlation between the religious affections or emotions and the grammar of prayer.

901. Schlatter, Adolf. Das christliche Dogma. Fourth Edition. Foreword to the New Edition by Wilfried Joest. Calwer Verlag, 1984. Schlatter discusses "feeling and blessedness" in terms of a theological anthropology, situated between a discussion of "knowing and truth" and "the human will and divine love." The division of various feelings is presented in terms of the opposition between pleasure and pain, such that a hierarchy distinguishing between lower and higher feelings is presented in terms of a corresponding division of goods and evils in relation to a cumulative result of feelings as happiness or unhappiness. Schlatter then discusses religious feelings as emerging with God-consciousness, namely, as thankfulness and fear of God, overcoming the distortions

affecting lower and higher feelings through the transformative power of the consciousness of God's goodness, wrath, and holiness.

902. Schleiermacher, Friedrich. **On Religion: Speeches to its Cultured Despisers**. Translated and edited by Richard Crouter. Cambridge Texts in the History of Philosophy. Cambridge: Cambridge University Press, 1996. This edition is a translation of the first edition that presented Schleiermacher's classic definition of the essence of religion as intuition and feeling.

903. ------. **The Christian Faith**. Edited by H. R. Mackintosh and J. S. Stewart. Philadelphia: Fortress Press, 1976. Schleiermacher's epoch-making work in Christian theology is pivotal for all later theological discussions concerning the relation between religion and the emotions. For Schleiermacher, the feeling of absolute dependence is piety, a constitutive dimension of common human experience. Christian piety is conceived as a modification of the feeling of absolute dependence in light of the consciousness of sin and grace.

904. Scholz, Heinrich. **Glaube und Unglaube in der Weltgeschichte. Mit einem Exkurs:** *Fruitio Dei*, **ein Beitrag zur Geschichte der Theologie und der Mystik.** Leipzig, 1911. The excursive essay on *fruitio Dei* [pp. 197-235], which accompanies Scholz' commentary on faith and unfaith in Augustine's "The City of God," presents a valuable overview of the essential elements of that notion in the history of theology and mysticism. The article examines the history of the notion prior to Augustine, Augustine's understanding, and the reception and utilization of this notion in subsequent theology and spirituality. It provides valuable references to texts and thinkers who utilize this notion.

905. Schwarz, Reinhard. *Fides, spes* **und** *caritas* **beim jungen Luther unter besonderer Berücksichtigung der mittelalterlichen Tradition.** Arbeiten zur Kirchengeschichte, Bd. 34. Berlin: Walter De Gruyter & Co., 1962. The monograph is a detailed examination of the development in Luther's understanding of the nature of and interrelations between the theological virtues of faith, hope, and love as evidenced principally in his lectures on the Psalms and the Pauline epistles. Extensive attention is given to Luther's reception and critical appropriation of antecedent medieval theological treatments of those virtues, especially with regards to the significance of the affections concerning the relation of faith to intellect and the will. Schwarz has a detailed excursus attending to the concept of affective knowledge in late medieval thought and Luther.

906. Shea, William M. **The Naturalists and the Supernatural: Studies in Horizon and an American Philosophy of Religion**. Mercer: Mercer University Press, 1984. Shea presents a theological dialogue on the nature of religion with the major representatives of the American naturalist philosophical tradition, namely, George Santayana, John Dewey, Frederick J. E. Woodbridge, and John H. Randall. Shea seeks to clarify the nature of religion through a clarification of the interrelations between basic terms of supernatural, feeling, acting, and thinking. His point is to engage and extend more adequately the naturalist usage of these terms in their understanding of religion as a process of unification. He underscores the understanding of feeling as a "knowing feeling" preceding and accompanying the overtly cognitional and volitional. It serves as the basis for overcoming the antithesis between naturalism and the Catholic understanding of the supernatural (as retrieved in modern Catholic theology, e.g., de Lubac and Rahner).

907. Shenck, David. "A Panegyric to Søren de Silentio." Soundings: An Interdisciplinary Journal 71 (1988): 581-599. The article examines the paradoxical interrelation between passion and reflection in Kierkegaard's authorship and the aesthetic strategy of indirect communication and edifying discourse in order to make possible noetic transformation of the individual.

908. Shultz, Werner. "Schleiermachers Theorie des Gefühls und ihre theologische Bedeutung." Zeitschrift für Theologie und Kirche 53 (1956): 75-103. Schultz presents a systematic exposition of the Schleiermacher's theory of feeling and its theological significance, which he relates to Schleiermacher's philosophical work concerning the relation between essence and appearance and its influence upon the development of his theory of feeling.

909. Simonson, Harold P. Jonathan Edwards: Theologian of the Heart. With a foreword to the ROSE edition by Martin E. Marty. Macon: Mercer University Press, 1982. Simonson's book critiques the interpretation of the Edwardsian understanding of the "sense of the heart" put forth by Perry Miller as essentially to be understood in terms of the philosophy of John Locke. He proposes to see the sense of the heart in Edwards as rather being in the tradition of Calvin and Augustine. He also attends to the relation between the affections and the imagination in Edwards in terms of the sanctified imagination that informs Edwards' understanding of religious language and use of such language in his sermons. Words are the "occasional" cause preparing the heart by creating an "emotional readiness for the apprehension of religious truth" (p. 14).

910. Smith, John Clark. The Ancient Wisdom of Origen. Lewisburg: Bucknell University Press, 1992. The book provides a helpful overview of Origen's account of spiritual development in the Christian life, especially in relation to the management and transfiguration of the senses, desires, and passions through self-control made possible through grace.

911. Solignac, Aimé. "Passions et Vie spirituelle." Dictionnaire de Spiritualité Ascétique et Mystique, Doctrine et Histoire, Vol. 12, pt. 1: Pacaud - Photius. Paris: Beauchesne, 1984. Pp. 339-357. The article focuses upon the understandings of the passions and the spiritual life in (1) the Greek and Roman philosophical traditions that were influential upon the early church fathers, (2) representative church fathers (chiefly Clement of Alexandria, Gregory of Nyssa, Lactantius, Ambrose, and Augustine), and French philosophers, moralists, and spiritualists in the 17th century (Nicolas Coeffetau, Jean-Francois Senault, Descartes, Pascal, and Malebranche). The author also provides brief notations of significant philosophers in modernity who have addressed the topic.

912. Spidlík, Tomas. The Spirituality of the Christian East: A Systematic Handbook. Translated by Anthony P. Gythiel. Cistercian Studies Series: No. 79. Kalamazoo: Cistercian Publications, Inc., 1986. The book provides a systematic overview of spirituality in Eastern Orthodox theology, especially of the role of the affections and passions in anthropology, the negative purificative praxis of asceticism, renunciation of the flesh and its passions, spiritual warfare for custody of the heart, apatheia and the purification of the passions, the positive praxis of the virtues and charity, and contemplation. The author provides a good bibliography of both primary and secondary sources on each of the above topics.

913. Spohn, William C. "Passions and Principles." Theological Studies 52 (1991): 69-87. The article examines the interplay between rationality and affectivity in

moral experience, contending that both reason and emotion tutor each other, in light of the recovery of the importance of the affective character of the moral agent in terms of character, disposition, and moral development. The article examines the nature of the moral assessment of the passions and the question as to whether or not the passions are educable.

914. Spohn, William C. "**The Reasoning Heart: An American Approach to Christian Discernment.**" Theological Studies 44 (1983): 30-52. The essay argues that moral discernment is based upon judgments of affectivity as distinguished from abstract judgments of rationality. The Christian tradition offers certain normative symbols and patterns of affectivity that serve as criteria for Christian discernment, correlated with fundamental religious convictions about God and Jesus Christ. Discernment, therefore, occurs within a normative context and is accountable to public tests presented by Scripture and the believing community. Spohn utilizes theological insights from Karl Rahner, H. Richard Niebuhr, and Jonathan Edwards.

915. **Steele, Richard B. "Narrative Theology and the Religious Affections." In Theology without Foundations: Religious Practice and the Future of Theological Truth. Edited by Stanley Hauerwas, Nancy C. Murphy, and Mark Nation. Nashville: Abingdon Press, 1994. Pp. 163-179, 327-332.** Steele argues that emotions are a constitutive element of human life in general and of Christian faithfulness in particular. He rejects what Lindbeck would term "experiential-expressivist" theories of the emotions as foundationalist in favor of a nonfoundational narrative theory of the emotions. Such a theory would see emotions as (1) entailing judgments of objects, (2) having reasons for being, not just causes, (3) being perduring character features, and (4) capable of moral evaluation and appraisal. A narrative theology, construing authoritative narratives as shaping the judgments of various communities, would likewise see those narratives as also shaping emotions.

916. **Stock, Ursula. "*Spes exercens conscientiam*. Sprache und Affekt in Luthers Auslegung des 6. Psalms in den *Operationes in psalmos*." In Lutheriana: Zum 500. Geburtstag Martin Luthers von den Mitarbeitern der Weimarer Ausgabe. Edited by Gerhard Hammer and Karl-Heinz zur Mühlen. Archiv zur Weimarer Ausgabe der Werke Martin Luthers: Texte und Untersuchungen, Bd. 5. Köln/Wien: Böhlau Verlag, 1984. Pp. 229-244.** A close analysis and exegesis of the relation between language and affect in Luther's interpretation of Psalm 6 in 1519 that attends to the affects of suffering and the alleviation of that suffering through hope exercising the conscience through words of promise.

917. **Stolt, Birgit. "*Docere, delectare* und *movere* bei Luther." Deutsche Vierteljahresschrift für Literaturwissenschaft und Geistesgeschichte 44 (1970): 433-474.** An examination of classical rhetoric in Luther and its relation to Luther's theology. The essay examines in particular the significance of the three classical functions of rhetoric – to teach (*docere*), to move (*movere*), and to delight (*delectare*). It provides important contextual information concerning theology and rhetoric for an understanding of the significance of the emotions in Luther's theology and sermons.

918. **Szabó, Titus. "L'Extase chez Les Théologiens du XIIIe Siècle." Dictionnaire de Spiritualité Ascétique et Mystique, Doctrine et Histoire IV/2: Espagne — Ezquerra. Paris: Beauchesne, 1961. Pp. 2120-2131.** The article is devoted to a presentation of the treatment of ecstasy in Bonaventure and Thomas Aquinas. It highlights Bonaventure's understanding of the perfect harmony between *cognitio* and

affectio in mystical ecstasy resulting in a *docto ignorantia*. The article also pays attention to Thomas' distinction between ecstasy and rapture and the difference between the indirect causality of divine love in relation to the cognitive faculty and the direct causality of divine love in relation to the appetitive faculty.

919. Tallon, Andrew. "Affectivity in Ethics: Lonergan, Rahner, and Others in the Heart Tradition." In **Religion and Economic Ethics**. Edited by Joseph F. Glower. The Annual Publication of the College Theological Society; Vol. 31 (1985). Lanham: University Press of America, 1990. Pp. 87-122. Tallon discusses the question of the justification of the role of reasons of the heart in moral decision-making in ethics. The article chiefly utilizes the work of Lonergan and Rahner on affectivity in relation to an articulation of knowledge by affective connaturality. The centrality of the role of the affective in ethics provides the basis for an existential hermeneutics in which there is a primacy of orthopraxis over orthodoxy.

920. ------. "The Heart in Rahner's Philosophy of Mysticism." **Theological Studies** 53 (1992): 700-728. The essay progressively explicates Karl Rahner's theory of the heart in his philosophy of mysticism through the concepts of affective intentionally, the affective connaturalaity of knowledge, and of habit as virtue. The interdependent unity of these notions provide the basis for the articulation of a phenomenology and metaphysics of the heart. The essay is an excellent explication of Rahner's thought, especially his discussion of the spiritual meaning of feelings in relation to the heart as perfected intellectus.

921. ------. "The Experience of Grace in Relation to Rahner's Philosophy of the Heart." **Philosophy & Theology** 7 (1992): 193-210. Tallon argues for a proper understanding of Rahner's metaphysics of cognition in terms of his philosophy of heart, where the "heart-mind" is the functional union of affective, volitional, and cognitive consciousness. The experience of grace is explicated in terms of the integration of affective, volitional, and cognitive intentionalities in the direction of the full actualization of finite spirit as intersubjective faith, hope, and love.

922. ------. "Religious Belief and the Emotional Life: Faith, Love, and Hope in the Heart Tradition." In **The Life of Religion: Philosophy and the Nature of Religious Belief**. Edited by Stanley Harrison and Richard Taylor. Washington, D.C.: University Press of America. 1986. Pp. 17-38. The essay explicates the relation between religious belief and the emotional life in terms of an analysis of Pascal's dictum "It is the heart that senses [feels] God, and not reason." Tallon argues that the heart is not a separate faculty besides that of reason, but rather that the heart is reason transformed by being graced by the gifts or virtues of the Spirit (faith, hope, and charity).

923. ------. "Connaturality in Aquinas and Rahner. A Contribution to the Heart Tradition." **Philosophy Today** 28 (1984):138-147. An explication of the Thomistic notion of connaturality and Rahner's appropriation of the notion of connaturality in terms of the theological and philosophical tradition's interpretation of the heart. Major attention is given to the relation between affectivity and connaturality.

924. Thévenaz, Jean Pierre. "Passion de Dieu, passions humaines et sympathie des choses: ethique et messianisme chez Jürgen Moltmann." **Revue de Théologie et de Philosophie** 119 (1987): 303-321. The article surveys the corpus of Moltmann's writings in terms of the centrality of the messianic passion of Jesus Christ and its

involvement in the reality of God and human reality. The article concludes with a discussion of the implications of Moltmann's position for an ethics of the passions.

925. **Thomas Aquinas. The Disputed Questions on Truth: Questions XXI-XXIX. Vol. III. Translated by Robert W. Schmidt, S.J. Chicago: Henry Regnery Company, 1954.** Particularly noteworthy are Thomas' discussion of the topic of the passions of the soul and his treatment of *gratis graium faciens*. In Question XXVI on "The Passions of the Soul," Thomas addresses the questions of how does the soul suffer when separated and joined to the body, whether passion is only in the appetitive power, grounds for contrariety and diversity of the passions of the soul, the four principal passions (hope, fear, joy, and sadness), merit and the passions, and the questions concerning the passions of Christ. In the following question on grace, Thomas has enlarged the concept of grace in order to give room for the divine gift of whole affections (*sanctas affectiones*), an advancement upon his treatments of grace in preceding texts.

926. **Thonnard, F.-J. "La vie affective de l'ame selon Saint Augustin." L'Année Théologique Augustinienne 13 (1953): 33-55.** The article explicates three domains of Augustine's depiction of the affective life of human beings: the passions, free will, and the instincts. The relation between the passions and free will is articulated in terms of what the author terms the "law of delectation" governing the movement of the affective life. For Augustine, the law of delectation is the law of love.

927. **Thunberg, Lars. Microcosm and Mediator: The Theological Anthropology of Maximus the Confessor. Foreword by A. M. Allchin. Second Edition. Chicago: Open Court Publishing, 1995.** Thunberg systematically explicates the trichotomy of Maximus' theological anthropology, especially in relation to his discussion of the passions. He richly presents the historical antecedents and background (e.g., Plato, Aristotle, the Stoics, Philo, Clement, Origen, and the Cappadocians) to Maximus' thought and its own distinctiveness. He examines in particular the relation of the passions to the psychology of the will, both in terms of the disintegration through the passions and the resulting generation of vices in light of self-love as well as the reintegration of the self through the transformation of the whole self through charity and the resulting transfiguration of the passions in the spiritual life and the life of the virtues. He also discusses the affective character of ecstasy in relation to mystical union and the deification of the human.

928. **Tillich, Paul. Systematic Theology. Three Vols. Chicago: The University of Chicago Press, 1965.** Tillich's classic work is significant for the topic of religion and the emotions in several ways. The existential character of theological claims as related to ultimate concern enables Tillich to affirm the reciprocal unity of faith and love, the relation between revelation and religion as the reception of revelation through the ecstasy of reason, and the multidimensional unity of the cognitive, aesthetic, affective, and volitional aspects of human existence. In his pneumatology, Tillich's emphasis on the multidimensionality of life enables him to overcome the danger of dualisms that have affected consideration of the emotions in the history of philosophy and theology and to be able to explicate the impact of the Spiritual Presence upon all the dimensions of life, including the affective element.

929. **------. The Courage to Be. New Haven: Yale University Press, 1952.** Tillich's Terry Lectures at Yale University present a classic treatment of the ontological and existential character of the courage to be in relation to the varied forms of anxiety and existential despair. That analyses are conducted in order to interpret faith through the

analysis of courage in its ontological sense as the self-affirmation of human nature, rather than as being one virtue amongst others. Tillich presents an ontology of anxiety in relation to human finitude that distinguishes the interdependence between anxiety and fear. He develops a typology of anxiety in relation to fate and death, emptiness and meaninglessness, guilt and condemnation.

930. ------. **The Dynamics of Faith.** World Perspectives, Vol. 10. New York: Harper & Brothers Publishers, 1957. Tillich defines faith as the state of being ultimately concerned. Faith as ultimate concern is the centered act of the total personality. Faith is not reserved for a particular function of the human's total being. In this manner the various distortions of the meaning of faith are prevented, whether they are intellectualistic, voluntaristic, or emotionalistic. Though faith has emotional or affective elements within itself, emotions are not the source of faith.

931. Tomás De La Cruz. "L'Extase chez Sainte Thérèse D'Avila." **Dictionnaire de Spiritualité Ascétique et Mystique, Doctrine et Histoire** IV/2: Espagne – Ezquerra. Paris: Beauchesne, 1961. Pp. 2151-2160. The article presents an interpretation of ecstasy in relation to the writings of St. Theresa of Avila, who exerted an enormous influence upon subsequent theoretical discussions of ecstasy, even though she did not herself present an explicit theory of ecstasy.

932. Tyrell, Bernard J. "Affective Conversion: A New Way of Feeling." In **The Human Experience of Conversion: Persons and Structures in Transformation.** Edited by Francis A. Eigo, O.S.A. Villanova: Villanova University Press, 1987. Pp. 109-142. The essay is concerned with the nature of affectivity and the meaning of the notion of a "conversion" of affectivity. His discussion of each of these topics is mediated by a discussion of other thinkers, namely, Lonergan, William Lyons, Robert Solomon, James Hillman, John Macmurray, and von Hildebrand. He proposes to understand higher intentional feelings as "apprehensive, discerning, discriminating, preferential responses to values."

933. Van der Ven, Johannes. **Formation of the Moral Self.** Studies in Practical Theology. Grand Rapids: Eerdmans Publishing Company, 1998. The book analyzes the moral dimension of the religious practice of the formation of the self. The author regards emotional formation as an integral element of the religious practice of education for moral character. The author presents a cognitive interaction theory of the emotions in relation to emotional development as an aspect of the stages of moral development, culminating in the unity of moral passions, the virtues, and narration. It is a text by one of the leading practical theologians of today.

934. Vögtle, A. "Affekt." In **Reallexikon für Antike und Christentum: Sachwörterbuch zur Auseinandersetzung des Christentums mit der antiken Welt,** Vol. 1: A und O - Bauen. Edited by Theodor Klauser. Stuttgart: Hiersemann Verlags, 1950. The article surveys the understandings of affect in both Greek and Roman as well as early Christian literature and thought. Within both the article provides a helpful overview of the understandings of human affect and the various affects, their significance or value, and the therapy and education of the affects. The overview of Christian thought also discusses the various understandings of the affects in relation to God and Christ. It also has a helpful bibliography of older secondary literature.

935. Völker, Walther. **Praxis und Theoria bei Symeon dem Neuen Theologen: Ein Beitrage zur byzantiner Mystik.** Wiesbaden: F. Steiner, 1974. A continuation of

his history of Greek-speaking mystical piety, the author is concerned to exposit the intimate unity between ascetic and moral praxis and the *theoria* of the knowledge of God as mystical vision. A lengthy analysis of the emotions is presented in terms of the doctrine of sins and the passions of *pathos*, the virtues (especially humility, *apatheia*, and love), and the "feelability" or affective character that accompanies the mystical vision and the dispositions following from that vision.

936. ------. **Gregor von Nyssa als Mystiker.** Wiesbaden: F. Steiner, 1955. This detailed and lengthy monograph is concerned with the explication of the mystical theology of Gregory of Nyssa in terms of the manifold influences of preceding Greek philosophical thought (especially Stoic philosophy) and Eastern Christian theology, especially that of the Alexandrian theologians. Following a synopsis of Gregory's ontology and concept of the image of God in christology and anthropology, prominent attention is given to the understanding of the "emotions" in relation to the essence and origin of sin, the gradual ascent towards perfection through the gnosis of faith and the ascetic cultivation of the virtuous life. Though Völker sees Gregory as dependent upon the Alexandrians for his philosophical understanding of the passions, he emphasizes the fundamental importance of the religious and theological understanding of *pathos* as separation from God in Gregory.

937. ------. **Maximus Confessor als Meister des geistlichen Lebens.** Wiesbaden: F. Steiner, 1965. A monumental study of the theology and the spirituality of Maximus the Confessor. Völker examines Maximus's systematic treatment of the spiritual life in relation to his creative reception and transformation of the antecedent tradition, from the Alexandrian theologians, Gregory of Nyssa amongst the Cappadocian theologians, Evagrius Ponticus, to Pseudo-Denys the Areopagite. He gives a detailed analysis of the passions in relation to Maximus's theological anthropology, doctrine of sin and its effects, the role of baptism and penance in the struggle against sin and the corrupted passions, the process of the transfiguration of the passions and the role of gnosis in that process of the active pursuit of perfection (*theosis*), and the relation of the emotions to mystical ecstasy.

938. ------. **Kontemplation und Ekstase bei pseudo-Dionysius Areopagita.** Wiesbaden: F. Steiner, 1958. Focusing on the relation between contemplation and ecstasy in the Areopagite's theology of the spiritual life, the author presents a fine discussion of the anagogic transfiguration of the passions in the soul's ascent towards God through the path of contemplative ecstasy.

939. ------. **Das Vollkommenheitsideal des Origenes: Eine Untersuchung zur Geschichte der Frömmigkeit und zu den Anfängen christlicher Mystik.** Beiträge zur historischen Theologie 7. Tübingen: J.C.B. Mohr, 1931. Völker sees the significance of Origen in terms of the intersection between the history of piety and the history of ethics, precisely as the initiator of a Christian mystical theology decisively shaping the Eastern church with an ascetic ideal of perfection for the Christian life. Pivotal in the pursuit of the ascetic ideal of perfection through Christian discipleship is the struggle against sins and the "passions of the flesh" in light of the ecstatic experience of Christian gnosis or faith.

940. ------. **Scala paradisi; Eine Studie zu Johannes Climacus und zugleich eine Vorstudie zu Symeon dem Neuen Theologen.** Wiesbaden, F. Steiner, 1968. This monograph is a systematic and historical-theological study of Johannes Climacus' famous ascetic and mystical treatise, *Scala Paradisi*, and a preparatory study for the

author's later work on Symeon the new theologian. It presents a thorough study of the historical and theological background which was influential upon the thought of Climacus, locating it in the history of Greek Christian piety and spirituality. It also gives a systematic examination of various emotions and passions in terms of Johannes Climacus' portrayal of the cardinal sins or vices, the nature of the struggle against sin, and the virtuous life and its particular virtues.

941. ------. **Fortschritt und Vollendung bei Philo von Alexandrien: Eine Studie zur Geschichte der Frömmigkeit.** Texte und Untersuchungen 49/1. Leipzig: Akademie-Verlag, 1938. The initial volume of Völker's multivolume project to unfold the history of mystical piety and spirituality that is devoted to laying the foundations for his examination of Greek-speaking Christian piety and spirituality in the Patristic period until the rise of Byzantine theology. This monograph on Philo of Alexandria examines the Stoic influences on Philo's Hellenistic Jewish piety and thought, especially in terms of the passions and the role of intellect in the control of the passions for the sake of the moral and spiritual process of advancement.

942. ------. **Der wahre Gnostiker nach Clemens Alexandrinus.** Texte und Untersuchungen 57. Leipzig: Akademie-Verlag, 1952. This vast and lengthy monograph on the mystical piety and spirituality of the "Christian gnosticism" of Clement of Alexandria presents a detailed analysis of the interrelation between sin and the passions of the flesh, the effect of faith and Christian gnosis upon the emotions, and the relation between ecstasy and gnosis in the theology of Clement. It also presents a detailed examination of the theological reception and critique of Hellenistic philosophy (especially Philo and the Stoics) by Clement.

943. ------. "Die Vollkommenheitslehre des Clemens Alexandrinus in ihren geschichtlichen Zusammenhängen." **Theologische Zeitschrift** 3 (1947): 15-39. The essay examines the doctrine of perfection in Clement of Alexandria and interprets it in terms of the relation between gnosis and love. Völker outlines the systematic interconnections of Clement's teaching in relation to other theological topics. The essay provides a helpful contextual background for understanding Clement's discussion of the passions, which was influenced by Philo and Stoicism.

944. Von Balthasar, Hans Urs. **The Glory of the Lord: A Theological Aesthetics, Vol. I: Seeing the Form.** Translated by Erasmo Leiva-Merikakis. Edited by Joseph Fessio, S.J. and John Riches. Edinburgh: T. & T. Clark, 1982. In the first volume of his monumental theological aesthetics, von Balthasar emphasizes the centrality of affectivity in his treatment of the subjective evidence of the experience of faith in terms of "Christian attunement" [*Einstimmung*], in which *con-sensus* as *cum-sentire* (to feel with) is prior *assentire* (to assent to), and his emphasis upon the necessary role of the spiritual senses in the aesthetic experience of faith, and its reciprocity between "receptivity to extraneous im-pression and the ex-pressing of the self onto the extraneous" (p. 244).

945. Von Hügel, Baron Friedrich. "Suffering and God." In **Essays & Addresses on the Philosophy of Religion, Second Series.** London: J. M. Dent & Sons, 1926. Pp. 165-214. Von Hügel examines the merits of theological claims being made concerning whether or not God suffers. Contending against Patripassianism and its claim that there is suffering in God, he argues that there is no suffering in God, but rather sympathy in God. He rejects the rationalist "either-or" between "suffering entails sympathy" and "non-suffering entails asympathy." Sympathy in God is founded in the

system of emotions in the personal life of God, the emotions being joy, love, and delectation.

946. Wadell, Paul J., C.P. The Primacy of Love: An Introduction to the Ethics of Thomas Aquinas. Mahwah: Paulist Press, 1992. In contrast to interpretations of Thomistic ethics as primarily an ethics of natural law, Wadell sees Thomas' ethics as an ethics of the virtues in which there is a distinction between, but not a separation of the moral and the spiritual life. This interpretative emphasis allows for the centrality of the consideration of the passions and the affections in the moral life (courage, hope, and anger) and their purificative, perfecting transformation through the infusion of the gifts of the Spirit, culminating in joy.

947. Wainwright, William J. "James, Rationality, and Religious Belief." Religious Studies 27 (1991): 223-238. Wainwright argues that James contended that some passionally grounded beliefs can be and are not only practically rational but also epistemically rational. His reading challenges interpretations of James presented by John E. Smith and Gerald Myers concerning whether the conditions under which passional human nature may or may not legitimately affect the construction and assessment of beliefs and arguments. The article also examines the advantages and disadvantages of James' approach, especially as to whether James' appeals to generic human needs, interests, and sentiments can only warrant generic religious hypotheses, neglecting the possible justification of convictions in terms of non-generic affections, and the limits of appeals to invariant features of human nature in light of postmodern suspicions concerning such claims.

948. Ware, Kallistos. "The Way of the Ascetics: Negative or Affirmative?" In Asceticism. Edited by Vincent L. Wimbush and Richard Valantasis with the assistance of Gary L. Byron and William S. Love. New York: Oxford University Press, 1995. Pp. 3-15. The article explores the ambiguities in the ascetical theology of Greek Christianity in relation to two constitutive elements of ascetic practice: "withdrawal" (*anachoresis*) and "self-control" (*enkrateia*). Is "withdrawal" world-denying or world-affirming? Is "self-control" repression of the emotions/passions or their transfiguration in *apatheia* as purity of heart? The author presents a theological defense of asceticism in terms of the positive construals of withdrawal and self-control.

949. Werkmeister, Lucyle. "Coleridge on Science, Philosophy, and Poetry: Their Relation to Religion." Harvard Theological Review 52 (1959): 85-118. The article examines the influence of Berkeley and Edmund Burke's "A Philosophical Inquiry into the Origin of our Ideas of the Sublime and the Beautiful" upon Coleridge's thoughts concerning the relation between science, philosophy, and poetry and the suggestive influence of them for his later theological account of the meaning and purpose for all human activities. Werkmeister emphasizes the significance of the role of feeling in Coleridge's understanding of the relation between poetry and religion, both of which appeal to the feelings.

950. Whitehead, Alfred North. Process and Reality : An Essay in Cosmology. Gifford Lectures, 1927-1928. Corrected Edition. Edited by David Ray Griffin and Donald W. Sherburne. New York: Free Press, 1978. Whitehead's metaphysical essay in cosmology is the application of the reformed subjectivist principle for the development of a philosophy of organism through the metaphysical generalization of the elements disclosed in the analysis of the experiences of subjects as actual entities. Actual entities are constituted in the process of the concrescence of operations terminating in

satisfaction. These operations are prehensions or feelings. These are the bedrock for Whitehead's depiction of the internal relatedness between God (as the supreme exemplar of the metaphysical categories) and the world. God is understood by Whitehead to have both a primordial as well as a consequent nature, such that God can be affected by the world and affectively relate to the world.

951. Wilken, Robert L. "Maximus the Confessor on the Affections in Historical Perspective." In Asceticism. Edited by Vincent L. Wimbush and Richard Valantasis with the assistance of Gary L. Byron and William S. Love. New York: Oxford University Press, 1995. Pp. 412-423. Wilken presents a historical overview of Maximus the Confessor's theological understanding of the affections in relation to his theological predecessors (especially Evragius of Pontus and Gregory of Nyssa) and explicates affinities between Maximus and Augustine concerning the emotions. It includes a discussion of the transformative effect of love upon the concupiscible passions (desire and delight) and the irascible passion of anger.

952. Wobbermin, Georg. The Nature of Religion. Translated by Theophil Menzel and Daniel Sommer Robinson with an Introduction by Douglas Clyde Macintosh. New York: Thomas Y. Crowell Company, 1933. In this book which is the second volume of his systematics according to the *religionspsychologische* method, Wobbermin addresses the question of religion in order to overcome two one-sided views: the separation of faith from religion in the so-called crisis theology of Karl Barth and Emil Brunner and the failure to consider the uniqueness of Christianity in the affective understanding of religion in Rudolph Otto. Wobbermin's motto is "back to Schleiermacher and forward to Schleiermacher." Wobbermin seeks to recast and supplement Schleiermacher's understanding of the essence of religion as the feeling of absolute dependence. Though the feeling of absolute dependence is as such the basic religious feeling, Wobbermin adds two additional feelings: the feeling of security and the sense of longing.

953. Wolff, Hans Walter. The Anthropology of the Old Testament. Translated by Margaret Kohl. Philadelphia: Fortress Press, 1974. A classic study of the vocabulary utilized for the being of the human and a presentation of the temporal ("biographical") and sociological dimensions of being human in the Old Testament. The topic of the emotions or "feelings" are examined chiefly in relation to Hebrew words for "spirit" and "heart." Wolff emphasizes the intertwining of affective, volitional, and intellectual (or rational) elements in the various senses given to the most common anthropological term used in the Old Testament, the heart.

954. Yeager, Diane M. "Passion and Suspicion: Religious Affections in "The Will to Believe." Journal of Religion 69 (1989): 467-483. An excellent essay defending James' assessment of the passional character of the "will to believe" and the possibility of the trustworthiness of the passions in the will to believe.

955. Zur Mühlen, Karl-Heinz. "Melanchthons Auffassung vom Affekt in den *Loci communes* von 1521." In Humanismus und Wittenberger Reformation: Festgabe anläßlich des 500. Geburtstages des Praeceptor Germaniae Philipp Melanchthon am 16. Februar 1997. Edited by Michael Beyer and Günther Wartenberg with the assistance of Hans-Peter Hasse. Leipzig: Evangelische Verlagsanstalt, 1996. Pp. 327-338. The article explicates Melanchthon's understanding of *affectus* and the centrality of the affections in his theological anthropology in the 1521 edition of the *Loci* in terms of his critical reception of medieval understandings

(especially Jean Gerson's *De theologia mystica*) and his theological articulation of the dialectic of sin and grace. The essay shows the reemergence of late medieval understandings of the affections in the later theology of Melanchthon which had been de-emphasized in the earlier theology.

956. Zur Mühlen, Karl-Heinz. "Die Affektenlehre im Spätmittelalter und in der Reformationszeit." In <u>Reformatorisches Profil: Studien zum Weg Martin Luthers und der Reformation</u>. Edited by Johannes Brosseder and Athina Lexutt with the assistance of Wibke Janssen, Volkmar Ortmann, and Jochen Remy. Göttingen: Vandenhoeck & Ruprecht, 1995. Pp. 101-122. The article presents an excellent overview of the significant treatments of the affections in late medieval theology and in Reformation theology. The representative figures treated from the late medieval period are Thomas Aquinas, Bonaventure, Pierre D'Ailly, Gabriel Biel, John Gerson, Gert Groote, Johannes Mauburnus, and Thomas à Kempis (for the *devotio moderna*). For Reformation theology, Zur Mühlen discusses Luther, Melanchthon, Calvin, and Zwingli. The article concludes with indications of the effective trajectories of these understandings of the affections in modernity.

957. Zwingmann, W. "*Ex affectu mentis.* Über die Vollkommenheit menschlichen Handelns und menschlicher Hingabe nach Wilhelm von Saint Thierry." <u>Cîteaux</u> 18 (1967): 5-37. This essay and the following essay by Zwingmann are without a doubt the most comprehensive treatment and compendium of material concerning the concept of *affectus* in the theology of William of St. Thierry. This article examines the relation between affections and the mind in relation to the perfection of human action and human devotion.

958. Zwingmann, W. "*Affectus illuminati amoris.* Über das Offenbarwerden der Gnade und die Erfahrung von Gottes beseligender Gegenwart." <u>Cîteaux</u> 18 (1967): 193-226. The second part of Zwingmann's comprehensive examination of *affectus* in the theology of William of St. Thierry. This essay examines William's notion of the illumination of the affections through love in relation to the manifestation of grace and the beatifying experience of God.

Philosophical Studies

959. Addis, Laird. "The Ontology of Emotion." <u>Southern Journal of Philosophy</u> 33 (1995): 261-278. The article claims that an emotion is an "object" of awareness, neither a type of awareness nor a state of consciousness, because an emotion is distinct from feeling an emotion. Those emotions that are "about" something are so only due to the genuine intentionality of an accompanying mental state that is the cause of the feeling. The author claims that this theory can explain how some emotions are "about" something, while others are not.

960. Alain [pseud. of Emile Chartier]. <u>Les Arts et les Dieux</u>. Edited by Georges Bénézé with a Preface by André Bridoux. Collection Bibliothèque de la Pléiade (No. 129). Paris: Gallimard, 1958. Especially noteworthy in this collection of Alain's writings are his writings on aesthetics: *Système des Beaux-Arts* [System of the Beautiful Arts] and *Vingt Leçons sur les Beaux-Arts* [Twenty Lessons on the Beautiful Arts]. They

include extended analyses of the relation between the arts and the passions, emotions, feelings, and sentiments by a philosopher in the French reflexive philosophical tradition.

961. ------. **Les Passions et La Sagesse: <u>Les Idées et les Âges - Les Sentiments familiaux - Les Aventures du coeur - Souvenirs de guerre - Mars ou la guerre jugée - Souvenirs concernant Jules Lagneau - Abrégés pour les aveugles - Platon, Descartes, Hegel - Quatre-vingt-un chapitres sur l'esprit et les passions - Entretiens au bord de la mer [1960]</u>.** Edited by Georges Bénézé with a Preface by André Bridoux. Collection Bibliothèque de la Pléiade (No. 143). Paris: Gallimard, 1960. Important, but often neglected texts by one of the great literary stylists and philosophy teachers in France, the teacher of Sartre, S. Weil, and Dufrenne. Particularly significant is the interrelation between Alain's discussion of the social matrix of sentiments in terms of the family (drawing upon the thought of Comte) and his discussion of the passions in relation to the individual.

962. Allen, Chad. "Smith's *The Felt Meaning of the World* and the Pure Appreciation of Being Simpliciter." <u>Journal of Philosophical Research</u> 21 (1996): 69-80. A review essay of Quentin Smith's *The Felt Meanings of the World* that analyzes Smith's groundwork for a metaphysical view intended as an alternative to nihilism, which Smith claims cannot account for the possibility of faculties other than reason, namely, feeling and intuition, as being sources of metaphysical insight. Smith's metaphysical view is a metaphysics of feeling concerned with the relationship between the world and our feelings through which one can become aware of what the world is, rather than a rational account of the existence of the world. Allen disputes Smith's contention that joy is the proper affective response to the pure existence of the world or Being *simpliciter*, wanting to maintain that a metaphysics of feeling renders such a claim incoherent.

963. Allen, R. T. "Governance by Emotion." <u>Journal of the British Society for Phenomenology</u> 22 (1991): 15-29. Author utilizes insights from Stephen Strasser's "Phenomenology of Feeling" to show that the emotions are necessary for the governance of action. Action through habit is a secondary possibility requiring antecedent guidance furnished by the emotions such that felt desires and aversions initiate action. Hope, fear, and self-confidence provide general aims for specific actions, while lack of confidence and resignation gives rise to abstaining from action.

964. Alquié, Ferdinand. **La Conscience affective.** A La Recherche de la Vérité. Paris: Librarie Philosophique J. Vrin, 1979. A study on the distinctive character of affective consciousness by one of the great students of classical French philosophy, its distinctiveness being that it is not a derivative of cognitive consciousness. The book also discusses love and reason, emotion and anguish, and the relations of affective consciousness to faith and ontological consciousness. It is an important text in the history of contemporary French philosophy on affectivity.

965. Alston, William P. "Emotion and Feeling." In <u>The Encyclopedia of Philosophy</u>, Vol. 1-2. Edited by Paul Edwards et al. New York: Macmillan Publishing Co., and The Free Press, 1967. Pp. 479-486. An article surveying the philosophical issues related to the study of emotion and feeling.

966. Aristotle. **The Complete Works of Aristotle: The Revised Oxford Translation.** Vol. 2. Edited by Jonathan Barnes. Bollingen Series LXXI, 2. Princeton: Princeton University Press, 1984. Considering the towering influence of

Aristotle in the subsequent history of philosophy and in contemporary discussions, one must consult especially his "Nicomachean Ethics" [translated by W. D. Ross and rev. by J. O. Urmson (pp. 1729-1867)] and the "Rhetoric" [translated by W. Rhys Roberts (pp. 2153-2269)].

967. Arregui, Jorge V. "On the Intentionality of Moods: Phenomenology and Linguistic Analysis." **American Catholic Philosophical Quarterly** 70 (1996): 397-411. Paper attempts to defend Wittgenstein's distinction between the cause and the object of an emotion from criticisms from the analytical and phenomenological traditions (e.g., A. Kenny and Strasser), that the connection between object and emotion does not obtain in the case of moods.

968. ------. "Descartes and Wittgenstein on Emotions." **International Philosophical Quarterly** 36 (1996): 319-334. Paper examines Wittgenstein's criticism of the epistemological approach of the Cartesian study of the emotions and contends that Wittgenstein distinguishes between the matter and the form of emotions, such that emotions and physiological changes are not two distinct events, but one event described in two different grammars or ways.

969. Armon-Jones, Claire. **Varieties of Affect.** Toronto: University of Toronto Press, 1991. Three currently dominant philosophical theories of the concept of affect are critically examined: the standard, the neo-cognitivism, and the objectual view. It is argued that these views radically distort our understanding of affective life. A new theory is developed which explains the cognitive nature of affective states, their special logic, their degrees of conceptual independence from objecthood, and the relationships between their objectless and object-directed forms. The book concludes by showing how the arguments presented challenge certain fundamental assumptions about the rationality and moral status of affect and require a revision of the conception of the good in affect.

970. Azouvi, François. **Maine de Biran: La Science de L'Homme.** Bibliothèque d'Histoire de la Philosophie. Paris: Librarie Philosophique J. Vrin, 1995. A superb historical and philosophical study of the genesis of Maine de Biran's reflective journey towards a new anthropology, which was and is so influential in subsequent French philosophical thought. For the purpose of this bibliography, the final section of the book is valuable for the treatment of feeling in Maine de Biran's reflections on the science of the interior man in relation to moral and religious philosophy.

971. Baier, Annette C. "The Ambiguous Limits of Desire." In **The Ways of Desire.** Edited by Joel Marks. Chicago: Precedent, 1986. Pp. 39-61. Baier examines the views of Hobbes, Descartes, and Hume in order to determine what might plausibly be affirmed concerning the relations between desires and emotions/passions, such as love. With their aid, she argues that any attempt either to identify desire, together with belief, as being the central psychological phenomena or to reduce the emotions/passions to them is a mistake to be resisted.

972. ------. "Hume, The Women's Moral Theorist," In **Women and Moral Theory.** Edited by Kittay, Eva Feder. Totowa: Rowman Littlefield, 1987. Pp. 37-55. The essay contrasts Hume's moral theory as the cultivation of proper character traits through the correction of the sentiments with Kant's and argues for its congeniality with the findings of Carol Gilligan on the psychology of moral development vis-à-vis Kohlberg's Kantian position.

973. ------. **A Progress of Sentiments: Reflections on Hume's "*Treatise.*"** Cambridge: Harvard University Press, 1991. In this major study of Hume, Baier examines the relation between Hume's presentation of cognitive abilities and disabilities in Book I ["Of the Understanding"] and his analysis and selective sanctioning of the repertoire of passions and sentiments in Books II ["Of the Passions"] and III ["Of Morals"]. Baier argues that, while in Book I reason narrowly construed in a rationalist sense fails the test of reflexivity, Hume presents a more social and natural reason that is included among the virtues.

974. **Barad, Judith. "Aquinas on the Role of Emotion in Moral Judgment and Activity."** The Thomist **55 (1991): 397-414.** The paper presents an account of Thomas' understanding of the role of emotion in moral judgment and activity, contending that Thomas presents an intermediate perspective that neither contends that emotions are the foundation for moral philosophy nor that they categorically should not enter into moral judgment. Barad argues that the strength of Thomas' position is that it can specify how emotions can both support as well as impair moral judgments by attending to the characteristic role each of the human faculties has in moral deliberation and activity.

975. **Barnes, Hazel. "Sartre on Emotions."** Journal of the British Society for Phenomenology **15 (1984): 3-15.** Noting that Sartre always distinguished between emotion manifestations as immediate affective impulses, emotional behavior, and emotional states, Barnes argues that whereas Sartre early on considered emotional behavior as ineffective and probably in bad faith, his later writings affirmed that emotional behavior could be effective in alliance with praxis. Barnes attributes the changes in the development of these views to his treatments of love.

976. **Barnouw, Jeffrey. "Passion as 'Confused' Perception or Thought in Descartes, Malebranche and Hutcheson."** Journal of the History of Ideas **53 (1992): 397-424.** The author examines the treatment and the development of the passions as "confused" thoughts or perceptions in Descartes, Malebranche, and Hutcheson. He explicates the new definition and application Descartes gives to this theme of classical philosophy and its subsequent reception and transformation in Malebranche and Hutcheson.

977. **Ben-Ze'ev, Aaron. "Appraisal Theories of Emotions."** Journal of Philosophical Research **22 (1997): 129-143.** The paper examines the assumption that evaluations or appraisals are the most important factor in emotions. The author argues that the assumption can imply three claims that are not necessarily related: (1) evaluative patterns distinguish one emotion from another; (2) evaluative appraisals distinguish emotion from non-emotions; and (3) emotional evaluations determine emotional intensity. The author argues that (1) and (3) are true, but (2) is false.

978. ------. **"The Nature of Emotions."** Philosophical Studies **52 (1987): 393-409.** Paper presents a general theory of emotions that takes into account their complexity. The author identifies two basic dimensions of emotional attitudes as mental states: feeling and intentionality. The intentional dimension is analyzed in terms of three factors: evaluative, cognitive, and motivational.

979. **Ben-Ze'ev, Aaron / Oatley, Justin. "The Intentional and Social Nature of Human Emotions: Reconsideration of the Distinction between Basic and Non-Basic Emotions."** The Journal of the Theory of Social Behavior **26 (1996): 81-94.** The article seeks to clarify the contemporary debate over the nature of basic and non-basic

emotions. It examines several senses of basic emotions, clarifying the nature of the relation between them. It argues that non-basic emotions are the result of the development of complex intentional capacities. The authors suggest that non-basic emotions are those involving a conception of self in which social comparisons between the self and others become central. They further argue that the emergence of social development also impacts upon basic emotions, such that social concerns acquire a centrality in them as well.

980.   Beyssade, Jean-Marie. "De l'émotion intérieure chez Descartes à l'affect actif Spinoziste." In Spinoza: Issues and Directions. The Proceedings of the Chicago Spinoza Conference. Edited by Edwin Curley and Pierre-François Moreau. Brill's Studies in Intellectual History, Vol. 14. Leiden: E. J. Brill, 1990. Pp. 176-190. A superb article concerned with explicating Descartes' understanding of interior emotion and its reception and transformation by Spinoza. It is an essay that explores the topic in both historical and systematic detail.

981.   ------. "La Classification cartesienne des passions." Revue Internationale de Philosophie 37 (1983): 278-287. The article is an explication of the order and structure underlying Descartes' classification and taxonomy of the passions of the soul.

982.   Bollnow, Otto-Friedrich. Das Wesen des Stimmungen. Second Edition. Frankfurt am Main: Vittorio Klostermann, 1949. Bollnow's monograph is chiefly significant for his critique of Heidegger's provocative identification of anxiety (*Angst*) as the center of the ontological condition of human existence, presenting a similar approach to the significance of affections and moods but with a more positive assessment of the importance of other moods.

983.   Bradley, James C. "'The Critique of Pure Feeling': Bradley, Whitehead, and the Anglo-Saxon Metaphysical Tradition." Process Studies 14 (1985): 253-264. The author explicates the transformative appropriaton of Bradley's theory of feeling by Whitehead. He contends that feeling is utilized by Whitehead as a principle of functional analysis in order to establish a philosophical cosmology, rather than as a rationally inaccessible metaphysical substratum.

984.   Bradley, James. "Relations, Intelligibilité et Non-contradiction dans la Métaphysique du Sentir de F. H. Bradley: Une Réinterpretation." Archives de Philosophie 54 (1991): 529-551. The article seeks to redress the inadequacies of previous interpretations of Bradley's treatment of relations in light of their failure to take into consideration the fact that his doctrine of relations as internal is predicated upon his theory of feeling. The article provides a detailed textual analysis of Bradley's texts in light of his discussions with his contemporaries.

985.   Brandt, Richard B. The Philosophy of Schleiermacher: The Development of His Theory of Scientific and Religious Knowledge. Second Greenwood Reprinting. Westport: Greenwood Press, 1971. This book is an examination of the development of Schleiermacher's early thought, tracing the interplay between his philosophical and theological thoughts, especially those concerning the relation among feeling, knowing, and religion.

986.   Brentano, Franz Clemens. Psychology from an Empirical Standpoint. Edited by Oskar Kraus and translated by Antos C. Rancurello, D. B. Terrell, and Linda L. McAllister; English edition edited by Linda L. McAllister. International

Library of Philosophy and Scientific Method. London, Routledge and Kegan Paul; New York, Humanities Press, 1973. Brentano presents a taxonomy of mental acts into three classes: ideas, judgments, and phenomena of love and hate (in which are comprised emotions, feelings, desires, and acts of the will) that adopt either a pro- or con-attitude toward what is judged.

987. Brusotti, Marco. **Die Leidenschaft der Erkenntnis: Philosophie und ästhetische Lebensgestaltung bei Nietzsche von *Morgenröthe* bis *Also sprach Zarathustra*.** Monographien und Texte zur Nietzsche-Forschung, 37. New York/Berlin: Walter de Gruyter, 1997. Lengthy and detailed investigation of the development of Nietzsche's understanding of "passion as knowledge." It provides rigorous exegetical analyses of Nietzsche's texts concerning the relation of passion to his understanding of knowledge and aesthetics.

988. Calhoun, Cheshire. "Cognitive Emotions?" **What is an Emotion? Classic Readings in Philosophical Psychology.** Edited by Cheshire Calhoun and Robert C. Solomon. New York: Oxford University Press, 1984. Pp. 327-342. The essay raises a number of objections to cognitive theories of emotion. The author contends that interpretative "seeings as . . ." and not beliefs constitute emotions. She denies the claim that beliefs are constitutive of emotions or that emotion ascriptions entail belief ascriptions. She claims that her proposal can account for the conflicts between emotions and beliefs more adequately than prevailing cognitive theories.

989. Calhoun, Cheshire and Robert C. Solomon, Eds. **What is an Emotion? Classic Readings in Philosophical Psychology.** New York: Oxford University Press, 1984. An excellent anthology of classical texts on the emotions from the history of philosophy, discussions between psychology and philosophy (e.g., Darwin, James, Dewey, Freud, and Schlachter and Singer), the continental tradition (Brentano, Scheler, Heidegger, and Sartre), and essays from the analytical tradition (Ryle, Bedford, Kenny, Thalberg, and the editors). An introductory essay sketches five models of theory: sensation, physiological, behavioral, evaluative, and cognitive theories. The collection also includes a good bibliography at the end.

990. Cataldi, Sue L. **Emotion, Depth, and Flesh: A Study of Sensitive Space. Reflections on Merleau-Ponty's Philosophy of Embodiment.** Albany: State University of New York Press, 1980. The author extends the insights of Merleau-Ponty's ontology of embodiment and James J. Gibson on the character of perceived depth for an understanding of the dynamics of emotional experience and how emotional and perceived depths are intermingled and related to changes in self-understanding.

991. Chenu, Marie-Dominique. "Les Passions vertueuses: L'Anthroplogie de Saint Thomas." **Revue philosophique de Louvain** 72 (1974): 11-18. The article by one of the great interpreters of the thought of Thomas Aquinas examines the thesis of the consubstantiality of the soul and the body in the human in terms of the morality of the passions. Chenu contends that Thomas claimed that the passions are the subjects of virtues and critiqued the dualism of *ratio inferior* and *ratio superior* in affirming that the passions are virtuous in light of the penetration of spirit and sensibilities.

992. Chisholm, Roderick M. "Brentano's Theory of Correct and Incorrect Emotion." **Revue Internationale de Philosophie** 20 (1966): 395-415. An excellent article explicating the criteria for distinguishing between correct and incorrect emotions in Brentano's psychology and ethics.

993. Cicero. **Tusculanae Disputationes (Tusculan Disputations)**. Text with English translation by J. E. King. Loeb Classical Library. Cambridge: Harvard University Press, 1927. An important source for the Roman reception of Stoic philosophy, which proved to be influential for subsequent philosophical and theological thought.

994. Cohen, Ted. Metaphor, Feeling, and Narrative." **Philosophy and Literature** 21 (1997): 223-244. The essay argues that metaphor can be a device for the communication and incitement of feeling. It also suggests that narratives can also have this effect through readers' metaphorical identifications with authors and literary characters.

995. Cooper, John M. "An Aristotelian Theory of the Emotions." In **Essays on Aristotle's "*Rhetoric*."** Edited by Amélie Oksenberg Rorty. Berkeley: University of California Press, 1996. Pp. 238-257. The essay is an excellent account of Aristotle's analysis of various emotions in Book II of the *Rhetoric* seeks to elicit certain patterns in those analyses that could provide the basis for a general theoretical account of the emotions which is not provided in any of his major ethical writings.

996. ------. "Plato's Theory of Human Motivation." **History of Philosophy Quarterly** 1 (1984): 3-21. The essay is a superb analysis of the tripartite understanding of the parts of the soul as reason, spirit (*thumos*), and appetite in Plato's *Republic*. The essay advances the thesis that competitiveness and the desire for esteem and self-esteem are an intrinsic form of human motivation, distinct from both reason and the appetites.

997. ------. "Plato's Theory of Human Good in the *Philebus*." **The Journal of Philosophy** 74 (1977): 713-730. The paper examines the nature of the good and its relations to both knowledge and pleasure in terms of Socrates' four ontological genera: indeterminates, determinates, mixed things of the union of indeterminate and the determinate, and the causes of mixed things. Cooper shows how this ontology resolves the dispute concerning whether pleasure or knowledge has priority in terms of the constitution of the good.

998. ------. "Pleasure and Desire in Epicurus." In **Reason and Emotion: Essays on Ancient Moral Psychology and Ethical Theory**. Princeton: Princeton University Press, 1999. Pp. 485-514. The essay explicates Epicurus' psychological theory of human motivation and action and its discussion of the passions, desires, and appetites. The essay advances the thesis that Epicurus was not a psychological hedonist as has been traditionally maintained by philosophers and classical scholars.

999. ------. "Posidonius on Emotions." In **Reason and Emotion: Essays on Ancient Moral Psychology and Ethical Theory**. Princeton: Princeton University Press, 1999. Pp. 449-484. The article defends the Stoic character of Posidonius' theory of the emotions wherein emotions are ultimately functions of the rational faculty, but notes the distinctive character of Posidonius' contribution advancing beyond previous Stoic theories of the action, especially that of Chrysippus.

1000. ------. "Some Remarks on Aristotle's Moral Psychology." **Southern Journal of Philosophy** 27 Suppl. (1988): 25-42. The article examines the historical and philosophical significance of Aristotles' moral psychology and its treatment of the non-rational character of desires and emotions, their independence from human reason, as alternative to the Stoic account of these phenomena as rational.

1001. Cooper, John M. and J. F. Procopé, Eds. Seneca: Moral and Political Essays. Cambridge Texts in the History of Political Thought. Cambridge: Cambridge University Press, 1995. This volume presents new translations of the most important of Seneca's "Moral Essays": *On Anger, On Mercy, On the Private Life*, and the first four books of *On Favours*. The general Introduction offers a good introduction and overview of Seneca's Stoic philosophy and discussion of the fundamental ideas, such as the emotions and passions, in his moral, social, and political philosophies.

1002. Cottingham, John. "The Intellect, the Will and the Passions: Spinoza's Critique of Descartes." Journal of the History of Philosophy 26 (1988): 239-257. The article explicates how Spinoza's critique of the distinction between perceptions and volitions breaks with both Aristotelian and Cartesian analyses of the soul. Yet it is argued that Spinoza's critique can be seen as a natural development of Descartes' thought, but one which does not sufficiently take into consideration Descartes' concept of freedom.

1003. ------. "Cartesian Ethics: Reason and the Passions." Revue Internationale de Philosophie 50 (1996): 193-216. The paper examines the relations between Cartesian science and Cartesian ethics, indicating how the innovations in the former produced a distinctive approach to ethics. The major link lies in Descartes' philosophical anthropology and its understanding of the human as embodied in terms of the passions. Cottingham superbly shows the ethical significance of Cartesian ethics in light of its attention to the passions, one in contrast to customary readings of Descartes.

1004. Craemer-Ruegenberg, Ingrid. "Begrifflich-systematische Bestimmung von Gefühlen. Beiträgen aus der antiken Tradition." In Zur Philosophie der Gefhle. Suhrkamp Taschenbuch Wissenschaft; 1074. Edited by Hinrich Fink-Eitel und Georg Lohmann. Frankfurt am Main: Suhrkamp Verlag, 1993. Pp. 20-32. The article provides a useful topological survey of the various semantic determinations associated with the ambiguity of the concept of "feeling" in ancient philosophy.

1005. Crocker, Robert. "Mysticism and Enthusiasm in Henry More." In Henry More (1614-1687) Tercentenary Studies. Edited by Sarah Hutton with a biography and bibliography by Robert Crocker. International Archives of the History of Ideas 127. Dordrecht: Kluwer Academic Publishers, 1990. Pp. 137-155. Crocker presents a richly detailed exposition of More's psycho-physiology of the purification of the passions and his understanding of true divine senses.

1006. Crossley, David. "Feeling in Bradley's *Ethical Studies*." Idealistic Studies 19 (1989): 43-61. Crossley examines Bradley's account of moral decisions in terms of felt harmonies or felt contradictions in light of his contention that moral principles cannot tell one what to do because of either their formal and empty character or as being generalizations not necessarily applicable in future situations. The essay provides an explication of Bradley's theory of feeling and its role in his theory of the psychology of moral development.

1007. Cudworth, Ralph. A Treatise concerning Eternal and Immutable Morality. With A Treatise of Freewill. Edited by Sarah Hutton. Cambridge Texts in the History of Philosophy. Cambridge: Cambridge University Press, 1996. An exemplary text presenting the understanding of the passions in Cambridge Neo-Platonism by one of the most important English philosophers in the seventeenth century. Opponent of Hobbes and Spinoza, Cudworth utilized Descartes' theory of the passions of the soul, yet also quite critical of Descartes.

1008. David, Anthony. "Le Doeuff and Irigaray on Descartes." Philosophy Today 41 (1997): 367-382. Article demonstrates how Michele Le Doeuff and Luce Irigaray, leading French feminist philosophers, appropriate elements of Descartes' thought.

1009. Deigh, John. "Cognitivism in the Theory of Emotions." Ethics 1045 (1994): 824-854. Article superbly traces the ascendancy of cognitivism in current philosophical accounts of the emotions in light of two major criticisms of feeling-centered conceptions long a dominant factor in British empiricism: the failure to account adequately for the intentionality of emotions and to present emotions as proper objects of rational assessment. The article questions, however, whether the success of these criticisms entails the validity of cognitivist conceptions of the emotions.

1010. Dent, N. J. H. The Moral Psychology of the Virtues. New York: Cambridge University Press, 1984. The author contends that the sense-desire, emotion, and rational desire are the three sources of human activity and that the differing relations between these three sources are constitutive of the various virtues. He further argues that virtuous dispositions include not merely acting on desire nor on the belief that something is right alone, but comprise a structure informed and ordered by right practical reason expressing the common assent of both the heart and the mind.

1011. Deprun, Jean. "Qu'est ce qu'une passion de l'ame?" Revue philosophique de la France et de l'Étranger 17 (1988): 407-413. An excellent examination of the different senses of "passion" in Descartes' treatise (as perceptions, sensations, and emotions) and the interrelation between them.

1012. Descartes, René. "The Passions of the Soul." In The Philosophical Writings of Descartes, Vol. 1. Translated by John Cottingham, Robert Stoothoff, and Dugald Murdoch. Cambridge: Cambridge University Press, 1985. Pp. 325-404.

1013. De Sousa, Ronald. The Rationality of Emotion. Cambridge, Mass.: MIT Press, 1987. Probably the best written book on the emotions and their role in the rational life, defending the possibility of assessing the emotions as rational and objective, and in the conduct of life. De Sousa argues that emotions are a kind of perception with roots in paradigm scenarios possessing an essentially dramatic structure. It is a standard work to come to grips with, discussing the emotions at different levels.

1014. Despland, Michael. The Education of Desire: Plato and the Philosophy of Religion. Toronto: University of Toronto Press, 1985. Linking classical approaches with those of modern Christianity, Despland presents how Plato understood religion as a way of educating human desires for the sake of well-being that comes from therapy of appetites that hinder the life of the mind and the pursuit of justice. He presents Plato's philosophy of religion as a therapy of words that educates desires in light of the reality of Eros and its destructive and constructive potential, individual and social.

1015. Dewey, John. Art as Experience. Introduction by Abraham Kaplan. The Later Works of John Dewey, 1925-1953, Vol. 10: 1934. Edited by Jo Ann Boydston et al. Carbondale/Edwardsville: Southern Illinois University Press, 1989. A major text presenting Dewey's understanding of the crucial importance of the role of the emotions in art as experience of the felt character of "qualitative meaning."

1016. ------. "Feeling." In **The Early Works of John Dewey, 1882-1898**, Vol. 2: **1887 - Psychology.** Carbondale/Edwardsville: Southern Illinois University Press, 1967. Pp. 215-297. Dewey's early formulation of a theory of feeling within the language of voluntaristic idealism, but one in which there are important themes in continuity with his later work: feeling as adjustment, as activity, and as interest.

1017. ------. "The Theory of Emotion. (I) Emotional Attitudes." **Psychological Review** 1 (1894): 553-569. The article presents a critique of Darwin's *Expression of Emotions in Man and Animals* in order to integrate it with the James-Lange theory of emotion through the use of William James' notion of the "psychologist's fallacy." He argues that emotions are "the reduction of movements and stimulation originally useful into attitudes."

1018. ------. "The Theory of Emotions. (II) The Significance of Emotions." **Psychological Review** 2 (1895): 13-32. Dewey extends the insights of the first part of his essay to present emotional experience as an integral part of the rational construction of action. Emotions are the interruption of an on going line of conduct where two tendencies are in tension with one another, and they are at the core of rational behavior. It is an interesting essay to compare with De Sousa's.

1019. Dorschel, Andreas. "Empfindung, Gefühl und Emotion: Zur analyse von Bewertungen." In **Mythos Wertfreiheit? Neue Beiträge zur Objektivität in den Human- und Kulturwissenschaften.** Edited by Karl-Otto Apel and Matthias Kettner in connection with the Istituto Italiano per gli Studi Filosofici. Frankfurt/New York: Campus Verlag, 1994. Pp. 157-173. The paper is concerned with distinguishing sensations, emotions, and feelings from one another in terms of their irreducible distinctiveness and the relations between them. The author presents several conjectures concerning their relation to the requirements of rational evaluation or appraisal, namely, that feelings and emotions have a relation to affirmation or denial, but that evaluation has a distinctive affinity with emotions, not sensations or feelings.

1020. ------. "Über die Intentionalität von Emotionen." **Zeitschrift für Philosophie und Praxis** (1996): 9-12. Utilizing insights from Wittgenstein, the author provides a careful analysis of the intentional objects of emotions and the distinction between the cause and the object of an emotion, that provides the basis for a critical examination of psychotherapeutic practices.

1021. Drost, Mark P. "Intentionality in Aquinas' Theory of Emotions." **International Philosophical Quarterly** 31 (1991): 449-460. The article presents a defense of the plausibility of Aquinas' contentions that "where there is a specific object, there is a specific emotion" and that "the object determines both the identity and the very nature of an emotion" from accusations of implausibility. The author argues that these claims are plausible when one distinguishes between the intentional object and the material object and by aspects of Aquinas' salient intentional account of the emotions.

1022. Dufrenne, Mikel. **Phenomenology of Aesthetic Experience.** Translated by Edward S. Casey [and others]. Northwestern University Studies in Phenomenology & Existential Philosophy. Evanston: Northwestern University Press, 1973. Dufrenne, a student of Alain, presents his masterful phenomenological analysis of aesthetic perception and of the primacy of feeling in aesthetic perception. He presents a critique of aesthetic experience in terms of the affective a priori which is both cosmological as well as existential. The affective a priori is explicated as the ontological bond between world and self. It is the foundational text for Dufrenne's other writings.

1023. ------. **Le poétique. Précédé de Pour une philosophie non théologique. Second ed., rev. and augm. Bibliothèque de philosophie contemporaine. Paris, Presses Universitaires de France, 1973.** While *The Phenomenology of Aesthetic Experience* examined the aesthetic experience of the work of art, this text is its complement, being the explication of the coming-to-be of the creation of the work of art in the poetic state of the artist and its affective and expressive character in relation to nature.

1024. ------. **The Notion of the A Priori. Translated with an Introduction by Edward S. Casey. Preface by Paul Ricoeur. Northwestern University Studies in Phenomenology & Existential Philosophy. Evanston: Northwestern University Press, 1966.** This text is the elaboration of a rethinking of the notion of the a priori as both objective (formal, material, perceived, and constituting) and subjective (know a priori, incarnate, corporeal, and social). Both a prioris are founded in the affinity between the human and the world that Dufrenne explicates in terms of sentiment. The text includes valuable discussions of Scheler and others.

1025. ------. **L'inventaire des à priori: recherche de l'originaire. Paris: C. Bourgois, 1981.** This text is the sequel to *The Notion of the A Priori* in which Dufrenne articulates the impossibility of providing an exhaustive system of the a priori because of the historicity of the a priori. Drawing upon Kant's division of the anthropological faculties as cognitive, volitional, and affective, he presents an inventory of these a priori that does not claim to be exhaustive.

1026. Duns Scotus. Duns Scotus on the Will and Morality. Selected and trans., with an Introduction, by Allan B. Wolter, O.F.M. Translation edition edited by William A. Frank. Washington, D.C.: The Catholic University of America Press, 1986. An excellent collection and translation of important ethical writings by Duns Scotus that includes an excellent bibliography of secondary examinations of Scotus' thought. It is especially useful for the examination of Scotus' discussions of the ethical significance of the affections for justice and the advantageous as well as its treatments of the will in relation to the appetites.

1027. Epicurus. Epicurus: The Extant Remains. Edited and translated by Ernest Barker. Oxford: Clarendon Press, 1946. An invaluable collection of the various texts of Epicurus.

1028. Emotion and the Arts. Edited by Mette Hjort and Sue Laver. New York: Oxford University Press, 1997. An interdisciplinary volume encapsulating the current debates concerning the role of beliefs, intentions, and judgments in emotional responses to art in various genres. The essays represent both social constructivist and cognitivist views of emotion in four major areas: "the paradox of fiction," "emotion and its expression in art," "the rationality of emotional responses to art," and "the value of emotion." The introductory essays are superb, and a substantial bibliography is included.

1029. Enç, Berent. "Hume on Causal Necessity: A Study from the Perspective of Hume's Theory of Passions." History of Philosophy Quarterly 2 (1985): 235-251. The essay examines Hume's views on causation by focusing on his notion that the idea of causal inference is the idea of a necessary connection derived from an impression of reflection or a passion. Hume's theory of passions is utilized to demonstrate the coherence in Hume's accounts of causation, which has the additional advantage of seeing the *Treatise* as a unified treatment of all the philosophical issues addressed.

1030. Epictetus. Discourses. Two Volumes. Text with English translation by W. A. Oldfather. Loeb Classical Library. Cambridge: Harvard University Press, 1925, 1928. These are writings devoted almost exclusively to the moral aspects of Stoic philosophy, advocating the peace of mind through the proper control of the passions by distinguishing between what is and what is not in one's control.

1031. Fell, Joseph P. Emotion in the Thought of Sartre. New York: Columbia University Press, 1965. The monograph is an examination of the development of Sartre's phenomenological theory of the emotions. Part I examines the early writings and Part II analyzes the treatment of emotion in *Being and Nothingness*. Part III is a critical examination of Sartre's theory, prosecuted with particular reference to Whitehead, James, and Dewey, contending that Sartre has falsely identified emotion with an act of consciousness.

1032. Feuerbach, Ludwig. Lectures on the Essence of Religion. Translated by Ralph Mannheim. New York/Evanston/London: Harper & Row, Publishers, 1967. For Feuerbach, the essence of religion is identical with self-consciousness, the consciousness the human has of its own essential nature, species. The nature of the human is constituted by that which is proper to the humanity of the human, namely, reason, will, and affection. For Feuerbach, religion has no distinctive dispositions or emotions peculiar to itself. What religion claims exclusively for its object are simply the same dispositions and emotions that the human experiences either in relation to itself, other humans, or to Nature. Feeling alone is the object of feeling, and feeling is sympathy that arises only in community, the love of human to human.

1033. Fillion, Lahille Janine. Le "*De ira*" de Sénèque et la philosophie stoicienne des passions. Paris: Klincksieck, 1984. The book is an excellent historical and philosophical treatment of the passions in Stoic philosophy, especially in its analysis of anger in Seneca's thought.

1034. Fink-Eitel, Hinrich. "Angst und Freiheit. Überlegungen zur philosophishen Anthropologie." In Zur Philosophie der Gefühle. Edited by Hinrich Fink-Eitel und Georg Lohmann. Suhrkamp Taschenbuch Wissenschaft, 1074. Frankfurt am Main: Suhrkamp Verlag, 1993. Pp. 57-88. The essay examines the confrontation between modern theories of the affects with Freud's psychoanalytic theory of anxiety and the affections after a survey of the treatment of the affects in the history of philosophy. The essay pays attention to the intentional-propositional character of the affections, their relation to time, their practical and voluntary aspects, and the individual-subjective and the social-intersubjective constitution.

1035. Floyd, Shawn D. "Aquinas on Emotion: A Response to Some Recent Interpretations." History of Philosophy Quarterly 15 (1998): 161-175. An analysis of Thomas' view of human emotion as involving two acts, a cognitive act of belief or judgment and a passion as an act of sense appetite occurring through bodily change. Author argues that, for Thomas, passion is not to be identified as emotion, but rather as a constitutive element of human emotion.

1036. Fontanelle, Jacques. "Modalisations et Modulations passionnelles." Revue Internationale de Philosophie 48 (1994): 341-362. The essay outlines the significant import that a semiotics of the passions has for an understanding of the theory of modalities. The essay concludes with the observation that a semiotics of the passions provides a better instrument for ordering the passions in contrast to the categorical taxonomies utilized in the seventeenth and eighteenth centuries.

1037. Forthomme, Bernard. "L'épreuve affective de l'autre selon Emmanuel Lévinas et Michel Henry." Revue de Métaphysique et de Morale 91 (1986): 90-114. A dialectical examination of the thought of Emmanuel Lévinas and Michel Henry concerning the affective proof of the alterity of the other, both in terms of their mutual differences and similarities.

1038. Fourier, Charles. The Passions of the Soul and Their Influence on Society and Civilization. Two Volumes. Translated by H. Doherty. London: H. Ballieve, 1851. A classic treatment of the social dimensions of the passions. Fourier identifies thirteen passions whose release from the repression of civilization will bring about the replacement of human misery and division with happiness and unity. These passions are (1) the five senses, (2) the social passions (ambition, friendship, love, and family feeling), (3) the distributive passions (the "cabalist" passion for intrigue and mystery, the passion for diversification, and the "composite" passion for combining pleasures), and (4) the passion for harmony which synthesizes the other passions.

1039. Frankenberry, Nancy. Religion and Radical Empiricism. SUNY Series in Religious Studies. New York: SUNY Press, 1987. The monograph presents an exposition of the traditions of radical empiricism in religious perspective (William James and John Dewey), theistic interpretations of Henry Nelson Wieman, Bernard Meland, and Bernard Loomer, and in the metaphysical perspectives of Charles Hartshorne and Buddhism. The essays attend to the import of the felt quality of experience in James, Dewey, and Whitehead.

1040. Frede, Michael. "The Stoic Doctrine of the Affections of the Soul." In The Norms of Nature. Edited by Malcolm Schofield and Gisela Striker. Cambridge: Cambridge University Press; Paris: Maison des Sciences de l'Homme, 1986. Pp. 93-110. The essay provides a synoptic discussion of the treatment of the affections of the soul in Stoic philosophy.

1041. Frings, Manfred S. Max Scheler: A Concise Introduction into the World of a Great Thinker. Second Edition. Milwaukee: Marquette University Press, 1996. The best introductory examination of Scheler's thought, especially the systematic aspects of his theory of feeling and its philosophical significance.

1042. Gardner, Harry M., Ruth Clark Metcalf and John G. Beebe-Center. Emotion: A History of Theories. First Greenwood Reprinting. Westport: Greenwood Press, Publishers, 1970. This text was first published in 1937, but it still presents today a useful history of theories of the emotions from the ancient Greeks, Aristotle, Patristic and Medieval thought, the Renaissance, Descartes, Malebranche, Spinoza, and Hobbes in the seventeenth century to the early twentieth century.

1043. Gilbert, Christopher. "Freedom and Enslavement: Descartes on Passions and the Will." History of Philosophy Quarterly 15 (1998): 177-190. The essay presents an interpretation of Descartes' understanding of the relation between the will and the passions in light of the apparent contradiction of his affirmation of the will as the source of the actions of the soul and that the passions can enslave the soul. Gilbert argues for a reading of Descartes that allows for consistency between the two affirmations.

1044. Gordon, Robert M. "The Passivity of the Emotions." Philosophical Review 95 (1986): 371-392. Excellent analysis of the ambiguities and misconceptions involved in the notion of the passivity of emotions which have contributed to the contention that emotions are voluntary actions (e.g., Solomon). Gordon explicates the systematic differences between emotions and action, although both are each causally dependent upon both cognitive and attitudinal states.

1045. ------. The Structure of Emotions: Investigations in Cognitive Philosophy. Cambridge Studies in Philosophy. Cambridge /New York: Cambridge University Press, 1987. A rigorously argued examination of the causal structures of beliefs, desires, and wishes underlying various emotions. Gordon emphasizes the propositional content of emotions and draws a distinction between "factive" (related to something that is or is believed to be the case) and "epistemic" (related to something that might be the case) emotions. He also offers an excellent criticism of the James-Schacter theory of emotion.

1046. Gouhier, Henri. "Le coeur qui sent les trois dimensions." In La Passion de la Raison: Hommage à Ferdinand Alquié. Published under the direction of Jean-Luc Marion in collaboration with Jean Deprun. Paris: Presses Universitaires de France, 1983. Pp. 203-216. A marvelous essay on the senses of the "heart" in Pascal's philosophy by one of the great masters of the history of philosophy in France.

1047. ------. Les Conversions de Maine de Biran, histoire philosophique du sentiment religieux en France. Paris, J. Vrin, 1947. Gouhier's study remains foundational for the development of Maine de Biran's thought as a series of intellectual conversions, culminating in renewed attention to the role of feeling in Maine de Biran's reflections in philosophy of religion that he developed towards the end of his life. Gouhier is especially attentive to the importance of affections in Maine de Biran's exposition of the interior man and the influence of Rousseau and Fenelon upon him.

1048. ------. La philosophie de Malebranche et son expérience religieuse, Histoire philosophique du Sentiment religieux en France. Paris: J. Vrin, 1948. A classic study of Malebranche's philosophy attentive to the religious sources that inform his Christian philosophy, indispensable for understanding the intertwining of metaphysical and theological issues contextualizing his examination of the passions of the soul.

1049. Green, O. H. "Actions, Emotions, and Desires." In Marks, Joel (ed.). The Ways of Desire: New Essays in Philosophical Psychology on the Concept of Wanting. Chicago: Precedent, 1986. Pp.115-131. Though the active/passive distinction seems plausible in the sense that what we do is in our control, as what happens to us is not, and seems important for notions of responsibility, Green argues that several ways of drawing the distinction are burdened with difficulties. He contends that an interpretation of the distinction between passivity and activity in terms of direct dependence on desires which are responsive to considerations of desirability is more adequate for understanding the interrelation between action, emotion, and desire.

1050. ------. The Emotions: A Philosophical Theory. Philosophical Studies Series, v. 53. Dordrecht/Boston/London: Kluwer Academic Publishers, 1992. In contrast to theorists who derive the intentionality of emotions from the beliefs to which they are related and see non-intentional phenomena to be constitutive of emotions and those who understand emotions to be evaluative beliefs or judgments, Green argues for the greater adequacy of a "Belief-Desire" theory, wherein emotions are interrelated structures of beliefs and desires, that can account for the hedonic character of emotional affectivity.

1051. ------. **"Wittgenstein and the Possibility of a Philosophical Theory of Emotion."** Metaphilosophy 10 (1979): 256-264. Green argues that Wittgenstein not only in the *Blue and Brown Books* and the *Philosophical Investigations* rejected theories identifying emotions with inner feelings and outward behavior, but also doubted the possibility of a theory of emotion. Green maintains that Wittgenstein does not establish that a satisfactory theory cannot be given and proposes a theory to which Wittgenstein's objections do not apply.

1052. Greenspan, Patricia. **Emotions and Reasons: An Inquiry into Emotional Justification**. New York: Routledge, 1988. The book puts forth, in contrast to Cartesian views of emotions and views of emotions as being essentially judgments or beliefs, the position that they should be understood as being states of comfort or discomfort with evaluative propositional content. Greenspan argues that emotions possess a special role in rational and moral motivation because of their nature as such states. They can be seen as being rationally justificatory in the sense of emotional appropriateness founded upon adaptiveness and rational self-interest in escaping discomfort and as empathetically motivating in instigating altruistic action.

1053. Greimas, Algirdas Julien, and Jacques Fontanille. **The Semiotics of Passion: From States of Affairs to States of Feeling**. Translated by Paul Perron and Frank Collins, with foreword by Paul Perron and Paolo Fabbri. Minneapolis: University of Minnesota Press, 1993. Greimas and Fontanille present a semiotics of the passions in order to assure an autonomy to the "pathemic" or "thymic" dimension interior to a theory of signification, such that a representation of the narrative dimension of discourse is not reduced to a logic of action and to a conception of the subject entirely determined by its doing. Their work presents a semiotic epistemology of the passions that reduces the hiatus between "knowing" and "feeling," "passion" and "action," and allows for a semiotic taxonomy of the passions. The theory elaborated is then examined in relation to the analysis of the passions of avarice and jealousy.

1054. Griffiths, P. E. **"Modularity, and the Psychoevolutionary Theory of Emotion."** Biology & Philosophy 5 (1990): 175-196. It is unreasonable to assume that our prescientific emotion vocabulary embodies all and only those distinctions required for a scientific psychology of emotion. The psycho-evolutionary approach to emotion yields an alternative classification of certain emotional phenomena. New categories are based on a set of evolved adaptive responses, or affect-programs. Though the structure of the adaptive responses is innate, the contents of the system are largely learnt.

1055. ------. **"The Degeneration of the Cognitive Theory of Emotions."** Philosophical Psychology 2 (1989): 297-313. The type of cognitive theory of emotion traditionally espoused by philosophers of mind makes two central claims. First, that the occurrence of propositional attitudes is essential to the occurrence of emotions. Second, that the identity of a particular emotional state depends upon the propositional attitudes that it involves. Griffiths argues that both claims are defective and irreparable. He argues that more fruitful approaches should be conducted in dialogue with neurobiology and cognitive science rather than in consort with the traditional propositional attitude psychology.

1056. ------. What Emotions Really Are: The Problem of Psychological Categories. Science and Its Conceptual Foundations. Chicago: The University of Chicago Press, 1997. Griffiths rigorously criticizes the "propositional attitude," "feeling," and "social constructivist" theories of the emotions and sets forth an evolutionary model of the emotions in conjunction with contemporary neurobiology and cognitive science, inspired by the semantics of kind terms whose initial impetus came from Kripke and Putnam's causal theories of meaning in the 1970's.

1057. Gueroult, Martial. Descartes' Philosophy Interpreted according to the Order of Reasons, Vol. 2: The Soul and the Body. Minneapolis: University of Minnesota Press, 1985. Gueroult's classic and massive explication of Descartes' thought provides a background for the treatment of the passions in Descartes in terms of the relation between the soul and the body.

1058. Guyer, Paul. "Pleasure and Knowledge in Schopenhauer's Aesthetics." In Schopenhauer, Philosophy, and the Arts. Cambridge Studies in Philosophy and the Arts. Cambridge: Cambridge University Press, 1996. Pp. 109-132. Paper presents Schopenhauer's claim that art affords not only the negative pleasure of release from pain associated with desire, but also the positive pleasure arising from the cognition of the forms of reality art presents. This accounts for the pleasure music offers through the representation of the will itself.

1059. Hammacher, Klaus. "Die Vollendung der Wissenschaftslehre in einer Affektenlehre: Eine ungenutzte Chance." Fichte-Studien 11 (1997): 379-396. Hammacher explicates the doctrine of affections and feeling in Part II of Fichte's *Grundlage der gesammten Wissenschaftslehre* (1794) that is devoted to the deduction of the practical and the foundations for ethics. Hammacher discusses the systematic possibilities which Fichte could have, but did not utilize in this section.

1060. Hankinson, James. "Actions and Passions: Affection, Emotion and Moral Self-Management in Galen's Philosophical Psychology." In Passions & Perceptions: Studies in Hellenistic Philosophy of Mind. Proceedings of the Fifth Symposium Hellenisticum. Edited by Jacques Brunschwig and Martha C. Nussbaum. New York: Cambridge University Press, 1993. Pp. 184-222. The essay is a detailed presentation and interpretation of Galen's account of the interrelation between affection, emotion, and the nature of moral self-management in his philosophical psychology.

1061. Hart, James G. "Axiology as the Form of Purity of Heart: A Reading of *Husserliana XXVIII*." Philosophy Today 34 (1990): 206-221. The essay discusses three topics in connection with the publication of Husserl's early lectures on ethics and value theory (1908-1914): the epistemic character of the "heart" as appreciative consciousness founded in passive and active motions of feeling, emotion, and will; the sense in Pascal and Scheler's claim that the heart has reasons that reason does not know; and the relation between the logical and the axiological.

1062. Haste, Helen. "Moral Responsibility and Moral Commitment: The Integration of Affect and Cognition." In The Moral Domain: Essays in the Ongoing Discussion between Philosophy and the Social Sciences. Edited by Thomas E. Wren in cooperation with Wolfgang Edelstein and Gertrud Nunner-Winkler. Studies in Contemporary German Social Thought. Cambridge: The MIT Press, 1990. Pp. 315-359. The author presents a critique of Kohlberg's cognitive model of moral development and attempts to present a model that integrates affect and cognition in which an affective experience can be the primary impetus to moral insight and motivation. Several case studies are offered.

1063. Hegel, G. W. F. Aesthetics: Lectures on Fine Art. Two vols. Translated by T. M. Knox. Oxford: Clarendon Press, 1975. An important text for the consideration of the relation between the emotions and aesthetics, especially in terms of Hegel's sustained arguments with Romanticism and their emphasis upon irony and feeling.

1064. ------. Faith and Knowledge. Translated by Walter Cerf and H. S. Harris. Albany: State University of New York Press, 1972. Hegel's critique of the philosophy of feeling of Jacobi and the philosophies of Fichte and Schelling.

1065. ------. Philosophy of Mind, being Part Three of the Encyclopedia of the Philosophical Sciences (1830) translated by William Wallace, together with the Zusätze in Boumann's Text (1845) translated by A. V. Miler. With a foreword by J. N. Findlay. Oxford: Clarendon Press, 1971. Particularly significant are Hegel's discussions of the "feeling soul" (the feeling soul in its immediacy, self-feeling, and habit) and the practical mind (practical sense or feeling, the impulses and choice, and happiness) within the discussion of the mind as subjective in the preparatory process of coming-to-consciousness of itself directed towards objective mind and culminating in absolute mind.

1066. ------. Lectures on the Philosophy of Religion, Vol. 1: Introduction and the Concept of Religion. Edited by Peter C. Hodgson. Translated by R. F. Brown, P. C. Hodgson, and J. M. Stewart with the assistance of J. P. Fitzer and H. S. Harris. Berkeley: University of California Press, 1984. This volume includes Hegel's lectures from 1821, 1824, 1827, and 1831 on the philosophy of religion. In particular this volume deals with introductory material and the concept of religion. For Hegel, religion is consciousness of God, whether it has the form of feeling, representation, or knowledge. Religious feeling necessarily gives rise to representation, culminating in doctrine. It is the basis of the further forms, but it is also the lowest and most indeterminate form of religion in relation to the content of religion. Hegel extensively addresses the question of the relation between feeling, representation, and thought.

1067. ------. Lectures on the Philosophy of Religion, Vol. 2: Determinate Religion. Edited by Peter C. Hodgson. Translated by R. F. Brown, P. C. Hodgson, and J. M. Stewart with the assistance of H. S. Harris. Berkeley: University of California Press, 1985. Hegel's lectures in this volume concern the nature of determinate religion and the process of its varied development in the history of religions: immediate religion or nature religion (e.g., the religion of magic, the religion of phantasy [Hinduism], the religion of good or light [Persian religion], and the religion of enigma [Egyptian religion]), the religions of spiritual individuality (e.g., the religion of sublimity [Judaism], the religion of beauty [Greek religion], and the religion of expediency [Roman religion]. Hegel's treatment of "fear of the Lord" in relation to the religion of sublimity and his discussion of the feeling of absolute dependence in relation to Judaism and Roman religion are of particular interest, especially as implicit critiques of Schleiermacher's construal of the feeling of absolute dependence.

1068. ------. Lectures on the Philosophy of Religion, Vol. 3: The Consummate Religion. Edited by Peter C. Hodgson. Translated by R. F. Brown, P. C. Hodgson, and J. M. Stewart with the assistance of H. S. Harris. Berkeley: University of California Press, 1987. Hegel's lectures on Christianity as the consummate religion revisit many of his earlier reflections on religion and feeling. Noticeable in this volume are his critiques of the emphasis upon religious piety in Pietism (as ingenuousness) and the suspicions addressed to religion by the Enlightenment (i.e., subjectivism without objective content) and his continuing critique of Schleiermacher. For Hegel, his opposition to feeling as the basic form of religious relationship lies in its receptive, dependent, and passive character, whereas the true character of the religious relationship should be active and participatory. The relationship should be one of awe or reverence, not fear or the feeling of absolute dependence, of freedom, neither dependency nor expediency.

1069. Heidegger, Martin. **Being and Time: A Translation of _Sein und Zeit_.** **Translated by Joan Stambaugh. SUNY Series in Contemporary Continental Philosophy. Albany: State University of New York Press, 1996.** Heidegger's classic work presents a fundamental ontology of Dasein as Being-in-the-world in which *Befindlichkeit* is understood as an equiprimordial existential of the Being-in as such of Being-in-the-world.

1070. ------. **The Fundamental Concepts of Metaphysics: World, Finitude, Solitude. Translated by William McNeill and Nicholas Walker. Bloomington, Ind.: Indiana University Press, 1995.** These lectures from 1929/30 are an important addition to Heidegger's analysis of Dasein that involves a lengthy existential phenomenological interpretation of boredom and anxiety. It is also a significant text in light of Jean-Luc Marion's critique of Heidegger's privileging of anxiety in a fundamental ontology.

1071. Heller, Agnes. **A Theory of Feelings. Translated by Mario D. Fenyö. Dialectic and Society. Assen: Van Gorcum, 1979.** The book is a presentation of a phenomenological theory of feelings in relation to an ethical discussion of the moral life and social theory of feeling by the Hungarian philosopher who was a student of Georg Lukacs. She argues that the fundamental meaning of feeling is of being involved in something. This provides the basis for a classification of feelings from an anthropological point of view that in turn provides the basis for a sociology of feeling (presented in terms of "the bourgeois world of feeling in general").

1072. Henry, Michel. **The Essence of Manifestation. Translated by Girard Etzkorn. The Hague: Martinus Nijhoff, 1973.** Henry's massive tome is the project of the establishment of an ontology of life as radical immanence, prosecuted in an extensive debate with Husserl and Heidegger. He argues that immanence as affectivity is the more radically prior basis for both Husserlian intentionality and the Heideggerian transcendence of Dasein. Affectivity is the essence of human being and not the interplay of empirical feelings, but is itself the very possibility of such feelings.

1073. ------. **The Genealogy of Psychoanalysis. Translated by Douglas Brick. Stanford: Stanford University Press, 1993.** Henry's study of the genealogy of Freudian psychoanalytic theory contends that Freud's theory of the unconscious is not a break with the Cartesian tradition, but a stage in the heritage of philosophical misunderstandings of the Cartesian cogito (from Kant, Schopenhauer, to Nietzsche). Henry is especially attentive to the issue of affectivity in this heritage, culminating in Freud's understanding of anxiety as the common denominator of all affects, the "anxiety of life's inability to escape itself."

1074. ------. **"Pathos-avec." In Phénoménologie matérielle. Epiméthée. Paris: Presses Universitaires de France, 1990. Pp. 137-179.** Henry, after an analysis and critique of Husserl's "Fifth Meditation" of "The Cartesian Meditations," which is devoted to the analysis of the experience of the other, elaborates a phenomenology of community as "pathetic" community in which the essence of community is explicated as affectivity.

1075. ------. **Philosophy and Phenomenology of the Body**. **Translated by Girard Etzkorn. The Hague: Martinus Nijhoff, 1975.** The French edition, the complementary thesis to *The Essence of Manifestation*, included the subtitle "Essay on the Biranian Ontology." Henry presents an interpretation of the significance of the thought of Maine de Biran on the body and effort as preliminary to a radical ontology of life as self-affection, a radical philosophy of immanence, inspired by Maine de Biran's suggestive reflections on activity and passivity.

1076. **Hobbes, Thomas.** *De corpore* **[1655]. In The English Works of Thomas Hobbes, Volume 1. Edited by W. Moleworth. London: John Bohn, 1839.** This edition follows an English translation of 1656. Hobbes examines the causes and the effects of the motions of the mind, namely, appetite, aversion, love, benevolence, hope, fear, anger, emulation, envy, and so forth. The emotions are analyzed in terms of the pursuit of pleasure and the avoidance of pain, the basic drives and desires informing Hobbes' psychology.

1077. ------. **Leviathan. Edited by Richard Tuck. Cambridge Texts in the History of Political Thought. Second Edition. Cambridge: Cambridge University Press, 1996.** The classic masterpiece by Hobbes in which one can see the socio-political philosophical issues in conjunction with his understanding of the emotions.

1078. **Hocking, William Ernest. The Meaning of God in Human Experience: A Philosophic Study of Religion. New Haven: Yale University Press, 1928.** This work is a distinctive and unique synthesis of idealism and pragmaticism that understands that religion, in relation to human experience, is simultaneously one of feeling and ideas. For Hocking, feelings are ideational, in that all positive feelings attain a terminus in knowledge and can do no work apart from the direction of a guiding idea.

1079. **Hoffman, Paul. "Three Dualist Theories of the Passions." Philosophical Topics 19 (1991): 153-200.** The essay examines the dualist theories of the passions of the soul in Descartes, Spinoza, and Malebranche by attending to the underlying more general metaphysical issues that inform their divergent accounts of the nature of the passions of the soul, their causes, their effects on freedom, and the methods advanced for the control of the passions.

1080. **Hume, David. Enquiries concerning Human Understanding and concerning the Principles of Morals. Reprinted from the posthumous edition of 1777 and edited with Introduction, Comparative Table of Contents, and analytical Index by L. A.Selby-Bigge. Third Edition. With text revised and Notes by P. H. Nidditch. Oxford: Clarendon Press, 1975.** Hume's *Enquiries* represents a re-working of his earlier treatise on human nature, though there appear to be significant differences between them. In the *Treatise* Hume ranked benevolence amongst the natural virtues and vices, but treats it as the chief of the social virtues in the *Enquiry*. Likewise the sections on self-love and its relation to the passions are more extensively treated in the *Enquiry* than in the other text. Hume suggests that benevolence is the primary passion and that self-love is the secondary passion. Also less space is devoted to demonstrating that moral distinctions are not derived from reason ("reason is the slave of the passions") than that they are derived from a sentiment of humanity. It includes also two appendices on self-love and moral sentiment.

1081. ------. **A Treatise of Human Nature: Being An Attempt to introduce the experimental Method of Reasoning into Moral Subjects.** Reprinted from the Original Edition in Three Volumes and edited with an analytical Index, by L. A. Selby-Bigge. Oxford: At the Clarendon Press, 1975. Hume's first masterpiece discusses the nature, origin, causes, and effects of the passions and emotions in Book II, following the examination of the understanding in Book I and preceding his discussion of morals in Book III. For Hume, the passions are secondary, or reflective impressions which proceed from original impressions by the interposition of its idea. He divides them into "direct" and "indirect" passions. Direct passions arise from good or evil, pain or pleasure while the indirect arise from the same but in relation to other qualities. Pride and humility, ambition and vanity, love and hatred, envy and pity, and malice and generosity, together with their dependent emotions, are indirect. Desire, grief, aversion, joy, hope, fear, despair, and security are direct passions.

1082. ------. **Essays: Moral, Political, and Literary.** World's Classics. Reprinted from the 1903 edition. London: Oxford University Press, 1963. An important collection of material, drawn from a range of Hume's publications, for consideration of the relation between Hume's discussion of the passions or emotions and social and political philosophy, especially in terms of his treatment of Epicurean, Stoic, and Platonic philosophy.

1083. ------. **Four Dissertations.** With a new introduction by John Immerwahr. I. The natural history of religion—II. Of the passions—III. Of tragedy—IV. Of the standard of taste. Originally published: London: A. Millar, 1757. Key texts (Bristol, England). Bristol, England: Thoemmes Press, 1995. The dissertation on the passions consists largely of verbatim extracts from Book II of the *Treatise*. It is significant in terms of what its grouping with the other dissertations implies for the overall character of Hume's philosophical position.

1084. ------. **The Natural History of Religion.** Edited, with an Introduction, by James Fieser. Library of Liberal Arts. New York: Macmillan, 1992. Hume presents his natural history of religion as a critique of understandings of natural religion as rational. He argues that the origins of religion are to be traced to the passions and ordinary hopes and fears of human life, namely, anxious concern for happiness, the dread of future misery, and fear of death in relation to the theater of nature.

1085. Hutcheson, Francis. **An Essay on the Nature and Conduct of the Passions and Affections, with Illustrations on the Moral Sense (Third Edition, 1742).** A Fascimile Reproduction with an Introduction by Paul McReynolds. History of Psychology Series. Gainesville: Scholars' Fascimiles & Reprints, 1969. A foundational text for the moral sense theory of ethics and for discussions of eighteenth-century thought.

1086. Ibana, Rainier R. A. "The Stratification of Emotional Life and the Problem of Other Minds according to Maz Scheler." **International Philosophical Quarterly** 31 (1991): 449-460. The paper claims that knowledge of other minds requires the serious consideration of the emotional life in order to understand a human person as a whole, where emotions, according to Scheler, correspond to an objective order of values. The author argues that sympathy allows for participation in the interior life of another, while empathy preserves the distinction between one's own emotions and those of another person. The author utilizes Edith Stein's critique of Scheler to suggest that a more adequate account of emotional life can be developed.

1087. Immerwahr, John. "Hume's 'Dissertation on the Passions.'" Journal of the History of Philosophy **32 (1994): 225-240.** Hume's dissertation is composed of rearranged selections drawn from Book II of the "Treatise," yet no consensus exists concerning the underlying purpose for the dissertation. The author argues that the purpose becomes clearer when the text is read in its original publication context, i.e., in relation to the "Natural History of Religion" and "Of Tragedy." It was to demonstrate the relevance of his theory of the passions to religion and aesthetics, especially in terms of its analysis of fear.

1088. ------. "Hume on Tranquilizing the Passions." Hume Studies **18 (1992): 293-314.** The article explicates Hume's preference for the calm passions over violent passions as a unifying theme in his writing. They are the key to moderation and stability in personal life, religion, and politics. Hume's belief that the passions can be softened by playing opposites against one another is shown to be a literary strategy behind the construction of many of his works, one intending to produce calm passions in the readers of his texts.

1089. Inwood, Brad. "Seneca on Emotion and Action." In Passions & Perceptions: Studies in Hellenistic Philosophy of Mind. Proceedings of the Fifth Symposium Hellenisticum. **Edited by Jacques Brunschwig and Martha C. Nussbaum. New York: Cambridge University Press, 1993. Pp. 150-183.** In a finely nuanced essay, Inwood examines Seneca's theory of the relation between emotion and action, underscoring the Chrysippan character of many of Seneca's arguments.

1090. Jacquette, Dale. "Hume's Aesthetic Psychology of Distance, Greatness, and the Sublime." British Journal of the History of Philosophy **3 (1995): 89-112.** Article examines Hume's efforts to account for the aesthetic impact of distance by way of Locke's associationist psychology in the historical context of the enlightenment interest in the categories of the beautiful and the sublime. The paper attempts to resolve the tension in Hume's claims concerning the effect of distance upon conception and the passions as opposed to aesthetic judgment through the notion that, for Hume, aesthetic response belongs to the mind's reason and reflection rather than to emotion and the passions.

1091. Jaggar, Alison M. "Love and Knowledge: Emotion in Feminist Epistemology." Inquiry **32 (1989): 151-176.** The paper argues that the Western epistemological tradition has obscured the role of emotion in the construction of knowledge by viewing it as epistemologically subversive, thereby undercutting the epistemic authority of women and other social groups culturally associated with emotion. The paper emphasizes the voluntary, active, and socially constructed aspects of emotion and its role in evaluation and observation and sketches how the emotions of such groups can lead to the development of a critical social theory.

1092. James, Susan. "Explaining the Passions: Passions, Desires, and the Explanation of Action." In The Soft Underbelly of Reason: The Passions in the Seventeenth Century. **Edited by Stephen Gaukroger. Routledge Studies in Seventeenth-Century Philosophy. London/New York: Routledge, 1998. Pp. 17-33.** An excellent article tracing how the role of the passions in motivating or initiating action was gradually replaced with the narrower conception of passion as desire, in conjunction with beliefs, as that which is explanatory of human action.

1093. ------. **Passion and Action: The Emotions in Seventeenth-Century Philosophy.** Oxford: Clarendon Press; New York: Oxford University Press, 1998. Superb examination of the understanding of emotions in seventeenth-century understandings of body and mind, reasoning, and action, especially in Hobbes, Descartes, Malebranche, Spinoza, Pascal, and Locke. It is especially valuable in presenting the reception of Aristotelian and Thomistic accounts of passion and action and the transformation of that reception in early modern philosophy that have been so influential for present discussions.

1094. James, William. "The Place of Affectional Facts in a World of Pure Experience." In **Essays in Radical Empiricism.** The Works of William James. Cambridge: Harvard University Press, 1976. James argues that the "pretended" spirituality of emotions and attributes of value really argue in favor of the concept of pure experience advocated by radical empiricism and that such an understanding is consistent with what he had maintained in his article on the physical basis of emotion.

1095. ------. **The Principles of Psychology.** Edited by Frederick H. Burkhardt as general editor, with Fredson Bowers as textual editor and Ignas K. Skrupskelis as associate editor. Works of William James. Cambridge, Mass.: Harvard University Press, 1983. This text provides an amplification and extended treatment of emotion, but now included within a systematic psychology.

1096. ------. **The Varieties of Religious Experience.** Introduction by John E. Smith. The Works of William James. Cambridge, Mass.: Harvard University Press, 1985. James' Gifford lectures are a classic statement of the sources of religion in feeling or sense of the divine as a study of human nature and defense the priority of religious affectivity as experience in relation to the secondary character of philosophy and theological formulations.

1097. ------. "What is an Emotion?" **Mind** 9 (1884): 188-205. James articulates an understanding of emotion's nature as the feeling of bodily changes following the experience of an exciting fact.

1098. Janet, Paul. **Les Passions et les Caractères dans la Littérature du XVIIe Siècle.** Bibliothèque Contemporaine. Paris: Calmann Lévy, 1888. Paul Janet presents an analysis of the psychology of the passions in classical seventeenth-century French literature and moralist texts from a philosophical perspective. He concentrates chiefly upon Racine, Molière, La Bruyère, and Bossuet.

1099. Jankélévitch, Vladimir. **Traite des Vertus.** Bibliothèque Générale de Philosophie. Paris: Éditions Bordas, 1949. While this text does not examine the notion of emotion per se, the author discusses various emotions in his monumental and encyclopedic presentation of the virtues that draws upon an amazing wealth of resources from the history of philosophy, theology, and literature. It is a modern classic text in French moral philosophy that is a reflective and literary tour de force.

1100. Kant, Immanuel. **Anthropology from a Pragmatic Point of View.** Trans., with an Introduction and Notes, by Mary J. Gregor. The Hague: Martinus Nijhoff, 1974. Kant distinguishes between the feelings of pleasure and displeasure and the appetitive powers of the passions and the affects. Of particular note, in his discussions of feeling and desire, are his presentation of taste as a social phenomenon and his discussion of the social passions as passions of inclination arising from human culture ("the manias for honor, for power [of domination], and for possession").

1101. Kenny, Anthony. Action, Emotion and Will. Studies in Philosophical Psychology. London/Henly: Routledge & Kegan Paul, 1963. An important text presenting criticisms of Descartes and the James-Lange theory of emotion that is developed through an analysis of intentionality and the role of the formal object.

1102. Koehn, Daryl. Rethinking Feminist Ethics: Care, Trust, and Empathy. London: Routledge, 1998. The author presents a critical analysis of the insights of feminist ethics concerning care, trust, and empathy and contends that they can best be maintained in a dialogical ethics and not as separate from a rule-based ethics.

1103. Köhl, Harald. "Die Theorie des moralischen Gefühls bei Kant und Schopenhauer." In Zur Philosophie der Gefühle. Suhrkamp Taschenbuch Wissenschaft; 1074. Edited by Hinrich Fink-Eitel und Georg Lohmann. Frankfurt am Main: Suhrkamp Verlag, 1993. Pp. 136-156. The article provides an excellent systematic comparison between Kant and Schopenhauer's theories of moral feeling as respect and sympathy/compassion respectively.

1104. Kremer-Marietti, Angèle. "De la passionalité." Revue Internationale de Philosophie 48 (1994): 275-287. The article is an essay commenting on the topic of "passionality" in light of Michel Meyer's book *Le Philosophie et les Passions: Esquisse d'une histoire de la nature humaine.*

1105. Kretzmann, Norman. "Aquinas on God's Joy, Love, and Liberality." Modern Schoolman 72 (1995): 125-148. The author discusses the complex nature of affective language predicated of God in Aquinas' philosophical and theological thought.

1106. Kühn, Rolf. Leiblichkeit als Lebendigkeit: Michel Henrys Lebensphänomenologie absoluter Subjektivität als Affektivität. Freiburg/Munich: Verlag Karl Alber, 1992. This massive text is a systematic investigation of the radical phenomenology of life in the writings of Michel Henry that center around the topic of affectivity, especially in relation to living bodiliness. It surveys all of the major texts by Henry and is an extremely helpful guide to understanding his thought and the difficulties it presents.

1107. ------. Studien zum Lebens- und Phänomenbegriff. Transzendentalphilosophie Heute; Bd. 6. Cuxhaven: Junghans-Verlag, 1994. Kühn provides a masterful developmental survey of the interrelations between the concept of life and the concept of phenomena in Hegel, Fichte, Husserl, Heidegger, and Scheler leading up to the philosophy of Michel Henry. It provides also a discussion of the issue of affectivity that comes to the fore in the interrelation of phenomenology and a philosophy of life.

1108. ------. "La Vie affective en Psychology et en Philosophie: L'Apport de Victor E. Frankl et de Simone Weil à une Théorie thérapeutique du Sentiment." Revue des Sciences Philosophiques et Théologiques 69 (1985): 548-562. The article shows a correspondence between the thought Frankl and Simone Weil placed upon the value of sentiment in a full emotional life. Kühn explicates in particular Weil's notion of consent (*con-sensus*) as the union of intellect and sentiment to justify responsible personal acts.

1109. **Lacroix, Jean. "Un philosophe du sentiment: Michel Henry." In Panorama de la philosophie française contemporaine.** Paris: Presses Universitaires de France, 1966. Pp. 164-170. An excellent, concise presentation of Henry's philosophy as a philosophy of sentiment.

1110. ------. **Les sentiments et la vie morale.** 8. ed. Collection SUP. Philosophe. Paris: Presses Universitaires de France, 1976. A classic twentieth-century French study of the nature and the role of the sentiments in the moral life that draws upon the major resources of the French philosophical tradition.

1111. **Lacroze, René. L'angoisse et l'émotion.** Paris: Boivin & Cie, Éditeurs, 1938. The book is divided into three parts. The first part, in dialogue with psychological theories, argues that many items associated with emotion (e.g., sensations, reaction, etc.) cannot account for the affective character of emotion. It can only be accounted for in terms of anguish as an a priori of human consciousness through a regressive analysis. The second part studies the principles governing the organization and development of elementary forms of affectivity, and the third part presents the metaphysical component of an affective philosophy that analyzes the origin of human anguish in the conditions of life and existence.

1112. **Langer, Suzanne. Feeling and Form: A Theory of Art.** New York: Charles Scribner's Sons, 1953. Langer presents an extension of the insights in her earlier work, *Philosophy in a New Key: A Study in the Symbolism of Reason, Rite, and Art* (1942), towards a characterization of art as the creation of forms symbolic of human feeling as expressive representation of "felt life."

1113. ------. **Mind: An Essay on Feeling.** Three vols. Baltimore: Johns Hopkins University Press, 1967, 1972, and 1982. Langer's final work is an exploration of the biological roots of human mentality as the locus for the role of feelings in the mind and especially in how the artist projects an idea of feeling through the expression of art.

1114. **Leighton, Stephen R. "Modern Theories of Emotion." Journal of Speculative Philosophy** 2 (1988): 206-224. The paper examines the plausibility of possible constituent elements of the emotions, such as desires, judgments, physiological changes, feelings, and behavior. It provides an assessment of each, with critical attention given to the relationship between feeling and physiological changes, and proposes an account in terms of judgments and feelings.

1115. **Levenson, Jerold. "Emotion in Response to Art." In The Routledge Encyclopedia of Philosophy, Vol. 3: Descartes, René - Gender and Science. Edited by Edward Craig. London/New York: Routledge, Pp. 273-285.** The article surveys the following topics: the nature of the emotions; the paradox of fiction in emotional response to representational art; the relation between music and feeling in abstract art; emotional response to tragedy; and emotion in the aesthetic appreciation of art.

1116. **Levi, Anthony. French Moralists: The Theory of the Passions, 1585 to 1649.** Oxford: Clarendon Press, 1964. An extensive and detailed analysis of the understanding of the passions in the evolution of the seventeenth-century thought of French moralists from Montaigne to Pascal, examining the influence of neo-stoicism, devout humanism, Senault, La Rochefoucald, Pascal, the relation between medicine and morals in de la Chambre, and the rationalism of Descartes.

1117. Levinas, Emmanuel. **Totality and Infinity: An Essay on Exteriority**. **Translated by Alphonso Lingis. Duquesne Studies: Philosophical Series, 24. Pittsburgh: Duquesne University Press, 1969.** Levinas' seminal work addresses the issue of affectivity in relation to the themes of interiority and economy. Through an analysis of enjoyment, Levinas contends that the enjoyment of solitude is the breach of totality and that affectivity is the ipseity of the I. The intentionality of enjoyment is contrasted with the intentionality of representation. Enjoyment precisely preserves exteriority which is suspended in the intentionality of representation.

1118. **Little, Margaret Olivia. "Seeing and Caring: The Role of Affect in Feminist Moral Epistemology."** **Hypatia 10 (1995): 117-137.** The article discusses the substantive and methodological import of affect in contemporary feminist moral epistemologies through the contrast of caring in relation to seeing.

1119. **Lloyd, A. C. "Emotion and Decision in Stoic Psychology." In The Stoics. Edited by John M. Rist. Berkeley: University of California Press, 1978. Pp. 233-246.** The author criticizes traditional representations of Stoic psychology of the passions and emotions as one-sidedly represented as intellectual. He contends that one could also state that the Stoics, just as they intellectualized the passions, also "made the intellect volitional and passionate" (p. 242).

1120. **Lloyd, Genevieve. "Rationalizing the Passions: Spinoza on Reason and the Passions." In The Soft Underbelly of Reason: The Passions in the Seventeenth Century. Edited by Stephen Gaukroger. Routledge Studies in Seventeenth-Century Philosophy. London: Routledge, 1998. Pp. 34-48.** Excellent article on Spinoza's account of the relation between reason and the passions with regards to the question of how they can engage each other, given the contrast between them. Lloyd argues that Spinoza's aim to liberate us from the passions is only possible through the transformation of reason as being itself affective, i.e., reason transforming passion into an active emotion, an affect. She notes this in his concept of *hilaritas* as reflective joy, the mind's understanding of itself as whole.

1121. **Locke, John. An Essay concerning Human Understanding. Edited with an Introduction, Critical Apparatus and Glossary by Peter H. Nidditch. Oxford: Clarendon Press, 1975.** A foundational text for the understanding of the emotions in the influential tradition of British empiricism. Locke's reflections concerning the emotions are important for his treatment of the problem of enthusiasm in the latter sections of the *Essay*.

1122. **Loock, Reinhard. "Gefühl und Realität: Fichtes Auseinandersetzung mit Jacobi in der *Grundlage der Wissenschaft des Praktischen*." Fichte-Studien 10 (1997): 219-237.** The essay analyzes Fichte's dispute with Jacobi in terms of his reception and transformation of Jacobi's understanding of feeling and reason. For Fichte, a transcendental deduction establishes that the system of sentiments is only produced by reason's necessary reflection upon its preconscious striving. The identity of reflection and sentiment enables Fichte to understand immediacy as reflected within the speculative system of reason, whereas Jacobi understood immediacy of feeling as the essence of reason.

1123. López-Dominguez, Virgina. "Die Deduktion des Gefühls in der *Grundlage der gesamten Wissenschaftslehre*." Fichte-Studien 10 (1997): 209-218. The study examines the position of feeling in Fichte's philosophy in terms of the parallelism between the deduction of feeling and the deduction of representation in both of which the "I" becomes conscious of both theoretical and practical products. Feeling is presented as the aspect of action which provides content to knowledge and a formal ethics and as that which, being neither accidental nor irrational, can give unity to the human being, especially as love.

1124. Löw-Beer, Martin. "Zur Einschätzung von Gefühlen und Gefühlsleben." In Zur Philosophie der Gefühle. Suhrkamp Taschenbuch Wissenschaft;1074. Edited by Hinrich Fink-Eitel und Georg Lohmann. Frankfurt am Main: Suhrkamp Verlag, 1993. Pp. 89-111. The article addresses the question of the criteria to be utilized in the appraisal of feelings and the affective life.

1125. Losonsky, Michael. "John Locke on Passion, Will, and Belief." British Journal of the History of Philosophy 4 (1996): 267-283. An exposition of the interrelation between passion, the will, and belief in Locke's philosophy.

1126. Lyons, William. Emotion. Cambridge: Cambridge University Press, 1980. An excellent and ample survey of physiological and cognitive analyses of emotion. The author presents a causal-evaluative theory of emotion and presents it in relation to various topics. The volume includes a quite comprehensive bibliography of texts from both philosophy and psychology.

1127. Malebranche, Nicholas. The Search after Truth. With Elucidations of the Search after Truth. Translated and Edited by Thomas M. Lennon and Paul J. Olscamp. *Elucidations of The search after Truth* translated and Edited by Thomas M. Lennon. Cambridge Texts in the History of Philosophy. Cambridge: Cambridge University Press, 1997.

1128. ------. "Traité de Morale." In Oeuvres, Vol. II. Edited by Geneviève Rodis-Lewis. Bibliothèque de la Pléiade 390. Paris: Éditions Gallimard, 1992. Pp. 423-647. Malebranche presents his treatment of the passions in his ethics in the discussion of virtue in the moral life as the habitual and dominant love of immutable order. This treatise is an important adjunct to his masterpiece "The Search after Truth."

1129. Macmurray, John. Reason and Emotion. Atlantic Highlands: Humanities Press, 1992. A reprinting of Macmurray's critique of dualistic oppositions between reason and emotion.

1130. Marion, Jean-Luc. "L'être et l'affection." Archives de Philosophie 43 (1980): 433-442. Marion presents a discussion of F. Alquié's differentiation of affective consciousness from intellectual consciousness such that affective consciousness is related to Being through the refusal of the objectification marking the representations of intellectual consciousness.

1131. ------. "L'angoisse et l'ennui: pour interpréter "Was ist Metaphysik?" Archives de Philosophie 43 (1980): 121-146. Over against Heidegger's claim that anguish or anxiety apprehends Being through nothingness and his explanation in the *Nachwort* (1943) that Dasein can interpret being through anxiety only through answering the claim of Being, Marion argues that such a possibility of answering implies the possibility of refusal that occurs in boredom, an existential determination indifferent to the ontological difference and the claim of Being.

1132. ------. God without Being: Hors-Texte. Translated by Thomas A. Carlson with a Foreword by David Tracy. Chicago: University of Chicago Press, 1991. Marion presents a phenomenology of affects to underscore the indifference of love to both the primacy of representation (in which affective intentionality is founded upon a prior representation and judgment of existence) and the question of Being in Heidegger. Marion utilizes a phenomenology of the affective domain of the Pascalian pathètique of misery, boredom, vanity, and melancholy to exhibit an "interspace, a space undetermined because belonging to the domain neither of the idol nor at the same time of the icon" (p. 110). He contends that the affectivity of that domain of boredom, vanity, and melancholy suspends and renders indifferent the ontological claim of the Heideggerian privileging of anxiety as the fundamental affection. An important text for Marion's philosophical and theological dispute with Heidegger.

1133. Marks, Joel, ed. The Ways of Desire: New Essays in Philosophical Psychology on the Concept of Wanting. Precedent Studies in Ethics and the Moral Sciences. Chicago: Preceedent, 1986. A valuable collection of essays (by Robert Audi, Annette C. Baier, Ronald De Sousa, Robert M. Gordon, and O. H. Green, Michael Stocker, et al.) on the nature and function of desire, rich in implications for the theory of emotions.

1134. Marks, Joel and Roger T. Ames, Eds. Emotions in Asian Thought. Albany: SUNY Press, 1995. The book seeks to redress the almost total lack of reference to non-Western accounts of the emotions by presenting comparative and Asian philosophical scrutiny of various relevant issues from both perspectives. The rich collection of essays includes an initial survey of recent work on the emotions in the West and an extensive summary essay by Robert C. Solomon.

1135. Mazis, Glen A. Emotion and Embodiment: Fragile Ontology. Studies in Contemporary Continental Philosophy, vol. 3. New York: Peter Lang, 1993. The monograph presents an expansion of Merleau-Ponty's ontology of the body in order to reappraise the traditionally undervalued epistemological role of the emotions. The book seeks to present a phenomenological analysis of the "world " of emotion in dialogue with literary works and various philosophies of emotion (e.g., James, Descartes, Sartre, Darwin, Heidegger, Solomon, and Levinas).

1136. McCormick, Peter J. Fictions, Philosophies, and the Problems of Poetics. Ithaca/London: Cornell University Press, 1988. In Chapter 4 ["Fictions and Feelings"], McCormick addresses the issue as to how the plight of fictional characters can properly be said to affect nonfictional persons. He utilizes the insights of Nelson Goodman and Paul Ricoeur on reference, truth, and world to develop a notion of reference as productive and truth as truth to life rather than truth as truth-functional, such that the feelings some works of art arouse can be taken as being both the intentional referents of uses of language in poetic works and the extensional referents of the contents of reader's emotions.

1137. ------. "Meinong and Aesthetic Feelings." In Modernity, Aesthetics, and the Bounds of Art. Ithaca: Cornell University Press, 1990. Pp. 252-273. McCormick's essay examines the problematic relationship between what literary truths are and how those truths are presented in literary works. The essay explores the implications of

Meinong's theory of emotional presentation for an understanding of the relation between the cognitive and the aesthetic. It focuses on the distinction between what literary works say and what they show. McCormick suggests that the literary truths shown in a literary work of art can be presented by aesthetic feeling.

1138. Meinong, Alexius. **On Emotional Presentation. Translated, with an Introduction, by Marie-Luise Schubert Kalsi. With a Foreword by J.N. Findlay. Northwestern University Studies in Phenomenology & Existential Philosophy. Evanston: Northwestern University Press, 1972.** Meinong's classic and complex study defends the autonomy of emotions as independent bearers of value in construing emotional presentation of dignatives, just as ideas are the presentation of objects and thoughts, the presentation of objectives.

1139. Meyer, Michel. "Introduction: De l'importance et de la résurgence des passions." **Revue Internationale de Philosophie 48 (1994): 269-274.** Introductory essay to a collection of essays on the passions that highlights the paradox of the philosophical interrogation of the passions in the present.

1140. ------. **Le Philosophie et les Passions: Esquisse d'une histoire de la nature humaine. Le Livre de Poche. Paris: Librarie Générale Français, 1991.** This is an ambitious history of the various theories of emotions or passions which provides a privileged place for examining the various enigmas of Western thought in the polarities of passion and reason, soul and body, nature and human nature, instinct and intelligence. A rich and fruitful journey through the history of theories of the emotions that is attentive to the moral, political, and metaphysical visions of the human in the great philosophers of the Western tradition.

1141. ------. "Le problème des passions chez Saint Thomas d'Aquin." **Revue Internationale de Philosophie 48 (1994): 363-374.** Meyer examines problematic structural features in Thomas Aquinas' discussion of the passions, especially concerning the passage from the concupiscible to the irascible.

1142. More, Henry. **Enthusiasmus triumphatus: or, a discourse of the nature, causes, kinds, and cure, of enthusiasme: written by Philophilus Parresiastes London and Cambridge [1656]. Reprinted Los Angeles: Clark Memorial Library, University of California, 1996.** An important text by one of the leaders of the movement called Cambridge Platonism that prominently deals with the emotions in his presentation of the cause and the cure of enthusiasm, the misconceit of being inspired, in philosophy and religion.

1143. Mulhall, Stephen. "Can there be an Epistemology of Moods?" **In *Verstehen* and Humane Understanding. Edited by Anthony O'Hear. Royal Institute of Philosophy Supplement: 41. Cambridge: Cambridge University Press, 1996. Pp. 191-210.** Drawing upon Nussbaum's work on narrative emotions, Heidegger's account of moods, and Stanley Cavell's work on Wittgenstein and Emerson, Mulhall articulates a cognitive theory of affectivity that reveals weaknesses in the Kantian tradition's conception of epistemology.

1144. Myers, Gerald E. "William James on Emotion and Religion." **Transactions of the Charles S. Peirce Society 21 (1985): 463-484.** The article raises the question of the relation between James' theory of emotion, commonly known as the James-Lange theory, to his theory of religion. The author concludes that the theory of emotion and the theory of religion are mutually coherent, but notes that James exaggerates the role of emotions in religion.

1145. Nash, Ronald Alan. "Cognitive Theories of Emotions." Nous 23 (1989): 481-504. Assuming that a theory of emotion should be cognitive and account for the passivity of emotion, the author distinguishes pure and hybrid cognitive theories. Whereas hybrid theories account for the passivity of emotion in terms of non-intentional states (e.g., bodily sensations or physiological change), pure theories analyze emotion solely in terms of intentional states. Nash criticizes the claim that only a hybrid theory can account for the passivity of emotion and proposes an alternative "pure" theory formulation that can account for the passivity of emotions.

1146. Neu, Jerome. Emotion, Thought & Therapy: A Study of Hume and Spinoza and the Relationship of Philosophical Theories of the Emotions to Psychological Theories of Therapy. London: Routledge & K. Paul, 1978. Provides an excellent treatment of the understanding of Hume and Spinoza's understandings of the emotions in relation to various theories of therapy. The monograph argues for a cognitive theory of emotion.

1147. Neuberg, Marc. "Les Traité des passions de L'âme de Descartes et les théories modernes de l'émotion." Archives de Philosophie 53 (1990): 479-508. The author attempts to show the methodological relevance of Descartes' "the Passions of the soul" for contemporary studies of the emotion. He claims that Descartes established the patterns being utilized presently by the competing "physiological" and "cognitive" theories of emotion and that Descartes' text provides illustrations of the difficulties inherent in these two approaches to the emotions.

1148. Nietzsche, Friedrich. "On the Genealogy of Morals." Translated by Walter Kaufmann and R. J. Hollingdale. In On the Genealogy of Morals and Ecce Homo. Ed., with Commentary, by Walter Kaufmann. Vintage Books Edition. New York: Random House, 1967. Pp. 1-163. Classic discussion of the emotions and the passions in light of a genealogical critique of morals in terms of the will-to-power. Nietzsche presents an analysis of guilt and bad conscience in terms of a theory of resentment.

1149. Noreña, Carlos G. Juan Luis Vives and the Emotions. Foreword by George Kimball Plochmann. Philosophical Explorations. Carbondale and Edwardsville: Southern Illinois University Press, 1989. An excellent account of the nature and the significance of the emotions in the Renaissance philosophy of Juan Luis Vives and his reception and transformation of the classical heritage.

1150. Nussbaum, Martha Craven. The Fragility of Goodness: Luck and Ethics in Greek Tragedy and Philosophy. Cambridge: Cambridge University Press, 1986. An excellent analysis of the fragility of goodness in terms of the intersection between Greek tragedy and philosophy (Plato and Aristotle), especially in relation to the tragic emotions of pity and fear elicited through catharsis.

1151. ------. "Narrative Emotions: Beckett's Genealogy of Love." Ethics 98 (1988): 225-254. Nussbaum presents a narrative theory of emotions which would mediate between the competing cognitive and social constructionist theories of the emotions. The writings of Samuel Beckett are utilized as a case study for the presentation of her narrative theory.

1152. ------. "Poetry and the Passions: Two Stoic Views." In **Passions & Perceptions: Studies in Hellenistic Philosophy of Mind. Proceedings of the Fifth Symposium Hellenisticum**. Edited by Jacques Brunschwig and Martha C. Nussbaum. New York: Cambridge University Press, 1993. Pp. 97-149. The article examines the critical ambivalence in Stoic philosophy concerning poetry in light of the relation between poetry's power of seduction and the passions. Whereas Posidonius seems to take a non-cognitive view of the moral significance of poetry, Chrysippan Stoicism (and Seneca and Epictetus) adopt a cognitive view of the role of poetry in education. Nussbaum notes the more positive regard for poetry amongst the Stoics, in contrast to the Epicureans and Skeptics, precisely for its pedagogical value in promoting self-recognition.

1153. ------. **The Therapy of Desire: Theory and Practice in Hellenistic Ethics**. Martin Classical Lectures. New Ser., v. 2. Princeton: Princeton University Press, 1994. Nussbaum's text is a major retrieval of the import of what she terms the "therapeutic arguments" of the Hellenistic schools of philosophy - the Epicurean, the Skeptic, and the Stoic schools. She limits her focus to the more or less orthodox development of these schools, utilizing Aristotle's ethical thought as contextual background for the presentation of each school's development. Her work is an excellent account of the subtlety of their analyses of the passions and the emotions, concluding that there is a conflict in Hellenistic philosophy between their call for detachment and commitment to engagement in addressing the problems of life.

1154. Oakley, Justin. **Morality and the Emotions**. New York: Routledge, 1991. A major monograph arguing for the moral significance of the emotions in their own right, even in spite of assumptions of the antipathy of the emotions to reason and moral responsibility. It seeks to overcome inadequate assumptions concerning the nature of emotions in many ethical theories in order to discern the fundamental role they play in the moral life and the extent to which one is responsible for one's emotions.

1155. Otto, Rudolf. **The Idea of the Holy: An Inquiry into the Non-Rational Factor in the Idea of the Divine and Its Relation to the Rational**. Translated by John W. Harvey. London/New York: Oxford University Press, 1958. A classic work in the history of religions concerning the nature of the holy as the *mysterium tremendum* in relation to affective experience. It was the companion text to Otto's presentation of the Kantian and Friesian philosophies of religion.

1156. ------. **The Philosophy of Religion, Based on Kant and Fries**. Translated by E. B. Dicker with a Foreword by W. Tudor Jones. London: Williams & Norgate Ltd., 1931. The book is Otto's presentation of his philosophy of religion in light of the critical philosophy of Kant and especially that of Fries and his modifications of the Kantian notion of the sublime in relation to religion.

1157. ------. **Religious Essays; A Supplement to "The Idea of the Holy."** Translated by Brian Lunn. London: Oxford University Press, 1931. Supplementary essays to "The Idea of the Holy" that present further treatment of the feeling of the holy, in particular an essay on Schleiermacher's thought.

1158. Parret, Herman. "Le timbre de l'affect et les tonalités affectives." **Revue Internationale de Philosophie** 48 (1994): 287-303. Parret presents an investigation of the frontier between affect and passion as it has been thematised by Immanuel Kant in his aesthetics. The essay concludes with observations of the understandings of affectivity in

Kant, Husserl, and Michel Henry, contending that Kant's aesthetics anticipated many of the conceptions articulated in the phenomenology of affectivity.

1159. Pascal, Blaise. Pensées and Other Writings. Translated by Honor Levi with an Introduction and Notes by Anthony Levi. The World's Classics. Oxford: Oxford University Press, 1995. Pascal presents his important reflections on the reasons of the sentiments of the heart and an analysis of the pathos and grandeur of human existence and its vanity, misery, and ennui.

1160. Perreiah, Alan B. "Scotus on Human Emotions." Franciscan Studies 56 (1998): 325-345. Paper contends that two affections of the will (*affectio iustitiae* and *affectio commodi*) are primitive and the basis for comprehending the other emotions (concupiscible and irascible). This claim is explicated through an examination of the emotions connected with moral virtues, countering Descartes' claim that the concupiscible and irascible emotions were foundational.

1161. Pfänder, Alexander. "Zur Psychologie der Gesinnungen." Jahrbuch für Philosophie und phänomenologische Forschung 1 (1913): 325-404 and 3 (1916): 1-125. Pfänder's text is a phenomenological critique of psychological reductions of sentiments to either acts of attention, striving, or willing or feelings of pleasure/displeasure. He elaborates an understanding of sentiments as directed towards objects. While positive sentiments are in union with their objects and affirmative of their objects, negative sentiments are adverse to their objects and involve the denial of their right to exist. He also examines the modifications of sentiments in conjunction with other psychical acts.

1162. Polanyi, Michael. Personal Knowledge: Towards a Post-Critical Philosophy. Harper Torchbooks – The Academic Library. New York: Harper & Row, 1964. Underscoring the active components of appraisal and commitment in scientific knowing, Polanyi discusses the intellectual passions as one of the tacit components, besides articulation and conviviality, in the art of scientific knowing.

1163. Plutarch. De libidine et aegritudine (Desire and Grief: Psychical or Bodily Phenomena?). Text with English translation by F. H. Sandbach. In Plutarch's "*Moralia*," vol. 15. Loeb Classical Library. Cambridge: Harvard University Press, 1939. The text offers a valuable historical presentation and Platonist critique of Stoic moral psychology in relation to the emotions of grief and anguish.

1164. Pradines, Maurice. Esprit de la Religion, Essai sur les Rapports des Disciplines humaines: Science, Morale, Philosophie, et des Disciplines mystiques: Magie et Religion. Philosophie de l'esprit. Paris: Aubier, Éditions Montaigne, 1941. A fascinating study, putting various disciplines into dialogue with one another, on the spirit (*ésprit*) of religion. Pradines situates the relation between emotions and sentiment as analogous to that between magic and religion.

1165. ------. Traité de psychologie générale. Vol. I. Le psychisme élémentaire. Third Edition. Vol. II. [Part 1] Le génie humain: ses oeuvres. [Part 2] Le génie humain: ses instruments. Logos, Introduction aux Études Philosophiques. 2. éd., rev. et corr. Paris: Presses Universitaires de France, 1948. Pradines examines emotions and sentiments within a framework of functional reciprocity uniting naturalism and idealism, a philosophy of life as well as a philosophy of spirit. For Pradines, all genesis is reciprocal generation, in which the appearance of the superior is not accounted for in terms of the inferior, but rather there is a reciprocal genesis of the inferior by the superior and of the superior by the inferior.

1166. Pritchard, Michael S. "Reason and Passion: Reid's Reply to Hume." The Monist 61 (1978): 283-298. The paper examines Thomas Reid's criticisms of Hume's theory of the passions, which imply that Hume's understanding of the role of reason in morality is deficient.

1167. Radcliffe, Elizabeth S. "Hume on Passion, Reason, and the Reasonableness of Ends." Southwestern Philosophical Review 10 (1994): 1-11. The article wrestles with the apparent conflict in Hume's account of motivation in the "Treatise" in which Book I discusses the influence of beliefs on the passions, while Book II presents the claim that reason is slave to the passions. The author attempts to reconcile the apparent tension by arguing that the feelings of pleasure and pain are motivating passions and that they are produced concurrently with beliefs, in contrast to the interpretations of Annette Baier and Nicholas Sturgeon that passions are the product of reason.

1168. Ratner, Carl. "A Social Constructionist Critique of the Naturalistic Theory of Emotion." The Journal of Mind and Behavior 10 (1989): 211-230. The doctrine that emotions are products of natural mechanisms is critiqued from a social constructionist perspective. Evidence marshaled in support of the naturalistic theory is also subjected to critical analysis and found to be inadequate. The author argues that, because emotion exemplifies psychological phenomena in general, the social constructionist theory that explains it is to be considered a worthy candidate capable of accounting for the whole range of psychological phenomena.

1169. Rauh, Frédéric. De la méthode dans la psychologie des sentiments. Paris: Félix Alcan, Éditeur, 1899. A philosophical classic examining the philosophical assumptions in the methodological treatment of the sentiments in psychology and moral philosophy at the turn of the century, especially the scientific assumptions in French psychology (e.g., Ribot, Paulhan, etc.). Though presented in a distinctively French idiom, it is a text remarkably relevant to contemporary discussions between psychology and philosophy concerning the emotions.

1170. Reboul, Olivier. L'Homme et ses passions d'après Alain, Vol. 1: La Passion. Publications de L'Université de Tunis Faculté des Lettres et Sciences Humaines; 6e Série: Philosophie, Vol. III. Paris: Presses Universitaires de France, 1968. A magisterial explication of the passions in Alain's philosophical reflections concerning the human. Part I examines passion in relation to personality, the imagination, signs, and the union of mind and body. Part II discusses the question of the ordering and classification of the passions, his interpretations of distress and boredom, hate, jealousy, envy, avarice, ambition, fanaticism, and love, and the remedies to the passions.

1171. ------. L'Homme et ses passions d'après Alain, Vol. 1I: La Sagesse. Publications de L'Université de Tunis Faculté des Lettres et Sciences Humaines; 6e Série: Philosophie, Vol. III. Paris: Presses Universitaires de France, 1968. Reboul examines the question of the human and the passions in relation to Alain's reflections concerning politics, the individual and society, art, religion, education, culture, freedom and the moral life.

1172. Rehm, David. "The Structure of the Emotions in Plotinus." American Catholic Philosophical Quarterly 71 (1997): 469-488. Analysis of Plotinus' treatment of the emotions in *Ennead* III.6 in relation to the effect of anger upon the soul and the nature of the relation between emotions and beliefs. The author argues there is a tension that arises in light of Plotinus' understanding of emotions as the outgrowth of beliefs.

1173. **Ricoeur, Paul.** "**The Antinomy of Human Reality and the Problem of Philosophical Anthropology.**" In The Philosophy of Paul Ricoeur: An Anthology of His Work. **Edited by Charles E. Reagan and David Stewart. Boston: Beacon Press, 1978. Pp. 20-35.** A significant statement of the underlying methodological framework that informs Rioeur's *Freedom and Nature* and his interpretations of emotion and affectivity, the idea of the reciprocity of the involuntary and the voluntary. The essay draws upon Plato's idea of the "mixed" from *Philebus*, Pascal's analysis of pathos, and Kant on the passions.

1174. ------. "**Thou Shalt Not Kill**": **A Loving Obedience.**" Thinking Biblically: Exegetical and Hermeneutical Studies. **Edited by Paul Ricoeur and André LaCocque. Translated by David Pellauer. Chicago: The University of Chicago Press, 1998. Pp. 111-138.** Ricoeur presents the issue of the affections in relation to the topic of love and its ethical import as loving obedience dispositionally engendering autonomy in responsibility towards others.

1175. ------. **Freedom and Nature: The Voluntary and the Involuntary. Trans., with an Introduction by Erazim V. Kohák. Northwestern University Studies in Phenomenology and Existential Philosophy. Evanston: Northwestern University Press, 1966.** Ricoeur examines the topic of emotion within a philosophical anthropology devoted to an eidetic analysis of the will. For Ricoeur, emotion is an involuntary which sustains voluntary action and which serves it in preceding and limiting it. Ricoeur utilizes Descartes' treatise on the passions of the will but within a framework of the reciprocity of the voluntary and the involuntary.

1176. ------. **Fallible Man: Grandeur and Limitation of an Ethical Vision of the World. Revised translation by Charles A. Kelbley and Introduction by Walter J. Lowe. New York: Fordham University Press, 1986.** Ricoeur's text presents a model of philosophical reflection upon the pathos of existence through a series of approaches towards the comprehension of a global disposition of human reality. Ricoeur articulates that global disposition as the affective fragility of the heart, which is the locus for human fallibility and the capacity for evil. Ricoeur presents a philosophy of feeling as the culmination of a philosophical anthropology.

1177. ------. "**The Metaphorical Process as Cognition, Imagination, and Feeling.**" Critical Inquiry **5 (1978): 143-159.** This is an important essay relating his philosophical work upon metaphorical language to his previous work on the reciprocal genesis of knowing and feeling. He explicates how the productive character of the metaphorical process schematizes the mutual promotion of knowing and feeling.

1178. ------. **Oneself as Another. Translated by Kathleen Blamey. Chicago: The University of Chicago Press, 1992.** Ricoeur addresses the issue of affectivity in relation to the enigmas of passivity in the last study of his published Gifford Lectures, which focuses on the ontological implications of oneself as another.

1179. ------. "**Preface: Response to My Friends and Critics.**" **Translated by Charles E. Reagan.** Studies in the Philosophy of Paul Ricoeur. **Edited by Charles E. Reagan. Athens: Ohio University Press, 1979.** Ricoeur responds to Solomon's essay on his position and he: (1) notes that emotions arise from the complementary relation between the voluntary and the involuntary; (2) distinguishes between the passivity of emotions and the passivity of the passions; and (3) suggests that feeling is a third affective entity, distinct from the passions and the emotions, as a metaphorical transposition of emotion.

1180. ------. "Le sentiment." In A L'école de la phénoménologie. Bibliothèque d'histoire de la philosophie. Paris: Librairie Philosophique J. Vrin, 1986. Pp. 251-265. Ricoeur explicates the character of the intentionality and the "inwardness" of feeling in this essay. Feeling is paradoxically described as the unity of a non-positional intention and an affection, of an intention toward the world and as an affection of the self.

1181. ------. "Sympathie et respect." Revue de Métaphysique et Morale 59 (1954): 380-397. Ricoeur critically addresses the ethical dispute between Scheler and Kant vis-à-vis the question of whether sympathy or respect should have primacy. Ricoeur argues for the ethical primacy of respect in relation to sympathy.

1182. ------. "The Unity of the Voluntary and the Involuntary as a Limiting Idea." In The Philosophy of Paul Ricoeur: An Anthology of His Work. Edited by Charles E. Reagan and David Stewart. Boston: Beacon Press, 1978. Pp. 3-19. An important methodological essay explicating the significance of "limit idea" for understanding the unity of the voluntary and the involuntary, especially in relation to the possibility of philosophical reflection upon the pathos and affectivity of human existence.

1183. Ricoeur, P. and A. J. Greimas. "Le Débat du 23 Mai 1989 entre A. J. Greimas et P. Ricoeur sur la Sémiotique des Passions." In Anne Hénault, Le pouvoir comme passion, avec le débat d'A. J. Greimas et Paul Ricoeur sur la sémiotique des passions. Formes Sémiotiques. Paris: Presses Universitaires de France, 1994. Pp. 195-216. Ricoeur and Greimas continue their conversation concerning hermeneutical and semiotic approaches in relation to the question of the nature and philosophical import of semiotics of the passions in Greimas and Fontenelle.

1184. Roberts, Robert C. "Aquinas on the Morality of Emotions." History of Philosophy Quarterly 9 (1992): 287-305. The article presents Aquinas' subtle account of the nature of the emotions and their susceptibility to moral evaluation as "cognitive" in which emotions are understood as perceptions of objects in their value aspect. Roberts claims that this subtle account is, however, weakened by its insistence upon the location of emotions in the sensory appetite. Instead, a consideration of the formal objects that identify the emotions in Thomas' analysis indicates that such objects often are accessible only through the faculties of the will and the intellect.

1185. ------. "Aristotle on Virtues and Emotions." Philosophical Studies 56 (1989): 293-306. Paper examines Aristotle's claims concerning the relations between virtues and emotions and contends that Aristotle, though noting differences between the virtues, presents a too homogenous account of the logical/psychological structure of the virtues in relation to the emotions. The author claims that the two connections between virtues and emotions (propriety of affect relation and the index relation) are not general in scope, but only true of some of the virtues.

1186. ------. "Existence, Emotion, and Virtue: Classical Themes in Kierkegaard." In The Cambridge Companion to Kierkegaard. Edited by Alastair Hannay and Gordon D. Marino. New York: Cambridge University Press, 1998. Paper examines several Kierkegaardian concerns in terms of their continuities with classical moral psychology, especially Aristotle's, and emphasizes the connection of the concepts of character, virtue, and practical wisdom with Kierkegaard's understanding of emotions in light of his attention to passion, pathos, and feeling.

1187. ------. "**Feeling One's Emotions and Knowing Oneself.**" **Philosophical Studies 77 (1995): 319-338.** Roberts presents a construal account of the distinction between emotion and feelings. The article contends that emotions are states of awareness of situation, inclusive of the self as part of that situation. Feelings, meanwhile, are states of awareness of the self in an emotional state. In terms of the construal account, six criteria are put forth for the truth of feelings.

1188. ------. "**Is Amusement and Emotion.**" <u>American Philosophical Quarterly</u> **25 (1988): 269-274.** Roberts contends that amusement and emotions are both construals and passions, but that while emotions are concern-based, amusement is to be characterized as interest-based. The difference between amusement and emotions accounts for why many emotions can motivate action, whereas amusement does not. This is also because emotions presume a dependence upon beliefs that is lacking for amusement.

1189. ------. "**Propositions and Animal Emotion.**" <u>Philosophy</u> **71 (1996): 147-156.** Author argues that animal emotions lacking syntactical language are concern-based construals in contrast to views that strictly relate emotions to propositions. The paper explores the relations between construals and propositions and distinguishes two kinds of propositional content for standard human emotions: defining and material propositions.

1190. ------. "**Some Remarks on the Concept of Passion.**" In <u>International Kierkegaard Commentary: *Two Ages*</u>. **Edited by Robert L. Perkins. Mercer: Mercer University Press, 1984.** Paper examines (1) the leading senses of "passion" in Kierkegaard's thought and the ways in which they are related to one another, (2) reflection as ally and enemy of passion, and (3) the passion-engendering features of Kierkegaard's own thought as "double" reflection.

1191. ------. "**What an Emotion Is: A Sketch.**" <u>The Philosophical Review</u> **97 (1988): 183-209.** Emotions are concern-based construals. Such a theory can account for the following: (1) emotions can be felt; (2) emotions are intentional states with propositional objects in which the objects of emotions can be propositionally specified; (3) typically emotions involve beliefs; (4) some emotions can beget dispositions for action and be explanatory of action; (5) voluntary control of some emotions is possible; and (6) emotions are unified states of mind, not sets of component elements.

1192. **Rorty, Amelie Oksenberg.** "**Hume: La Réconciliation philosophique de la Raison et des Passions.**" <u>Bulletin de la Societé française de Philosophie</u> **85 (1991): 121-151.** Rorty argues that Hume, in his "Treatise on Human Nature," introduces a set of oppositions – between reason and the imagination, reason and the passions, etc. – only in order to demonstrate that the terms are psychologically interdependent.

1193. ------, ed. <u>Explaining Emotions</u>. **Topics in Philosophy 5. Berkeley: University of California Press, 1980.** An excellent anthology of essays that approaches the problem of the conceptual apparatus to be employed in classifying and characterizing the emotions from several perspectives, namely, neurophysiology, psychology, social psychology, and philosophical psychology. The collection includes a very helpful bibliography.

1194. Ross, Stephen David. **Inexhaustibility and Human Being: An Essay on Locality.** New York: Fordham University Press, 1989. The author discusses the emotions within the presentation of a philosophical naturalism that must include human experience as part of nature, such that the emotions are an irreducible form of reason, as a form of human being that is inexhaustible.

1195. Rousseau, Jean-Jacques. **Religious Writings.** Edited by Ronald Grimsley. Oxford: Clarendon Press, 1970. An important collection of texts by Rousseau, especially in terms of his understanding of religion and the role of affectivity and the sentiments therein.

1196. Ryle, Gilbert. **The Concept of Mind.** Chicago: University of Chicago Press, 1984 [Reprint of the 1949 edition]. Ryle unfolds a classic critique of the dogma of the "ghost in the machine" view of emotions as internal or private experiences. He argues that the word "emotion" designates several different kinds of things: inclinations, moods, agitations, and feelings.

1197. Saeson, J. E. "Descartes' Influence on John Smith, Cambridge Platonist." **Journal of the History of Ideas** 20 (1959): 258-263. The author presents an historical study of the influence of Descartes' treatise on the passions of the soul upon Smith's thought.

1198. Salien, Jean-Marie. "Dialectique de la Raison et des Passions dans la Pensée de Jean-Jacques Rousseau." **International Studies in Philosophy** 12 (1980): 55-60. The article presents an analysis of the dialectical interdependence of the faculties of passion and reason in Rousseau's account of the moral evolution of the human from natural innocence to evil.

1199. Sandkaühlen, Birgit. "Oder hat Vernunft den Menschen?" Zur Vernunft des Gefühls bei Jacobi." **Zeitschrift für philosophische Forschung** 49 (1995): 416-429. The essay presents an analysis of the interrelations between reason and feeling in the philosophy of Jacobi, in which he elevated feeling as the organ of philosophy and as the fundamental presupposition underlying concrete human reason. The author explicates Jacobi's position in comparison with Spinoza, Hume, Fichte, and Hegel.

1200. Sarot, Marcel. "God, Emotion, and Corporeality: A Thomist Perspective." **The Thomist** 58 (1994): 61-92. The article is devoted to an analysis of Thomas's theory of human and divine emotion. The article contends that, since, for Thomas, emotions require or presuppose corporeality, God, being incorporeal, cannot have emotions. This conceptual connection between emotions and corporeality is corroborated, the author claims, by contemporary theories of emotion. The essay discusses the implications for contemporary philosophical-theological discussions and debates concerning the impassability of God.

1201. Sartre, Jean-Paul. **Being and Nothingness: An Essay on Phenomenological Ontology.** Translated by Hazel E. Barnes. New York: Philosophical Library, 1956. A modern classic with rich phenomenological analyses of anxiety and bad faith.

1202. -----. Jean-Paul. **The Emotions: Outlines of a Theory of the Emotions.** Translated by Bernard Frechtman. New York: Philosophical Library, 1949. Sartre proposes a phenomenological theory of the emotions defending a view of the emotions as conscious intentional acts constituting a world for which one must accept responsibility.

Sartre criticizes understandings which construe emotions as being physiological phenomena and psychological states of consciousness.

1203. Scheler, Max. **The Nature of Sympathy.** **Translated by Peter Heath; Introduction by Werner Stark. London: Routledge & Kegan Paul, 1954. Reprinted, Hamden: Archon Books, 1970.** Scheler examines the nature of inter-human emotional relations. He distinguishes four types of inter-human emotional experiences: community of feeling, fellow-feeling, psychic contagion, and emotional identification. Scheler is critical of naturalistic theories of love and provides a phenomenological critique of Schopenhauer and Nietzsche in relation to sympathy.

1204. ------. **Ressentiment. Translated by William W. Holdheim. First edition edited with an Introduction by Lewis A. Coser. New York: Free Press of Glencoe, 1961. Reprint: New York: Schocken Books, 1972. Second edition: Introduction by Manfred S. Frings, Marquette University Press, 1994.** A classic study investigating ressentiment as the source for value-deception through false valuations. Ressentiment, for Scheler, is the reactive, psychical self-poisoning that ranges in intensity of feeling from revenge to envy and from enviousness and malice to ressentiment proper. These degrees of intensity are determined by the decrease of cognition and distinction of the object that is resented.

1205. ------. **Formalism in Ethics and Non-Formal Ethics of Values. A New Attempt Toward A Foundation of An Ethical Personalism. Translated by Manfred S. Frings and Roger L. Funk. Northwestern University Studies in Phenomenology and Existential Philosophy. Evanston: Northwestern University Press, 1973.** Scheler's classic critique of the Kantian formalism in ethics and argument for a non-formal ethics of value. Scheler argues that values as a priori are given immediately to intentional feeling, being the intentional objects of feelings. Scheler argues for the irreducibility of the apprehension of values in feelings - feelings are not deducible either from reason or the will.

1206. ------. **On Feeling, Knowing, and Valuing: Selected Writings. Edited and with an Introduction by Harold J. Bershady. Heritage of Sociology. Chicago: University of Chicago Press, 1992.** This anthology is an excellent and useful compilation of selected writings of Scheler on feeling, knowing, and valuing and the interrelations between them.

1207. ------. **"Ordo Amoris." In Selected Philosophical Essays. Trans., with an Introduction, by David R. Lachterman. Northwestern University Studies in Phenomenology and Existential Philosophy. Evanston: Northwestern University Press, 1973. Pp. 98-135.** Influenced by Pascal, Scheler presents an axiological hierarchy of values and of feelings in relation to love and hatred, the movement from lower to higher values and from higher to lower values respectively.

1208. Schmidt, Alfred. **Die Wahrheit im Gewande der Lüge: Schopenhauers Religionsphilosophie. Serie Piper 639. Munich/Zurich: Piper Verlag, 1986.** Discussion of Schopenhauer's philosophy of religion that includes discussions of the relation between his ethics, in which the affections play a prominent role, and his treatment of religion.

1209. Schmitz, Hermann. **"Gefühle als Atmosphären und das affektive Betroffensein von ihnen." In Zur Philosophie der Gefühle. Edited by Hinrich Fink-

Eitel und Georg Lohmann. Suhrkamp Taschenbuch Wissenschaft; 1074. Frankfurt am Main: Suhrkamp Verlag, 1993. Pp. 33-56. The article provides a helpful treatment of the issues surrounding feelings as atmospheric moods.

1210. Schopenhauer, Arthur. **On the Basis of Morality.** Translated by E.F.J. Payne with an Introduction by David E. Cartwright. Rev. ed. Providence: Berghahn Books, 1995. This text presents Schopenhauer's critique of the Kantian moral philosophy and his presentation of an ethics founded upon compassion or sympathy (*Mitleid*).

1211. ------. **The World as Will and Representation.** Two vols. Translated by E.F.J. Payne. New York: Dover Publication, 1958-1959. Significant in Schopenhauer's masterpiece is his treatment of emotions, sentiments, and affections vis-à-vis the interrelations between his aesthetics (presented in Book III) and ethics (Book IV). Aesthetic experience through the contemplation of the work of art liberates from egoistic desires of the will to life. And compassion is the ethical alternative to the malice arising from egoism. It is a rich text in terms of description of various emotions, affections, and passions.

1212. Schrag, Calvin. **Experience and Being: Prolegomena to a Future Ontology. Northwestern University Studies in Phenomenology and Existential Philosophy.** Evanston: Northwestern University Press, 1969. Schrag presents an intentional analysis of the equiprimordial, tripartite structure of human experience as felt, willed, and cognitional through the rejection of a faculty psychology. Schrag argues for feelings as bearers of intentionality that is disclosive of a world and that they are temporal in character.

1213. Sedgwick, Sally S. "Can Kant's Ethics Survive the Feminist Critique?" **Pacific Philosophical Quarterly** 71 (1990): 60-79. In light of recent discussions of Kant's ethics that have drawn attention to his claim that emotion may be an important motivating factor in the moral life of a rational agent and that empirical content may exercise a role in guiding the application of the moral law, the author argues that these discussions fail to meet the challenge of feminist critiques that contend that emotion is a constitutive element of moral agency.

1214. Seidler, Michael J. "Kant and the Stoics on the Emotional Life." **Philosophy Research Archives** 7, no. 1479 (1981). The essay presents an interpretation of Kant's relationship to the Stoics concerning the affective dimension of the moral life. The essay seeks to show that Kant drew upon a number of Stoic themes and distinctions (e.g., between affects and passions) in order to reincorporate the affective dimensions of being human into his account of the fully moral life that appeared to have been excluded in the *Critique of Practical Reason*.

1215. Shaffer, Jerome A. "An Assessment of Emotion." **American Philosophical Quarterly** 20 (1983): 161-174. Shaffer understands an emotional state to be a composite of physiological processes which are caused by a beliefs and desires nexus. Ethical and rational assessment is appropriate only for the complex of beliefs and desires, not the emotion itself. The author further claims that emotions are not necessary for action for only desires and beliefs are necessary and sufficient for action.

1216. Shibles, Warren. **Emotion in Aesthetics.** Philosophical Studies Series. Dordrecht: Kluwer Academic Publishers, 1995. A systematic and detailed presentation of a cognitive-emotive theory of aesthetic emotion in which aesthetic emotion and aesthetic value are based upon evaluative judgments, discarding a mentalistic theory of meaning in favor of an association theory of meaning appropriate to aesthetic expression.

1217. Smith, Quentin. The Felt Meanings of the World: A Metaphysics of Feeling. West Lafayette: Purdue University Press, 1986. To combat nihilism, the author proposes a new metaphysics of feeling that explicates the meanings of the world through how they are appreciated in moods and affects. He argues that each feature of the world is a felt meaning in that each feature is a source of a particular feeling-response if and when it appears. The features of the world emphasized are its being in time (appreciated in joy), its purposeless existence (appreciated in despair), and its non-dependence upon that to which it appears (appreciated in reverence).

1218. Solomon, Robert C. "Emotions, Nature of." In The Routledge Encyclopedia of Philosophy, Vol. 3: Descartes, René - Gender and Science. Pp. 281-285. The article provides a helpful introduction to the questions of the nature of emotion, the intentionality of emotions, the individuation of emotions, and the rationality of emotions.

1219. ------. "Emotions, Philosophy of." In The Routledge Encyclopedia of Philosophy, Vol. 3: Descartes, René - Gender and Science. Pp. 285-290. The article provides a survey of the treatment of the emotions in the history of philosophy in terms of the relation between reason and the emotions through the metaphor of master and slave. The article focuses Plato to the Stoics, Descartes to Nietzsche, and on discussions in the twentieth century.

1220. ------. "On Kitsch and Sentimentality." Journal for Aesthetics and Art Criticism 49 (1991): 1-14. Solomon argues a qualified apology for both kitsch and sentimentality by contesting the undeserved suspicion of the emotions that underlies a number of objections to kitsch and sentimentality.

1221. ------. "On Emotions as Judgments." American Philosophical Quarterly 25 (1988): 183-191. Article presents a defense of cognitive theories of emotion against the objection that cognition or belief is at best a necessary, but not sufficient condition for having an emotion.

1222. ------. "Paul Ricoeur on Passion and Emotion." In Studies in the Philosophy of Paul Ricoeur. Edited by Charles E. Reagan. Athens: Ohio University Press, 1979. Pp. 1-20. An analysis of Ricoeur's discussion of passion and emotion as principally to be found in Ricoeur's *Freedom and Nature: The Voluntary and the Involuntary*. Solomon sees the absence of a systematic theory in Ricoeur's position and suggests what such a systematic theory if developed would look like through a comparison of Ricoeur and Sartre.

1223. ------. The Passions: Emotions and the Meaning of Life. Indianapolis: Hackett Publishing Company, 1993 [1977]. One of the books chiefly responsible for the revival of interest in the emotions as an important philosophical topic. Influenced by Sartre, Solomon contends that the passions have been systematically misunderstood as physiological disturbances or psychological interruptions and proposes that they are self-chosen phenomenological structurings of reality as experienced. The theory of emotions as judgments is applied in brief analyses of different emotions. The new edition also includes revisions of the prior editions, specifically, the elimination of the more speculative phenomenological aspects.

1224. ------. "Sartre on Emotions." In the Philosophy of Jean-Paul Sartre. Edited by Paul Arthur Schilpp. The Library of Living Philosophers, Vol. XVI. La Salle: Open Court, 1991. Pp. 211-228. Solomon presents an excellent overview, analysis, and appreciative critique of Sartre's understanding of the emotions, drawing upon both early and later writings of Sartre.

1225. Sontag, Frederick. Emotion: Its Role in Understanding and Decision. American University Studies. Series V, Philosophy; vol. 11. New York: Peter Lang Publishing, Inc., 1989. Sontag attempts to retrieve the role of emotions in understanding and decision in light of the disparagement of emotion in modern philosophy. His philosophical retrieval of the emotions engages in dialogue with the psychoanalytic theories of Freud and Jung.

1226. Spader, Peter H. "The Primacy of the Heart: Scheler's Challenge to Phenomenology." Philosophy Today 29 (1985): 223-229. A defense of Scheler's claim that access is obtained to non-formal values as the objective grounds of moral decisions only through particular intentional affective acts, through the heart, not the head, against the criticism put forth by Stephen Strasser.

1227. Spinoza, Benedict de. A Spinoza Reader: The Ethics and Other Works. Ed. and trans, by Edwin Curley. Princeton: Princeton University Press, 1994. This anthology of texts by Spinoza presents the full text of his *Ethics* in a readily accessible and affordable edition of Edwin Curley's superb translation. An essential text in the history of philosophy for a consideration of the emotions.

1228. Stephens, G. Lynn. "Cognition and Emotion in Peirce's Theory of Mental Activity." Transactions of the Charles S. Peirce Society 16 (1981): 131-140. Stephens examines Peirce's endeavor to perform the reduction of emotion to cognition in light of his claim that every mental activity can be reduced to cognition. He argues that Peirce, though establishing various analogies between emotion and cognition, finally withdraws the claim that the thought process in emotion is an instance of valid reasoning and does not present a cognitivist understanding of emotion.

1229. Sterling, Marvin C. "The Cognitive Theory of Emotions." Southwest Philosophical Studies 10 (1979): 165-176. The author criticizes two claims advanced by Robert C. Solomon for a cognitive theory of emotion in his book *The Passions*: (1) that emotions are things we invariably do if they are judgments, and (2) that one is invariably responsible for one's emotions if they are judgments. He argues that, even if Solomon is right on his account of emotion as judgment, it does not necessarily follow that emotions are always actively done and that one is always responsible for them.

1230. Stevens, John A. "Posidonian Polemic and Academic Dialectic: The Impact of Carneades upon Posidonius' *Peri pathon*." Greek, Roman, and Byzantine Studies 34 (1993): 229-323. The essay is a lengthy and detailed argument for the profound influence of Carneades upon Posidonius' understanding of the passions.

1231. Stocker, Michael [with Elizabeth Hegeman]. Valuing Emotions. Cambridge Studies in Philosophy. Cambridge: Cambridge University Press, 1996. The book is a valuable congruence and integration of various philosophical, psychoanalytic, and cultural anthropological resources in interdisciplinary collaboration. It argues for the irreducibility of affectivity in examining how emotions reveal values in contrast to the claims of emotivism and naturalism. Making extensive use of Aristotle, Part II examines the relation between emotions and values, and Part III provides case studies of particular emotions in relation to the interdependence of emotions and psychology (empathy, sympathy, shame, and painful emotions), affectivity and self concern (pride, anger, pity, fear, and self-pity), and Aristotle's presentation of the angry man.

1232. Strasser, Stephan. **Phenomenology of Feeling: An Essay on the Phenomena of the Heart**. Foreword by Paul Ricoeur. Translated with an Introduction by Robert Wood. Duquesne Studies. Philosophical Series, Vol. 34. Pittsburgh: Duquesne University Press; Atlantic Highlands, N.J.: distributed by Humanities Press, 1977. The most systematic phenomenological theory of feeling, developed in critique of Scheler's phenomenology of feeling and psychological theories of emotion and which seeks to develop a "thymic" philosophical anthropology. Strasser addresses feeling in terms of a total picture of the self-realization of the human which involves three levels of analysis: the pre-intentional, the intentional, and the level of spirit. An excellent bibliography is included.

1233. Tallon, Andrew. **Head and Heart: Affection, Cognition, and Volition as Triune Consciousness**. New York: Fordham University Press, 1997. The author develops a phenomenological analysis of the intentionality of affective consciousness and its distinctiveness as an essential constitutive element of human consciousness, in equal partnership with cognition and volition. The proposal for a triune consciousness is then the basis for the construal of the connaturality of affection and cognition and how affectivity works in relation to habitude and finitude. The book provides also an excellent survey of continental discussions of affectivity.

1234. ------. "Intentionality, Intersubjectivity, and the Between: Buber and Levinas on Affectivity and the Dialogical Principle." **Thought: Fordham University Quarterly** 53 (1978): 292-309. The author argues for a complementarity in the positions of Buber and Levinas in the notion of intentionality as affectivity and in locating it in the between. In this manner the author contends that the complementarity allows for the correction of possible excesses in each of their positions.

1235. ------. "The Concept of the Heart in Strasser's Phenomenology of Feeling." **American Catholic Philosophical Quarterly** 66 (1992): 341-360. An essay devoted to explicating the centrality and the philosophical significance of the concept of the "heart" in Strasser's phenomenology of feeling. He explicates the heart as affective consciousness, the point of intersection between the motion of *bios* and its desire of *epithumia* with the motion of the *eros* of *logos*, that expresses itself as affective intentionality toward the other.

1236. ------. "The Meaning of the Heart Today: Reversing a Paradigm according to Levinas and Rahner." **Journal of Religious Studies** 11 (1984): 59-74. The author sets forth a reversal of the model of the human conceived primarily in terms of intellect. He argues that the heart is a more adequate model of the human because affectivity is the most fundamental form of intentionality. He draws upon Levinas, but especially Rahner in order to advocate the concept of affective connaturality.

1237. ------. "Nonintentional Affectivity, Affective Intentionality, and the Ethical in Levinas' Philosophy." In **Ethics as First Philosophy: The Significance of**

Emmanuel Levinas for Philosophy, Literature and Religion. **Edited by Adrian T. Peperzak.** **New York: Routledge, 1995. Pp. 107-121.** The author presents an explication of the relation of affectivity and the ethical in Levinas' philosophy guided by a discussion of the relation between affectivity and intentionality.

1238. ------. "Triune Consciousness and Some Recent Books on Affectivity." *American Catholic Philosophical Quarterly* **70 (1996): 243-273.** The author reviews texts on emotion by Quentin Smith, Sue L. Cataldi, and George Turski from the perspective of his understanding of triadic consciousness as constituted by an operational synthesis of affection and cognition mediated by volition.

1239. Taylor, C. C. W. "Emotions and Wants." *The Ways of Desire: New Essays in Philosophical Psychology on the Concept of Wanting.* **Edited by Joe Marks. Chicago: Precedent, 1986. Pp. 217-231.** Paper explores the various ways in which emotions involve desires. Emotions are classified into (a) appetitive, involving desires for a state of affairs not realized, and (b) possessive, where the emotion is a reaction to the satisfaction of a desire. Further, in some emotions the element of desire is the desire to dwell on an object in thought. The existence of these emotions, which are forms of enjoyment, suggests to the author that physiological changes are not necessary features of emotion.

1240. Taylor, Charles. *Sources of the Self: The Making of the Modern Identity.* **Cambridge: Harvard University Press, 1989.** This text is an excellent resource for comprehending the shifts in understanding the emotions in light of its hermeneutical explication of the sources in the Western intellectual tradition informing the meaning of modern identity of the self. Taylor gives great attention to the treatment of the emotions in his magisterial work.

1241. Taylor, Gabriele. *Pride, Shame, and Guilt: Emotions of Self-Assessment.* **Oxford: Clarendon Press; New York: Oxford University Press, 1985.** A provocative analysis of pride and humility, shame, and guilt and remorse as emotions of self-assessment. She argues that emotions of self-assessment are to be conducted in terms of identificatory beliefs as that which makes emotional experience rationally intelligible in order to determine the possible reasonableness of experiencing an emotion on a particular occasion. A valuable discussion of the relation between emotions and beliefs.

1242. Thomas Aquinas. *Summa Theologiae.* **60 vols. Latin text with English translation, Introductions, Notes, Appendices, and glossaries. Cambridge: Blackfriars; New York: McGraw Hill, 1964-1975.** The primary texts for Thomas Aquinas' discussion of the passions in relation to the moral life can be found primarily in the First Part of the Second Part of the *Summa* in questions 22-48 within his treatment of human action.

1243. Thomas, James. "Spinoza's Theory of Expression." *Prima Philosophia* **10 (1997): 425-432.** Paper explicates Spinoza's use of the verb "*exprimere*" (to express) in his *Ethics* as according best with the sense of "to involve or presuppose." The paper develops the implications of Spinoza's theory in order to contend that the emotion expressed in a work of art is capable of objective determination by considering the understanding of life the work of art involves.

1244. Timmermans, Benoît. "Descartes et Spinoza: de l'admiration au désir." **Revue Internationale de Philosophie** 48 (1994): 327-340. The essay examines the shift from Descartes' consideration of admiration or wonder as the first of all the passions to Spinoza's affirmation of desire as the most essential of the primitive passions. Timmermans argues that the changes in Spinoza from Descartes should be understood as a generalization of the Cartesian problematic in which the context (in which the passions are inscribed) is "enlarged" from passion to affect such that a more positive moral and political role is allowed.

1245. Turski, George W. "Experience and Expression: The Moral Linguistic Constitution of Emotions." **Journal for the Theory of Social Behavior** 21 (1991): 373-392. In relation to the emphasis upon the semantic-conceptual aspect of emotions, Turski examines how emotional experience can be structured through language. Utilizing the insights of developmental psychology and De Sousa's concept of "paradigm scenarios," he contends that emotions possess a dramatic-narrative structure that is essentially metaphorical in character. The paper concludes with comments to the effect that the correlation between emotional experience and language does not always have a close fit.

1246. ------. "Emotions and Responsibility." **Philosophy Today** 35 (1991): 137-152. Beginning with an exposition of Aristotle's and Sartre's notions of responsibility and a discussion of the utility of the action-passion distinction for assessments of responsibility, Turski proposes a hermeneutic approach to the emotions in which responsibility is a function of self-transforming reflective practice set within the context of a developmental-normative theory of motivation and human nature.

1247. ------. **Toward a Rationality of Emotions: An Essay in the Philosophy of Mind**. Series in Continental Thought 21. Athens: Ohio University Press, 1994. The book presets insights into emotions through an examination of their relation to various features of being human: intentionality, expression and language, sense of self, responsibility, self-deception, value cognition, and moral agency. Rather than presupposing a description of rationality in relation to the emotions, the author proposes to allow a potential understanding of rationality to be informed by the aforementioned analyses of the emotions, reflecting the underlying conviction of rationality as being complex and multifaceted, not singular. The book utilizes both analytical and phenomenological traditions.

1248. Van Hooft, Stan. "Scheler on Sharing Emotions." **Philosophy Today** 38 (1994): 3-17. The paper attempts to account for Scheler's claim that two persons can share the same feeling by understanding it to mean that persons interpret their individual feelings as shared emotions in shared situations. The author argues that this is only possible and can make sense (that two persons share the same emotion) if they care about the same relevant things.

1249. Wainwright, William J. **Reason and the Heart: A Prolegomenon to a Critique of Passional Reason**. Cornell Studies in the Philosophy of Religion. Ithaca: Cornell University Press, 1995. Wainwright presents an argumentative challenge to the position in the contemporary debate concerning the rationality of religious belief that maintains that objective reason alone is sufficient for the assessment of the evidence upon which religious belief rests. Through the examination of the thought of Jonathan Edwards, William James, and John Henry Newman, Wainwright argues that emotion can guide reason such that reason only functions properly when informed by a rightly disposed heart. Whether one assents to the arguments offered, it is valuable in terms of its analysis of the aforementioned figures.

1250. Wallace, R. Jay. **Responsibility and the Moral Sentiments.** **Cambridge: Harvard University Press, 1994.** Arguing against the claim that accountability requires freedom of the will, Wallace contends that fairness in holding persons responsible depends upon their rational competence, the power to comprehend moral reasons and, hence, control their behavior, which is compatible with determinism. His skillfully prosecuted argument develops through a consideration of the emotions as reactive and nonreactive, moral and nonmoral.

1251. Walton, Douglas N. **The Uses of Emotion in Argument.** **University Park: Pennsylvania State University Press, 1992.** Instead of dismissing commonly used appeals to emotion, pity, fear, sentimentality, and *ad hominem* attacks as inherently fallacious, Walton argues that each use of such appeals must be judged on its own merits. He presents over fifty case studies to discuss the subtler features of the problem of emotional fallacies. He argues that such presumptive reasoning presents in these appeals, while tentative and subject to default, do not necessarily have to be classified as being fallacious argumentation.

1252. Weberman, David. "Heidegger and the Disclosive Character of the Emotions." **Southern Journal of Philosophy 34 (1996): 379-410.** The article presents a reconstruction of Heidegger's theory of the emotions in order to critique contemporary cognitivist understandings of the emotions through an examination of emotion's disclosive character concerning the self, other selves, and the world.

1253. Welsch, Wolfgang. **Aisthesis: Grundzüge und Perspektiven der Aristotelischen Sinneslehre.** **Stüttgart: Klett-Cotta Verlag, 1987.** This text provides a lengthy analysis of *aisthesis* in Aristotle that is extremely important for the philosophical context framing Aristotle's discussion of the emotions.

1254. Wetzel, Marc. "Action et passion." **Revue Internationale de Philosophie 48 (1994): 341-362.** The author examines four plausible theses concerning the relations between action and passion that have been articulated in the history of philosophy. The various proposals are examined in light of the tendencies both to oppose as well as to coordinate passion with action.

1255. Whitehouse, P. G. "The Meaning of 'Emotion' in Dewey's Art as Experience." **Journal of Aesthetics and Art Criticism 37 (1978): 149-156.** The essay explicates in a helpful manner the various senses characterizing the notion of emotion as utilized in Dewey's William James lectures on "art as experience".

1256. Williston, Byron. "Descartes on Love and/as Error." **Journal of the History of Ideas 58 (1997): 429-444.** Article examines Descartes' treatment of love in the "Treatise on the Passions," showing that the passion of love may be a guarantor of the correctness of moral judgments concerning beloved objects in the formulation of moral judgments.

1257. Windelband, Wilhelm. **"Das Heilige. (Skizze zur Religionsphilosophie)."** **Präludien: Aufsätze und Reden zur Philosophie und ihre Geschichte.** **Vol. 2. Seventh Edition. Tübingen: Verlag von J. C. B. Mohr, 1921.** The essay presents a

Neo-Kantian interpretation of the notion of religious feeling for a philosophy of religion and response to the Neo-Friesian position advanced by Rudolph Otto.

1258. Wolf, Ursula. "Gefühle im Leben und in der Philosophie." In Zur Philosophie der Gefühle. Suhrkamp Taschenbuch Wissenschaft; 1074. Edited by Hinrich Fink-Eitel und Georg Lohmann. Frankfurt am Main: Suhrkamp Verlag, 1993. Pp. 89-111. An excellent essay on the philosophical issues surrounding the role of feeling in life, especially in relation to moral philosophy.

Index of Authors

Authors indexed by entry number

Abu-Lughod, Lila, 450, 451
Addis, Laird, 959
Adler, Elaine June, 1
Agaësse, Paul, 659
Akira, Omine, 452
Alain [pseud. of Emile
   Chartier], 960, 961
Alexiou, Margaret, 2
Ali, S. Ameer, 286
Allen, Chad, 962
Allen, R. T., 963
Allen, Robert Raymond, 560
Al-Qatam, Abdulla Abdalli, 8
Alquié, Ferdinand, 964
Alston, William P., 965
Anderson, Douglas R., 660
Anderson, Gary A., 3
Anderson, Marston, 180
Appadurai, Arjun, 453
Appasamy, A. J., 4
Arapura, G., 287
Archimandrite Chrysostomis, 661
Archimandrite Sophrony, 662
Aristotle, 966
Armon-Jones, Claire, 969
Armstrong, Robert Plant, 454
Aronson, Harvey B., 288
Arregui, Jorge V., 967, 968
Ashforth, Adam, 561
Attivissimo, Donna Ann, 336
Aune, David Charles, 5
Avalos, Hector I., 6
Averill, James R., 337, 338
Azouvi, François, 970

Babés, Leïla, 49, 455
Baier, Annette C., 971, 972, 973
Bailey, Cyril, 7
Bailey, F. G., 456
Baillie, John, 663
Baker, Robert O., 664
Baloian, B. E., 8
Barad, Judith, 974
Barker-Benfield, G. J., 131

Barnard, G. William, 339
Barnes, Hazel, 975
Barnouw, Jeffrey, 976
Baroni, Helen J., 457
Barth, Brigit, 340
Barth, Karl, 665
Bartlett, Anne Clark, 50
Basu, Helen, 224
Bateson, Gregory, and Mary
   Catherine Bateson, 458
Baumgärtel, F., and J. Behm, 666
Bayer, Oswald, 667
Becker, Aimé, 668
Beckman, David M., 225
Bedard, André, 669
Beecher, Marguerite and
   Willard Beecher, 341
Behari, Bankey, 289
Beintker, Horst, 670, 671
Beit-Hallahmi, Benjamin, 226, 342
Bell, David N., 672
Bell, Joseph N., 9
Bellah, Robert N., 562
Bellah, Robert N., Richard
   Madsen, and William M.
   Sullivan, 563
Bennett, Peter, 227, 459
Ben-Ze'ev, Aaron, 977, 978
Ben-Ze'ev, Aaron, and Justin
   Oatley, 979
Beonio-Broccheri,
   Mariateresa Fumagalli, 51
Berger, Peter L., and Thomas
   Luckman, 64
Bernard, Charles-A., 673
Bernard, Charles André, S.J., 674, 675
Bettini, Maurizio, 10
Beyssade, Jean-Marie, 980, 981
Bharati, Agehananda, 290
Bhattacharyya, Manjula, 52
Bhattacharyya, N. N., Ed., 53
Bhogle, Shalini, 343

Bieritz, Karl-Heinrich, 676
Binski, Paul, 54
Bisson, Thomas N., 55
Bland, Lucy, 181
Blowers, Paul M., 677
Bochet, Isabelle, 678
Boddy, Janice, 460, 461
Boden, Margaret A., 345
Boer, P. A. H. de, 11
Boles, John C., 132
Bollnow, Otto-Friedrich, 982
Bondi, Richard, 679
Borchert, James, 228
Bowra, Sir Maurice, 56
Bradley, James, 983, 984
Brandt, Richard B., 985
Breitweiser, Robert Mitchell, 133
Bremard, Henri, 291, 292
Bremmer, J. N., 12
Brenner, Athalya, 13, 14
Brentano, Franz C., 986
Brice, Eugene W., 15
Briffault, Robert, 293
Brooks, Charles R., 229
Brown, Michael F., 565
Browning, Don S., 680, 681
Brunner, Emil, 682
Brusotti, Marco, 987
Brutz, Judith L., 566
Buehler, Arthur F., 294
Bultmann, Rudolf, 683
Burgess, Andrew J., 684
Burnaby, J., 685
Butler, Jonathan M., 182

Caldwell, Sarah Lee, 462
Calhoun, Cheshire, 988
Calhoun, Cheshire and Robert C. Solomon, Eds., 989
Call, Vaughn R. A., and Tim B. Heaton, 567
Calvin, Jean, 686
Campbell, John Angus, 183
Campbell, Joseph, 346
Campbell, Ted A., 134
Camporesi, Piero, 135
Capps, Donald, 347, 348, 349
Carmel, Sara, and Elizabeth Mutran, 568
Carroll, Michael P., 69

Cataldi, Sue L., 990
Chagnon, Napoleon A., 463
Chamberlain, Ava, 687
Champakalakshmi, R., 57
Champion, Françoise and Danièle Hervieu-Léger, Eds., 295, 570
Chatillon, Jean, 688
Chatterjee, Chinmayi, 296
Chenu, Marie-Dominique, 991
Cherry, Keith, and David H. Smith, 350
Ching, Julia, 297
Chisholm, Roderick M., 992
Christian, William A., Jr., 58, 59, 230
Christodoulou, Joan, 184
Cicero, 993
Clapper, Gregory S., 136, 689, 690, 691
Clark, Anna, 185
Clark, Candace, 571
Cleary, M., 692
Clulow, Christopher F., 572
Coe, David K., 298
Cognet, Louis, 693
Cohen, Charles Lloyd, 60
Cohen, Ted, 994
Coles, Robert, 352
Colish, Marcia L., 694
Collins, Randall, 573, 574
Colonna, Fanny, 575
Comaroff, Jean, 464
Conkin, Paul K., 186
Conn, Walter E., 353, 695, 696, 697
Connolly, Thomas, 61
Cooper, John M., 995, 996, 997, 998, 999, 1000
Cooper, John M. and J. F. Procopé, Eds., 1001
Copestake, David R., and H. Newton Malony, 354
Coppins, Attracta Anne, 62
Corrigan, John, 137, 138, 187
Cottingham, John, 1002, 1003
Coursen, Herbert R., Jr., 63
Coxhead, Nona, 355
Craemer-Ruegenberg, Ingrid, 1004

Crane, R. S., 64
Crapanzano, Vincent, 465
Crawford, Mark E., Paul J. Handal, and Richard L. Wiener, 577
Crawford, Michael J., 139
Creel, Richard E., 698
Crocker, Robert, 1005
Cross, Whitney R., 188
Crossley, Daid, 1006
Crouzel, Henri, 699
Csordas, Thomas J., 356
Cudworth, Ralph, 1007
Culligan, Kevin, 700
Cuthbertson-Johnson, Beverley, David D. Franks, and Michael Dornan, Eds., 643

Damann, Ernst, 231
Danforth, Loring M., 467
D'Arcy, Martin C., 701
Darwin, Charles, 357
David, Anthony, 1008
David, E. Valentine, 468
Davidman, Lynn, 578
Davies, Stevan L., 16
Davies, Wendy, 65
Davis, Charles, 358
Davis, Scott, 469
De Sousa, Ronald, 1013
De St. Aubin, Ed., 359
De Wette, Wilhelm Martin Leberecht, 704, 705
Dechanet, J.-M., O.S.B, 702
Deigh, John, 1009
Delitzsch, Franz, 703
Delumeau, Jean, 299
Denby, David J., 140
Denison, J. H., 300, 301
Dent, N. J. H., 1010
Deprun, Jean, 1011
Derné, Steve, 232
Descartes, René, 1012
Desjarlais, Robert R., 471, 472
Despland, Michael, 1014
Destro, Adriana, 17
Devlin, Judith, 189
Dewey, John, 1015, 1016, 1017, 1018

Dhavamony, Mariasusai, 302
Diamond, Stephen, 360
DiBlasio, Frederick A., 580
Dick, Lois Chapman, 361
Didier, Béatrice, 141
Diederich, Martin, 706
Dillon, Michele, 581
Dinet, Dominique, 142
Dockhorn, Klaus, 707
Docking, Jeffrey R., 582
Dodds, E. R., 18
Doi, Kenji, 708
Dollimore, Jonathan, 303
Domingues, Patricia L., 583
Domino, George, and Yoshitomo Takahashi, 584
Dorner, Isaak August, 709, 710
Dorschel, Andreas, 1019, 1020
Doud, Robert E., 711
Doyle, Barry M., 234
Dreyer, Elizabeth, 712, 713
Drost, Mark P., 1021
Duby, Georges and Philippe Braunstein, 66
Duff, Robert W., and Lawrence K. Hong, 585
Dufrenne, Mikel, 1022, 1023, 1024, 1025
Duncan, Margaret Beaton, 143
Dunlap, Knight, 362
Dunn, Paul, 363
Duns Scotus, 1026
Dupre, Louis, 714
Dupuy, Michel, 715
Durkheim, Emile, 586, 587
Dusenbery, Verne A., 235

Ebersole, Gary L., 144, 473
Edwards, Jonathan, 716, 717, 718, 719
Ekman, Paul, and Richard J. Davidson, Eds., 408
Elder, E. Rozanne, 720
El-Helou, Mohamed W., and Peter R. Johnson, 588
Ellison, Christopher G., 589
Ellwood, Gracia Fay, 364
Enç, Berent, 1029

Englehardt, Carol Marie, 190
Epictetus, 1030
Epicurus, 1027
Erben, Andreas, 590
Erdt, Terrence, 721
Erikson, Erik H., 67, 236
Erol, Nese, and Nail Sahin, 365
Esler, Philip F., 19
Eulogio De La Virgen Del Carmen, 722, 723
Evans, Arthur, 20
Evans, Donald, 724, 725
Ewing, Katherine P., 237

Fabry, Heinz-Josef, 726
Fairchild, Hoxie Neale, 68
Farley, Edward, 727
Farley, Wendy, 728
Farron, S., 21
Febvre, Lucien Paul V., 69
Feld, Steven, 474
Fell, Joseph P., 1031
Ferguson, Harvie, 304, 729
Feuerbach, Ludwig, 1032
Fields, Stephen, S. J., 730
Fiering, Norman, 731
Fillion, Lahille Janine, 1033
Fink-Eitel, Hinrich, 1034
Finn, Thomas M., 22
Fiorenza, Francis, 732
Fisher, Gene A., and Kyum Koo Chon, 591
Fleischer, Manfred P., 238
Flood, Gervin, 239
Floyd, Shawn D., 1035
Flynn, Maureen, 145
Fontanelle, Jacques, 1036
Fortes, Meyer, 240
Forthomme, Bernard, 1037
Foster, Lawrence, 191
Fourier, Charles, 1038
Fowler, James W., 733
Fox, Nili S., 23
Fragola, Anthony N., 367
Frank, Robert H., 592
Frankenberry, Nancy, 734, 1039
Franklin, Stephen T., 735
Frazer, James George, 475
Frede, Michael, 1040

Frembgen, Jurgen Wasim, 241
French, Hal W., 192
Freud, Sigmund, 368, 369
Frey-Wehrlin, C. Toni, 370
Frings, Manfred S., 1041
Frohnhofen, Herbert, 736
Fromm, Erich, 371

Gager, John G., 24
Galanter, Marc, 593
Gallard, Martine, 372
García-Ruiz, Jesús, 594
Gardner, Harry M., Ruth Clark Metcalf, and John G. Beebe-Center, 1042
Garrity, Robert Michael, 70
Gatyas, Kenton Bernard, 147
Geertz, Clifford, 476, 477, 478
Gemünden, Petra von, 737
George, Kenneth M., 479, 480
Gerlach, Luther P., 242
Ghazzal, Zouhair, 71
Gilbert, Christopher, 1043
Gildea, Marianna, 72
Gill, Frederick C., 148
Gillepsie, V., 738
Gilman, James E., 739
Gilmour, John, 740
Gilpin, W. Clark, 73
Gilson, Étienne, 741
Gispert-Sauch, G., 305
Githieya, Francis Kimani, 243
Goddrich, Michael E., 74
Goffman, Erving, 595
Goldenberg, Naomi R., 373
Goldenweiser, Alexander, 481
Goldin, Frederick, 75
Goldstein, Jan, 193
Goodman, Elizabeth Kushi, 596
Goodman, Felicitas D., 482, 483
Goodman, Felicitas D., Jeannette H. Henney, and Esther Pressel, 484
Gordon, Robert M., 1044, 1045
Gorringe, Timothy, 306
Goswami, Bhagabat Kumar, 25

Index of Authors

Gouhier, Henri, 1046, 1047, 1048
Graf, Friedrich W., 742
Graham-Pole, John, Hannelore Wass, and Sheila M. Eyberg, 597
Grasmick, Harold G., Robert J. Bursik, and John K. Cochran, 598
Gratton, Henri, 743
Greaves, Margaret, 76
Greeley, Andrew, 599
Green, O. H., 1049, 1050, 1051
Greene, Donald, 149
Greenspan, Patricia, 1052
Greer, Bruce A., and Wade C. Roof, 600
Gregg, Robert C., 744
Gregory of Nyssa, 745, 746
Greimas, Algirdas Julien and Jacques Fontanille, 1053
Greven, Philip, 150, 374
Griffin, William Paul, 26
Griffith, R. Marie, 244
Griffiths, P. E., 1054, 1055, 1056
Groves, Nicholas, 747
Gueroult, Martial, 1057
Guettler, Amy E., 27
Gugerli, David, 151
Guillaumont, Antoine, 748
Gunther, Candy, 194
Gustafson, James M., 749, 750
Guyer, Paul, 1058

Hagerty, Bonnie M., Reg A. Williams, James C. Coyne, 601
Haller, William, 77
Halligan, Frederick R. and John J. Shea, Eds., 366
Halperin, Daniel Tzvi, 485
Hambricke-Stowe, Charles, 152
Hamilton, Malcolm B., 602
Hamlin, William M., 78
Hammacher, Klaus, 1059
Hamm-Ehsani, Karin, 153
Hankinson, James, 1060

Harak, G. Simon, 752
Hardison, O. B., Jr., 79
Hardy, Alister, 375
Hardy, Friedhelm Ernst, 80, 307, 308, 309
Häring, Bernard, C.S.S.R, 751
Harner, Sandra, and Warren W. Tryon, 486
Harrell, David Edwin, Jr., 245
Harris, Grace Gredys, 487
Hart, James G., 1061
Hartshorne, Charles, 753
Haste, Helen, 1062
Hattur, Matt, 81
Hausherr, Irénée, 754
Havran, Michael J., 154
Hayward, Douglas James, 488
Heelas, Paul, 489
Hegel, G. W. F., 1063, 1064, 1065, 1066, 1067, 1068
Heidegger, Martin, 1069, 1070
Heisig, James W., 376
Heller, Agnes, 1071, 1072, 1073, 1074, 1075
Henderson, David, 490
Henry, James P., 377
Hermann, Wilhelm, 756
Heschel, Abraham J., 757
Heyd, Michael, 155, 156
Hildebrand, Dietrich von, 758, 759
Hill, Peter C., 378
Hilliard, David, 46
Hinton, Rebecca Ann, 82
Hjort, Mette and Sue Laver, Eds., 1028
Ho, Shun-Yee, 83
Hobbes, Thomas, 1076, 1077
Hochschild, Arlie Russell, 604
Hocking, William Ernest, 1078
Hoffman, Gerhard and Alfred Hornung, Eds., 247
Hoffman, Paul, 1079
Hoffman, W. Michael, 761, 762, 763
Holland, Ronando W., 248
Hollywood, Amy, 84
Holm, Nils G., Ed., 249
Holmer, Paul L., 764

Hölte, Ragnar, 760
Homans, Peter, 379, 380, 491
Hood, Ralph W., Jr., 381
Horváth, Tibor, S.J, 765
Hughes, Jonathan, 85
Huidberg, Flemming Friis, 28
Hume, David, 1080, 1081, 1082, 1083, 1084
Huntington, Richard, and Peter Metcalf, 382
Hutch, Richard A., 766
Hutcheson, Francis, 1085
Hyers, M. Conrad, 310

Ibana, Rainier R. A., 1086
Imber-Black, Evan, 605
Immerwahr, John, 1087, 1088
Inge, William Ralph, 767
Ingebretsen, Edward J., 311
Inwood, Brad, 1089
Irvine, Judith T., 383
Ivánka, Endre von, 768

Jackson, Hugh, 195
Jackson, Stanley W., 384
Jacobs, Janet L., 385, 386
Jacquette, Dale, 1090
Jaggar, Alison M., 1091
James, Susan, 1092, 1093
James, William, 387, 388, 1094, 1095, 1096, 1097
Janet, Paul, 1098
Janet, Pierre, 389
Janet, Richard J., 196
Jang, Nam Hyuck, 492
Jankélévitch, Vladimir, 1099
Janowiak, Sharon Marie, 606
Javalgi, Rajshekhar G., Bob Cutler, and Naresh K. Malhotra, 607
Javelet, Robert, 769, 770, 771
Jensen, Lene Arnett, 608
Jetté, Fernand, 772
Jewett, Robert, 773
Jilek, Wolfgang G., 493
Joest, Wilfried, 774
Johansson, Rune E. A., 390
Johnson, Doyle Paul, and Larry C. Mullins, 609
Johnson, Elizabeth, 775
Jones, Serene, 776

Jordan, Gregory E., 86
Jung, C. G., 391, 392
Jung, Patricia Beattie, 777, 778

Kahn, Jack, 393
Kant, Immanuel, 1100
Kapferer, Bruce, 494, 495
Kaufman, Peter Iver, 87
Kaufmann, Gordon D., 779
Keaty, Anthony W., 780
Kemper, Theodore D., 610
Kenny, Anthony, 1101
Kent, John, 197
Kerner, Karen, 250
Khair, Gajanan S., 496
Kierkegaard, Søren, 781, 782, 783, 784, 785, 786
Kiernan, Jim, 251
Kim, Man-Poong, 88
Kimbrough, David L., 497
Kinneavy, James L., 787
Kirchmeyer, Jean, 788
Kirkpatrick, Lee A., 394, 395
Kirschner, Suzanne R., 396
Klaniczay, Gábor, 89
Kleinman, Arthur and Byron Good, Eds., 466
Klenow, Daniel J., 611
Kligman, Gail, 498
Klostermaier, Klaus Konrad, 90
Knowles, David, 312
Knox, R. A., 313
Koehler, Théodore, 789, 790, 791
Koehn, Daryl, 1102
Köhl, Harald, 1103
Kohut, Heinz, 397
Kolenda, Pauline, 252
Koltun-Fromm, Ken, 198
Konkola, Kari Sueros, 91
Köpf, Ulrich, 792, 793
Körtner, Ulrich H. J., 794
Koteskey, Ronald L., 795
Kracke, Waud H., 499
Kratz, Corinne A., 500
Kremer-Marietti, Angèle, 1104
Kretzmann, Norman, 1105
Kreuzer, Johann, 796

Index of Authors

Kristeva, Julia, 398
Kselman, Thomas A., 199
Kühn, Rolf, 797, 798, 799, 1106, 1107, 1108
Kunz, Erhard, 800

Labouvie-Vief, Gisela, 399
Lacroix, Jean, 801, 1109, 1110
Lacroze, René, 1111
Lactantius, 802, 803
Laderman, Carol, 501
Laderman, Carol, and Marina Roseman, 532
Laing, Annette Susan, 157
Lamm, Julia A., 804
Land, Steven J., 805
Landman, Christina, 253
Laney, James T., 806
Langer, Otto, 807
Langer, Suzanne, 1112, 1113
Lasch, Christopher, 254
Lash, Nicholas, 808
Latvus, Kari, 29
Lauritzen, Paul, 809, 810, 811
Lawrence, Patricia B., 503
Lazarus, Richard S., and Bernice N., 504
Leaver, Robin A., 158
Leavitt, John, 505
LeClerc, Jean, 92
Lee, Jae Hoon, 400
Lefèvre, André, 812
Lefkowitz, Mary R., 93
Leiby, James, 200
Leighton, Stephen R., 1114
Lesnick, Daniel R., 94
Levenson, Jerold, 1115
Leverenz, David, 95
Levi, Anthony, 1116
Levinas, Emmanuel, 1117
Levy, Eric P., 813
Levy, Jerrold E., Raymond Neutra, and Dennis Parker, 507
Levy, Robert I., 508
Lewis, I. M., 509
Lewis, Jan, 201
Lewis, Paul, 814
Lilla, Salvatore R. C., 815
Lindholm, Charles, 255

Link, Hilde K., 510
Little, Lester K., 96
Little, Margaret Olivia, 1118
Lloyd, A. C., 1119
Lloyd, Genevieve, 1120
Lobel, Diana Nicole, 97
Lock, Margaret, 511
Locke, John, 1121
Lokhande, Ajit, 98
Lonergan, Bernard, 816
Lonsdale, Steven H., 30
Loock, Reinhard, 1122
López-Dominguez, Virgina, 1123
Lorenz, Rudolf, 817
Losonsky, Michael, 1125
Lovejoy, David S., 99
Löw-Beer, Martin, 1124
Loyer, François, 202
Lutz, Catherine A., 512, 513
Lutz, Catherine A., and Lila Abu-Lughod, Eds., 502
Lutz, Catherine and Geoffrey M. White, 514
Lynch, Owen M., 256
Lyons, William, 1126

Maccoby, Hyam, 31
MacDonald, Jerry P., 612
MacDonald, Margaret Y., 32
MacDonald, Michael, 159, 160
MacDonald, Michael, Ed., 129
Macmurray, John, 1129
Macquarrie, John, 818, 819
Macquire, Daniel C., 820, 821
Magai, Caroln and Susan H. McFadden, Eds., 603
Majumdar, Bimanbehari, 100
Malebranche, Nicholas, 1127, 1128
Malinowski, Bronislaw, 517
Mallimaci, Fortunato, 613
Mangano, Mark J., 33
Mansfield, Bruce, 314
Mansfield, Mary C., 101
Mantzaridis, Georgios I., 822
Marcus, Ivan C., 102
Marett, R. R., 518, 519
Marglin, Frédérique A., 520

Marion, Jean-Luc, 1130, 1131, 1132
Marks, Joel, Ed., 1133
Marks, Joel and Roger T. Ames, Eds. 1134
Marten, A. Lynn, 103
Martycz, Virginia Kennedy, 614
Maslow, Abraham H., 401
Masson, J. Moussaieff, 34, 521
Masson, Jeffrey Moussaieff, and Susan McCarthy, 522
Matsumoto, David, 402
Maurer, Wilhelm, 823
Maxsein, A., 824
May, Henry F., 315
Mazis, Glen A., 1135
Mazzaroni, Christina, 316
Mazzela, David Samuel, 161
McCandless, J. Bardarah, 825
McCanley, Deborah Vansau, 203
McCarthy, Vincent A., 826, 827
McCormick, Peter J., 1136, 1137
McDaniel, June, 257, 515
McDonough, Peter, 258
McGaffey, Wyatt, 259
McGinn, Bernard, 828, 829
McGinn, Bernard, Ed., 830
McGoldrick, Monica, Rhea Almeida, and Paulette Moore Hines, 615
McIntire, Sandra, 104
McKenzie, Alan T., 204
McLoughlin, William G., 317
McWilliams, Warren, 831
Mead, George Herbert, 403
Meinong, Alexius, 1138
Meissner, W. W., 404, 405
Meland, Bernard, 832, 833, 834, 835
Mellor, Philip A., and Chris Shilling, 616
Menon, Usha, and Richard A. Shweder, 523
Meslin, Michel, 836
Metzger, Günther, 837
Meyer, Michel, 139, 1140, 1141
Michel, Patrick, 260
Milgrom, Jacob, 35
Milhaven, John Giles, 105, 838
Miller, John, 162
Miller, Perry, 163, 164
Miller, Randolph Crump, 839
Miller, William Ian, 617
Millet, Olivier, 840
Minces, Juliette, 618
Minnis, Alastair J., 841
Minor, John E., 261
Miquel, P., 842
Mockler, Anthony, 106
Moltmann, Jürgen, 843, 844
Monad, Paul Kleber, 107
Montmasson, E., 845
Moore, Leonard J., 262
Moran, W. L., 36
More, Henry, 1142
Morel, Georges, 846
Morgan, Michael L., 37
Morissey, Michael P., 847
Morris, Linda Louise, 619
Mosher, Robert E., 620
Motta, Roberto, 524
Mounteer, Carl A., 406
Mouroux, Jean, 848
Mudford, Peter, 205
Mueller, John J., S.J, 849, 850
Muellner, Leonard, 38
Muffs, Yochanan, 39
Mulder, J. A. Niels, 263
Mulhall, Stephen, 1143
Muller, Richard A., 851
Myers, Fred R., 264
Myers, Gerald E., 407, 1144
Myers, Scott M., 621

Nadeau, Janice Winchester, 622
Narayanan, Vasudha, 40
Nash, Ronald Alan, 1145
Nasuruddin, Mohammed Ghouse, 265
Nellas, Panayiotis, 852
Nelson, Timothy John, 266, 623
Nemesius of Emesa, 853
Netherton, William D., 108

Neto, Felix, 624
Neu, Jerome, 1146
Neuberg, Marc, 1147
Neumann, Erich, 409
Newman, Martha G., 109
Niebuhr, H. Richard, 854
Niebuhr, Richard R., 855, 856, 857, 858
Nielsen, Stevan Lars, and Albert Ellis, 410
Nietzsche, Friedrich, 1148
Nilsson, Martin Persson, 41
Noble, H.-D, 859
Nock, Arthur Darby, 42
Noffke, Suzanne, O.P, 860
Noreña, Carlos G., 1149
Nurbakhsh, Javad, 318, 319,
Nussbaum, Martha Craven, 1150, 1151, 1152, 1153
Nuttall, Geoffrey F., 861, 862
Nygren, Anders, 863

Oakley, Justin, 1154
Oatley, Keith, and Jennifer M. Jenkins, 411
Oberman, Heiko A., 864, 865
Obeyesekere, Gananath, 526, 527, 528
Okorocha, Cyril C., 267
Olthius, James H., 866
O'Neil, Mary, 110
Orellana, Sandra L., 111
Ortner, Sherry B., 529, 530
Ostow, Mortimer, 412
Otto, Rudolf, 1155, 1156, 1157
Owen, John, 867, 868
Ozment, Steven E., 869

Paisley, A. G., 45
Paloutzian, Raymond F., and Aris S. Janigan, 413
Pande, Susmita, 112
Pannenberg, Wolfhart, 870
Parish, Steven M., 268
Park, George, and Cheryl Brown, 269
Park, Kristin, 625
Parkes, Colin Murray, Pittu Laungani and Bill Young, Eds., 470

Parret, Herman, 1158
Parrott, W. Gerrod, and Rom Harré, 626
Parsons, William B., 414, 415
Pascal, Blaise, 1159
Payne, Rodger M., 165
Pearson, Roger, 270
Peletz, Michael G., 531
Pelton, Robert D., 271
Perella, Nicholas James, 322
Perreiah, Alan B., 1160
Perry, Bruce F., 416
Peter Homans, Ed., 351
Peters, Larry, 272
Petroff, Elizabeth Alvilda, 113, 114
Pétursson, Pétur, 273
Pevey, Carolyn, Christine L. Williams, and Christopher G. Ellison, 627
Peyroux, Catherine, 115
Pfänder, Alexander, 1161
Pfister, Oscar, 323
Piette, Albert, 628
Pitts, Walter F., 274
Plutarch, 1163
Polanyi, Michael, 1162
Polhemus, Robert M., 206
Pomi, Massimo, 417
Porter, Jean, 871
Porter, Roy, 166
Pourrat, P., 872
Pradines, Maurice, 1164, 1165
Pressman, Peter, John S. Lyons, and David B. Larson, 418
Preul, Reiner, 873
Priest, Robert Joseph, 533
Principe, Walter, C.S.B, 874
Pritchard, Michael S., 1166
Proudfoot, Wayne, 875, 876, 877
Puig, Maria Elena, 629

Quaife, G. R., 167
Questier, Michael C., 116
Quiroga, Diego, 534

Rabinowitz, Richard, 207
Raboteau, Albert J., 208
Rack, Henry D., 209

Radcliffe, Elizabeth S., 1167
Radcliffe-Brown, A. R., 535
Radday, Yehuda T. and
　Athalya Brenner, Eds., 43
Rahner, Karl, 878, 879, 880,
　881
Rajabally, Mohamed H., 419
Ramsey, Janet Lauchnor, 630
Rank, Otto, 420
Ratner, Carl, 1168
Rauh, Frédéric, 1169
Rawlinson, Andrew, 324
Rawlyk, G. A., 210
Rayburn, Carole, 421
Reboul, Olivier, 1170, 1171
Rehm, David, 1172
Reimers, Adrian J., 422
Reynolds, Charles H., and
　Ralph Norman, Eds., 576
Reynolds, Terence Paul, 882
Richards, P. Scott, Randy K.
　Hardman, Harold Frost,
　424
Ricoeur, Paul, 1173, 1174,
　1175, 1176, 1177, 1178,
　1179, 1180, 1181, 1182
Ricoeur, P., and A. J.
　Greimas, 1183
Rieff, Philip, 631, 632
Riesèbrodt, Martin, 633
Riesman, David, 634
Riggs, Cheryl, 117
Rivers, Isabel, 168
Rizzuto, Ana-Maria, 425
Robb, Paul V., S.J, 891
Roberts, Robert C., 883, 884,
　885, 886, 887, 888, 889,
　890, 1184, 1185, 1186,
　1187, 1188, 1189, 1190,
　1191
Robins, Roger, 211
Roche, Aloysius, 325
Rohls, Jan, 892, 893
Rorty, Amelie Oksenberg,
　1192
Rorty, Amelie Oksenberg,
　Ed., 1193
Rosaldo, Michelle Z., 536,
　537
Rose, Paul Lawrence, 118
Ross, Christopher F. J., 426
Ross, Stephen David, 1194
Rothko, Christopher Hall, 427
Rousseau, Jean-Jacques, 1195
Rousselot, Pierre, 894
Rozett, Martha Tuck, 119
Rozin, Paul, Linda Millman,
　and Carol Nemeroff, 538
Rubin, Julius H., 326
Ruello, Francis, 895
Ryder, Mary R., 169
Ryle, Gilbert, 1196

Sabersky, Dorothy, 896, 897
Sabini, J., and M. Silver, 635
Saeson, J. E., 1197
Sahin, Nesrin H., Ayseguel
　Durak Batiguen, and Nail
　Sahin, 636
Sala, Raymond, 170
Salien, Jean-Marie, 1198
Saliers, Don E., 898, 899, 900
Sanders, Cheryl J., 275
Sandkauhlen, Birgit, 1199
Sanford, A Whitney, 120
Sarbin, Theodore R., 428
Sarot, Marcel, 1200
Sartre, Jean-Paul, 1201, 1202
Saussy, Carroll, and Barbara
　J. Clarke, 429
Scharlach, Andrew E., and
　Esme Fuller-Thomson, 637
Scheidlinger, Saul, 430
Scheler, Max, 1203, 1204,
　1205, 1206, 1207
Schervish, Paul G., Raymond
　J. Halnon, and Karen
　Bettez Halnon, 638
Schlatter, Adolf, 901
Schleiermacher. Friedrich,
　902, 903
Schmidt, Alfred, 1208
Schmitz, Hermann, 1209
Schneider, Carl D., 431
Schoenfeldt, Michael, 121
Scholz, Heinrich, 904
Schopen, Ann, and Brenda
　Freeman, 432
Schopenhauer, Arthur, 1210,
　1211
Schrag, Calvin, 1212
Schwab, Reinhold, and Kay

Index of Authors

U. Petersen, 433
Schwartz, Theodore, Geoffrey M. White, and Catherine A. Lutz, 525
Schwarz, Reinhard, 905
Scribner, Bob, 122
Sedgwick, Eve Kosofsky and Adam Frank, Eds., 434
Sedgwick, Sally S., 1213
Seed, Patricia, 171
Seeley, Paul Alan, 212
Seidler, Michael J., 1214
Shaffer, Jerome A., 1215
Sharda, S. R., 327
Sharma, Krishna, 328
Sharpe, Kevin, 172
Shaw, Nancy Joy, 213
Shea, William M., 906
Sheehy, Noel, 435
Shenck, David, 907
Shibles, Warren, 1216
Shiefflin, Edward L., 276
Shobha, Savitri Chandra, 123
Shultz, Werner, 908
Shumaker, John f., 423
Shuman, Carolyn R., Glenn P. Fournet, Paul F. Zelhart, 639
Shweder, Richard A., 539, 540, 541, 542
Shweder, Richard A., and Edmund J. Bourne, 543
Siegel, Lee, 544
Simmel, Georg, 640
Simon, Ulrich, 329
Simonson, Harold P., 909
Simpson, Michael A., 641
Singer, Irving, 330, 331
Sizer, Sandra S., 214
Slater, Philip E., 642
Smith, A. J., 124
Smith, Edwin W., 332
Smith, John Clark, 910
Smith, Quentin, 1217
Smith, Robert C. and John Lounibos, Eds., 44
Sober, Elliot, and David Sloan Wilson, 436
Solignac, Aimé, 911
Solomon, Robert C., 1218, 1219, 1220, 1221, 1222, 1223, 1224
Sommerville, John C., 173
Sontag, Frederick, 1225
Sorokin, Pitirim, 644, 645
Southard, Samuel, Ed., 579
Spader, Peter H., 1226
Spae, Joseph J., 333
Spears, Timothy B., 215
Spero, Moshe H., and Roberto Mester, 437
Spidlík, Tomas, 912
Spinoza, Benedict de, 1227
Spiro, Melford E., 545, 546
Spohn, William C, 913, 914
Spurr, John, 174
Squarcini, Federico, 547
Starzomski, Rosalie C., 646
Steele, Richard B., 915
Steemers, J. C., 277
Stein, Michael, 647
Stein, Murray, 438
Steinberg, Mark D., 278
Stephens, G. Lynn, 1228
Sterling, Marvin C., 1229
Stevens, John A., 1230
Stevenson, Robert M., 125
Stock, Ursula, 916
Stocker, Michael, with Elizabeth Hegeman, 1231
Stolt, Birgit, 917
Strasser, Stephan, 1232
Strongman, K.T., and L. Strongman, 648
Stubley, Peter, 216
Sutherland, Cherie Olga, 649
Switzer, David K., 439
Symington, Neville, 440
Szabó, Titus, 918

Tallon, Andrew, 919, 920, 921, 922, 923, 1233, 1234, 1235, 1236, 1237, 1238
Tan, Leshan, 548
Taylor, C. C. W., 1239
Taylor, Charles, 1240
Taylor, Gabriele, 441, 1241
Taylor, Henry Osborn, 126
Thévenaz, Jean Pierre, 924
Thoits, Peggy A., 650
Thomas Aquinas, 925, 1242
Thomas, James, 1243

Thompson, Martie P., and
  Paula J. Vardman, 651
Thonnard, F.-J., 926
Thunberg, Lars, 927
Tillich, Paul, 928, 929, 930,
Timmermans, Benoît, 1244
Tolbert, Elizabeth Dawn, 279,
  549
Tomás De La Cruz, 931
Tomkins, Silvan S., 442
Toomey, Paul M., 550
Torgovnick, Marianna, 551
Trawick, Margaret, 280
Trevarthen, Colwyn, 443
Turley, Briane K., 217
Turner, H. W., 282
Turner, Victor, 552, 553
Turski, George W., 1245,
  1246, 1247
Tuzin, Donald, 554
Tyrell, Bernard J., 932

Ueno, Yuji, 555
Uffenheimer, Rivka Schatz,
  218
Ulanov, Ann Belford, 444,
  445
Ullman, Chana, 446

Van der Ven, Johannes, 933
Van Hooft, Stan, 1248
Vergote, Antoine, 447
Versnel, H. S., 46
Veysey, Lawrence, 219
Victor, Jeffrey S., 652
Viswanathan, Gauri, 220
Vögtle, A., 934
Voipio, Aarni, 283
Völker, Walther, 935, 936,
  937, 938, 939, 940, 941,
  942, 943
Von Balthasar, Hans Urs, 944
von der Luft, Eric, Ed., 755
Von Hügel, Baron Friedrich,
  945

Wach, Howard M., 221
Wach, Joachim, 653
Wadell, Paul J., C.P, 946
Wainwright, William J., 175,
  947, 1249

Wallace, R. Jay, 1250
Walton, Douglas N., 1251
Wanagffelen, Thierry, 127
Ward, W. R., 176
Ware, Kallistos, 948
Watson, Samuel J., 222
Watts, Fraser N., 448
Weber, Max, 654, 655
Weberman, David, 1252
Weeramunda, A. J., 284
Weisberger, Bernard A., 223
Wekker, Gloria, 556
Welsch, Wolfgang, 1253
Werkmeister, Lucyle, 949
Werner, Karel, 334
Westerkamp, Marilyn, 177
Wetzel, Marc, 1254
White, Geoffrey M., 557
Whitehead, Alfred North, 950
Whitehouse, Harvey, 558
Whitehouse, P. G., 1255
Wiethaus, Ulrike, 128
Wijeyewardene, Gehan, 285
Wilken, Robert L., 951
Williston, Byron, 1256
Windelband, Wilhelm, 1257
Wobbermin, Georg, 952
Wolf, Ursula, 1258
Wolff, Hans Walter, 953
Wolff, Larry, 178
Wolfson, Eliot R., 130
Woolley, Geoffrey H., 335
Wu, David Y. H., 559
Wuthnow, Robert, 656, 657,
  658

Yeager, Diane M., 954
Youngs, J. William T., Jr.,
  179
Yuen, Shing-Chung Royan,
  47

Zur Mühlen, Karl-Heinz, 955,
  956
Zwingmann, W., 957, 958

Index of Topics

Topics indexed by page number

Aborigines, 58
aesthetics, 52, 64, 88, 90, 123, 132, 151, 162, 171, 174, 179, 190, 194, 203, 211
affection, 35, 36, 44, 62, 72, 90, 123, 126, 127, 129, 131, 135, 145, 147, 153, 159, 161, 185, 189, 192, 199, 200, 207, 214, 215
affections, 31, 39, 43, 72, 122, 123, 124, 125, 126, 127, 128, 131, 132, 133, 134, 135, 136, 137, 138, 139, 140, 141, 142, 143, 145, 146, 147, 148, 149, 150, 152, 155, 156, 157, 158, 159, 160, 161, 162, 163, 164, 165, 168, 172, 173, 174, 178, 184, 185, 186, 187, 189, 204, 206, 210, 211
affective theory, 75
affectivity, 50, 121, 123, 124, 127, 128, 130, 134, 135, 137, 139, 141, 145, 146, 147, 149, 151, 153, 155, 156, 159, 165, 166, 167, 169, 171, 175, 188, 191, 192, 195, 196, 197, 198, 200, 201, 203, 206, 207, 209, 214, 215
Africa, 53, 54, 56, 58, 59, 60, 76, 87, 88, 89, 92, 94, 95, 102, 104
African Americans, 47, 52, 56, 58, 59, 103, 110, 112
African Methodist Epicopal Church (AME), 113
African religious ideas, 52
African spirit churches, 55
Afro-Brazilian religion, 92, 98
AIDS, 71, 73, 110
Aikido, 103
Aladura, 60
Al-Ghazzali, 61
allegory, 39

altruism, 74, 84, 98, 108, 116, 118
Ancestor worship, 59
Andaman Islanders, 99
Anfechtung, 123
anger, 22, 23, 24, 26, 30, 33, 34, 36, 38, 46, 56, 59, 60, 61, 69, 72, 77, 81, 82, 83, 84, 87, 89, 92, 93, 96, 97, 98, 99, 105, 107, 108, 111, 117, 131, 136, 137, 145, 147, 148, 155, 157, 172, 173, 185, 192, 206, 214
Anglicanism, 43, 47
anguish, 77, 86, 151, 175, 197, 199, 204
Anschauung, 135
anxiety, 26, 31, 38, 57, 58, 61, 72, 74, 77, 78, 80, 81, 82, 84, 92, 95, 99, 104, 107, 110, 113, 133, 143, 144, 145, 149, 151, 158, 168, 178, 185, 191, 199, 200, 209
apatheia, 130, 134, 137, 150, 155, 165, 170, 172
apathy, 130, 133, 134, 136, 139, 142, 154
Appalachia, 94
appetitive faculties, 132, 150
Argentina, 112
Aristotle, 22, 31, 69, 109, 138, 159, 168, 175, 180, 186, 202, 203, 207, 208, 214, 216, 217
art, 24, 43, 60, 71, 87, 103, 110, 135, 162, 182, 184, 189, 197, 200, 201, 204, 205, 211, 215, 217
artificial intelligence, 70
asceticism, 72, 125, 128, 144, 150, 165, 172
Asia, 60, 91, 96, 101
Australia, 48, 55
authority, 27, 36, 40, 42, 53, 55, 59, 62, 80, 81, 91, 107, 108, 115, 118, 194

avarice, 137, 188, 205
awe, 24, 29, 31, 53, 67, 79, 145, 149, 191

Bacchanalia, 23
Bacchus, 25
Bali, 90, 114
Bantu, 59, 67
baptism, 60, 170
Barth, Karl, 122
Basil of Caesarea, 136
Bateson, Gregory, 87
beauty, 32, 130, 131, 132, 190
Bedouin love poetry, 86
Beguines, 38
Bellah, Robert, 104, 106, 110, 111
benevolence, 30, 49, 105, 192
bereavement, 89, 105, 106, 110, 113
Bernard of Clairvaux, 30, 34, 35, 38, 41, 51, 123, 124, 126, 128, 132, 135, 137, 141, 144, 145, 149, 151, 155, 162, 163, 169, 186, 209
bhakta, 34, 64
bhakti, 21, 24, 26, 28, 36, 38, 53, 57, 62, 63, 64, 66, 67, 101, 102, 118
biology, 78, 86, 89, 95, 102, 108
bliss, 25, 72, 79, 80, 88
Bliss, 24, 64, 72
Blondel, Maurice, 146
body, 23, 26, 27, 32, 38, 39, 40, 42, 71, 72, 73, 75, 88, 90, 93, 95, 96, 98, 114, 125, 128, 136, 141, 144, 146, 154, 155, 168, 179, 189, 192, 195, 200, 201, 205
boredom, 116, 191, 200, 205
bravery, 27
Brazil, 88, 92
Brunner, Emil, 125
Buddha, 61, 67, 101
Buddhism, 28, 33, 61, 67, 76, 77, 87, 89, 96, 98, 101, 118
Bunuel, Luis, 74

Bunyan, John, 44

Caitanya movement, 33
Calvin, John, 126, 142, 153, 155, 156, 165, 174, 211
Campbell, Joseph, 70
candomblé, 59, 98
Cappadocians, 124, 136, 168, 170
care, 71, 73, 89, 113, 116, 117, 148, 196, 216
caritas, 36, 67, 126, 140, 157, 164
Carthusians, 32
Cassian, John, 122, 128, 137
Catholic (Roman Catholic), 22, 25, 30, 31, 32, 35, 36, 39, 42, 44, 45, 47, 50, 55, 57, 59, 60, 63, 65, 66, 72, 74, 83, 94, 107, 109, 112, 116, 117, 123, 124, 129, 136, 137, 138, 164, 176, 184, 205, 214, 215
character, 41, 42, 49, 50, 114, 115, 123, 124, 125, 128, 130, 133, 138, 139, 141, 142, 143, 145, 147, 148, 149, 151, 152, 153, 154, 155, 156, 158, 159, 160, 161, 163, 166, 168, 169, 170, 173, 175, 176, 179, 180, 181, 182, 184, 185, 188, 189, 191, 193, 194, 195, 197, 206, 207, 208, 211, 216, 217
charisma, 72, 108, 118
child-rearing, 42, 50, 75, 85
Chile, 113
China, 27, 46, 63, 89, 101, 103, 112, 114, 116
Christian evangelicalism, 30
Christian identity, 23
Christian visions, 28
Christianity, 21, 24, 25, 26, 28, 29, 31, 34, 35, 38, 44, 51, 53, 58, 62, 63, 64, 65, 66, 67, 68, 70, 72, 80, 81, 84, 88, 89, 91, 92, 93, 95, 103, 112, 113, 114, 118, 126, 127, 129, 151, 157, 172, 173, 182, 190

Index of Topics 233

Christians, Freethinking, 43, 46, 91, 163
Cistercians, 36, 123, 132, 135, 136, 137, 147, 151, 163, 165
Class differences, 51
Clement, 134, 138, 144, 148, 165, 168, 171
cognition, 24, 56, 75, 98, 100, 130, 149, 151, 167, 189, 210, 212, 213, 214, 215, 216
community, 34, 48, 53, 54, 55, 93, 94, 101, 104, 106, 110, 111, 113, 135, 154, 166, 185, 192, 210
compassion, 25, 58, 61, 96, 97, 117, 118, 132, 133, 142, 147, 148, 162, 196, 211
compunction, 29
concupiscible emotions, 173, 201, 204
confidence, 37, 82, 91, 106, 111, 147, 175
Confucianism, 33, 46, 62, 118
consolation, 73, 136
constructivism, 25, 27, 29, 36, 38, 44, 48, 52, 63, 64, 65, 96, 99, 104, 108, 118, 125, 142, 172, 183, 194, 202, 205
contempt for the world, 63
conversion, 24, 26, 29, 33, 37, 40, 41, 43, 44, 51, 58, 69, 70, 78, 80, 81, 86, 92, 107, 116, 128, 135, 142, 149, 150, 162, 169
courage, 27, 138, 147, 168, 172
covenant, 21, 25
Creole, 103
Crusades, 28
Cuba, 114
cults, 82, 87, 88, 92, 102, 103, 108, 118
cursing, 30, 34, 115

dance, 25, 54, 58, 59, 87, 92, 93, 94, 97, 98
Dante, 29, 38, 69

Darwin, Charles, 46, 72, 84, 110, 179, 183, 200
Dasein, 191, 199
death, 28, 31, 39, 41, 48, 58, 59, 63, 66, 67, 71, 73, 76, 81, 82, 84, 89, 94, 97, 99, 105, 107, 108, 109, 110, 111, 112, 113, 116, 117, 128, 162, 163, 169, 193
Deism, 30
delight, 42, 66, 139, 166, 173
delirium, 43, 47
Denmark, 59
depression, 72, 76, 78, 82, 85, 89, 92, 110
dervishes, 61
Descartes, Rene, 69, 125, 138, 154, 165, 175, 176, 177, 178, 181, 182, 186, 187, 189, 192, 195, 196, 197, 198, 200, 202, 204, 206, 209, 212, 216, 217
desire, 33, 37, 49, 62, 63, 70, 72, 73, 74, 76, 77, 82, 86, 87, 88, 93, 102, 104, 105, 124, 126, 132, 136, 144, 146, 155, 162, 173, 176, 180, 182, 187, 189, 195, 196, 200, 214, 215, 216
despair, 24, 33, 37, 51, 52, 82, 97, 98, 118, 133, 143, 151, 163, 168, 193, 212
Despair, 33, 52, 98, 118, 143
devotion, 23, 26, 27, 28, 29, 32, 34, 35, 37, 52, 57, 60, 62, 63, 64, 67, 72, 88, 93, 126, 174
Diderot, 40
Dionysiac religion, 25, 26, 27, 65
disenchantment, 23
disgust, 88, 99, 100, 112
distress, 25, 29, 72, 82, 86, 95, 106, 108, 117, 205
Donne, John, 33, 37, 38
Douglas, Mary, 99
dread of the divine, 58
dreams, 60
Durkheim, Emile, 76, 96, 105, 106, 107, 108, 111, 112

ecstasy, 23, 25, 27, 31, 32, 34, 37, 38, 39, 51, 52, 56, 57, 58, 59, 61, 64, 66, 77, 79, 90, 91, 92, 94, 96, 98, 102, 109, 123, 132, 136, 139, 141, 144, 157, 160, 163, 166, 168, 169, 170, 171
Edwards, Jonathan, 40, 45, 65, 127, 131, 132, 133, 140, 148, 156, 159, 165, 166, 216
Egypt, 95
Elias, Norbert, 64
embodiment, 88, 92, 94, 96, 112
Emerson, Ralph Waldo, 50, 121, 201
empathy, 59, 78, 146, 194, 196, 214
empiricism, 69, 77, 182, 186, 195, 198
England, 32, 33, 34, 35, 37, 38, 40, 41, 42, 43, 44, 45, 47, 49, 51, 53, 110, 133, 135, 153, 193
Enlightenment, 40, 42, 66, 67, 191
ennui, 199, 204
enthusiasm, 29, 32, 34, 37, 41, 42, 44, 45, 46, 47, 50, 51, 56, 65, 73, 106, 111, 113, 118, 144, 198, 201
envy, 33, 70, 74, 84, 85, 86, 95, 96, 97, 115, 131, 137, 192, 193, 205, 210
Epicureans, 22, 147, 203
epistemology, 188, 201
Erikson, Erik, 71, 94
eros, 64, 79, 129, 157, 214
eroticism, 22, 34, 37, 63, 67, 74, 97, 101, 154
eternity, 38, 74, 145
ethics, 79, 93, 116, 118, 128, 137, 139, 147, 148, 149, 158, 159, 167, 168, 170, 172, 179, 181, 189, 193, 196, 199, 210, 211
evangelicalism, 39, 47, 49, 50, 51, 55, 65, 66, 88, 92
evil, 43, 52, 67, 73, 79, 82, 93, 98, 104, 112, 115, 118, 133, 144, 147, 150, 193, 206, 209
experimental religion, 29
Eygpt, 86

family, 22, 23, 30, 35, 42, 43, 47, 50, 53, 59, 60, 82, 86, 94, 104, 106, 111, 113, 114, 115, 117, 175, 186
fanaticism, 40, 47, 205
fantasies, 34, 56, 81, 85
fear, 23, 25, 29, 31, 35, 39, 44, 53, 56, 57, 58, 59, 66, 67, 68, 70, 71, 72, 73, 74, 77, 79, 80, 81, 82, 84, 90, 92, 93, 96, 97, 99, 102, 105, 106, 107, 109, 110, 112, 117, 123, 126, 132, 134, 137, 138, 144, 145, 155, 156, 161, 163, 168, 169, 175, 190, 191, 192, 193, 194, 202, 214, 217
fear of death, 39, 41, 47, 63, 71, 73, 81, 82, 90, 93, 97, 106, 109, 138, 193
fearlessness, 63
feeling, 23, 25, 29, 32, 34, 37, 38, 40, 41, 48, 49, 51, 53, 54, 57, 59, 60, 67, 70, 71, 73, 74, 75, 77, 79, 80, 81, 82, 86, 90, 91, 96, 97, 98, 99, 103, 104, 105, 106, 108, 110, 111, 113, 115, 117, 118, 119, 130, 132, 134, 138, 139, 142, 143, 149, 150, 154, 157, 158, 163, 164, 167, 169, 172, 173, 175, 179, 183, 188, 191, 192, 195, 197, 199, 200, 204, 205, 208, 209, 210, 211, 216
feeling of absolute dependence, 62, 127, 130, 131, 160, 162, 164, 173, 190, 191
female divinity, 36
female ecstatics, 98
female heroes, 41
female prophets, 46
feminine, 71, 76, 79, 88

feminism, 58, 76, 88, 103, 106, 142, 148, 182, 196, 198, 211
feminist critiques, 76, 105, 106
Finland, 60, 102
firewalking, 89, 98
forgiveness, 106
fortitude, 137
France, 28, 31, 33, 35, 38, 40, 44, 45, 47, 48, 50, 61, 62, 74, 101, 106, 113, 136, 146, 165, 175, 176, 182, 184, 187, 191, 192, 195, 197, 204, 205, 207
Franciscans, 32, 34, 130, 139, 204
Freud, Sigmund, 34, 61, 70, 71, 72, 74, 76, 78, 79, 81, 82, 97, 109, 110, 114, 179, 185, 191, 213
frui Deo, 121, 149
fruits of the Spirit, 123, 161
fundamentalism, 76, 115, 118
funeral rites, 21

Geertz, Clifford, 76, 90
Gefühl, 129, 135, 147, 159, 162, 183, 198
gender, 23, 39, 79, 88, 99, 103, 117
Gerson, Jean, 29, 142, 144, 150, 158, 174
Ghana, 52, 60
glossolalia, 59
Gnosticism, 23, 56, 63, 148
goddesses, 22
gratitude, 113, 116, 117
Great Awakening, 39, 40, 41, 43, 45
Greece, 21, 22, 24, 25, 89
greed, 74, 93
Gregory of Nazianzus, 136, 138
Gregory of Nyssa, 124, 136, 144, 151, 155, 165, 170, 173
grief, 21, 24, 27, 31, 39, 73, 77, 78, 89, 91, 94, 96, 105, 109, 110, 115, 116, 136, 155, 193, 204
Guatemala, 109

guilt, 23, 25, 29, 33, 34, 47, 54, 57, 61, 67, 69, 74, 82, 85, 86, 96, 98, 125, 144, 158, 161, 169, 202, 215

Hadewijch, 35, 153
hagiography, 31
happiness, 58, 63, 64, 77, 79, 83, 94, 96, 101, 104, 108, 109, 113, 114, 116, 146, 163, 186, 190, 193
hate, 23, 107, 108
hatred of evil, 147
healing, 33, 43, 52, 55, 59, 60, 72, 76, 79, 88, 89, 90, 92, 93, 94, 99, 108, 110, 113, 149
heart, 29, 35, 38, 40, 52, 59, 64, 67, 70, 77, 80, 85, 87, 92, 93, 94, 104, 108, 122, 124, 125, 126, 127, 128, 129, 130, 131, 132, 133, 134, 137, 139, 141, 148, 149, 150, 154, 155, 156, 159, 162, 165, 167, 172, 173, 182, 187, 189, 204, 206, 213, 214, 217
heart religion, 29, 35, 40
heaven, 33, 58, 64, 71, 81, 83, 101
Hebrew, 21, 22, 23, 25, 26, 27, 133, 139, 173
Hegel, Georg, 138, 147, 175, 190, 191, 196, 209
Heidegger, Martin, 81, 145, 149, 178, 179, 191, 196, 199, 200, 201, 217
hell, 33, 39, 66, 71, 73
Hellenism, 37, 136, 141, 144, 157, 171, 189, 194, 203
Hellenistic mystery cults, 37
Henry, Michel, 146, 186, 196, 197, 204
hermeneutics, 122, 130, 139, 152, 167, 207, 215
Hinduism, 32, 33, 35, 53, 56, 59, 63, 70, 87, 89, 94, 95, 96, 97, 100, 101, 112, 118, 190
history, 22, 23, 26, 27, 31, 33, 35, 37, 38, 39, 43, 44, 45,

49, 50, 51, 52, 53, 55, 57, 58, 60, 61, 62, 63, 64, 65, 66, 67, 76, 78, 85, 93, 94, 101, 118, 124, 133, 141, 145, 148, 155, 157, 159, 162, 164, 168, 170, 171, 175, 176, 179, 185, 186, 187, 190, 193, 195, 201, 203, 212, 213, 217
honor, 44, 54, 118, 196
hope, 24, 25, 57, 67, 75, 77, 82, 101, 111, 118, 123, 124, 132, 145, 147, 149, 155, 161, 162, 163, 164, 166, 167, 168, 172, 192, 193
Hugh of St. Victor, 141, 144
Hume, David, 49, 125, 131, 139, 159, 176, 177, 184, 185, 192, 193, 194, 202, 205, 208, 209
humiliation, 27, 35, 56, 112
humility, 77, 97, 131, 137, 170, 193, 215
humor, 26, 49, 78
hymns, 28, 40, 50, 104
hysteria, 25, 38, 47, 53, 65, 95

identity, 23, 28, 33, 48, 70, 75, 76, 83, 84, 93, 104, 106, 109, 113, 133, 158, 183, 188, 198, 215
Ignatius Loyola, 29, 123, 138, 162
imagination, 31, 79, 88, 105, 165, 205, 208
immortality, 38, 82
immutability, 40, 130
impassability, 128, 130, 133, 151, 209
impurity, 21
India, 21, 24, 25, 28, 32, 33, 35, 38, 51, 52, 53, 54, 56, 57, 60, 64, 66, 70, 87, 88, 93, 96, 97, 101, 102
indignation, 27, 83
individuation, 76, 77, 78
Indonesia, 91, 92
intellect, 33, 123, 128, 129, 139, 140, 141, 155, 160, 164, 171, 197, 198, 207, 214
intentionality, 174, 177, 182, 187, 191, 196, 198, 200, 207, 211, 212, 214, 215, 216
interiority, 45, 137, 138, 198
intimacy, 30, 74, 87
intuitionism, 122
Iran, 115
irascible emotions, 173, 201, 204
Irish, 45, 47, 71, 84, 112
Islam, 27, 28, 30, 61, 70, 81, 87, 88, 89, 91, 95, 96, 99, 106, 112, 114, 118
Israel, 21, 22, 24, 26, 52, 71, 105
Italy, 27, 36

Jacobitism, 35
James, William, 26, 45, 48, 52, 56, 61, 66, 69, 71, 75, 77, 90, 92, 99, 110, 121, 125, 128, 134, 135, 137, 144, 145, 146, 147, 151, 152, 153, 157, 159, 169, 172, 173, 178, 179, 183, 185, 186, 187, 189, 193, 194, 195, 196, 200, 201, 202, 215, 216, 217
Japan, 56, 79, 87, 95, 107, 109, 111, 116
Javanese religion, 90
jealousy, 21, 23, 25, 31, 57, 70, 85, 99, 104, 145, 188, 205
Jehovah's Witnesses, 52
Jesuits, 35, 79
Job, 71, 77, 78
jokes, 26
Josephus, 22
joy, 21, 22, 25, 26, 27, 29, 35, 42, 50, 51, 52, 55, 61, 64, 72, 89, 91, 97, 101, 103, 109, 123, 132, 134, 138, 139, 145, 150, 151, 152, 161, 163, 168, 172, 175, 193, 196, 198, 212
Judaism, 21, 22, 23, 24, 25, 26, 34, 35, 38, 48, 51, 62,

Index of Topics   237

66, 68, 70, 71, 75, 83, 89,
  106, 107, 112, 171, 190
Judeo-Christian culture, 76,
  105
judgment, 66, 82, 159, 166,
  177, 179, 184, 188, 197,
  212, 213, 217
Julian of Norwich, 37
Jung, Carl G., 71, 74, 75, 77,
  80, 83, 85, 102, 110, 114,
  142, 151, 213

Kali, 88, 97
Kant, Immanuel, 147, 176,
  184, 191, 195, 196, 203,
  204, 206, 207, 211
kardia, 122, 137, 141
Kenya, 92, 94, 95
Kierkegaard, Soren, 125, 126,
  133, 140, 143, 144, 145,
  150, 151, 156, 161, 162,
  165, 207, 208
King, Martin Luther, Jr., 56,
  107
knowledge, 31, 74, 78, 85, 88,
  98, 104, 110, 122, 126,
  127, 128, 129, 135, 138,
  140, 146, 147, 149, 150,
  151, 152, 153, 154, 155,
  160, 161, 162, 164, 167,
  170, 179, 180, 190, 192,
  193, 194, 199
Kongo, 57
Korea, 79, 93
Krishna, 37, 52, 53, 67, 88,
  102

Lactantius, 69
laity, 37, 43, 44, 45, 47
lament, 27, 32, 60, 87, 102
language, 25, 26, 29, 30, 34,
  79, 86, 88, 94, 101, 114,
  123, 124, 134, 137, 139,
  142, 143, 148, 151, 156,
  157, 163, 165, 166, 183,
  196, 200, 206, 208, 216
Laotzu, 101
latitudinarianism, 30, 41, 44
laughter, 22, 23, 24, 33, 49,
  64, 97
Lawrence, D. H., 102, 114

Locke, John, 40, 165, 194,
  195, 198, 199
loneliness, 70, 71, 73, 75, 78,
  81, 83, 84, 110, 111, 113,
  115, 116
love, 21, 25, 26, 27, 28, 29,
  30, 31, 32, 33, 34, 35, 36,
  38, 41, 43, 44, 46, 47, 48,
  49, 53, 55, 57, 59, 60, 62,
  63, 66, 67, 69, 71, 72, 74,
  78, 80, 82, 86, 88, 92, 93,
  96, 97, 100, 101, 108, 109,
  116, 118, 123, 126, 129,
  130, 131, 132, 133, 134,
  135, 136, 137, 138, 139,
  140, 141, 143, 144, 145,
  146, 147, 149, 151, 154,
  157, 162, 163, 164, 167,
  168, 170, 171, 172, 173,
  174, 175, 176, 177, 179,
  185, 186, 192, 193, 199,
  200, 205, 206, 210, 217
love charms, 36
love of God, 67, 136
loyalty, 74, 107, 110, 111,
  117
lust, 137
Luther, Martin, 30, 55, 56, 67,
  71, 107, 123, 124, 126,
  130, 138, 141, 142, 150,
  152, 157, 158, 164, 166,
  174

madness, 22, 32, 43, 44, 57,
  65, 87, 95
magic, 36, 67, 93, 95, 97,
  100, 190, 204
Malay, 99
malice, 193, 210, 211
Malinowski, Bronislaw, 97,
  110
Mary, Blessed Virgin, 32, 34,
  35, 36, 38, 39, 44, 47, 53,
  57, 69, 87, 99, 195
Maximus the Confessor, 124,
  138, 144, 153, 154, 168,
  170, 173
Mayans, 36, 109
meditation, 84
Mediterranean, 23, 62

melancholy, 31, 32, 42, 66, 71, 76, 78, 90, 133, 151, 200
Melanesia, 92, 97, 102
mental illness, 43, 66
Methodism, 41, 43, 44, 48, 50, 51, 58, 89, 113
Mexico, 44, 63, 91
Micronesia, 96
Milton, John, 31, 38
misery, 101, 151, 186, 193, 200, 204
Mithraic liturgy, 22
modesty, 97, 100
monasticism, 34, 61, 98, 121, 144
moods, 51, 66, 91, 125, 143, 149, 150, 151, 158, 176, 178, 201, 209, 211, 212
moral philosophy, 116, 133, 177, 195, 205, 211, 218
moral psychology, 180, 204, 208
moral theology, 137, 138
Mormonism, 47, 63
motherhood, 50, 48, 70, 71, 78, 82, 83, 85, 88, 97, 106, 109
mourning, 21, 29, 32, 35, 39, 53, 60, 71, 77, 84, 90, 91, 93, 99, 106, 110, 112, 116
music, 24, 29, 43, 60, 87, 89, 92, 93, 102, 189, 197
mysticism, 21, 22, 23, 26, 27, 34, 35, 36, 45, 47, 51, 61, 62, 63, 64, 65, 66, 67, 69, 72, 74, 77, 79, 80, 81, 87, 88, 109, 122, 128, 131, 135, 136, 138, 144, 145, 147, 151, 153, 154, 157, 160, 163, 164, 167, 168, 170, 171
mystics, 27, 30, 32, 61, 63, 65, 151

native American, 76, 89, 93, 94, 95, 102
near-death experience, 73, 113, 117
Nepal, 89, 90, 92, 98
New Age, 89, 104

New England, 44, 49
New Guinea, 60, 90, 102, 103
new religious movements, 104, 111
New Testament, 122, 123, 125, 135, 144, 152, 157
Newman, John Henry, 36, 45, 137, 143, 216
Niebuhr, Reinhold, 107
Nigeria, 87
nirvana, 77, 101
nuns, 27, 99

oceanic feeling, 74, 81, 97
Old Testament, 22, 23, 24, 26, 67, 133, 173
Origen, 128, 130, 134, 138, 144, 160, 165, 168, 170
Orthodox Christianity, 39, 106, 125, 136, 137, 150, 155, 165
Otto, Rudolf, 31, 68, 71, 139, 152

Paganism, 23, 24, 25, 26, 38
pain, 32, 37, 39, 41, 79, 80, 82, 85, 116, 134, 163, 189, 192, 193, 205
Palestinian Intifada, 108
Papua New Guinea, 90, 103
Pascal, 154, 165, 167, 187, 189, 195, 197, 204, 206, 210
passibilism, 128
passion, 22, 27, 32, 40, 41, 43, 49, 50, 56, 64, 71, 74, 77, 86, 87, 88, 93, 95, 97, 98, 99, 102, 103, 108, 112, 115, 125, 132, 134, 147, 151, 162, 165, 167, 168, 173, 177, 179, 182, 185, 186, 187, 188, 192, 195, 198, 199, 201, 203, 205, 207, 208, 209, 212, 216, 217
passions, 21, 49, 74, 87, 101, 104, 121, 122, 124, 125, 126, 128, 130, 133, 135, 136, 138, 139, 141, 143, 146, 148, 150, 154, 155,

Index of Topics

156, 157, 158, 159, 160, 165, 166, 167, 168, 169, 170, 171, 172, 173, 175, 176, 177, 178, 179, 180, 181, 185, 186, 187, 188, 189, 192, 193, 194, 195, 196, 197, 198, 199, 201, 202, 203, 204, 205, 206, 207, 208, 209, 211, 212, 213, 215, 216
peak experience, 79, 91
Peirce, Charles S., 80, 121, 201, 213
penance, 35, 170
pentecostalism, 55, 58, 59, 92, 113, 122, 147,
personality, 78, 82, 83, 98, 100
Peru, 99
piety, 26, 32, 33, 36, 37, 38, 42, 43, 44, 45, 47, 50, 53, 56, 66, 126, 133, 137, 142, 147, 157, 162, 164, 170, 171, 191
pilgrimage, 59, 96, 98
Plato, 22, 25, 69
Plotinus, 134, 205
pneumatology, 123, 130, 131, 132, 154, 157, 158, 168
poetry, 27, 30, 32, 38, 86, 172, 203
Polynesia, 99
popular religion, 28, 33, 43, 47, 98
possession, 87, 88, 89, 93, 94, 95
power, 27, 34, 40, 63, 70, 73, 75, 78, 86, 87, 88, 89, 91, 93, 94, 97, 98, 100, 104, 107, 124, 137, 138, 147, 153, 159, 161, 164, 168, 196, 202, 203, 217
prayer, 21, 24, 33, 40, 42, 50, 78, 83, 97, 116, 118, 147, 163
preaching, 29, 34, 40, 45, 46, 51, 59, 156
Pride, 33, 85, 193, 215
prophecy, 26, 29, 34, 47, 139
prophet, 30, 34, 57, 139
Protestantism, 32, 33, 37, 38, 39, 40, 42, 45, 47, 48, 50, 55, 63, 66, 91, 107, 108, 122, 130, 133, 138, 151, 156
psychoanalysis, 70, 71, 72, 74, 75, 76, 78, 85, 88, 93, 98
Puerto Rican, 112
Puritan, 29, 30, 31, 34, 39, 41, 42, 44, 50, 157, 158
Puritanism, 31, 39, 50, 133
Puritans, 29, 31, 34, 42, 44, 64, 115
purity, 28, 130, 137, 154, 172
Pushti Marg, 52, 88

Quakers, 65, 104

racism, 70, 107
rage, 24, 83, 88, 93
rapture, 66, 79, 141, 150, 167
rasa, 57, 58, 97
rational religion, 45
rationality, 32, 51, 82, 97, 102, 105, 127, 139, 149, 160, 165, 166, 176, 184, 212, 216
reason, 22, 26, 27, 40, 43, 44, 45, 80, 84, 87, 88, 106, 118, 121, 125, 129, 132, 136, 138, 139, 140, 142, 147, 148, 149, 154, 155, 157, 166, 167, 168, 175, 177, 180, 182, 185, 189, 192, 194, 198, 199, 201, 203, 205, 208, 209, 210, 212, 216
Reformation, 37, 38, 45, 55, 66, 150, 157, 158, 173, 174
regret, 27, 51, 161
religious experience, 34, 49, 58, 59, 70, 71, 72, 76, 77, 79, 80, 83, 86, 122, 126, 131, 134, 140, 145, 147, 150, 152, 153, 154, 155, 159, 162
religious language, 134
religious thrill, the, 91
remorse, 25, 85
Renaissance, 27, 28, 29, 31, 32, 37, 38, 186, 202

repentance, 29, 39, 134, 137, 161
resignation, 27, 143, 175
revivalism, 48, 50, 55, 63, 65, 118
revivals, 40, 45, 46, 47, 48, 66
rhetoric, 44, 96, 124, 130, 139, 166
Ricoeur, Paul, 98, 99, 142, 184, 200, 206, 207, 212, 214
ritual, 21, 23, 24, 25, 29, 39, 46, 47, 52, 56, 57, 58, 59, 72, 75, 76, 77, 80, 81, 84, 85, 87, 88, 89, 90, 91, 92, 93, 94, 95, 97, 98, 99, 102, 103, 104, 105, 106, 107, 108, 109, 110, 111, 114, 116, 117
romantic love, 67
Romanticism, 23, 41, 42, 162, 190
Russia, 60, 95, 102, 116

sadness, 29, 32, 51, 89, 94, 95, 96, 97, 99, 100, 101, 111, 168
saints, 28, 32, 52, 66, 111, 116, 158
Sanskrit, 24, 25, 26, 62, 63, 64, 97
Santa Isabel, Solomon Islands, 103
santéria, 59, 114
Sartre, Jean-Paul, 145, 175, 177, 179, 185, 200, 209, 210, 212, 213, 216
Scandanavia, 60
schizophrenia, 57
Schleiermacher, Friedrich, 62, 122, 127, 129, 130, 131, 135, 138, 147, 152, 156, 159, 160, 162, 164, 165, 173, 178, 190, 191, 203
secularization, 40, 44, 62, 84, 105, 116, 152
self, 27, 30, 33, 35, 37, 42, 46, 48, 49, 50, 54, 56, 57, 58, 59, 61, 64, 69, 71, 72, 74, 75, 76, 77, 78, 79, 80, 82, 83, 84, 85, 86, 87, 88, 90, 91, 93, 94, 98, 99, 100, 101, 104, 106, 108, 109, 111, 113, 114, 115, 116, 117,123, 124, 125, 126, 128, 129, 130, 131, 132, 138, 142, 143, 144, 145, 151, 158, 161, 162, 163, 165, 168, 169, 171, 172, 175, 178, 179, 180, 184, 185, 188, 189, 190, 192, 203, 207, 208, 210, 212, 214, 215, 216, 217
self-hate, 56
self-love, 30, 72, 138, 192
semiosis, 188, 207
Seneca, 69, 181, 185, 194, 203
Senegal, 76
sensibility, 30, 34, 39, 152
sentiment, 29, 30, 40, 41, 74, 77, 86, 90, 96, 97, 99, 105, 108, 146, 184, 187, 193, 196, 197, 198, 204, 207
sentimentalism, 30, 32, 41, 42, 43, 46, 62
sentimentality, 60, 212, 217
sentiments, 30, 77, 86, 99, 104, 108, 148, 154, 172, 175, 176, 177, 197, 198, 204, 205, 209, 211
serenity, 66
sexual desire, 23
sexual emotion, 62
sexual jealousy, 99
sexual obsession, 74
sexual passion, 50, 88, 103, 112
sexuality, 23, 41, 61, 64, 85, 88, 103, 107
Shaiva sectarianism, 60
Shakers, 92
Shakespeare, William, 29, 33, 38
shamanism, 56, 57, 59, 79, 90, 92, 93, 96, 99, 102
shame, 23, 33, 53, 54, 58, 66, 67, 72, 77, 82, 84, 85, 96, 97, 98, 100, 109, 112, 114, 214, 215
shyness, 97

Index of Topics

sin, 25, 63, 72, 82, 83, 107, 138, 143, 144, 150, 151, 158, 162, 163, 164, 170, 171, 174
Sioux, 94
Soka Gakkai, 56, 62
Solomon, Robert C., 103, 169, 179, 187, 200, 206, 212, 213
song, 28, 88, 89, 90, 91, 92, 94, 104
sorcery, 25, 47
sorrow, 27, 34, 60, 63, 66, 73, 76, 78, 85, 87, 90, 93, 102, 105, 132, 145, 150
soul, 22, 31, 32, 38, 39, 49, 50, 78, 90, 98, 100, 128, 129, 136, 137, 140, 141, 144, 146, 148, 149, 150, 154, 155, 160, 168, 170, 178, 179, 180, 181, 182, 186, 187, 189, 190, 192, 201, 202, 206, 209
Spain, 28, 29, 41, 53
Spanish Inquistion, 41
spirit possession, 59, 88, 92, 95, 98, 113
spirits, 43, 48, 55, 58, 59, 67, 82, 88, 90, 160
Spiritualism, 63
spirituality, 30, 34, 62, 65, 82, 99, 104, 111, 113, 119, 123, 126, 128, 130, 132, 137, 140, 145, 147, 153, 159, 161, 162, 164, 165, 170, 171, 195
spontaneity, 26, 43, 72
Sri Lanka, 61, 89, 93, 94, 96, 98
St. Augustine, 31, 38, 126
St. Bonaventure, 38, 130, 131, 133, 144, 160, 162, 163, 166, 174
St. Cecilia, 29
St. Francis of Assisi, 35, 38
St. John of the Cross, 30, 128, 132, 154, 155
St. Perpetua, 34
Stoics, 22, 127, 128, 137, 140, 146, 147, 168, 170, 171, 180, 181, 185, 186, 193, 198, 203, 204, 211, 212
stress, 83, 118
subjectivism, 34, 44, 50, 70, 76, 99, 104, 111, 122, 135, 141, 142, 143, 146, 156, 159, 171, 184, 185, 190
subjectivity, 30, 51, 133, 142, 151
sublime, 53, 61, 194, 203
Sudan, 88
suffering, 41, 42, 49, 73, 78, 79, 82, 83, 85, 87, 93, 94, 97, 116, 118, 130, 133, 134, 139, 142, 148, 153, 156, 166, 171
Sufism, 35, 38, 52, 54, 55, 56, 61, 62, 65, 66, 67
Sunday, Billy, 46, 104
symbolism, 32, 58, 60, 94, 98, 99, 102, 106, 135, 149, 197
symbols, 22, 29, 56, 75, 84, 89, 90, 91, 98, 99, 102, 104, 106, 108, 114, 124, 126, 156, 166
sympathy, 35, 80, 105, 116, 129, 131, 139, 171, 185, 193, 196, 207, 210, 211, 214

taboos, 26, 67, 90
Tahiti, 95
Tamil, 26, 28, 60, 63, 64, 89, 94, 96
Tanzania, 76
temperament, 42, 65
temperance, 137
terror, 65, 80, 102, 163
Thai Buddhists, 61
theological anthropology, 123, 125, 136, 141, 145, 150, 151, 153, 154, 155, 163, 168, 170, 173
Theosophy, 63
Thomas Aquinas, 69, 76, 123, 126, 129, 138, 140, 142, 144, 149, 152, 155, 158, 159, 162, 166, 167, 168, 172, 174, 177, 179, 183, 185, 196, 201, 207, 215
Tillich, Paul, 145, 168, 169

Tomkins, Silvan, 72, 84, 85
tragedy, 29, 32, 67, 87, 153, 193, 197, 202
trance, 47, 52, 59, 60, 61, 62, 87, 88, 91, 92, 93, 94, 98, 113
Transylvania, 94
trickster, 59
trust, 71, 72, 80, 122, 124, 132, 152, 196
Tukurama, 34
Tunisia, 71
Turkey, 114, 115

Unification Church, 108
Unitarianism, 51

Vaisnava tradition, 26, 57, 62, 63, 101
values, 60, 70, 76, 79, 88, 90, 95, 98, 99, 104, 106, 107, 111, 114, 115, 117, 118, 139, 169, 193, 210, 213, 214
Venezuela, 88
vices, 38, 125, 136, 138, 168, 171, 192
virtue, 32, 40, 65, 91, 99, 131, 132, 136, 139, 140, 147, 158, 161, 167, 169, 199, 208
virtues, 38, 53, 66, 125, 130, 131, 137, 138, 139, 140, 155, 158, 159, 160, 161, 164, 165, 167, 168, 169, 170, 171, 172, 177, 179, 182, 192, 195, 204, 207

visions, 27, 32, 53, 60, 81, 82, 201
volition, 77, 149, 214, 215

weeping, 24, 29, 35, 39, 53, 66, 90, 99
Weil, Simone, 146, 196
Wesley, John, 40, 44, 50, 58, 126, 127
Wesleyanism, 50
Whitehead, Alfred North, 130, 134, 135, 151, 153, 172, 173, 178, 185, 186
wholeness, 64, 71, 74, 77, 79, 142
William of St. Thierry, 123, 129, 132, 135, 144, 151
witchcraft, 38, 44, 47, 95, 104
witches, 44
women, 22, 25, 27, 32, 33, 36, 38, 39, 41, 44, 45, 46, 47, 48, 53, 55, 56, 60, 65, 70, 76, 78, 83, 85, 86, 88, 89, 90, 95, 96, 99, 100, 102, 103, 104, 106, 107, 108, 110, 112, 113, 114, 115, 116, 142, 148, 151, 176, 194
wonder, 29, 31, 70, 81, 152, 216
wrath, 25, 58, 139, 164

Yanomamö, 88, 95

Zambia, 102
Zen, 64, 72, 87

About the Authors

JOHN CORRIGAN is Professor of Religious Studies and American Studies at Arizona State University. He has served as regular or visiting faculty at the University of Virginia, Harvard, Oxford, The University of London, University College (Dublin) and the University of Wittenberg-Halle. He is the author or coauthor of eight books on academic subjects and has written three screenplays produced for cable television. He is coeditor of the online *Journal of Southern Religion*, codirector of *The American Religious Experience* web site, and North American religions editor of The Electronic Cultural Atlas Initiative, based at the University of California, Berkeley.

ERIC CRUMP is Associate Professor of Systematic Theology at the Lutheran Theological Seminary in Gettysburg, Pennsylvania. He is currently doing research on affectivity and faith in relation to a theological aesthetics as the intersection between pneumatology and theological anthropology.

JOHN KLOOS is Professor of Religious Studies at Benedictine College. He is the author of studies of popular religion, religious initiation, and public piety, and *A Sense of Deity* (1991), an interpretation of the social psychology of American revolutionary Dr. Benjamin Rush, M.D. Currently at work on the themes of rebirth and renewal in person and community, he is writing on the poetry of Seamus Heaney, and on stories of self-making in popular culture.